The American Poet

Weedpatch Gazette
For 2001

Samuel D. G. Heath, Ph. D.

iUniverse, Inc.
New York Bloomington

The American Poet
Weedpatch Gazette For 2001

iUniverse books may be ordered through booksellers or by contacting:

iUniverse
1663 Liberty Drive
Bloomington, IN 47403
www.iuniverse.com
1-800-Authors (1-800-288-4677)

ISBN: 978-1-4401-4399-1 (sc)
ISBN: 978-1-4401-4400-4 (ebook)

Printed in the United States of America

iUniverse rev. date: 05/08/2009

Contents

Chapter One

I thought it was the beginning of a promising friendship with the lady until the subject of abortion came up. When she learned that I oppose abortion, it was all over. Immediately. No discussion. It was an unwanted pregnancy and she had an abortion as a means of contraception.

I wasn't given an opportunity to explain, unemotionally, that I oppose abortion on the basis of logic as a callous devaluing and desensitizing of life, all life, that abortion as a means of contraception promotes violence when the unborn are considered "things" to be discarded like unpleasant, inconvenient, and odious "trash," that I believe abortion, just as with capital punishment or divorce involving children, things impacting on a whole society, should be subject to a process of consideration with a view to the advancement of civilization rather than as easy as buying a bottle of shampoo.

Capital punishment is a very emotional issue, as is abortion. But I consider these to be issues that have an enormous impact on the progress of civilization. I favor national standards being applied to such things, rather than state-to-state, often arbitrary, rules of law.

I used to be a strong advocate of capital punishment, but like the killing of the unborn, I no longer see how a civilization can advance on the basis of such a thing. Remove murderers from society permanently, by all means. But I don't think the mechanisms will ever be in place that the State can ever be trusted to apply the taking of life fairly as long as the rule of "How much justice you can afford" is the rule.

Further, things like abortion on demand, capital punishment, circumcision, the striking of children in the name of "discipline" are barbaric practices that cannot possibly promote civilized behavior.

We have made enormous advances in knowledge without commensurate advances in wisdom, as Nobel-winning physicist Michio Kaku and others have pointed out. Is abortion on demand a wise thing for a society or nation? I don't think so. I believe those things like contraception, the preventing of unwanted pregnancies, far better suited to a society that considers itself civilized.

But when a California judge made mandatory contraception a part of sentencing a child-abusing welfare and alcohol and drug abusing unmarried mother, the ACLU stepped in with the argument: In America, we do not interfere with reproductive rights!

But the ACLU did not consider any rights of the unborn when this agency supported abortion on demand in Roe v. Wade.

As an educated and literate, civilized man, I have examined human history and come to a startling thought! I find myself in agreement with Kaku and others: Our advances in science and technology have not been commensurate with advances in either civilized behavior or wisdom!

Given the recent development of the brain function of self-recognition and self-consciousness, may it be possible our brains will eventually develop to the point where travel in time will be possible by the use of our minds as in the film "Somewhere In Time?" Even for some now as in the film?

No, I do not believe in UFOs, Astrology, or man-made religions. But I do believe there are amazing discoveries to be made under the oceans and ice caps, in astronomy and science. And I have learned that what was science fiction to me as a child is now, in many cases, fact. As a result, I have become somewhat more tolerant of the seemingly "impossible."

I wonder whether our brains are evolving more quickly? It took a long time to progress from Sumer to science. In the not too distant past we have had Confucius, Pythagoras, Archimedes, Socrates, Plato and Aristotle. Then there were Newton and most recently Einstein. The tremendous leap of science, could it be due to more quickly developing brains subject to multi-tasking heretofore unknown and unneeded?

Writing, as we know it and developed from the Greeks, is of very recent invention and played the most important role; this ability to convey the learning of one generation to another with ever more complex ideas finding expression in writing, which would explain why it took so long from Sumer to science.

It may be that the exercising of our minds by intellectual stimulation has caused a rapid growth in brain growth and function. If so, this would explain the explosion of technology. The Renaissance, the Enlightenment, the writings of men like Copernicus and Kepler, the calling into question of ancient beliefs that led to scientific thinking and discoveries, the great writers like Shakespeare and those following, all these things began to accelerate ever more complex thinking and discoveries... and quite possibly, an acceleration of brain growth and function.

If brain growth and function has been enhanced at an accelerating rate by the rapid increase in multi-tasking, in technology and science, the leaving off of superstitious beliefs leading to questions of things like origins, who knows how quickly things may change in the very near future? Things like the recent slowing of light to 38 mph (followed by an experiment stopping light completely) hold promise of unimagined possibilities for humanity! The speed of light was thought to be a universal constant. This may now be in question. Particularly when taken together with recent discoveries in Dark Matter and Vacuum Energy, the Holy Grail of physics, a Grand Unification Theory, may be on the threshold of attaining! The very stars begin to be within our reach!

Will advances in the understanding and use of light be of help in something like time travel? There is no discounting Einstein's thought of the relationship between space, matter, and time. And if our brains are actually growing at an increasing rate due to enhanced thinking and discoveries to meet an increasing technology, who knows what resources of our minds may become available to us? The curing of diseases, the expression "mind over matter" may take on a whole different perspective.

But it remains a demon-haunted world in which three billion people have never so much as received a phone call! A demon-haunted world in which people still kill others in the name of God!

As long as things like abortion on demand and the death penalty without national standards, divorce with little consideration for children, molestation treated as of little consequence, as long as such things remain in America, we will continue on a path of violence and barbarism in spite of our science and technology, in spite of the often "veneer" of civilized thought and behavior.

***

I've mentioned how close I have grown to those of my friends and loved ones passed on, how my conversations with them have become so real at night as I go to sleep.

These friends include people like old "Pappy" and Thoreau.

Both Newton and Einstein said they were able to see further than others because they had stood on the shoulders of those passed on.

I can say the same, and it may be that Einstein especially might have meant more than he said, just as I do.

What if? What if my affinity for Emerson, Thoreau, and others is peculiar in the sense that those passed on do in fact join me, as with my loved ones, in helping me to see so far? I've lived long enough to know how peculiar it is for anyone to develop the kind of connection I have with Thoreau, for example. In spite of his manifest faults, I read, and re-read his Walden and other works like letters from a close friend. And Emerson, I have grown much closer in my affinity to and understanding of this giant of a man. I no longer wonder that some call him the greatest intellect America ever produced!

What exactly is death? Is the veil, whatever it consists of, so very, very thin? That I am, in fact, conversing with my friends and loved ones? Just what does change at death? Are these others "where" and/or "what?" Is there a "sea of consciousness" and/or "universal lyre?" Are these others only able to communicate with a special few? And if so, how are these "few" decided?

What if it all depends on how we regard others, of how we treat others... the making of our own heaven or hell depending?

Well, such things occupy my mind, and they do so without my consciously seeking them out. I know you think on such things as well. It's one reason I can so easily lose myself in writing, especially the novel.

Odd thing about the equation: So many people claim: "Oh, well of course, I know that!" Or, as one fool said to me: That's in the Bible! Others make claims to it being in this writing or that but can't ever seem to find out where?

The very originality of the thing makes many envious that they had never thought of it. But when it comes to the fact that wisdom is impossible of attainment without that other half of humanity being included in philosophy leading to the decision making processes of government on the basis of equal value, well, men hate it and women try to excuse it. Facing this, I realized what an enormous challenge gaining real wisdom will be for the human race.

Over time, I have become accustomed to people like belittling the genius of the equation. Their minds are far too small to grasp the real significance of it. Knowledge plus Wisdom equals Peace (k+w=p)

We are a society that seems to think that intellectualism is the ability to answer a few of the questions on Jeopardy.

Brain "fingerprinting?" What about "false memory?"

If I really converse with Emerson and Thoreau, does this only have relevance and application in this life? What will we talk about on the other side?

A 6 million year old hominid, what do such discoveries portend? Recent studies in granite formation indicate the continents may have formed very quickly, rather than over long, geologic periods of time.

Newly discovered huge amphibian fossils; some with 600 and more teeth. Flying dinosaurs (more properly flying reptiles like those fossils found in South America with up to forty-foot wingspans), but can flying dinosaurs be totally discounted?

New Fossil Suggests Bird Feathers Evolved From Dinosaur Scales

December 7, 2000

WASHINGTON—Birds' feathers appear to have evolved from dinosaur scales well over 100 million years ago, Chinese scientists have shown, based on a fossil bird found in the Yixian mountains of northern China.

The bird, scientific name Protopteryx fengningensis, dates from the Early Cretaceous period and was about the size of a starling.

The U.S. magazine Science printed Thursday the account by the two scientists Fucheng Zhang and Zhonghe Zou.

Protopteryx, the most primitive of the enantiornithine birds that were dominant in the period, had feathers that were halfway between long scales and properly developed flight feathers.

Enantiornithines developed in parallel with other birds, but the line then died out. The prototype feathers were mainly to keep the bird warm, but were also used to flutter short distances.

Fucheng and Zhonghe argued in the article that feathers in the ancestry of modern birds would have developed from elongated scales into a second stage where a central shaft developed. Barbs or branches would then have grown to the sides, then branched out in a fourth stage into the tiny structures known as barbules and barbicel.

Another team of paleontologists recently found fossil remains of a feathered dinosaur in northeastern China. It was about the size of a crow and smaller than Archaeopteryx, the first bird in the fossil record.

Writing in the British magazine Nature, its discovers, Xing Xu, Zhonghe Zou and Xiaolin Wang, said Microraptor zhaoianus appeared to be a key link between the dinosaurs and today's birds.

The hypothesis that birds are descended from dinosaurs was strongly doubted by some paleontologists until quite recently.

***

I think it probable that if ancient civilizations like Atlantis and Mu existed, cataclysmic destruction left only a handful of survivors that reverted to primitivism to exist. The recent discovery of pottery 16,000 years old, the discovery of ancient monoliths off the coast of Japan, indicate that while ancient civilizations may have advanced significantly, they did not advance technologically beyond being able to discern astronomical data and the building of impressive structures.

But did such civilizations ever develop a written language beyond that of pictorial? Possibly not. It may be that hieroglyphs such as those of Egypt are a holdover from the lack of such abstract written expression in lost, ancient civilizations. This may have precluded technological advancement such at that of modern times.

It may be that these ancient civilizations did not develop a thorough system of mathematics such as algebra and calculus. This would have precluded their being able to develop a system of physics capable of real understanding of the principles of the mechanics of what is called natural law. To have never reached the mathematics of Newton and Einstein would have prevented technological innovations.

I believe ancient, lost civilizations not only were lacking advanced physics, technology and abstract written expression, I believe they were more given to mythology and superstition, much like that of Cro-Magnon, and this prevented much advancement. I think the hold over of religious beliefs and rites carried on by other resulting civilizations evidence this in things like the building of pyramids and things like human sacrifice.

Recent attention to magnetotactic bacteria:

New report offers compelling evidence of Mars life. Close-up view of a meteorite that has provided tantalizing evidence of fossilized life on Mars. December 14, 2000. By Richard Stenger CNN.com Writer.

The presence of extraordinary magnetic fossils in a meteorite from Mars suggests that the planet once hosted primitive life, scientists reported this week.

The only known sources of such microscopic magnetic crystals on Earth are certain types of bacteria that produce them to seek food and energy.

Magnetite, the mineral form of black iron oxide, is created through natural forces on our planet. But magnetite crystals like those produced exclusively by a class of aqueous bacteria are different.

They are chemically pure and free of defects. "The process of evolution has driven magnetotactic bacteria to make perfect little bar magnets, which differ strikingly from anything found outside biology," said Joseph Kirschvink, a geobiologist who took part in the NASA-funded study.

"In fact, an entire industry devoted to making small magnetic particles for magnetic tapes and computer disks has tried and failed for the past 50 years to make similar particles," he said in a statement.

The microorganisms arrange the magnet crystals in their cells as miniature compasses, which direct them along naturally occurring magnetic fields towards hospitable environments.

The magnetic samples came from the oldest identified red planet meteorite, a potato-sized igneous rock with an estimated age of 4.5 billion years. Life could have thrived on the planet at the time, scientists theorize.

"Mars is smaller than Earth and it developed faster. Consequently, bacteria able to produce tiny magnets could have evolved much earlier on Mars," said Simon Clement, another scientist who investigated the meteorite.

Kirschvink, Clement and other planetary scientists published their findings in the December issue of Geochimica et Cosmochimica Acta, the journal of the Geochemical Society and the Meteoritical Society.

The meteorite landed more than 13,000 years ago in Antarctica, according to researchers, where it remained buried in ice until its discovery in 1984.

NASA scientists created a stir in 1996 when they announced they had discovered microscopic fossils of life in the meteorite, known as ALH84001.

Critics have countered that terrestrial life could have contaminated the rock after it reached Earth. But later research demonstrated that the samples came from an uncontaminated section of the meteorite, the report authors said.

***

Is it possible that the increasing technology of modern science that depends so heavily on electro/magnetism pervading our world may be damaging to our own brains? Does such a thing account for the beaching of whales and dolphins whose brains are dependent on similar "food-seeking" and survival mechanisms as those found in magnetotactic bacteria?

CNN.com - Health - University of Kentucky center probes chemical communication in the brain - January 1, 2001. LEXINGTON, Kentucky (AP) -- Greg Gerhardt doesn't mind being called a "brainiac."

As a professor of anatomy and neurobiology at the University of Kentucky, Gerhardt is the first to admit he's fascinated by the brain and how its cells communicate.

He came to the university in 1999 to create the Center for Sensor Technology, where researchers work to gain knowledge of the fundamental processes that occur during chemical interactions among nerve cells in the brain.

Gerhardt hopes that a better understanding of the communication process will lead to breakthroughs in the treatment of such neurological disorders as Parkinson's disease, Huntington's disease and Alzheimer's.

"We don't understand the actual chemical signaling going on in the brain that allows you to move or think," Gerhardt said. "The new technologies that we are developing here will allow us to enter the world of chemical communication between cells.

"We're going to figure out why neurodegenerative diseases have such a big impact on people's lives. The brain's circuitry is being destroyed by these illnesses. By better understanding the communication process, we can better repair the damage to the brain at the cellular level."

Don Gash, chairman of the College of Medicine's Department of Anatomy and Neurobiology, said the center is a prestigious addition to the university.

"It's great to be at the forefront of such exciting research," Gash said. "We are actually building instruments here in Lexington that are going to be used throughout the world. People who want to do this kind of research in London or Switzerland or wherever in the future are going to be looking to us for the technology and the expertise, and that's exciting." Gerhardt originally established the center in 1991 at the University of Colorado Health Sciences Center. But after joining the College of Medicine in 1999, he arranged to transfer the Colorado center's National Science Foundation funding to the University of Kentucky.

Research at the Center for Sensor Technology is centered on the development and use of high-tech sensors and other state-of-the-art equipment, such as tiny microelectrodes, for studies of brain function.

The microelectrodes can be implanted in various regions of the brain to measure tiny amounts of chemicals such as dopamine, norepinephrine, serotonin, glutamate and nitric oxide. "We design and build these very small sensors to understand how cells in the brain, called neurons, actually communicate with one another," said Gerhardt, who also serves as director of the university's Morris K. Udall Parkinson's Disease Research Center.

"These cells are very small, about a third of the size of a human hair. So in order to go into that environment and listen to how neurons speak, we have to develop by hand these very tiny sensors that are even smaller than the neurons themselves.

"In fact, with Harvard we are working on a procedure to actually use the sensors during neurosurgery as a tool to understand more of what's wrong with the brain of a person that has Parkinson's or epilepsy."

The sensors measure lightning-quick chemical interactions that nerve cells use to exchange signals. These molecules are recorded by the tiny sensors and transmitted to a computer program where researchers can monitor the reactions in real time.

Studies are under way using sensors implanted into the brains of laboratory rats, which allow researchers to monitor what is going on in the animals' brains while they are in motion and at rest.

A more detailed picture of the neurological signaling system could lead to better understanding of schizophrenia, depression, aging, aggression, drug abuse and even smell and taste, Gerhardt said.

"We really don't understand a lot about smell and taste systems and how they operate," he said. "Right now, we're working with a marine biological laboratory on a study of lobsters and how they smell. As it turns out, a lobster is a good model system to understand many of the signaling properties that take place in the human nose to trigger smells.

"When an odor enters your nose, it binds to odor receptors. There then is a chemical interaction that takes place to signal the brain to identify that smell. It is a very rapid process, and you need very fast recording methods to be able to watch how that occurs. These sensors allow us do that."

***

Why the dinosaurs: Trial and error in creation?

Emerson: A fixed point from which all else must go out?

With so much uncertainty concerning origins, it makes it impossible to begin with certainty about many things. A fixed point for the beginning of the universe, once (if) established, would probably explain things. But if we are working backward to an explanation by science, that may be satisfactory. Right now science seems plagued with a lack of a workable life philosophy that would temper its findings. May this be because women have not yet earned their place in philosophy? I think this is at least in part the reason.

I know that science hasn't yet discovered all there is to know in particle physics, science hasn't yet determined the nature, if it exists, of dark matter and vacuum energy; there is not as yet a Grand Unification Theory that works. And there is the matter of continued work on brain function and the genome.

So it is that much remains unknown, much is uncertain. How is that thinking people make such outrageous claims of certainty when such claims are nothing but beliefs? Perhaps Aquinas realized this, provoking him to say just before he died that "all he had done was nothing but straw?"

Yet even great thinkers like Emerson were guilty of this. But if he had known the science of today, would that of helped? Not, I believe, without a complete philosophy which logic dictates must include women and children based on equal value to men.

***

There is the possibility that a great meteor or comet may spell finis to the earth. Great cataclysmic events or plagues may do the same. But human beings will continue to work and learn which would seem the sensible thing to do since we have no control, as yet, over things like meteors, plagues or volcanoes.

But I believe only a complete philosophy that includes women will enable us to put our science, knowledge, to the best use (wisdom).

I wish there were someone to talk to about such things. But maybe it is best that I struggle with all these thoughts in solitude. I don't know.

Where and how did "religion" a belief in god or gods, goddesses originate? Why is it so natural to cry out My God! Prayer seems quite natural.

***

I came across a great quote from Oliver Cromwell that pretty well describes my position: A man never rises as high as when he knows not whither he is going.

As I walk about in the house and outside, I know I don't know "whither I am going." But the most important thing I can do at this point in my life is to think, and try to put my thoughts, which may be of God and loved ones, friends, now passed on, into writing; new thoughts; new ways of looking at things.

Perhaps this is why I find myself constantly saying to myself "I don't know." The constant thinking is provoked by this "not knowing." I am seeking answers. And even this seeking may be of some other source rather than me.

I find much in the writings of men like Emerson and Thoreau. But they didn't know either; they joined me in the seeking process. A man is never so free as when seeking the truth? Perhaps.

***

January 12, 2001

I read in Strachey on Boswell where he writes that while many want to confess, few have the power to do so. He writes that it takes rare clarity of vision in order to confess. It brought to mind the story Thoreau told of the wise man that wanted to know the number of his faults so he could reduce them but could not come to the end of the number of them.

So it was that I wondered if, in an attempt to be honest and factual, I find it ever more difficult to analyze my own faults and thoughts. There is just too much that I do not know. And I am increasingly aware that the problems we face do not admit of simplistic solutions.

Just tonight I was watching TLC and the program was about other planets and the possibilities of life on them. But the admission was made that we do not yet know how life began on our own planet.

I continually wonder how we began? And just what made the difference between modern Homo sapiens and those early hominids? We seem to have been around such a relatively short time. Are we an experiment of Gods? And where did they originate, if so?

I think it's an appreciation of my own ignorance that makes me wonder about such things. It certainly makes it increasingly difficult for me to reach any decisions about many things. As soon as I think to confess a fault, I wonder at the things that led to such a fault, how others contribute to our faults. This is not an attempt to excuse; it's an attempt to understand. No wonder Strachey wrote what he did. It would require extreme "clarity of vision" to really understand and confess.

I believe the Amendment is the right direction, but I also believe women must take their place in philosophy before there is any hope of peace. Most certainly religion offers no answers; quite the contrary, religion promotes violence in the name of God. But drawing on my own experience in religion, I think people use religion as an excuse to avoid the hard, legitimate questions- Intellectual laziness.

But back to confession, I know I used religion as an excuse for many a failure to be responsible for my own actions. But I used the religion I had been taught as a child. The Bible and Jesus were my religion. These were lies, but they were lies I had been taught to believe as a child by people that loved me. I went on to teach, use and perpetuate these lies to my own children and others. I now cringe at the self-deceptions and hypocrisy of my own life and the hurt I caused in the lives of others, especially my children.

Now being aware that I have enough clarity of vision to make such a confession, I can't help but believe that I may be able to go even further in confession, understanding, and discovery.

And, perhaps, with this kind of understanding I'm not as inclined to always condemn myself out of hand. I could, for example, beat myself to death for not being a better husband and father. But in many cases it would have required the help and cooperation of wives and children to be so. Again, not to excuse myself for my own selfishness, but wouldn't it have helped if I had been taught better? Especially if I had not been taught the lies and prejudices of the religion I used to justify so much of my own wrongdoing?

And those that loved and taught me these errors; wouldn't they have done better if others had not misled them?

So it becomes difficult to speak with certainty about such things. It becomes difficult with age, experience, learning, to be dogmatic about many things. I have to stop and think. Even then I often have to qualify and qualify, and often say, "I don't know."

Aquinas came to the end of his life pronouncing his life's work as "nothing but straw." I believe I understand. And it explains why such deep thinkers come to the same pass. Once you try to make real meaning of life and death, of origins, you must realize how very limited someone like Aquinas was in understanding. But even with the best of present science, we still don't know many things. We don't really know what constitutes "life."

In trying to make sense of such things, Fitzgerald wrote magnificently but came to the end pronouncing Hemingway an expert in success but himself an expert in failure. I think because Scott was driven to search much deeper than Earnest. And the deeper we search; it seems the more prone to failure.

How to make sense of what separates us from the earliest hominids? How to make sense of life and death? If heaven there be, if life after death, how is such a future existence equalized among persons? The dead Ethiopian child, starved, and the opulent, well educated American that dies at a ripe old age?

Why should I be alive and my daughter Diana killed at such a young age? Death does not seem to be very discriminatory. And yet so many are willing to ascribe "our time being in God's hands." It does not make sense.

The origin of evil: Another conundrum. And why the good has not yet overcome the evil? I know the good does not attempt a concentrated effort to overcome evil. Why not? The lack of wisdom? The lack of a common philosophy that includes both men and women as of equal value? All the theories of UFOs, co-existing universes, etc. At what point in human development did romantic love evolve? What is its origin?

January 18, 2001 Nature Journal

Brain: 'I' is to the right.

Next time you look in a mirror or at a photo of yourself, spare a moment to thank your right hemisphere. For this is the part of your brain you are probably using to recognize your face, according to Julian Paul Keenan and colleagues of Harvard Medical School in Boston.

Keenan's group studied patients who were having their brain hemispheres individually anaesthetized to investigate their epilepsy — a process called the 'Wada' test. While the left or right hemisphere was anaesthetized, the researchers showed the patients photos of themselves morphed to blend their faces with that of a famous person, such as Marilyn Monroe.

Afterwards, when forced to choose between a picture of themselves and a picture of the famous person, those whose right hemispheres had been anaesthetized thought they had been shown a photo of the famous person during anesthesia. If the left hemisphere had been anaesthetized the subject claimed that the photo they'd seen was of himself or herself.

The researchers also saw more activity in the right hemispheres of healthy controls when the pictures contained elements of the controls' own faces. The results are published in this week's Nature.

Neuroscientists have long suspected that the right hemisphere is the seat of self-recognition. There is a rare condition, 'asomatopagnosia', in which patients deny or misidentify their own extremities, which is also associated with damage to the right hemisphere.

Only humans and the higher apes (chimpanzees and orangutans) can distinguish their own face in the mirror. Other monkeys can learn to interpret mirror images of others — turning to see a person enter a room when they spot the reflection in a mirror — but can't learn to recognize themselves.

This is believed to reflect the fact that parts of the right hemisphere (the fronto- temporal cortex) evolved only very recently. Indeed, even humans do not begin to show compelling evidence of self-recognition until they reach 18–24 months old — which is when the prefrontal cortex begins to mature.

"It is conceivable that a right-hemisphere network gives rise to self-awareness which may be a hallmark of higher-order consciousness," Keenan's team concludes.

"Self-awareness, consciousness and mind are an expression of the same underlying process," agrees Gordon G. Gallup, who works on self-awareness in animals at the State University of New York." At about the time that children learn to recognize themselves, they begin to show other evidence of self-conception, such as using personal pronouns, smiling after mastering a task and engaging in self-conscious play."

Keenan, J. P., Nelson, A., O'Connor, M., Pascual-Leone, A. Self-recognition and the right hemisphere.

***

Scientists bring light to a halt in the lab

January 19, 2001, CAMBRIDGE, Massachusetts -- Physicists announced this week that they have managed to stop light, which blazes through the universe at 186,000 miles (300,000 km) per second when unimpeded.

In separate experiments, two teams of researchers said that they brought light particles to a halt and then speed them back up to their usual blistering speed.

Scientists said they hope the achievement could speed the development of super-powerful "quantum computers," which would calculate millions of times faster than present-day counterparts, and inventions that no one has yet dreamed of.

Lene Vestergaard Hau of Harvard University and the Rowland Institute of Science led one of the experiments. Ronald L. Walsworth and Mikhail D. Lukin of the Harvard-Smithsonian Institute for Astrophysics led the other.

Both laboratories are in Cambridge, Massachusetts. The results will be published in upcoming issues of the journals Nature and American Physical Letters.

Physicists who did not participate in the experiments said the two research papers make an important contribution to understanding the properties of light. However, any practical applications are far off, they said.

'Optical molasses'

"It's a real first," said Stanford physicist Stephen Harris, who collaborated on a 1999 experiment with Hau that slowed light to 38 mph.

"These experiments are beautiful science."

In the latest experiments, researchers took steps to not only slow light to a virtual crawl, but to stop it completely.

To do so, they created a trap in which atoms of gas were chilled magnetically to within a few-millionths of a degree of absolute zero and a consistency they described as "optical molasses." Hau's group used sodium atoms, while Walsworth's group used rubidium, an alkaline metal.

Normally, the gas atoms would absorb any light directed into the trap. The researchers solved this problem by aiming a "control" laser beam into the gas, which transformed it from opaque to a state known as electromagnetic ally induced transparency, or EIT.

Then they shined a second, probe laser that operated at a different frequency. When the wave of light particles hit the gas atoms, the particles slowed dramatically.

To stop the probe light entirely, the researchers waited until it had entered the vessel, encountered the gas atoms and imprinted a pattern into the orientation of the spinning atoms.

Then the scientists gradually reduced the intensity of the control beam.

As a result, the probe light dimmed and then vanished. But information in the light particles still was imprinted on the atoms of sodium and rubidium, effectively freezing or storing it, according to Hau.

Reconstituting light:

Then the scientists gradually restored the control beam. The light that had been stored in the spinning atoms was reconstituted and continued its journey through the vessel. "It's as if you stretched a silk thread across a railroad track and a train vanishes into it," said University of Colorado physicist Eric Cornell, who reviewed the Hau study for Nature.

"You wait and then -- bam! -- the train reappears and goes zooming down the track," Cornell said. "It's not at all what you would expect from a pulse of light."

About 50 percent of the light -- and its information -- was retrieved in the regenerated light pulse, scientists said. That might not be good enough for a practical computing system, but it demonstrates how such a system might store and ship data.

"Nothing is ready to be picked up by the optical communications industry," Harris said. "It needs further invention."

The quantum question

The unique properties of the stopped light could be used to make ultra-fast quantum computers.

Here, the light pulse does get dimmer and dimmer and slower and slower, Stein said. "The light does disappear but instead of getting absorbed in the usual way as it heats up atoms, it goes to storing its information in the atoms in the form of something called spin."

This little change could work just like the switches in computers. "You could store zeros and ones just like they are stored in computers," Stein said.

But it would happen much faster and, using the sometimes-weird laws of quantum mechanics, one photon could have more than one "on-off" position at the same time.

Stein said the applications, beyond the use of light in a quantum computer, are not clear. But the same was true of lasers when they were first invented.

"No one foresaw their use in supermarket scanners and so on," he said.

Manipulating light's properties is a subject of intensely competitive research. In July, physicists in Princeton, New Jersey, apparently pushed a laser pulse through a vapor of cesium atoms so it traveled faster than the conventional speed of light.

Bill Delaney: Harvard scientist stops light

January 25, 2001. CNN Boston Bureau Chief Bill Delaney reports on the recent breakthrough by a Harvard scientist who figured a way to stop light for the first time in history.

Q: How was light stopped and what are the implications of this scientific feat?

DELANEY: Harvard scientist Lene Hau has created a way in her laboratory in Cambridge, Massachusetts, to stop light for the first time in history.

When you look at a glass of water with a spoon in it, the spoon will look bent from a certain angle. In that example, what you're seeing is light slowing down. Light slows down in certain media, like water, and will create certain effects like the appearance of the bending of the spoon, but it doesn't slow down much.

About a year-and-a-half ago, Lene Hau figured out how to slow light down all the way down to 38 miles per hour from the pace light usually travels at 186,000 miles per second. That was her first breakthrough.

She's now gone a critical step farther. Using a glob of sodium atoms in an intricate device she created -- which looks like a giant pinball machine on a table, a collection of mirrors and lasers -- Hau has now shot a beam of light into this glob of sodium atoms, cooled just above absolute zero, and the light stopped.

The light actually stalled out inside the glob of sodium atoms, particularly at an instant when the light hits the sodium atoms, it is simultaneously hit with another laser -- what's called a coupling laser.

This all sounds pretty abstract, but it has a very practical application in the world of computers. If you can control the vast energy source of light, if you can stop it and therefore manipulate it, you can create -- at least theoretically -- a whole new generation of super-fast computers, lightning-fast computers, known as quantum computers.

Instead of storing information on a disk, these quantum computers would store and transmit information along optical fiber. Light would store information.

Q: Would these quantum computers be available to the average consumer?

DELANEY: Like most technological breakthroughs, they would likely start out on a more sophisticated level of computer, a type of new generation of super computers.

But like so much technology, what starts out on a very advanced level not accessible to the ordinary person could eventually work its way down to the average person using a computer. What it works out to is using optical fiber and light technology to store and send information. Light is a much more powerful source and could store much more information and move at inconceivably fast speeds.

Another advantage of light-based computers, scientists tell us, is that it will be virtually impossible to break into this system and steal information.

It's all very complex, but it all boils down to conceivably a new generation of computers almost infinitely faster than anything we've ever seen.

And it all starts on a lab on the shores of the Charles River in Cambridge, Massachusetts, where for the first time in history of science light has been stopped.

Q: How long has this scientist been trying to stop light?

DELANEY: Lene Hau has actually been working on experiments with light for about three or four years, which is not a very long time when you're talking about experimental science. She's worked very long hours, and had a lot of hit-and-mostly-miss experiments until about a year-and-a-half ago when they figured out a way to slow light down. It is interesting to ask what happens to light when it's slowed down and when it's stopped.

Q: That's very interesting: What happens to light when it stops? Does it disappear?

DELANEY: It's not too easy for a layman to grasp when Lene Hau begins to talk about the different levels of the atom in explaining how light is stopped. But, in effect, light does disappear when it's stopped. It stalls out. It can be reactivated by, in effect, opening a gate. I mentioned the coupling laser.

The cloud of sodium atoms must be intermingled with this coupling laser to actually stop the light. The coupling laser slams down into the cloud of sodium atoms to stop the light. When the coupling laser is then slammed off, the light again reactivates itself and begins to travel again. That's the bare bones of how this works.

Q: What are the ethical concerns in the scientific community with stopping light?

DELANEY: I asked Lene Hau: Are you changing reality? Are you taking this basic fundamental property of all reality -- light -- and obliterating what exists in existing light?

She said what they are doing is a kind of magic, but on the other hand, it needs to be understood that we are dealing with very, very tiny quantities of light. It's not as if this can be extrapolated to mean that the light flowing off a person's face or off a tree could ultimately be captured or stopped -- almost like some kind of science-fiction manipulation of light. This is a very limited control of light involving this super-cooled sodium that eventually may have implications for super-fast computers.

***

Complacency

Karl Marx was, in spite of much misguided thinking, nevertheless a thinker: Religion as the opiate of the masses. Religion is indeed a source of complacency, a convenience to ease conscience and excuse personal responsibility. My "friend" the Episcopal Priest excuses his own wrongdoing on the basis of religion; but my pointing this out easily angers him. He does not want to accept the personal responsibility of his own wrong actions.

And no one can be a real friend on the basis of religion any more than they can on the basis of alcohol or drug addiction. I have lived to see virtually every kind of immoral act, lying, cheating, stealing, betrayal, and all these excused on the basis of blaming God through religion.

It is religion, as a superstition, that makes the world such a demon-haunted one and dangerous. And the convenience of religion cannot be denied. Beyond the self-deception of easing conscience, for many it makes for a hiding place from much of the ugliness of the world; and for some, from the ugliness of themselves.

January 25, 2001

Last night I was reading in philosophy. It occurred to me that philosophy with the Greeks like Socrates had a beginning in writing. His ideas and questions led to the Who am I, where did I come from, where am I going, what is the purpose of the universe, etc. expressed in writing.

It took centuries for such written expressions of thoughts and questions to overcome superstitions and religious prejudices and men like Kant and others to deal with them from a perspective of the growing field of science. It was science that freed men from dogmatic theology. As long as thinking was confined by religion, real progress in philosophy was impossible.

With real progress in philosophy that could consider science and factor it in, I only have to think about 2001 A Space Odyssey. You will recall the scene suddenly shifting from the ape throwing the bone in the air and the next scenes opening on a space station. There were millions of years intervening between the two events. But from 1,500 AD to the present computer-driven science and technology was a comparative snap of the fingers in time. The past century surpassed all others combined. And how quickly may things change now?

It is because of this that I believe it took a philosophy, humanity, freed of the constraints of religion, to achieve such phenomenal scientific growth in such a relatively short period of time. But the looming specter of knowledge without commensurate wisdom remains.

Now, I can even entertain the idea of time travel… but in what sense? Last night I wondered if I could go back, to what time would I like to travel? Bakersfield with the folks now passed on? Probably. I would like to revisit the era of WWII as experienced as a child, living with the folks and Ronnie, the whole aura of Bakersfield during this period of time. Our little church and grocery store, the people then, the sense of excitement, these are things I would like to experience again.

I would also like to revisit the mining claim before the lake went in and I had the river and forest all to myself.

Then there are certain periods of time as a child in different places while traveling with mom and the various stepfathers… the time in San Pedro, Las Vegas, and others, places like the camps along old Route 66.

But this has to do with loved ones and friends already passed on, not those like my children still living. Would I want to go back in time to be with them when they were still small? Maybe to try to correct mistakes I made as their father?

I would like to relive the good times with people I love now gone on. There are things I would change. But the argument is whether the things changed in the past would change the future. And most would agree that such a thing would be at the very least dangerous and perhaps even catastrophic.

But I would try to save people like those two little girls in Belgium and so many others.

Then again, perhaps if such a thing becomes possible, it will by some mechanism be limited to only those people and events where change for the better could be assured?

Or, consider whether we may be able to visit in some form, call it spirit, which may enable us to experience but not change things? I would certainly like to be able to sit down and talk with my loved ones and friends now gone on. I do this now but get no audible response. Are they in a place where they can hear me and at least share their thoughts with me? Would that be the place I would be visiting as opposed to time travel as we think of such?

Reasonable, responsible, and thoughtful people have written much concerning the enormous complexities that present themselves when considering the implications of time travel.

But only recently, with things like the slowing of light in the laboratory, has such speculation been possible within the framework of serious consideration.

Films and time travel. Do films, books, plays allow us to travel in time; old photographs or things? Is it only in our imagination? As I watch an old Fred Astair and Ginger Rogers movie like Top Hat, I can easily imagine mom enjoying it with me. Or some piece of music, or reading the old Pogo cartoon books that Ronnie and I enjoyed together. The things Grandad and I enjoyed together. Grandma reading to Ronnie and me by a coal oil lamp, Tody's love of birds, is it only in our minds that we go back to those things or do we somehow enjoy them still with those we love?

Perhaps this has some bearing on the ancient beliefs in ghosts, spirits, and may account for some experiences involving the supernatural and paranormal like Psi that people have today.

There do seem to be historical "bounces" of paranormal perception throughout history, replete with exceptional people like Socrates, Alexander the Great, Newton and Einstein, even the seeming paradoxes of the Hitler's gaining power. In times past, some of these were considered conjurors, seers, shamans, people possessed of unexplained "powers."

No one that has studied Psi would entirely discount things like déjà vu, precognition, prescience, out of body experiences, premonition, clairvoyance, even seeing "ghosts" of some kind. While most knowledgeable and reputable researchers easily discount most such claims, enough throughout history remain to give a certain amount of credence to some of these. Savants may be peculiarly susceptible to some of these things.

What if? What if present brain function is increasing at such a rate as to make such things eventually commonplace? The following may have a direct bearing on this and seems to validate my contention that intellectual stimulation does in fact promote actual brain growth and function:

***

Study uncovers mystery cell's role in wiring the brain. January 25, 2001. WASHINGTON (AP) -- Stanford University scientists have filled an important gap in understanding how the brain works, discovering what prompts nerve cells to build the vital connections they need to communicate.

Glial cells, long thought to be just some passive scaffolding for the brain's all-important neurons, are directly responsible for how many connections neurons form so they can talk to each other, the scientists report in Friday's edition of the journal Science.

The surprise discovery could lead to better understanding of how memory forms, and perhaps shed new light on what causes certain brain diseases such as epilepsy or Lou Gehrig's disease.

"I'll bet money that there is going to be some disease that is a breakdown in this regulation," said Dr. Charles Stevens, a neurobiologist who wasn't involved in the new research and calls it a major finding.

More immediately important is the basic understanding of how glial cells affect those vital neuron connections called synapses, he said.

"If you want to understand how the brain computes, you have to understand how they form," explained Stevens, who is with the Salk Institute for Biological Studies in La Jolla, California.

Glial cells make up most of the brain's cells -- for every one neuron there are 10 glia, says Stanford lead researcher Dr. Ben Barres. The scientific dogma was that they only supported neurons, perhaps by providing nutrition, but nobody really knew.

So Barres and postdoctoral student Erik Ullian set out to uncover the function of a main glial cell called an astrocyte.

Neurons are nerve cells that send and receive messages by swapping chemical signals, such as signals that say you're suffering pain or move that leg to walk or retrieve that memory. To do that communicating, neurons first must form synapses.

Scientists once thought neurons were wired to simply build as many synapses as needed. Not so, Barres' team discovered -- young neurons form only a few immature synapses when there are no astrocytes nearby, he said.

But add astrocytes to neurons in laboratory dishes and suddenly they form seven times more synapses, and strong, healthy ones, Barres said. Ullian confirmed the finding with another experiment in which he took astrocytes away and the synapses promptly started shriveling.

"People really have not had a good feel for how the brain controls the number of synapses -- is the neuron just born with it or are there environmental signals?" Barres said. "Our results show absolutely clearly that environmental signals can have a profound effect on how many synapses neurons can have."

What does it mean for brain research? "We're very interested in the possible disease implications," he said. Under the microscope, numerous brain diseases show "gliosis," an abnormal accumulation of glia in the brain-injured area. Perhaps glia overreact to an injury, causing neurons to form too many synapses and thus triggering the over firing that means an epileptic seizure, Barres theorized.

Or consider degenerative diseases like Lou Gehrig's, in which neurons initially die in just one area before the disease spreads. Could overreacting glia kill those additional neurons by over stimulating them?

Then there's the question of memory. Many scientists believe memories are stored by building or strengthening synapses. Astrocytes signal neurons to build synapses by secreting a protein.

If Barres could identify that protein -- he has experiments under way to try -- then scientists could test both the disease and memory theories.

***

Giordano Bruno (1548-1600) burned at the stake as a heretic for his philosophy questioning dogmatic theology.

Immanuel Kant (1724-1804), perception and reason, nature the creature and humankind the creator, the mind causing action; and if action, subject to laws of the mind, which, if understood, may very well have a "physics" of its own, a "physics of the spirit."

It is of the utmost importance that Kant knew the work of Newton. This influenced Kant tremendously and had to have had a great impact on his philosophical thought. Kant and Newton must have influenced Emerson and Thoreau.

A major omission in Kant's thinking was his low opinion of women and the fact that he never married. These, as with Thoreau, were decided flaws that show themselves in their respective philosophies. A complete philosophy must include the input of both halves of humanity on a basis of equal value.

But given that it was not possible for women to make their contribution to philosophy during the time frame, another factor should be considered in the rapid increases in science and technology; that of the contributions women have been increasingly able to make.

Beginning to make their voices heard in literature, women gradually began to make their place in the professions, including medicine and science. Madam Curie immediately comes to mind.

While not yet having earned a place of equal value in philosophy, I believe the contributions of women have had a direct impact on the rapid acceleration of science and technology, on the increase of brain growth and function. It may even prove to be that women are more sensitive than men in some areas that make a great contribution to a more complete acceleration of brain growth and function for humanity as a whole.

The Stoics may have been on to something when they thought of philosophy having geometric design. If you take away the religion, what remains may well be that of philosophy having geometric design. Rational, logical thought would certainly lend itself to geometry, as does the best of music. The geometrical design found in all of nature, including the brain and that of the brain that is "self awareness" seems to follow geometrical precision when at its best form.

It is my thought of a "spiritual physics" that melds with the physics of the universe that causes me to speculate on things like time travel, of the potential for the mind to accomplish marvelous things, things that are not as yet understood but seen to happen, things like "miraculous" healings for example.

Kant argued to separate what could be known from the metaphysical. But he couldn't know the progress that science would make in reconciling the two. Much that was once thought metaphysical has become a part of the body of science. But as a brilliant man, he would be able to understand much of the science that gave us X-rays and nuclear energy.

The human capacity for the ideas of the ideals of truth, beauty, justice, and virtue has caused problems for philosophers. Once you enter this area of thought, you are in a world of ideas that do not always lend themselves to a strict empiricism.

Something else has always been at work in poetry, for example, that treats with ideals not known in a practical sense in physics, or nature red in tooth and claw.

Still, the ideals persist; they are there. For this reason I believe we will eventually have a "spiritual physics" ever much as real as the present physics and totally compatible with it. Subatomic particle research is already opening doors of understanding approaching what I call spiritual physics.

Even those things in imagination, like the pot of gold at the end of a rainbow or fairies dancing in a forest have a kind of truth to them. It is a kind of truth that seems inextricably entwined with our thoughts and hopes of immortality, of the eventual triumph of good over evil.

While it remains absolutely essential that mere belief be separate from actual knowledge, it is at least as important to realize that peace, for example, cannot be achieved by knowledge alone; it must be accompanied with wisdom (something I believe to be the essential attribute of spiritual physics), the application of knowledge to the best ends.

Thus a strictly empirical pragmatism is not suitable to beings capable of imagination and dreams, nor especially for beings capable of entertaining thoughts of ideals of truth and beauty.

Nor can accounts of either "angels" or "demons" be dismissed out of hand. And the use of drugs throughout history to induce states of mind (altered states of consciousness) more susceptible to influences not readily accessible otherwise should be taken into account when considering the desire of human beings to reach beyond the merely physical world.

Apart from the abuse of drugs and alcohol for other purposes, it does seem that at least some of the present use of drugs is for the purpose of trying to reach out beyond the physical self and world much as some artists and writers have done. That this use (and abuse) of drugs has reached such epidemic proportions may in part and in fact be due to increasing brain growth and function.

There has always been a natural tendency among many to resist change. The Luddites of old represent a rebellion to technology that is very much in evidence now. The restraints of religion since ancient times and even at present bears witness to this reluctance toward change.

But with increasing awareness of human potential due to increased brain growth and function, the use of drugs in order to enhance "spiritual physics" may have some credence.

It does seem the spirit of searching beyond ourselves has been a major occupation of humankind. It was a compulsion of great minds like those of Conan Doyle and Thomas Edison. It was the driving compulsion of Newton and Einstein. Things like the pyramids and other similar structures found all over the world bear testimony to this fact of "searching." With the beginnings of organized philosophy, such searching has become increasingly focused and sensible, most especially once science became a "partner" in the search of philosophy.

Kant did, more than other philosophers, lead in causing those following to be less dogmatic in assertions of knowledge. While Socrates opened the door to questioning ideas and beliefs held as fact without any proof, Kant went the further step of questioning all things without the stricture of religion. As a result, many things were open to honest and legitimate examination for philosophy that had been held in abeyance before his writings like Critique of Pure Reason.

As a "Transcendentalist" Kant believed in reaching beyond the physical for answers. Emerson and Thoreau went even further, but a new era of science was beginning to blossom in the time of these men in which their minds were capable of exploring further.

Of most importance in a search for truth, dogmatism was beginning to give way to scientific examination. The demand for proofs of assertions began to strip away what were only beliefs. The Scopes Trial in very recent history is a glaring example of how difficult it is to separate beliefs from knowledge.

But the more we learn, the more there seems to learn. An appreciation of our ignorance is essential to real learning. As a consequence, where I am lacking in certitude, I have become far more circumspect in expressing my own thoughts on some subjects. There is far more need for me to do more thinking and less speaking.

It is in writing that the best formulation of thought takes place. It is no wonder that little progress in philosophy, or science, could take place until writing became a fully functional tool. And with such a phenomenal tool, humanity began to be able to free itself from the ignorance and superstitions that held sway for thousands of years.

And while much remains to be done to rid the world of the kinds of ignorance and superstitions that lead to people killing each other in the name of God and leads to superstitious beliefs that retard real knowledge and wisdom, there would never be hope of doing so without writing.

But logic would seem to dictate that the other half of humanity, women, are going to have to take their place in philosophy on the basis of equal value and the compatibility of differences before a complete philosophy is possible. The greatest thoughts of the greatest thinkers, as long as they are all men, can only go so far.

When theology reigned as the "Queen of the Sciences" real science had no place as such. Now that theology has had to give place to a more enlightened world where real science has earned its place, the King of Disciplines, Philosophy, has made accommodation to further enlightenment. But as I have pointed out, while knowledge grows, wisdom seems an orphan, divorced from knowledge.

And it will probably remain so until women do earn their place in philosophy.

God as an *a priori* first cause has been challenged by science but cannot be entirely discounted since this remains an area of speculation. And it cannot be said that science is antithetical to the existence of God or Gods as a first cause. But as science and philosophy continue to bond finding increasingly common ground leading to a spiritual physics, presumptive apologetics concerning first causes fall away as we discover more of the actual workings of the universe.

Religion served a purpose when science was absent. But with the increased understanding of the very mechanics of the universe, religion was no longer necessary as a "comfort zone" on which to rely for those things that began to be explained by the scientific method. And a religious dualism, one that made God the prime cause for both good and evil, which haunted Hawthorne and Melville was never satisfactory to reason by any definition. But it did breed many skeptics, agnostics, and atheists.

Still, in a world where half the population of over six billion has never received a phone call, it can be understood that religion continues to have a profound presence and influence. But as technology, particularly by means of media, makes continued advances, more and more people come under its influence.

But it undeniably has the power to influence for evil as well as good. It makes for the possibility of nuclear annihilation; it can persuade a society that there are no moral absolutes, that perversion is acceptable in a society, that abortion as a means of contraception is acceptable.

There is so much yet to learn. But whether Kant, Emerson, or Heisenberg et al, I always remember the words of a man that knew he was going to his death. He didn't become a world-renowned philosopher and most would say he gave his life in a wrong cause. But there is no discounting the truth of his last testament concerning the need of a better "conductor" for the "Universal Lyre."

Ensign Heiichi Okabe

22 February 1945

I am actually a member at last of the Kamikaze Special Attack Corps.

My life will be rounded out in the next thirty days. My chance will come! Death and I are waiting. The training and practice have been rigorous, but it is worthwhile if we can die beautifully and for a cause.

I shall die watching the pathetic struggle of our nation. My life will gallop in the next few weeks as my youth and life draw to a close...

...The sortie has been scheduled for the next ten days.

I am a human being and hope to be neither saint nor scoundrel, hero nor fool – just a human being. As one who has spent his life in wistful longing and searching, I die resignedly in the hope that my life will serve as a "human document."

The world in which I live was too full of discord. As a community of rational human beings it should be better composed. Lacking a single great conductor, everyone lets loose with his own sound, creating dissonance where there should be melody and harmony.

It is Philosophy, the King of Disciplines, to which humanity looks for new ideas that hold promise of the melody and harmony Ensign Okabe spoke of. To consider Emerson and Melville, for example, it is preposterous to believe that new things, new thoughts, are not possible. Socrates was condemned to death and Bruno burned at the stake for their legitimate questions and new ideas. And it is always well to keep in mind the words of both Newton and Einstein that they stood on the shoulders of giants past in order to see further than other men.

But to use Emerson's own words of caution proving his wisdom, it is also of the utmost importance that the prestige of sages past does not deter us from breaking with the past when it is proved false. Time and stature are no guarantees of the truth, but what is presented as the truth must always be subject to the most intense interrogation.

So it is well, to consider Emerson's thoughts on the subject, to keep society large in our souls, but friendships few, as those real friends to the philosopher will be those whose actions, not just their words, prove them to be legitimate contenders for truth and beauty.

Beauty in the eye of the beholder is a combination of the cognitive and imagination. And while given to a degree of subjectivity, certain standards do apply when choosing between that which is beautiful and that which is patently ugly.

Truth of an absolute may be found in love, but love can turn to hatred. As with degrees of love, so there are degrees of beautiful.

The greatest of philosophical searches may be said the seeking of absolute harmony in which there are no discrepancies, no difficulties or argument with definitions of love, truth, and beauty, where the cognitive is in full agreement with the imagination and recognized and acknowledged by all, and this in turn leads to a coalescing with natural laws in which physics and spiritual physics come together and meld as whole and complete, the two becoming one with the capacity to reach the stars and making the origin of all things comprehensible.

Since it is at this point that infinity, immortality, eternity, become comprehensible terms, it is obvious that the direction in which brain growth and function should be encouraged by increasing intellectual stimulation as well as imagination be acknowledged and acted upon. But the imagination must be tempered, and nourished, by the cognitive; hence the necessity of the progress of both the physics of nature and the physics of the soul or spirit. The cognitive makes it possible to recognize the flower or rainbow, but the imagination gives them meaning of beauty. As beings filled with intimations of immortality and fired with the spark of divinity, we would not want to have one without the other.

Beauty in the eye of the beholder is a combination of the cognitive and imagination. And while given to a degree of subjectivity, certain standards do apply when choosing between that which is beautiful and that which is patently ugly.

Truth of an absolute may be found in love, but love can turn to hatred. As with degrees of love, so there are degrees of beautiful.

The greatest of philosophical searches may be said the seeking of absolute harmony in which there are no discrepancies, no difficulties or argument with definitions of love, truth, and beauty, where the cognitive is in full agreement with the imagination and recognized and acknowledged by all, and this in turn leads to a coalescing with natural laws in which physics and spiritual physics come together and meld as whole and complete, the two becoming one with the capacity to reach the stars and making the origin of all things comprehensible.

Since it is at this point that infinity, immortality, eternity, become comprehensible terms, it is obvious that the direction in which brain growth and function should be encouraged by increasing intellectual stimulation as well as imagination be acknowledged and acted upon. But the imagination must be tempered, and nourished, by the cognitive; hence the necessity of the progress of both the physics of nature and the physics of the soul or spirit. The cognitive makes it possible to recognize the flower or rainbow, but the imagination gives them meaning of beauty. As beings filled with intimations of immortality and fired with the spark of divinity, we would not want to have one without the other.

This reminds me of a letter I recently sent a lovely lady:

Toward the end of the 30s Nelson Eddy and Jeanette MacDonald were heralded the King and Queen of Hollywood… and rightly so. And Wanting You remains, to me, the most beautiful love song ever done. And no one has ever been able to duplicate the music or screen romance of Eddy and MacDonald.

The sheer beauty of the combination of the two that sends the spirit soaring and promises hope in the face of hopelessness is that "something" lost to the last couple of generations. But I am determined that it will not die with me. I want this for my children, for all children. The very majesty of such a thing must be preserved.

The tragedy of it all is that so many know this, but the cynicism of the age prevents them from reaching out to the stars. The stars are still there regardless the cynicism. And if heaven does not hold promise of this, it is a cheat!

***

February 9, 2001

While I have learned to exercise caution regarding dogmatic statements, "pontificating" if you will, last night as I was reading Emerson's Address to Divinity Students again the thought came to me that he had made the dogmatic statements opposing many errors, which no longer needed to be stated by me.

There is a need for dogmatism when confronting evil and egregious error. In Emerson's time there was much religious superstition and error that needed to be confronted, an age of science and reason was dawning but much darkness remained. But Emerson and others have said much that needed to be said and I do not have to repeat such worthies, particularly since those errors are no longer a problem of the proportion they were then. I suppose this has had an impact on my reluctance to be dogmatic in many cases.

True enough, as I have matured and become better educated the tendency has been to become more cautious in making dogmatic statements. With increasing age, expanding education and maturity, there is an increasing awareness of the complexity of many things once thought simple.

I often resort to Lincoln and his culminating wisdom exhibited in his unsurpassed, sublime Gettysburg Address. The very founding of our nation, the "Great Experiment in Democracy" Alexis Tocqueville referred to, required the amazing group called our Founding Fathers. Deficient as they were in many things, the most obvious the refusal to abolish slavery by the Constitution, they were nevertheless the product of the some of the best of the ideas and ideals of the time. The very genius of men like Franklin, Jefferson, Adams, Hamilton, the truly amazing character of Washington, all these exhibited the result of a growing intellectualism leading to the thought so well considered and defended by Lincoln that a people could govern themselves.

Lincoln was, more than any other, cognizant of the very genius of such an ideal. Time had passed, and Lincoln had rooted himself in that ideal of self-government. He was the inheritor of the ideals of the wisdom of the Founding Fathers. And as the inheritor, he took possession and improved the inheritance, surpassing those "Fathers" as any parents would want of their child.

Lincoln and Emerson were contemporaries. No two men could have been further apart in background and education. And while many biographers of Lincoln give him little credit for metaphysical transcendentalism, no one who is thoroughly familiar with the writings of each man can fail to make the connection between them.

I find myself in today's minority, that of Herndon's, that Lincoln had a courtly love, a true Sir Walter Scott love, for Ann Rutledge and never recovered from the melancholy of her untimely death. I agree with Herndon because I think I know Lincoln as only a poet can know him. Such a love would impact Lincoln in a way comparable to the stories of Camelot. I believe Lincoln carried his Lady's Colors next to his heart for the rest of his life and impacted on every decision he made, and comes to full flower in his most sublime expression of the soul that loves in the Gettysburg Address. I believe his was the kind of love, the purest love that found vent in the greatest poetry ever written, in his profound and final commitment to the ideals of the Founding Fathers, and surpassing them to the ideals of unity and freedom.

Unlike Emerson, Lincoln's business became politics. And he was an astute politician. But no one questioned his integrity or honesty, even in the usual spoils system or deal-making characteristic then as now.

But I have wondered how differently things might have been for us had Lincoln been educated as Emerson? Would we have known Lincoln now for surpassing Dostoevsky or Tolstoy in literature? Would we be thinking of Lincoln the Great Philosopher instead of the Great Emancipator? Certainly he left enough to entertain such thoughts.

Thomas Edison admired Thomas Paine because of his stand against religion. I consider *Aes Triplex* by Robert Louis Balfour Stevenson a reasonable look at death. And toward the end of his life, Edison did believe a machine could be invented that would allow the departed to speak to us.

I take comfort in talking to my loved ones and friends now gone on before me. But, so far, no audible replies. This does not mean that they don't influence my thoughts. If so, it would explain much of my work and writing, especially my concern for children.

Chapter Two

I was just thinking about the hospital administrator that walked out of his office one day and never came back. He left a $72,000 a year job to become a street person in Northern California. His family could never get him to return to his home or job. He explained: This is my life. And it was.

And I recall the fellow in a sanitarium that spent his entire day, every day, walking around a tree. He would clasp the trunk in his left hand and circle the tree counter-clockwise and as he passed a low limb, would reach up and slap it with his right hand. This was his life.

I used to know a young woman, quite lovely but disabled, that spent every day at a bar sipping wine and playing the game machines. She told me: This is my life. And it was.

Well, in one perspective this is much like the story of bemoaning not having shoes until you see someone with no feet. And true as this is, if you live in a relatively affluent society and still find your life without meaning, filled with ennui and the "blues" as such a state of mind is sometimes called, it can lead to hopelessness that your life is of real value or of accomplishing any thing of value with your life.

But much of such hopelessness is predicated on the world itself not seeming to accomplish anything of real value, of not having any real meaning. Of such thinking comes the basis of some nihilistic philosophy.

In my solitude (great old song) I find myself wanting to enter a dialogue and make some of the following suggestions:

I would argue that the dinosaurs were not a good idea, that nature red in tooth and claw was not a good idea. I would kill all mosquitoes and glassy-winged sharpshooters. I would get rid of the mice, rats, gophers and all the snakes that feed on them. I see nothing beautiful in a hippo or elephant, the great cats that tear and rend to feed, the bears you can never trust, these are part of the failures of creation or evolution whichever you choose.

In respect to either creation or evolution, an ancient hominid six million years ago or "Lucy" four and one-half million years ago, I have to ask why? Things like this and the dinosaurs seem more like creation or evolution gone awry, much like trial and error. And had the dinosaurs not become extinct? Where would that have led… reptilian Newtons and Rembrandts?

As the world has never been kind to children, so I would point out that the world has never been kind to the softer and gentler, the poetic higher aspirations of humanity. I would have settled for the rainbows and butterflies without the dinosaurs, volcanoes, earthquakes, and flies.

Perhaps, as with Thoreau, this is in part because the idea of feeding on slaughtered animals is not convenient to my imagination; that I believe we could achieve a higher degree of success as human beings if we could leave off the killing and raising of animals for slaughter. As a child, I was raised in an environment with animals and fowl meant for butchering and eating and was taught to do my share of dispatching and preparing these creatures for the table. During WWII I am certain the dinner tables in Kern County, California, including ours, saw their share of horse and mule meat. We were even treated to the odor of a meat packing plant just up the road from us.

I hadn't yet read Upton Sinclair's The Jungle, I hadn't visited the abattoirs where the cattle were killed and butchered, but even if I had I don't think such a visit would have persuaded me to leave off the eating of animals. My childhood was spent in raising animals for food, the hunting of creatures like quail and deer to eat. In other words, this was part of my culture, my society; and as such, fully approved by my elders, who taught me this was normal, natural, and healthy.

But I no longer believe this. Not because of the threat of E. coli, BSE, lysteria, trichinosis, or salmonella, but because it no longer seems civilized to me. And what need of cattle, hogs, and sheep when fruits, vegetables, cereals and soy products have developed to the point where they could easily supplant red meat?

One cannot read Charles Lamb's Dissertation "Upon a Roast Pig" without thinking of Jonathan Swift's Modest Proposal or the humor of Sam Clemens. Granted that none of these wrote to the point of encouraging the leaving off of eating animals, I believe that if they had the information in hand that we possess today, they may well have lent their pens to encouraging vegetarianism. The very barbarism of some of the people and societies these men wrote of lead me to think they would give serious consideration to my own suggestions in this regard.

But to go beyond these and my friend Henry Thoreau, I believe that we as human beings should control nature red in tooth and claw and bring it into submission to a kinder and gentler nature, a true balance of nature for the first time in the history of the world. A human kind that could split the atom and walk on the moon seems incongruous to one that does not devote attention to bringing nature into submission and relieve it from bloodshed, both of animals and people.

I believe Emerson and his often reluctant, resentful, and envious disciple Thoreau were correct in pointing out the need for people to live in harmony with nature and the giving of attention to the soul, but the present condition of nature makes such a thing impossible. As does the greed and selfishness, the ignorance and prejudices of too much of humanity. And I would include among these those that consider themselves "environmentalists" and "animal lovers" that refuse the logic of confronting the problem of nature red in tooth and claw. If a bear, like a dinosaur, ever served a useful purpose, which I do not believe, the "purpose" is long past. And if tigers and alligators are your "thing," I have to ask why? I'll take the koalas, pandas, bunnies and baby ducks (with controlled breeding) and eliminate the predators; including dogs and cats.

Both natural and catastrophic selection had their parts to play in the earth becoming what it is and for life to become what it is. But once Homo sapiens developed to a certain point, human selection began. Humans began to decide which animals and plants to breed and cultivate; a beginning if you will of bringing the earth into submission. The justifiable fear of "Frankenstein-like" genetic engineering is now a force with which to reckon. But as a tool for good, the prospects for "subduing" the earth loom on a grander scale!

But what about pets? I hear people say. To which I reply: Well, what about them? I love animals, I have a cat, but for the greater good of humankind I believe we could well dispense with such. I'll take the bunny. At least the bunny doesn't prey on other animals; and Jimmy Carter notwithstanding bunnies don't attack people.

Of course the howls of protest can be heard immediately at such a suggestion. "Balance of Nature!" I hear the cry. Where? I ask in return. If Nature were ever balanced, I defy anyone to dispassionately show me where!

But a real balance of nature is within the power of humankind. I would far rather the bluebird and mockingbird, the quail and partridge, than hawks and blue jays.

Think for a moment why any creature like a lion should be thought "beautiful?" Is it because of some primeval and barbaric bloodlust in humanity, some long-past worship of power in beasts reflective of a similar corruption in our own nature? Immediately I think of bear-baiting, bull, cock, and dog fighting that seems to appeal to the very basest of human nature. Not to mention the butchering of animals and people as sacrifices to mythological "gods."

Granting that there are responsible people that own and train guard and attack dogs, what does it say for a society that feels it needs such animals? And in far too many cases, the owners of such animals are not responsible, are not the best representatives of a civilized society.

As to the environment, let the peoples of the world pay attention to birth control and their eating habits, like the enormous consumption of animals, let the world pay attention to the need of these being addressed before they try to solve the global problems of pollution and the environment would not be in danger. Getting rid of the "animals" in our societies, the lawless criminals that prey on human beings, and walking, even "sauntering" as per Thoreau, once more might come back into vogue without such reliance on automobiles, which have become not only modes of transportation, but steel and glass shells of relative safety, of homes away from home. Why, the nations might find they don't even need guns and nuclear arsenals.

The myth of God supposedly telling human kind to subdue the earth has real merit, but every Dominion Theology following, being religious, has never been able to overcome the fatal flaw of dualistic thinking that makes God responsible for both good and evil. Hawthorne and Melville, despite their genius, both made shipwreck on this paradoxical rock.

But the fable of the Garden included Adam and Eve being vegetarians and the shedding of the blood of animals being the result of disobedience to the will of God. Our teeth, for example, are far better designed for the masticating of cereals, fruits, and vegetables than that of predators for the tearing and rending of flesh.

Indeed we should subdue the earth and have dominion over it. We are capable of doing so, we are capable of eliminating the weeds and thistles, the beasts of prey, of an agriculture that would be more than sufficient for our needs once these other problems like birth control, both human and animal, are acknowledged, confronted and overcome.

And it isn't just the argument that it takes eight pounds of grain to produce one pound of meat that is at issue; particularly when you factor in the issue of unproductive mouths, an issue that does have to be considered necessitating birth control. What is needed is an entirely new way, a new philosophy if you will, of thinking about diet that incorporates all the logical factors impinging on health. Logically it makes no sense for any culture to encourage non-productive welfare births, for example, that has little chance at success, but on the contrary is more likely to sap the resources of a society and enlarge a criminal population, a distasteful fact, but still a fact.

But rather than address such an inflammatory fact, responsible people and the leadership lack the will to confront it, blaming instead institutions such as the schools and social services for not performing miracles. I am not a friend of the way our schools and social services do business. But in all fairness, they are asked to do the impossible under the circumstances.

Such a thing as the lack of responsible birth control measures is patently and inherently unhealthy for any culture or society. Any discussion of "human rights" must begin to take into account those that have no regard for personal responsibility for their actions or the rights and property of others. Here in America we are encouraging hoards of barbarians and vandals by insanely encouraging irresponsibility and a lack of accountability on the part of individuals, the media, and on the part of the leaders of our institutions and government.

It would be legitimate for those being forced to pay the bill for welfare to ask this question: Who made the decision that welfare as a way of life should include reproductive rights without hope of being able to support the resulting children?

Oliver Wendell Holmes, the world-famed jurist and the only one with whom most would equate John Marshall (Millions for defense, but not one cent for tribute) favored sterilization in some cases and argued his point with the acute precision and intelligence for which he was known and properly honored.

The father of Justice Holmes was an intimate of such luminaries of intellectualism as Emerson, Whittier, Lowell, Longfellow, Prescott, Agassiz, and Hawthorne. Being raised in such a surrounding of great minds, Justice Holmes himself had the companionship of men like Henry and Brooks Adams and Henry and William James, so it is no wonder that he would be drawn in large measure to philosophy and would count Emerson, credited as the greatest thinker and writer America ever produced, as his mentor.

But Justice Holmes would never have countenanced the barbarism of a Hitler, for example, that would use forced sterilization for "ethnic cleansing" and political aims. But then the power of a dictator is not subject to any law. Holmes couldn't have foreseen the medical advances of contraception that would make it practicable to use contraceptive drugs rather than irreversible surgery to achieve the desired end for the public good. Had he been able to do so, there is no doubt the famed Supreme Court Justice would agree that in some cases court ordered contraception was imminently sensible, right, and just.

Before some readers might be too quick to disagree, I call their attention to what FDR said of Justice Holmes: For him, law was an instrument of just relations between man and man. And President Roosevelt said this of the man that found a just cause in sterilization, which recognized that in a just society the responsibility for the public welfare had to take cognizance of such a thing no matter how unpalatable for too often misguided social conscience.

The logic of the position of court ordered contraception is irrefutable on the facts alone. Only the emotionally irrational and immature, or those with a vested interest in continuing to advocate "drones" to live off the productive efforts of others would argue against such logic. It brooks no argument that those that continue to breed with no thought to taking care of the resulting offspring should not have "rights" that supercede those that live responsibly. To attempt to argue that there is such a thing as "reproductive rights" at the expense of others and without concomitant personal responsibility is to reveal an utter selfishness that carried to the extreme would destroy any nation!

I would ask the reader to consider the questions of why our leadership seems dedicated to a so-called "war on drugs" that all agree is un-winnable, why it seems dedicated to building more prisons rather than addressing the root cause of the growing populations of criminals, most coming from the city ghettos and barrios? Yet this same leadership takes exception to the far more humane argument that I am certain Justice Holmes would make in favor of court ordered contraception for those that refuse to be responsible for their own actions and continue to feed off that responsible segment of society. Thus it is that the rich get richer and the poor get poorer. As some wit put it: Why work when I can steal; though no politician facing election or reelection dares call it "theft" when so many feed at the public trough.

Sam Clemens opposed women being given the franchise because he knew politics to be a "dirty business." He said "Judas Iscariot was only a premature congressman!" and "The only honest politician is one that hasn't had time to sell out!" One only has to read Claude Bowers' "The Tragic Era" to understand such cynicism and agree.

But, then, to try to carry any argument on the basis of emotion alone is to lose the argument though it may win the day. Though in winning the day on this basis is invariably to bring pain and suffering to the innocent. Such is the case of abortion as a means of contraception, something that encourages violence and the devaluing of life, while at the same time refuses to discuss logically this issue of "reproductive rights." But the illogic of this position is to prove the paucity of intellectualism in America today and reinforces the idea that we have evolved a power structure of authority that is more concerned with maintaining its position than it is with the future of our posterity and our nation.

Tragically, we can hardly credit any in positions of authority here in America with the minds of a Ralph Waldo Emerson or Justice Oliver Wendell Holmes. Any discussion of this subject of "reproductive rights" would quickly prove the point. What we have as a curse that cannot be endured forever is a lack of those in authority with such intellectual capacity, let alone the courage of their convictions.

But pretenders to intellectualism such as Rosenblatt, Will, Buckley, et al abound and the time would fail to list them. For those really interested in my accusation and would like to dispute it I ask only this: Name one of these pretenders that are willing to take on the argument concerning the fact that women are not found in the numbers and on the basis of equal value in the King of Disciplines, Philosophy! But to be fair, neither Emerson nor Holmes seemed to have noticed this omission. Their failure to take notice of this might be excused on the basis of the times in which they lived (though personally I believe they should have noticed such a blatant omission). But such an excuse is no longer acceptable.

As a result, before any attack my position concerning court ordered contraception and the lack of true intellectualism in America I ask the above question be considered before going on the offensive (I might also suggest they ponder the problem of the paucity of women in the United Nations and exercise their "intellect" in this direction as well).

There is something terribly wrong in a society that keeps producing children no one wants, children of parents who believe it is the responsibility of society to care for and such parents are rewarded for their irresponsibility by producing children that have little chance of becoming productive adults. If personal responsibility for such children is not taken by their parents the case for forced contraception is not only logical, but it is humane. I have nothing against orphanages or foster homes; I do have something against a system and those that make them necessary for millions of unwanted children. I do have something against those and a system that promotes violence and a devaluing of life through abortion as a means of contraception.

But speaking of violence and devaluing life, a vegetarian world of people and beasts… In all logic, what's wrong with the idea? I do believe a generation born and raised in such a manner according to the suggestions I have offered would consider the previous generations of animal killers and eaters savage and barbaric! Not to mention the crude TV commercials of people eating in a disgusting manner with full sound effects.

But, then, just looking at the violence now so graphically portrayed in films, "games," and TV would quickly convince them of the barbarism and savagery of previous generations, together with the fact that people considering themselves "civilized" are still killing one another in the name of God because of their religious prejudices, and over something some call a "Holy Land."

I believe I was taught better and tried to teach my children better. As I would tell them: My love or friendship is not contingent on people agreeing with me. But I do require that they not be disagreeable in making their disagreement known to me.

I was a young man when I built a house by hand. I now realize there was more to it than the need I felt to build a house. I think I was following Thoreau's idea that a man needs to build his own house in order to learn and understand things about himself and nature, about humanity and poetry that can be learned by applying his hands and mind to such a task.

In building that house I confess there was a touch of Poe's Domain of Arnheim. But I chose a remote location on five acres closer to nature. And while it would have all the amenities of modern living, I would not have considered the project in a city. My ideals were those I entertained as a boy living in the Sequoia National Forest when I longed for my own cabin in the wilderness.

It would not have occurred to me as a boy to consider the thoughts of Emerson on the subject, though I now realize such thoughts were latent in me at the time, but now my mind does turn to him often and the following passage helps to explain the way I felt as a boy when I had that forest to explore on my own and lived the life of a "mountain man," both in fact as well as in my imagination in which J.F. Cooper and Zane Grey were my boon companions.

From Self-reliance:

When a man lives with God, his voice shall be as sweet as the murmur of the brook and the rustle of the corn. And now at last the highest truth on this subject remains unsaid; probably cannot be said, for all that we say is the far off remembering of the intuition. That thought, by what I can now nearest approach to say it, is this. When good is near you, when you have life in yourself, - it is not by any known or appointed way; you shall not discern the footprints of any other; you shall not see the face of man; you shall not hear any name; - the way, the thought, the good, shall be wholly strange and new. It shall exclude all other being. You take the way from man, not to man. All persons that ever existed are its fugitive ministers. There shall be no fear in it. Fear and hope are alike beneath it. It asks nothing. There is somewhat low even in hope. We are then in vision. There is nothing that can be called gratitude, nor properly joy. The soul is raised over passion. It seeth identity and eternal causation. It is a perceiving that Truth and Right are. Hence it becomes a Tranquility out of the knowing that all things go well. Vast spaces of nature; the Atlantic Ocean, the South Sea; vast intervals of time, years, centuries, are of no account. This which I think and feel underlay that former state of life and circumstances, as it does underlie my present and will always all circumstances, and what is called life and what is called death.

Though a classicist in his own right, when Thoreau made reference to the myth of Pallas Athena (Minerva) springing forth from the head of Zeus, I wonder if he wasn't borrowing from this thought of Emerson's? Emerson himself may have had the myth in his own mind in the above passage since he was a well-qualified, expert classicist.

I wonder if Emerson really was as brilliant as people said, and still say, that his was the greatest intellect America ever produced? I believe so. And I believe the above proves it. Few would dispute the claim that he was the greatest writer and thinker of his age.

At that, it is probable that Emerson spoke/wrote better than he knew. Real genius often does. And while it was not possible for him to know the things that I do today, while he could not know the direction history would take, he had obviously understood those things that would lead to my idea of the Amendment, the equation, and the need of women in philosophy, much as the myth of Minerva's origin.

And while I wonder if such ideas are the product of my own thinking or soul, or the ideas of those gone on before me that know the truth and suggest them to me, I believe Emerson is correct in saying that such truth is beyond the ordinary kin of what we would call the intellect alone; a kind of "intuition of the soul," a "living with God?" I do wonder.

As with those "Intimations of Immortality" that Wordsworth wrote of, it does seem to me that the Amendment and women and philosophy, the equation k+w=p, are not from my intellect, or "knowing." They seem to have sprung unbidden by any conscious effort on my part, of any conscious effort at deducing the answers to the ills of humanity… the intuition of the soul…?

But such thoughts are properly considered "metaphysical," or more charitably simply fanciful and beyond our present science to explain. What Emerson described could well be construed as madness. And it has been so described many times throughout history. But many things once considered madness are now taken for the greatest good sense of the finest minds.

Yet there are those things, such very human things that get in the way of "living with God," of being open to those "intuitions of the soul." It may be that the genius of Thoreau was unhorsed by these things because in spite of his own genius, in spite of his claiming to want to settle for being free of the need to "sell his baskets," in spite of my personal feelings about him as a friend and soul-brother and the constant re-reading of Walden, there is a certain envy and resentment of Emerson in the great teacher of Simplicity in Living and the author of Civil Disobedience.

Thoreau did envy his great mentor Emerson. He smarted under what he felt was the failure of Emerson and others to appreciate his genius and "buy his baskets." As Emerson so well said in eulogizing Thoreau, he almost counted it a fault in him that he "had no ambition." By this, Emerson, using the gentle way of speaking for which he was so well known, was talking about Thoreau's ego that insisted others should buy his baskets on his terms.

But my dear friend Henry could not seem to exercise the "ambition" to overcome his ego. There was too much justification for James Russell Lowell's criticism of him that "… there was no excuse for his unbounded egotism," that he lived on the "windfalls of Emerson's orchard."

But I wonder; had Thoreau married and had children perhaps family would have sustained him, perhaps have even led his own genius to becoming his own man? There is nothing like a wife and children that so well serves the purpose of teaching invaluable lessons of life providing a man is not too selfish and egocentric to learn such lessons.

In how many ways has genius been undone by this fault, this tragic flaw, of Thoreau's pained ego. And what a lesson there is for all of us in such a tragedy. We rightly honor Henry for the legacy of his writings, without which English literature would be so much the poorer. But we would be foolish indeed to accept them carte blanche.

But more than the desire to escape the enormous demands of technology and hurried pace of modern living, the decline of real learning and scholarship contributed to making Henry a favorite because of the very thing he contemptuously called "easy reading," while his mentor and the greater man, Emerson, because he is not such easy reading, began to fade, even recently called by one self-appointed university "scholar" a "hobby for antiquarians."

It wasn't necessary, of course, for men like Gandhi and M.L. King Jr. to know these faults of Thoreau in order to appreciate his Civil Disobedience and find direction and inspiration from the tract. But they could have found the inspiration, even the very thoughts, for the tract in Emerson. And I ask myself, would Civil Disobedience have even been in Thoreau's mind had it not been for the thoughts and words of his mentor? I don't believe so, notwithstanding the story about Thoreau's "prisons."

Sometime claims of "standing on the shoulders of giants" notwithstanding, where the masters that could have taught Shakespeare, Newton, Emerson, or Lincoln? It is good advice for some to follow their own genius. But it is no disgrace to not be a Shakespeare, Newton, Emerson, or Lincoln, only to ape them, and in so doing to think or call their genius your own.

But imagine, if you will, attempting to enter into a dialogue with others who are not capable of entertaining the great and new ideas that spring forth like Minerva, perhaps from some intuition of the soul or living with God? The ideas, for example, of actually subduing nature to the point where vicious animals, predators, attack dogs and the like are eliminated, of a society that will no longer tolerate criminals in its midst, that no longer raises and kills animals for food, these are things on too far a grand scale for the majority of people to consider. But does the inability of the great majority of humankind to understand and accept such grand ideas invalidate their logic and wisdom? Of course not.

The idea of the Amendment, for example, is on such a scale. The idea of women finally earning their place in philosophy leading to men and women exhibiting such cooperation with each other in the leadership of nations on the basis of equal value in the United Nations is on such a scale. The very concepts are too hard, too complex and even too fearful for the great majority of people to understand and accept.

But this does not invalidate the logic and wisdom of such concepts any more than the idea when first advanced that the earth revolved around the sun notwithstanding the fact that men like Copernicus were thought mad or heretic. Imagine, if you will, some of the things considered mad or impossible just fifty years ago? Personal computers, the Internet, cloning and mapping the human genome, all theoretical at best, the stuff of science fiction, all now realities, all opening doors to unimaginable possibilities!

And if we can consider overcoming disease, for example, why not consider subduing nature to the point where predators, including the human ones, where nature red in tooth and claw, are no longer a part of civilized society?

Benito Mussolini kept a copy of The Prince on his nightstand. I keep copies of Walden and To Kill A Mockingbird on mine. Does this mean that I'm blind to Machiavelli or Mussolini's thoughts concerning human nature and politics? No; of course not. These facets of human nature are there to contend with … and in many cases to overcome.

I make a pot of pulse and find, as in the fable of Daniel and his friends, that it sustains life just as well as a sirloin steak. Thoreau pointed out the foolishness of the farmer that said meat was necessary to build bones, all the while ignoring the strength in the bones of his ox. This to say that just as there is a need to re-think the "wisdom" of the past regarding diet, there is a need to re-think many things regarding the subduing of nature, both that in creation and in ourselves.

Unlike the fanciful, I am not attempting an apologetic for the implausible. On the contrary, such things as I have suggested are altogether plausible, even being discussed right now in one manner or another. But instead of UFOs and ancient, supposedly advanced civilizations, the ideas I have offered are predicated on an enlightenment based on facts unprecedented in history, facts that are coming to light through the disciplines of archeology, paleoanthropology, astronomy, subatomic particle research, and studies in medicine and brain function that are leading us to conclusions which make my suggestions all the more plausible.

To credit Emerson's genius he knew as a young boy that life was ahead of theology and that people knew more than preachers taught. Sam Clemens had come to the same conclusion as, I am sure, Lincoln had as well.

Wisdom had always taught that the doctrines of the fathers should always be submitted to the rigors of testing, that what was held as "truth" by sages of the past must not be held solely on the basis of the prestige of the teacher as Emerson himself warned.

There are absolutes, unchangeable, so well exemplified in the Golden Rule that we should do unto others, as we would have them do unto us. Few would argue the wisdom of this dictum of truth. But, of course, this is neither Emerson's point nor mine. The point being, obviously, that while knowledge increases, accommodation to new learning is essential to progress in civilization and the testing of past knowledge against new must be an ongoing process. This is the path of wisdom.

As a child, my loved ones and elders taught me many things that were untrue. That they did so out of love and good intentions did not make these things true. But because they loved me, I believe they rejoice in my discovery of errors, that I have better knowledge of some things than they did. Had they known better, they would have done better. It is, therefore, my obligation and duty to do better in honor to them if nothing else. And it is certainly my obligation and duty to do better for the sake of my own children.

There is a kind of dualism in nature in which the discovery of one half at least suggests, as Emerson pointed out in his Compensation, another to make it whole. Male and female need each other to make a whole, and the discovery of something incomplete suggests something else to make it complete. It sometimes happens that, as Lincoln said, you "wear an idea thin" in trying to make complete sense of it. In such cases, one thing leads to another, and often another, and another, and another until the whole of it is complete, the pieces of the puzzle are in place and the entire picture seen at last.

The yin and yang or yea and nay, the cause and effect, action and reaction, good and evil, virtue and vice, the give and take of things are discovered by experience and research. But to ask the hard, difficult yet legitimate questions about life and the universe is beyond most. It is not easy to leave a "comfort zone" in which the mind and soul are not restless for answers. In such cases, it may well be that some kind of "intuition of the soul" or "living with God" is required. And to understand a truth is often to first contend against it because to live is to progress; real life is not static.

But with every new influx of light comes new darkness to confront and overcome; with every step of progress comes new difficulties that challenge.

The threat of nuclear annihilation looms as Nobel-winning physicist Michio Kaku and others warn. And the FBI traitor Robert Philip Hanssen was correct in his assessment of America that the U.S. is a powerfully built but retarded child.

What else can you make of a nation that rewards illegitimate births, irresponsibility and a lack of self discipline, accountability, and refuses to close its borders to illegal aliens, that continues to advocate policies and laws that place a premium on ignorance rather than encourage the best and the brightest?

Even now we continue to live with the embarrassment of an ex-president and his wife that made us a laughingstock to the world and continues to shame us and defies pejorative adjectives but the word "tawdry" keeps coming to mind.

Even now we face an energy crisis in this country. But our leaders are willing to spend billions to protect nations that are dedicated to their own wealth, and making the traitors here at home wealthy. "Retarded child" is a charitable phrase under the circumstances. The Founding Fathers would weep and hang their heads in shame!

Chapter Three

While I have learned to exercise caution regarding dogmatic statements, "pontificating" if you will, last night as I was reading Emerson's Address to Divinity Students again the thought came to me that he had made the dogmatic statements opposing many errors, which no longer needed to be stated by me.

There is a need for dogmatism when confronting evil and egregious error. In Emerson's time there was much religious superstition and error that needed to be confronted, an age of science and reason was dawning but much darkness remained. But Emerson and others have said much that needed to be said and I do not have to repeat such worthies, particularly since those errors are no longer a problem of the proportion they were then. I suppose this has had an impact on my reluctance to be dogmatic in many cases.

True enough, as I have matured and become better educated the tendency has been to become more cautious in making dogmatic statements. With increasing age, expanding education and maturity, there is an increasing awareness of the complexity of many things once thought simple.

I often resort to Lincoln and his culminating wisdom exhibited in his unsurpassed, sublime Gettysburg Address. The very founding of our nation, the "Great Experiment in Democracy" Alexis Tocqueville referred to, required the amazing group called our Founding Fathers. Deficient as they were in many things, the most obvious the refusal to abolish slavery by the Constitution, they were nevertheless the product of the some of the best of the ideas and ideals of the time. The very genius of men like Franklin, Jefferson, Adams, Hamilton, the truly amazing character of Washington, all these exhibited the result of a growing intellectualism leading to the thought so well considered and defended by Lincoln that a people could govern themselves.

Lincoln was, more than any other, cognizant of the very genius of such an ideal. Time had passed, and Lincoln had rooted himself in that ideal of self-government. He was the inheritor of the ideals of the wisdom of the Founding Fathers. And as the inheritor, he took possession and improved the inheritance, surpassing those "Fathers" as any parents would want of their child.

Lincoln and Emerson were contemporaries. No two men could have been further apart in background and education. And while many biographers of Lincoln give him little credit for metaphysical transcendentalism, no one who is thoroughly familiar with the writings of each man can fail to make the connection between them.

I find myself in today's minority, that of Herndon's, that Lincoln had a courtly love, a true Sir Walter Scott love, for Ann Rutledge and never recovered from the melancholy of her untimely death. I agree with Herndon because I think I know Lincoln as only a poet can know him. Such a love would impact Lincoln in a way comparable to the stories of Camelot. I believe Lincoln carried his Lady's Colors next to his heart for the rest of his life and impacted on every decision he made, and comes to full flower in his most sublime expression of the soul that loves in the Gettysburg Address. I believe his was the kind of love, the purest love that found vent in the greatest poetry ever written, in his profound and final commitment to the ideals of the Founding Fathers, and surpassing them to the ideals of unity and freedom.

Unlike Emerson, Lincoln's business became politics. And he was an astute politician. But no one questioned his integrity or honesty, even in the usual spoils system or deal-making characteristic then as now.

But I have wondered how differently things might have been for us had Lincoln been educated as Emerson? Would we have known Lincoln now for surpassing Dostoevsky or Tolstoy in literature? Would we be thinking of Lincoln the Great Philosopher instead of the Great Emancipator? Certainly he left enough to entertain such thoughts.

***

Giordano Bruno (1548-1600) burned at the stake as a heretic for his philosophy questioning dogmatic theology.

Immanuel Kant (1724-1804), perception and reason, nature the creature and humankind the creator, the mind causing action; and if action, subject to laws of the mind, which, if understood, may very well have a "physics" of its own, a "physics of the spirit."

It is of the utmost importance that Kant knew the work of Newton. This influenced Kant tremendously and had to have had a great impact on his philosophical thought. Kant and Newton must have influenced Emerson and Thoreau.

A major omission in Kant's thinking was his low opinion of women and the fact that he never married. These, as with Thoreau, were decided flaws that show themselves in their respective philosophies. A complete philosophy must include the input of both halves of humanity on a basis of equal value.

But given that it was not possible for women to make their contribution to philosophy during the time frame, another factor should be considered in the rapid increases in science and technology; that of the contributions women have been increasingly able to make.

Beginning to make their voices heard in literature, women gradually began to make their place in the professions, including medicine and science. Madam Curie immediately comes to mind.

While not yet having earned a place of equal value in philosophy, I believe the contributions of women have had a direct impact on the rapid acceleration of science and technology, on the increase of brain growth and function. It may even prove to be that women are more sensitive than men in some areas that make a great contribution to a more complete acceleration of brain growth and function for humanity as a whole.

The Stoics may have been on to something when they thought of philosophy having geometric design. If you take away the religion, what remains may well be that of philosophy having geometric design. Rational, logical thought would certainly lend itself to geometry, as does the best of music. The geometrical design found in all of nature, including the brain and that of the brain that is "self awareness" seems to follow geometrical precision when at its best form.

It is my thought of a "spiritual physics" that melds with the physics of the universe that causes me to speculate on things like time travel, of the potential for the mind to accomplish marvelous things, things that are not as yet understood but seen to happen, things like "miraculous" healings for example.

Kant argued to separate what could be known from the metaphysical. But he couldn't know the progress that science would make in reconciling the two. Much that was once thought metaphysical has become a part of the body of science. But as a brilliant man, he would be able to understand much of the science that gave us X-rays and atomic energy.

The human capacity for the ideas of the ideals of truth, beauty, justice, and virtue has caused problems for philosophers. Once you enter this area of thought, you are in a world of ideas that do not always lend themselves to a strict empiricism.

Something else has always been at work in poetry, for example, that treats with ideals not known in a practical sense in physics, or nature red in tooth and claw.

Still, the ideals persist; they are there. For this reason I believe we will eventually have a "spiritual physics" ever much as real as the present physics and totally compatible with it. Subatomic particle research is already opening doors of understanding approaching what I call spiritual physics.

Even those things in imagination, like the pot of gold at the end of a rainbow or fairies dancing in a forest have a kind of truth to them. It is a kind of truth that seems inextricably entwined with our thoughts and hopes of immortality, of the eventual triumph of good over evil.

While it remains absolutely essential that mere belief be separate from actual knowledge, it is at least as important to realize that peace, for example, cannot be achieved by knowledge alone; it must be accompanied with wisdom (something I believe to be the essential attribute of spiritual physics), the application of knowledge to the best ends.

Thus a strictly empirical pragmatism is not suitable to beings capable of imagination and dreams, nor especially for beings capable of entertaining thoughts of ideals of truth and beauty.

Nor can accounts of either "angels" or "demons" be dismissed out of hand. And the use of drugs throughout history to induce states of mind (altered states of consciousness) more susceptible to influences not readily accessible otherwise should be taken into account when considering the desire of human beings to reach beyond the merely physical world.

Apart from the abuse of drugs and alcohol for other purposes, it does seem that at least some of the present use of drugs is for the purpose of trying to reach out beyond the physical self and world much as some artists and writers have done. That this use (and abuse) of drugs has reached such epidemic proportions may in part and in fact be due to increasing brain growth and function. There has always been a natural tendency among many to resist change. The Luddites of old represent a rebellion to technology that is very much in evidence now. The restraints of religion since ancient times and even at present bears witness to this reluctance toward change.

But with increasing awareness of human potential due to increased brain growth and function, the use of drugs in order to enhance "spiritual physics" may have some credence.

It does seem the spirit of searching beyond ourselves has been a major occupation of humankind. It was a compulsion of great minds like those of Conan Doyle and Thomas Edison. It was the driving compulsion of Newton and Einstein. Things like the pyramids and other similar structures found all over the world bear testimony to this fact of "searching." With the beginnings of organized philosophy, such searching has become increasingly focused and sensible, most especially once science became a "partner" in the search of philosophy.

Kant did, more than other philosophers, lead in causing those following to be less dogmatic in assertions of knowledge. While Socrates opened the door to questioning ideas and beliefs held as fact without any proof, Kant went the further step of questioning all things without the stricture of religion. As a result, many things were open to honest and legitimate examination for philosophy that had been held in abeyance before his writings like Critique of Pure Reason.

As a "Transcendentalist" Kant believed in reaching beyond the physical for answers. Emerson and Thoreau went even further, but a new era of science was beginning to blossom in the time of these men in which their minds were capable of exploring further.

Of most importance in a search for truth, dogmatism was beginning to give way to scientific examination. The demand for proofs of assertions began to strip away what were only beliefs. The Scopes Trial in very recent history is a glaring example of how difficult it is to separate beliefs from knowledge.

But the more we learn the more there seems to learn. An appreciation of our ignorance is essential to real learning. As a consequence, where I am lacking in certitude, I have become far more circumspect in expressing my own thoughts on some subjects. There is far more need for me to do more thinking and less speaking.

It is in writing that the best formulation of thought takes place. It is no wonder that little progress in philosophy, or science, could take place until writing became a fully functional tool. And with such a phenomenal tool, humanity began to be able to free itself from the ignorance and superstitions that held sway for thousands of years.

And while much remains to be done to rid the world of the kinds of ignorance and superstitions that lead to people killing each other in the name of God and leads to superstitious beliefs that retard real knowledge and wisdom, there would never be hope of doing so without writing.

But logic would seem to dictate that the other half of humanity, women, are going to have to take their place in philosophy on the basis of equal value and the compatibility of differences before a complete philosophy is possible. The greatest thoughts of the greatest thinkers, as long as they are all men, can only go so far.

When theology reigned as the "Queen of the Sciences" real science had no place as such. Now that theology has had to give place to a more enlightened world where real science has earned its place, the King of Disciplines, Philosophy, has made accommodation to further enlightenment. But as I have pointed out, while knowledge grows, wisdom seems an orphan, divorced from knowledge.

And it will probably remain so until women do earn their place in philosophy.

God as an a priori first cause has been challenged by science but cannot be entirely discounted since this remains an area of speculation. And it cannot be said that science is antithetical to the existence of God or Gods as a first cause. However, as science and philosophy continue to bond finding increasingly common ground leading to a spiritual physics; presumptive apologetics concerning first causes fall away as we discover more of the actual workings of the universe.

Religion served a purpose when science was absent. But with the increased understanding of the very mechanics of the universe, religion was no longer necessary as a "comfort zone" on which to rely for those things that began to be explained by the scientific method. And a religious dualism, one that made God the prime cause for both good and evil, which haunted Hawthorne and Melville was never satisfactory to reason by any definition. But it did breed many skeptics, agnostics, and atheists.

Still, in a world where half the population of over six billion has never received a phone call, it can be understood that religion continues to have a profound presence and influence. But as technology, particularly by means of media, makes continued advances, more and more people come under its influence.

But it undeniably has the power to influence for evil as well as good. It makes for the possibility of nuclear annihilation; it can persuade a society that there are no moral absolutes, that perversion is acceptable in a society, that abortion as a means of contraception is acceptable.

God On Trial

In one sense, there has never been a time in human history that God has not been on trial though it most often is confused with "worship." However, such worship is most properly viewed from the perspective of Emerson and his disciple Thoreau who rightly accused those in the churches of "blaspheming God in prayer, song, and sermon." My own experience of many years in the churches, including those supplying a pulpit, confirms the accusation. To my own deep regret, I was among the "blasphemers" though much of religious beliefs might charitably be called "earnest nonsense."

My defense is that I was raised to believe the things I did by people that loved me and certainly meant me no harm. Does this justify the preaching of myths and superstitions in the name of God? No. But I believed them and preached them, just as orthodox Jews and Moslems believe and teach the hating of each other in the names of Jehovah and Allah, making my own contribution to a "demon-haunted world" by doing so.

It is the most difficult of tasks to separate belief from knowledge. For the religious, especially, the two are confused. But if you study the Scopes Trial, you get a good idea of the difficulties as well as an understanding of what it is to put God On Trial.

The trial of teacher John Scopes (known both as the Scopes and the Monkey Trial) in Dayton, Tennessee began on July 10, 1925. It was assured notoriety because of the lawyers involved: William Jennings Bryan and Clarence Darrow.

The ACLU had tendered an offer to support any teacher that would violate the Tennessee law forbidding the teaching of evolution in the schools. The governor signed this measure that made it unlawful to teach any theory of the beginning of life but the Biblical doctrine of divine creation into law on March 13, 1925. As you can see, it didn't take long for it to be challenged and brought to trial.

Bryan and his supporting fellow Bible believers did indeed call the ensuing event a "putting of God on trial." The trial was a main element of Nobel-winning author (though he refused the Pulitzer for Arrowsmith) Sinclair Lewis' Elmer Gantry in which Christians horsewhip the character Frank Shallard nearly to death for doubting the Bible and entertaining ideas of evolution. And despite the many advances in science, in spite of the Monkey Trial and the work of people like Sinclair Lewis, this absurd law in Tennessee was not repealed until 1967!

Whatever the religion, each does in fact put God on trial. Not all religious views, most in contradiction with each other, can be correct; though the calling of anything "correct" that is only a matter of belief is an error. And in the process of making claims for a particular religious belief in contradiction to others, the claimants do put God on trial.

Of course, disease, death, disasters are the "work of God" according to religious people. And in attempting to make him responsible is to put him on trial. Every act of violence, according to the religious, is "the work and will of God, Jehovah, Allah, Vishnu, and so on" though many attempts to "explain" it differently such as the distinction of the "permissive will of God" have been made through the often tortured and agonizingly convoluted apologetics of believers.

"Scriptures" of various kinds throughout history would make God a bloodthirsty tyrant and despot. In the Jewish Scriptures, the Old Testament to Christians, God commanding the Israelites to kill every man, woman, and child in Canaan is a good example. One of my "favorites" is found in I Kings chapter eighteen where Elijah joyfully slays the false prophets (either 450 or 850 depending on how you read the account. Whichever, it was not a good time to be on the wrong side of Elijah).

Another real favorite is Psalm 137:9 *Happy shall he be, that taketh and dasheth thy little ones against the stones.* The Israelites never did hold with the Babylonians and there was a certain holy delight in thinking of smashing out the brains of their babies against rocks. The imprecatory Psalms are replete with such holy delights. Not to mention the Apocalypse; which would make fun reading for the Marquis de Sade.

In any event, when the song Give Me That Old Time Religion is sung I can't help thinking of the wholesale slaughter of people commanded by the god of some religions. Nor can I help thinking of his approval of things like polygamy and slaveholding, the stoning of people to death because some particular day was "holy" to Jehovah.

No doubt the murders throughout history, and still ongoing, in the name of God are "God's will" as well to the religious... including the burning of "heretics" and "witches" by good Christians... apparently the bloodlust of God wasn't satisfied by the numbers murdered in his name before Jesus became the excuse for "holy executions." Many at the time of the Scopes Trial were more than willing to do murder in the name of God and Jesus for the sake of the "holy integrity" of the "Holy Scriptures"... and they still are. So it is that Jews and Christians are more than willing to abrogate the commandments concerning "idol worship" by making their "holy books" such idols of worship.

Didn't both North and South have the will of God on their side during the Civil War? Didn't the religious of the period put God on trial during this fratricide and attempt at national suicide? But as Lincoln so well pointed out, God's favor and will might not have been on the side of either those in the North or the South.

But to quote Emerson (Heroism) on the subject:

The disease and deformity around us certify the infraction of natural, intellectual and moral laws, and often violation on violation to breed such compound misery... insanity that makes (a man) eat grass; war, plague, cholera, famine, indicate a certain ferocity in nature, which, as it had its inlet by human crime, must have its outlet by human suffering. Unhappily almost no man exists who has not in his own person become to some amount a stockholder in the sin, and so made himself liable to a share in the expiation.

At this date one hundred and sixty years after Emerson penned these words, I have the advantage of seeing somewhat further into the wisdom with which he wrote better than he could have known. In the capacity of such a "seer" I have invited readers to consider "nature red in tooth and claw" as well; for it is nature itself that would bring God to trial if the beliefs of the religious were adhered to strictly.

It was Emerson that put the case so succinctly. And to paraphrase: The view of the "righteous" is that "sinners" get their reward now; the righteous in the hereafter. The righteous would sin now and be rewarded if they had the courage to do so. But they will aid and abet the sinners by withholding their efforts for justice now, by going to church and blaming God for the lack of justice in the world, bringing him to trial and accusing him for such a lack of justice and judgment now.

It does seem grossly unjust for the righteous to blame God and put him on trial for what is patently our responsibility. It is our responsibility, not that of God, to confront evil and overcome it. And it does seem God is used and abused on the part of "good people" as an excuse for not doing so.

But I would far rather see God in the role of Creator in the sense of brush and canvas, of hammer and chisel, the wheel and the clay, attempting through trial and error to bring about beauty and order; for even if the flight of the butterfly seems erratic, there is a pattern of reason to be discerned in its flight if known only to itself by instinct.

I have asked myself if such an "instinct" might not be an attribute of God? And if so, why should God ever be brought to trial by the illogical assumptions and beliefs of the religious? Though I would argue with God why he would put such a dainty and beautiful bloom on the cruel goat's head sticker plant, the bane of all barefoot children... trial and error? I do wonder?

If there be required expiation of sin, should not the guilt and expiation be solely the responsibility of the perpetrators? And as Emerson tried to explain, shouldn't it be a whole society when it is the "body of believers" that is in error, even if that body is composed of an electorate that refuses to be responsible in electing honorable people to positions of authority over them?

It is proverbial and commonplace that a person will die for the sake and in the cause of a lie. We in the West deride the ignorant superstitions of the fanatics of the Moslem religion who become "suicide bombers." But in so doing, we choose to ignore the same kind of fanaticism among those that call themselves "Christian" or Jews that are willing to kill those that threaten their religious beliefs. In all of this religious hatred and prejudice, it does not seem to occur to the multitude of such believers that they continually put God on trial before all of humanity.

To call anything "holy" or "sacred" and to commit murder or wage war over such things is a contradiction at best, and insane at the worst! And to commit actual atrocities in the name of God is to put him on trial, to pray for the destruction of those that are only enemies because they disagree with your own religious beliefs is to put God on trial.

I wish Emerson were here to give us his thoughts on such grand accomplishments like the space station, the great advances in medicine and subatomic particle research, the mapping of the human genome. Then, he could look at the Taleban in Afghanistan, Israel and the Palestinians, India and Pakistan, where people are still waging "holy wars" in the name of God.

Even as I write on this date of March 3, 2001, the Taleban are in the process of destroying ancient sculptures of Buddha and the United Nations is trying to intercede on behalf of these ancient works. The rest of the world looks on and rightly recognizes these acts of religious fanaticism for the barbaric thing it is. Uncivilized! Yes, thoroughly uncivilized, and scandalously so.

Still, the Taleban have only to witness the constant stream through the media of the "worship" of sports, rock stars, drugs, sex, and violence on the part of the West in order to justify in their minds their own brand of barbarism. And how many have given God the "credit" for winning an Oscar or a football game?

As to morality, the Taleban leaders must certainly feel far superior to the example set by the Clintons. To have watched President and Mrs. Clinton walking into church with Bibles ostentatiously displayed in their hands, to watch the unfolding of such sordid and tawdry displays of behavior of a United States President totally lacking any shame for his lies and immorality including the brokering of pardons to the likes of the hated Jewish arms dealer with Russian Mafia connections Marc Rich and a top cocaine dealer among others would make most feel morally superior. To witness the pardon deal made by President and Mrs. Clinton with Hassidic Jews to ensure her election as a United States Senator would be especially hateful to Moslems, and to any with a sense of morality or even simple justice.

The way the Clintons justify the remark of Sam Clemens that Judas Iscariot was only a "premature congressman" in their betrayal of the American people, it can easily be understood why the Taleban, among others like Saddam Hussein, would think of America as the Great Satan where power and influence including that of the President are for sale and not subject to any standards of morality. When FBI traitor Robert Philip Hanssen called America "a powerfully built but retarded child" it can certainly be understood why many nations agree with his assessment.

But though civilized people agree that the Taleban are totally lacking in civilized behavior, that they are guilty of the most ignorant of religious beliefs, hatreds, and barbaric practices more suitable to some sub species of humankind, the minds and motives of their Islamic fundamentalism is little different except in degree than that of those of the ilk of the Clintons or the kind of "sophisticated" fanaticism that still believes the writings of men are to be held as the "holy word of God" in books like the Christian Bible and the Jewish Torah. The fanaticism of worshipping men like Moses, Jesus, and Mohammad is still a holdover of the dark minds of a nearly primeval past.

As long as "holy" books and "holy" men or women are reverenced and worshipped they are no less idols than the statues of Buddha the Taleban are set on destroying. But such is the darkness of the minds of multiplied millions that refuse the light of knowledge and wisdom, so it is that the mutilation of babies through the barbarism of circumcision as a religious act, the worship of persons and books as idols, so it is that such darkened minds make their contribution to a continuing demon-haunted world, a world that knows nothing of the wisdom of peace.

Whether the Taleban, a judge that wants the Ten Commandments on the walls of public buildings and prayer in the schools, whether beliefs in so-called "holy" persons and books, the mutilation of babies through circumcision, the waging of war in the name of God, the use and abuse of God by politicians, despots and tyrants as their stock in trade, it is God himself that remains on trial and we have made no substantive progress in civilization toward the goal of world peace since the infamous Monkey Trial or in spite of the Space Station and mapping the human genome.

The Great Wall of China stands as a memorial of an attempt to stem the hoards of "barbarians." The Berlin Wall was an infamous act of barbarism. But the wall of religious hatreds and prejudices remains more intractable and impervious to reason than any man-made structures, and a "wall" more shameful both to God and to humankind than any made by hands.

***

Only humans and the higher apes (chimpanzees and orangutans) have the capacity of self-recognition such as being able to distinguish their own face in a mirror. This self-awareness of self-recognition is quite phenomenal in nature. But at what point in our human development do we begin to truly become self-conscious and -aware?

As far as we know, in all of nature only humans become so acutely self-conscious and –aware that they become capable of philosophical thinking, of thoughts of life after death and immortality, of questions concerning the meaning of life and the universe, questions concerning the possibility of a Creator and the nature of such a Creator or Creators.

Are we divinity transmuted? If so, are we transmuted through several progressions as from the earliest hominids? A kind of parallel to this might be found in Mary Wollstonecraft Shelley's Frankenstein... or, perhaps, in the first imaginations capable of thinking of spirits, gods and goddesses in various forms.

I am not considering reincarnation, which I disbelieve, but transmutation. Were we possibly transmuted through a process of trial and error until a species was achieved capable of the transmutation of divinity? If so, given the estimated time from the beginning of the universe humanity occupies only the last few seconds of the last day of the last month of the universal year, an unimaginable length of time to achieve a creature capable of such transmutation of divinity!

I have attempted to make the case (TAP 3, 2001) for human selection, as opposed to natural or catastrophic selection, in subduing the earth. At this point in time, barring some limiting world catastrophe such as a meteorite, disease, or nuclear warfare, humanity has it within its power to continue to select, as it has done through things like hybridization and, now, genetic engineering, what species should survive or be altered and which should be exterminated, or at least absolutely controlled to the best benefit of humankind.

It would seem that if there is a case to be made for transmuted divinity, though it has taken an unimaginable length of time for it to be accomplished, modern Homo sapiens has the developed capacity for such.

Is it the transmuted divinity in us that strives for immortality; that strives through science to grow replacement organs or even to clone new bodies, to cure all disease, to attempt to overcome death through things like hGH treatment or some kind of genetic version of Dr. Frankenstein's experiment? Could a transmuted divinity be, after all, the thing that makes it so natural to pray and call out to God, particularly in extremis?

Is it in such divinity transmuted that we find the cause of the very rare geniuses, the Platos, Shakespeares, Michelangelos, and the Newtons, in the arts and sciences? Is it this transmuted divinity that enables those of only ordinary, or less, even far less, capacity to appreciate beauty and entertain thoughts beyond the ability of words?

There is a struggle for even those of rare ability to verbalize or write of the tantalizing hints of thoughts not quite clear, thoughts that seem they must be there but become phantoms once you attempt to seize them. Emerson and many other thinkers, philosophers and poets, consumed many pages, even entire books, attempting to do so, often finding themselves chasing these phantoms in circles.

And like these worthies, I also seem to glimpse such "phantoms" in pondering the origin of the universe, of life, of God and the nature of God. The very idea of the meaning of life gives rise to such phantoms, shades of thought that seem to dissolve or remove themselves to another hidden place once you put out your hand to touch or seize them, so formless and without definition, such flickering shadows as those cast by the light of a guttering candle in the mind, which while such dim light reveals their presence, they flee any attempt to shine a brighter light upon them, and so keep hidden the true form and identity of the object that casts the phantom shadow.

Most are familiar with the kind of hide-and-seek some thoughts seem to play with our minds. But this is not what I mean. I mean the kind of rare thoughts that derive from a form of intuition, a "knowing" the object must be there, but it proves so very elusive as to make you ponder the question of whether it was really there after all, a "something" like buried treasure but there is no treasure map. Nor do you have any evidence that it is, in fact, treasure at all or only worthless rags? Nevertheless, this kind of "intuition" drives the treasure seeker as though he was indeed seeking some pearl of great price.

Phantoms of intuition may be discovered hovering about in the concepts of love, truth, beauty, compassion, peace and justice, those ideals such words convey that may very well have their basis in divinity transmuted.

But to date, no "philosopher's stone" capable of transmuting the "lead" of such words into the "gold" of absolute realities has been discovered. Those tantalizing and formless phantoms abound, but resist attempts to touch or capture in order to give them life.

I think it may be that the human race has not yet reached its potential to capture such phantoms and give them life. I think it may require women earning their place in philosophy to do so. It may require an absolute seeking for peace to do so. It will, I "know in my bones," intuition if you will, that it will take wisdom to capture such phantoms.

The grotesque and macabre attempt at a "Frankenstein's Creature" may be proof of the transmuted divinity of intuition, of a "knowing in the bones" that the phantoms hovering about the ideals can be revealed, recognized, and given life. But I believe it will take the combination of knowledge and wisdom to reveal, recognize, and give them life, a combination of knowledge and wisdom that constitutes the true philosopher's stone to turn the base material into gold as in my equation Knowledge plus Wisdom equals Peace (k+w=p).

We may be, in fact, the only creatures that "whistle through a graveyard," the only creatures that sense "phantoms," that try through various mechanisms to contact those gone on before us. While other creatures may dream, human beings are the creatures capable of carrying out their dreams, turning them into realities… a "proof" of transmuted divinity? But no other creatures are capable of turning nightmares, particularly toward each other, into realities; which may be the evidence of a transmuted depraved divinity as well.

Chapter Four

Gatsby

Like the ending of Fitzgerald's masterpiece The Great Gatsby, I often find myself fighting against the current of the times, trying to go back and recapture the past. And like Fitzgerald himself, I have not grown so old and disillusioned that I wouldn't still like to believe in love. Even at the time of Harper Lee's Pulitzer-winning To Kill A Mockingbird there was a key element in the era in which her story was cast reminiscent of the time of Gatsby, the element of stability in America.

It takes the stability of the past to make sure progress toward a future. But such stability is based on the foundation of family. For those that have had such stability, the times in which we now live do not hold the same certainty of the future with which so many of my generation were blessed.

Apart from academic literary and social criticism, both Fitzgerald and Lee did manage to capture important elements of what made America work that held promise of a future. Certainly the Market crashed and brought a cataclysmic end to the euphoria of the twenties, the ugly specter of racism in the thirties continued to raise its ugly head, and after the Great War another world war remained to be fought.

Sinclair Lewis would expertly portray the hypocrisy of religion in Elmer Gantry and John Steinbeck would limn the condition of the poor from the Dust Bowl in his unsurpassed work The Grapes of Wrath. Yes, America had problems; problems of frightful dimensions, in the not distant past and there were those like Woody Guthrie trying as these others to raise the social consciousness of Americans. But the emphasis remained on home and family, on those values that had made America a great nation in spite of its several failings, failings made so apparent by the works of Fitzgerald, Lewis, Steinbeck, Lee, and so many others. But despite such failings, these great writers also expertly and with great sensitivity, described those attributes that made America great.

Alexander Pope wrote: "Vice is a monster of such frightful mien, as to be hated needs but to be seen." Then Pope adds his caveat that once vice gains a foothold and becomes too familiar it is embraced. Contemporary America certainly evidences the truth of this. Those things considered vices in the twenties and thirties are now embraced and the vices of the past are touted as quaint anachronisms born of naiveté.

Among those "quaint anachronisms" was the shame of welfare as a way of life, divorce, illegitimate birth, and abortion. But once these vices gained a foothold and society began embracing these things and started down the path of making them acceptable, they have made monumental contributions to the loss of the stability of the home, the foundation of any society and the loss of which leads to the loss for hope of a future.

Yes, I admit to fighting the current of time, of the longing for a time I still remember when there were such things as family values and lying, cheating, stealing, the perversion of homosexuality were considered shameful and disgraceful. In spite of the ugliness of much in the America I recall as a child, the need for the stability of the home was not in question. It took such stability for what were considered virtues to be taught and have any relevance.

Now, vice of every description having been seen too oft and having become too familiar with its face, as Pope warned, is embraced. And although many might accuse me of a nostalgic longing for the simple verities of the past, can any legitimately tell me that children are now born into a better world than the one for which I long?

How I wished that once George W. Bush became President, we had a leader that would denounce the perversion of William Clinton, would denounce the disgrace and shame this shameless and conscienceless man and his wife had brought to America!

But it was not to be. I have discovered that the phrase "We must move ahead" has become the political equivalent of "I don't dare criticize lest my own dirty laundry be exposed!" But I'm old enough to recall a time when the "Glass House" was the White House and we had leaders that could fearlessly denounce such perversion of office.

Far from the "Bully Pulpit," the Presidency has become an embarrassment for America and has struck fear and suspicion in the hearts of other world leaders. Lacking leaders in this nation that are free of scandal themselves there are none that dare confront the scandal of others in order to restore trust and integrity to our elected offices. And no amount of "Dear Abby" or attempting to use God for political gain, or even with the best of intentions, will suffice to cure the problem of our departure from the past emphasis on stable and virtuous homes.

My great-grandmother would often warn my brother and me of the path to perdition beginning with a boy's taking a pencil that did not belong to him. We were fortunate to have such a great-grandmother; we were fortunate to be raised in such a way as to know embarrassment if caught in a lie, to be able to blush at off-color stories. We were fortunate to have been taught that lying, stealing, cheating were wrong and shameful things… this in spite of our living in the dirt-poor area of Little Oklahoma in Southeast Bakersfield and being surrounded by characters so well described by Steinbeck.

Would any of you say that my great-grandmother intended, or did, harm to my brother or me by trying to instill a sense of shame in us for doing such things? But it took a woman of her own personal integrity to make the story of that boy and the pencil real in our lives. How many children today have such an influence in their lives? Where is the influence of someone like my great-grandmother evidenced in the homes of America today or in the lives of our leaders?

Education from TAP 2000

When it comes to our children, there should not be any politically sectarian boundaries. And whether you agree with my proposed amendment for the protection of children or not, I know you will agree that our children are suffering from a failed system of public education.

It was in another life it seems that I sat with California State Senator Ed Davis in his office in Sacramento. We had established a warm correspondence when he was LAPD Chief of Police and I was a fledgling freshman teacher at David Starr Jordan in the Watts district of South Central Los Angeles.

By the time of this meeting, I was no longer the naive young man who thought the problems in education would be relatively easy to fix. The travesty of the sixties in education such as Innovative Designs In Learning, which cast out the things that had worked and instituted the things that made no sense whatsoever, had done their dirty work. Children were going to pay the price of the adult abrogation of responsibility for their education.

The sacred cows remain the same, the universities that produced a failed system of public education which were untouchable then and are equally untouchable today in spite of the damning indictment of them through research and writing like that of Professor Reginald G. Damerell and so many others including myself.

I focused on Accountability in Education in my own Ph.D. dissertation only to discover it was such a hot button no publisher would touch it. Only one Ed. publisher at the time was honest enough to tell me that the material in my dissertation was such an indictment of the schools he didn't dare publish it!

I discovered that the school systems from the universities on down are so rife with corruption and such cronyism and nepotism as to be inbred to the point of impotence. Then I discovered that legislators were dedicated to asking the very people who created the problems in education for answers to the very problems they had created! Insane on the face of it!

And while I would never accuse the educational hierarchy of the purposeful destruction of public education, I do say they could not have better designed a system for failure had they done so intentionally!

I found that schools are not held fiscally accountable because of such creative bookkeeping it is impossible to audit them and the money is embezzled at will in the amount of countless hundreds of millions of dollars every year throughout California alone. The fox that guards the henhouse, the State Department of Education, has its reasons for not wanting this publicized, not the least of these being the public outcry it would cause together with the potential loss of so much federal funding.

I discovered first hand how tenure was abused to the point that the worst teachers who wouldn't have been allowed to continue to work a week in the private sector were guaranteed jobs for life in education, especially in the universities, and children and college students paid the price for such incompetence and lack of accountability throughout the entire system of public education.

I was at ground zero when Special Education began to be the cash cow for schools, a blank check no one questioned as empire building at its very worst became the norm in the public schools. Had I not personally witnessed what I have in this system alone, I don't think anyone could fictionalize the enormous boondoggle of this single education bureaucracy!

I began to try to tell parents and legislators like Ed Davis and Gary Hart, governors like Pete Wilson and Gray Davis, that the problems for children in education were not as bad as they thought, they were far, far worse!

I saw our classrooms being filled with teachers, products of the universities, who could not spell or do arithmetic and no one dared say anything about it! Why not? Because virtually every leader throughout society is a university graduate and would never criticize the institutions on which their own academic credibility and future success were based!

And teachers such as me with industry backgrounds knew the Ivory Tower mind-set was incapable of preparing children for real life. And most teachers who witnessed the terrible destruction of education would not speak out for fear of losing their jobs or becoming pariahs.

It has become the stock in trade of politicians to talk about educational reform. But politics being the trade of generalities does not deal with specifics and politicians always evade answering in specifics because they do not have any specifics when it comes to educational reform (or a host of other problems)! But no one knows better than I the enormity of the problems in education and the enormity of what will be required to fix them.

But as long as our children are defrauded of an education because politicians refuse to deal with the specifics, or even worse, have no idea of what the specifics are, I will continue to be a voice raised against the tragedy of ignorance that has invaded America and become the legacy of so-called educators and their crony political quislings passed on to our children.

Governor Gray Davis saw fit to thank me personally and pass my critique of To Kill A Mockingbird on to State Senator Gary Hart, the head of California's Education Committee. Senator Hart sent me a personal Thank You note.

Politicians have always been very gracious in thanking me for my concerns about our children and their education. But not a single one has ever followed through by doing the hard things my own research and experience proves need to be done. One school board president who tried to institute just a couple of the needed reforms I had suggested lost in the next election because of this.

In spite of my cautionary words, he didn't believe the furor this would cause among teachers who actively campaigned (illegally of course) against him in their very classrooms, even sending home with their pupils flyers produced in the school audio/visual department and taking out ads in the local paper against this man's re-election.

Of course, things were made pretty hot for me as well. I was betraying my kind and biting the hand that fed me.

It is easy to do the trend-forecast of where the present concerns about the latest enormously expensive and tragic boondoggle of education, that of Special Education, will lead. Nowhere. Once the noise dies down, it will be back to business as usual. The educational hierarchy from the universities on down depends on this.

Oh yes, audits there will be. A few arrests may even be made for blatant offenses and thefts that cannot be hidden no matter the creative book- and record-keeping. The lawsuits will proliferate and taxpayers will foot the bill as usual while the guilty in the schools from the universities on down will wring their hands and refuse to accept any responsibility.

But as in the case of the I.R.S. and California's Social Services, particularly Child Protective Services, the enormity of the task will make any meaningful audits virtually impossible. The educational hierarchy knows and depends on this to, as one principal told me, *do their own dirty laundry and not expose it to the public.*

His refreshing, albeit self-serving, candor reminded me of that of a Downey Chief of Police who told me in an interview: We're not here to help people; we're here to slam the door on them!

Like expressed concern about child abuse, the problems in the Evil Empire of Special Education will sell papers and make for News at Eleven and political rhetoric for a while. And then, quietly fade away until someone sees a way of making headlines and political hay of it once more.

Harper Lee addressed the failure of the schools in Thirties' Alabama. I witnessed it as a teacher in Sixties' California. And not just during my tenure in the war zones of the ghetto of Watts and the barrio of East San Jose, but places like lily-white Castro Valley and throughout Stanislaus County. And, of course, my home county of Kern, the target of Edward Hume's Pulitzer-winning book.

It was in my home County of Kern that a group of high school seniors applauded me for telling them: Any real education you get here will be because you earnestly desire and work for it, not because this school is really prepared and dedicated to giving you an education.

These seniors knew the truth of what I was telling them. Their applause was for my being the only adult school authority to make to them such a bald and honest confession of the failure of the school system to provide them the opportunity for an education, to have in fact defrauded them of an education.

The applause caught the attention of teachers and administrators. When they discovered the reason for it, I was not invited back. But I knew that would be the result. I have always been known as a high roller on behalf of the kids against the system. It is one reason I have worked in so many different school systems in spite of reaching tenure in two of them.

Tragically for our children and young people, my words to that group of seniors would apply with equal truth in schools across America. And while young people like the class of seniors mentioned know the truth, and will applaud me for telling it like it is, it doesn't win me any friends among adult authorities who should be my friends for my honesty.

The enormous fraud of Special Education has succeeded because those outside the system have no idea of what it is really all about. To understand how this is possible, you must understand that the field of education as a whole has its own manufactured language, a foreign language if you will, that admits of no outsiders learning it.

There is an incredible amount of paranoia in both Social Services and the schools. While working in Child Protective Services, I'll never forget my visits to the schools. Because of my experience in Special Ed. I knew the language and what to ask for concerning things like Individual Education Plans (IEPs). There was an absolute look of horror on one principal's face when he realized I was knowledgeable of such things. He was used to being able to dance around other CPS personnel who didn't know what questions to ask.

But CPS workers seldom visit the schools and don't know the system. And the schools rely on this kind of ignorance on the part of Social Services and the general public as well as parents and politicians. It is this kind of ignorance that enables the schools to continue to perpetrate this enormously successful con game of Special Education.

The con would not be so successful if parents and politicians were knowledgeable enough to ask the hard questions and demand answers. But they aren't. And I'm often in the position of asking myself: Does anybody really care?

But ignorance can be a real killer. When Robert Duvall made the picture The Apostle, I pointed out the weakness of the film was in his having never been raised a true believer in the charismatic religion. As a result, he simply was not believable in the role. He didn't really know the language and manners of the charismatic Christian.

But this did not prevent his being able to fool those like Siskel and Ebert who gave the film two thumbs up; thus displaying their own ignorance of charismatic Christianity.

Even the genius of Sinclair Lewis in Elmer Gantry could not succeed in fooling those born and raised as true believers. And while the lessons in both Duvall's film and Lewis' novel are universal and as such well worthwhile, the believability in their works falls short because of the lack of real experience.

It is this lack of real experience that dooms the efforts of parents and politicians who would genuinely like to make a contribution to reform in education.

Such people are unaware that unlike true academic subjects, education is itself lacking any empirical body of knowledge and has borrowed wholesale from legitimate disciplines in an attempt to legitimize itself. The resulting language of education is to be compared with a corrupt kind of pidgin, a virtual gobbledygook best compared with meaningless psycho-babble and its own kind of fraternal understandings available only to members of the club.

The system of Special Ed. particularly is a Byzantine labyrinthine monstrosity of nonsense within a larger system of nonsense. The language of Special Ed. is representative of the whole Alice in Wonderland field of education that reflects the language of the Jabberwocky. But unlike that delightful children's piece, the nonsensical words and phrases of Special Ed. make the pretense of sensibility.

In no other field of education is this smoke screen of pretended expertise of knowing what you are talking about when you do not through an invention of the imagination so evident as in Special Ed.

If things are ever going to take a turn for the better in education, they will only do so when political leaders take on the responsibility for confronting this enormous fraud and call it what it is: An Enormous Fraud!

The entire system of education must be called to account and held accountable. But it will take leaders of rare courage and a genuine concern for the welfare of America's children to bring this to pass. If I did not believe there were a few leaders of whom this is true, I would not have burdened them with my concerns.

It was known in 1954 that the bottom 15 per cent of college graduates were going into the field of education and nothing was done to correct this. Those responsible in the universities did nothing to change this and encourage the best and brightest to enter our classrooms. Today, we live with the result of this failure of the universities to act and be responsible. Not to mention the failure of the political leadership; which should have known and done better.

I expect better of those who have a genuine concern for children than I do of the amoral and literally silly - to use the most charitable word - leadership in the universities which gave us this failed system of public education and has even helped to perpetuate the enormously expensive and counter-productive continuing fraud of Special Education.

Only leaders who are genuinely concerned for the future of America, our children, are going to be able to confront this tragedy for our children and our nation and change things for the better. But elected leaders choose this political vocation and are elected for this very purpose.

A few years ago, when asked what she considered the greatest threat to America Marilyn vos Savant answered: The hyphenated American. Our presidential election for year 2K gives one pause to wonder...

Today, in politically correct terms, Ms. Savant would be called a racist for such a remark. But watching Jesse Jackson and many other African-Americans in Florida would seem to prove her contention. And what about those calling themselves Jewish-Americans? And what about the dual citizenship granted to Jews? Where is their real allegiance, to America or Israel? And am I to be called racist and anti-Semitic for raising such legitimate questions?

But who would argue that this election clearly evidences a House Divided? The power base of the Democrats would seem to be that of a welfare society continuing to demand they be supported by ever bigger government handouts and those like Jesse Jackson and Joseph Lieberman who play the race card, accusing all that do not agree with being racists. And to demonize Republicans, supporters are made to be the rich and powerful, their iron heel on the necks of the poor and minorities. If Lincoln could view the situation, I believe his comments on a House Divided would immediately come to mind.

Brain studies and child abuse

It has long been known that environment, as well as heredity, has an effect on mental growth and ability. Recent studies in brain function are beginning to open a door of understanding to this phenomenon.

We are now able to add the factor of child abuse to diminished mental ability. If a child is subjected to abuse, it is now known that a damaging and stultifying effect on the brain results, what I call "mental dystrophy."

Books like "The Mozart Effect" have made the point that proper stimulation of the brain results in increased mental ability, much like disciplines of memorization, mathematics, and games such as chess that challenge intellectual capabilities. I would include those things that challenge and stimulate the imagination and curiosity.

It has been long known that the earliest stimulation of brain growth, literally pre-natal and during infancy has a pronounced effect on later mental ability. But only recently has the effect of child abuse on actual damage to the brain been the subject of scientific study.

By "child abuse" can include through the broadest definition being deprived of the kind of environment and stimuli that would contribute to healthy mental growth. If the environment is one of drug and alcohol abuse, it is easily recognized and acknowledged that such a thing is certainly detrimental to, even destructive of, mental growth. What is not so easily accepted is the fact that an environment of destructive noise like that of loud and harsh Rock music, often with lyrics dedicated to irresponsible promiscuous sex, drugs, and violence, may be just as detrimental.

Physical abuse is most certainly brain retarding, as is the lack of those things like good literature and music, the lack of any emphasis on mental disciplines such as memorization and mathematics, the lack of emphasis on what we call the "fine arts" that promote civilized thinking and behavior.

In the case of "mental dystrophy," the lack of "nutrition" for the brain, the lack of those things that challenge intellectually, is becoming the focus of studies of brain function.

The schools, and not just parents, have a vested interest in such studies. Parents are the principal, responsible parties in ensuring "nutrition" for the mental growth of their children. But in loco parentis, the law of must hold the schools accountable as well.

It should be obvious that the lowering of educational expectations and standards by fiat of laws such as Affirmative Action, a case of social engineering at its very worse, contributed mightily to mental dystrophy. In a misguided and ill-thought attempt at justice, the universities, government, and the courts visited a plague of ignorance and illiteracy upon the whole of American society.

Why a Constitutional Amendment?

This is one of the most frequent questions I am asked.

To begin, there is nothing in our Constitution specifically addressed to the needs and rights of children. It was taken for granted by the framers of the Constitution that family and society were all the protection children needed. And for its time, this was true.

But virtually everyone would agree that the times have changed in this regard. And had the Founding Fathers known how things would change, I have no doubt whatsoever that the proposed amendment would have been included in the Bill of Rights.

Fortunately, those Founding Fathers made provision for future needs to be addressed by the amendment process. So it was that slavery was ended and women were given the right of the franchise.

As a society, as Americans, we face a most critical question concerning our future, and that future is our children.

In far too many ways, we have become a society that actually seems to hate children, rather than cherishing them. This must change.

The great majority of people agree that the most basic and fundamental of all human rights is the right of a child to be raised in lawfully, protected innocence. For this reason an addition, if you will, to the Bill of Rights is in order and morally needed.

No nation has ever done such a thing by its foundational charter of government. But at no time in history has such a thing cried out to be done!

And it is America, as the leader of nations, which all other nations look to for moral leadership. As the freest nation in history with a noble tradition of individual freedom and personal responsibility, the world has a right to look to America for such leadership.

And it is for this reason that the amendment is a call to We the People, as individual citizens and not the elected leadership, to act on behalf of our children, the future of our nation.

I believe We the People are better qualified than the elected leadership to recognize what is best for our children. We The People are the responsible parties for our children and our Constitution gives us the chance to act for ourselves in spite of an often-corrupt leadership that acts as though it was not answerable to the will of the people.

For this reason and many others, I do not want such a leadership to pass another law. I want Americans, by the right given us as American Citizens, to do what is right for our children by making a statement to this leadership and the world that We the People, Americans and not Congress, are able to stand and do what is right for our children.

Certainly it would be far easier to ask the federal leadership to make a law rather than to go through the arduous process of an amendment. But I contend Americans are better than we give ourselves credit, that Americans will recognize the absolute necessity of giving children their rightful place in our Constitution.

This is the path of nobility for a noble people, this is the chance to show the world that we, as Americans, do indeed cherish our young and recognize our place as the true leaders of responsible freedom and liberty.

In this respect, as it was in the founding of this nation, it is our duty as Americans to make our voices heard over the political glittering generalities and the mouthing of meaningless platitudes which promise much and deliver nothing on behalf of children and families.

We hear the leadership crying: Children are our most precious resource; they must be given a national priority. But where do we see this actually happening? We don't!

The amendment is the first step for American citizens, themselves, taking personal responsibility and action before the entire world for our young.

If America is to lead in the fight for human rights, if America is to lead in a workable doctrine of morality for the future of the world and world peace, nothing can give us better credentials and credibility as a people than the passage of this amendment.

The fact that this is an act of individual American citizens coming together in common cause for the sake of our children will speak volumes of our sincerity as a society to the other nations of the world.

A nation that has been so richly blessed and has long been a beacon of hope to the world has a duty, an obligation, to set such a precedent for all other nations to follow.

We have a reputation for sticking up for the underdog, for hatred of the coward and bully. And there is no more cowardly bully than the monster that preys on the most defenseless of victims: Children!

If we work together as Americans, we can take this step to guarantee our children their emancipation from slavery to the molester and his ilk. And in so doing, we have taken the necessary step to prove to our children and the world that we do love and cherish our children.

There is no question that our children have come to question this, that they have been losing hope of a future, that they are too often growing up in a callous and uncaring society where there is no protection for them, no absolutes of morality.

The amendment will speak volumes to our children and the world of the real love and concern we have for them. As Americans, we can do no less. We owe our children and the children of the world no less.

Samuel D. G. Heath, Ph. D.

Americans for Constitutional Protection of Children

CHAPTER FIVE

WHAT HAPPENED TO THE PAST GREAT CIVILIZATIONS?

Virtually everyone is interested in the possibility of UFOs and space aliens having visited earth in ages past. There are people that interpret some ancient monuments, writings, inscriptions and pictures in and on stone as depicting such visitations.

We wonder why some very ancient civilizations suddenly disappeared? There are those that believe some of these ancient civilizations reached a very a high level of technology and the arts. To only look to the age of the great pyramids gives one pause to wonder?

Nobel-winning physicist Michio Kaku makes the point that if there were advanced civilizations in space, beyond our world and galaxy, they probably reached the point of nuclear energy and destroyed themselves. This, he says, is probably why we have had no contact with such civilizations.

Many look to religious writings, astrology, and people like Nostradamus and Edgar Cayce for answers to some of these questions. Yet, I am the first to admit that people often look for esoteric answers to such seemingly complex questions and as the old bromide has it, miss the forest for the trees. I believe this has been true in my own case.

So it is that as much as I highly regard the opinion of that great physicist Kaku, I have to take exception to his conclusion about nuclear energy. What happened to great extraterrestrial civilizations is probably what happened to these past great civilizations here on earth

Thanks to Mexico's President Vincente Fox passing out survival kits to illegal aliens in order to make it easier for such criminals to make it into the United States, I think I have found the answer to these monumentally perplexing questions.

These past great civilizations did indeed reach the highest levels of technology and the arts, whether of extraterrestrial help or not. But once reaching such a great and high plateau, even reaching the level of civilization that we enjoy here in America, they implemented the most sought-after hallmark of an advanced state of civilized society, WELFARE as a way of life, and imploded never to rise again.

Eddy and MacDonald

Beauty in the eye of the beholder is a combination of the cognitive and imagination. And while given to a degree of subjectivity, certain standards do apply when choosing between that which is beautiful and that which is patently ugly.

Truth of an absolute may be found in love, but love can turn to hatred. As with degrees of love, so there are degrees of beautiful.

The greatest of philosophical searches may be said the seeking of absolute harmony in which there are no discrepancies, no difficulties or argument with definitions of love, truth, and beauty, where the cognitive is in full agreement with the imagination and recognized and acknowledged by all, and this in turn leads to a coalescing with natural laws in which physics and spiritual physics come together and meld as whole and complete, the two becoming one with the capacity to reach the stars and making the origin of all things comprehensible.

Since it is at this point that infinity, immortality, eternity, become comprehensible terms, it is obvious that the direction in which brain growth and function should be encouraged by increasing intellectual stimulation as well as imagination be acknowledged and acted upon. But the imagination must be tempered, and nourished, by the cognitive; hence the necessity of the progress of both the physics of nature and the physics of the soul or spirit. The cognitive makes it possible to recognize the flower or rainbow, but the imagination gives them meaning of beauty. As beings filled with intimations of immortality and fired with the spark of divinity, we would not want to have one without the other.

Oliver Wendell Holmes

Justice Oliver Wendell Holmes was often a dissenting voice for the Supreme Court. But quite often in his dissenting opinions he became the conscience of America and his decisions often gave an integrity and dignity to our High Court it may not have enjoyed otherwise.

I can't help believing that it is the lack of such conscience, dignity and integrity that plagues our government at all levels today; that prevents leaders from speaking out against the corruption that so infests our institutions. To judge others honestly, you must honestly judge yourself first. And it would seem the vast majority of our leadership comes up wanting, that makes our elected leaders so fearful of speaking out against such openly wanton corruption lest they themselves be exposed that has so blatantly betrayed the people and the ideals of America.

The myth of God supposedly telling human kind to subdue the earth has real merit, but every Dominion Theology following, being religious, has never been able to overcome the fatal flaw of dualistic thinking that makes God responsible for both good and evil. Hawthorne and Melville, despite their genius, both made shipwreck on this paradoxical rock.

But the fable of the Garden included Adam and Eve being vegetarians and the shedding of the blood of animals being the result of disobedience to the will of God. Our teeth, for example, are far better designed for the masticating of cereals, fruits, and vegetables than that of predators for the tearing and rending of flesh.

Indeed we should subdue the earth and have dominion over it. We are capable of doing so, we are capable of eliminating the weeds and thistles, the beasts of prey, of an agriculture that would be more than sufficient for our needs once these other problems like birth control, both human and animal, are acknowledged, confronted and overcome.

And it isn't just the argument that it takes eight pounds of grain to produce one pound of meat that is at issue; particularly when you factor in the issue of unproductive mouths, an issue that does have to be considered necessitating birth control. What is needed is an entirely new way, a new philosophy if you will, of thinking about diet that incorporates all the logical factors impinging on health. Logically it makes no sense for any culture to encourage non-productive welfare births, for example, that has little chance at success, but on the contrary is more likely to sap the resources of a society and enlarge a criminal population, a distasteful fact, but still a fact.

But rather than address such an inflammatory fact, responsible people and the leadership lack the will to confront it, blaming instead institutions such as the schools and social services for not performing miracles. I am not a friend of the way our schools and social services do business. But in all fairness, they are asked to do the impossible under the circumstances.

Such a thing as the lack of responsible birth control measures is patently and inherently unhealthy for any culture or society. Any discussion of "human rights" must begin to take into account those that have no regard for personal responsibility for their actions or the rights and property of others. Here in America we are encouraging hoards of barbarians and vandals by insanely encouraging irresponsibility and a lack of accountability on the part of individuals, the media, and on the part of the leaders of our institutions and government.

It would be legitimate for those being forced to pay the bill for welfare to ask this question: Who made the decision that welfare as a way of life should include reproductive rights without hope of being able to support the resulting children?

Oliver Wendell Holmes, the world-famed jurist and the only one with whom most would equate John Marshall (Millions for defense, but not one cent for tribute) favored sterilization in some cases and argued his point with the acute precision and intelligence for which he was known and properly honored.

The father of Justice Holmes was an intimate of such luminaries of intellectualism as Emerson, Whittier, Lowell, Longfellow, Prescott, Agassiz, and Hawthorne. Being raised in such a surrounding of great minds, Justice Holmes himself had the companionship of men like Henry and Brooks Adams and Henry and William James, so it is no wonder that he would be drawn in large measure to philosophy and would count Emerson, credited as the greatest thinker and writer America ever produced, as his mentor.

But Justice Holmes would never have countenanced the barbarism of a Hitler, for example, that would use forced sterilization for "ethnic cleansing" and political aims. But then the power of a dictator is not subject to any law. Holmes couldn't have foreseen the medical advances of contraception that would make it practicable to use contraceptive drugs rather than irreversible surgery to achieve the desired end for the public good. Had he been able to do so, there is no doubt the famed Supreme Court Justice would agree that in some cases court ordered contraception was imminently sensible, right, and just.

Before some readers might be too quick to disagree, I call their attention to what FDR said of Justice Holmes: For him, law was an instrument of just relations between man and man. And President Roosevelt said this of the man that found a just cause in sterilization, which recognized that in a just society the responsibility for the public welfare had to take cognizance of such a thing no matter how unpalatable for too often misguided social conscience.

To repeat what I have said elsewhere, the logic of the position of court ordered contraception is irrefutable on the facts alone. Only the emotionally irrational and immature, or those with a vested interest in continuing to advocate "drones" to live off the productive efforts of others would argue against such logic. It brooks no argument that those that continue to breed with no thought to taking care of the resulting offspring should not have "rights" that supercede those that live responsibly. To attempt to argue that there is such a thing as "reproductive rights" at the expense of others and without concomitant personal responsibility is to reveal an utter selfishness that carried to the extreme would destroy any nation!

I would ask the reader to consider the questions of why our leadership seems dedicated to a so-called "war on drugs" that all agree is un-winnable, why it seems dedicated to building more prisons rather than addressing the root cause of the growing populations of criminals, most coming from the city ghettos and barrios? Yet this same leadership takes exception to the far more humane argument that I am certain Justice Holmes would make in favor of court ordered contraception for those that refuse to be responsible for their own actions and continue to feed off that responsible segment of society. Thus it is that the rich get richer and the poor get poorer. As some wit put it: Why work when I can steal; though no politician facing election or reelection dares call it "theft" when so many feed at the public trough.

Sam Clemens opposed women being given the franchise because he knew politics to be a "dirty business." He said "Judas Iscariot was only a premature congressman!" and "The only honest politician is one that hasn't had time to sell out!" One only has to read Claude Bowers' "The Tragic Era" to understand such cynicism and agree.

But, then, to try to carry any argument on the basis of emotion alone is to lose the argument though it may win the day. Though in winning the day on this basis is invariably to bring pain and suffering to the innocent. Such is the case of abortion as a means of contraception, something that encourages violence and the devaluing of life, while at the same time refuses to discuss logically this issue of "reproductive rights." But the illogic of this position is to prove the paucity of intellectualism in America today and reinforces the idea that we have evolved a power structure of authority that is more concerned with maintaining its position than it is with the future of our posterity and our nation.

Tragically, we can hardly credit any in positions of authority here in America with the minds of a Ralph Waldo Emerson or Justice Oliver Wendell Holmes. Any discussion of this subject of "reproductive rights" would quickly prove the point. What we have as a curse that cannot be endured forever is a lack of those in authority with such intellectual capacity, let alone the courage of their convictions.

But pretenders to intellectualism such as Rosenblatt, Will, Buckley, et al abound and the time would fail to list them. For those really interested in my accusation and would like to dispute it I ask only this: Name one of these pretenders that is willing to take on the argument concerning the fact that women are not found in the numbers and on the basis of equal value in the King of Disciplines, Philosophy! But to be fair, neither Emerson nor Holmes seemed to have noticed this omission. Their failure to take notice of this might be excused on the basis of the times in which they lived (though personally I believe they should have noticed such a blatant omission). But such an excuse is no longer acceptable.

As a result, before any attack my position concerning court ordered contraception and the lack of true intellectualism in America I ask the above question be considered before going on the offensive (I might also suggest they ponder the problem of the paucity of women in the United Nations and exercise their "intellect" in this direction as well).

There is something terribly wrong in a society that keeps producing children no one wants, children of parents who believe it is the responsibility of society to care for and such parents are rewarded for their irresponsibility by producing children that have little chance of becoming productive adults. If personal responsibility for such children is not taken by their parents the case for forced contraception is not only logical, but it is humane. I have nothing against orphanages or foster homes; I do have something against a system and those that make them necessary for millions of unwanted children. I do have something against those and a system that promotes violence and a devaluing of life through abortion as a means of contraception.

***

We have a new phrase, the "sleaze factor." With the fall of Jesse Jackson, it immediately comes to mind. Together with the "deal" struck to let Clinton off the hook for lying and not being indicted the "sleazes," mainly politicians, are very "forgiving" of Jackson and Clinton. I suspect that virtually all of these are so guilty themselves that they put on the hypocritical face of being "charitable."

Reverse racism

Very few people outside the systems of entertainment and the universities know of the inordinate power of homosexuals within these. But when you wonder at the violent cartoon shows on TV, these are the product of the power of homosexuals who have taken over so much of children's programming.

The agenda of homosexuals is to promote their perversion and their target audience is children. The TV show Park Place is a perfect example of this.

You may well wonder at the part violence plays in this since the perception of so-called Gays, who are anything but gay in the correct use of the term, is one of non-violence. Thanks to Tom Hanks and Leonardo DiCaprio et al, every pervert is a sensitive artist.

Nothing could be further from the truth. Yet Hollywood and the universities promote this Big Lie. And since perversion has infected so much of our state and federal legislatures, it explains why so many in these institutions support the homosexual agenda.

As a deist, I believe in God but I despise systems of religion as superstition and no better than things like astrology, and having done far more harm than good throughout history. So I can hardly have a personal religious bias myself in regard to perversion.

But I do have a logical basis, one not dependant on whether one believes in God or not, upon which to confront homosexuals for the bullying tactics they employ. For example, how is it that a perfectly logical and normal revulsion to perversion is now called homophobic? Who made this a politically correct term? And for what purpose? One only has to look to the universities and the propaganda tactics of Hitler and Goebbels to understand this.

Thanks to the universities, the judiciary and Hollywood, it is politically correct to support perversion and incorrect to support family and family values. It is correct to attack white racism and incorrect to attack minority racism.

While racism on the part of whites against those of color is rightly denounced, where are the mobs of protesting marchers denouncing the racism of blacks against whites? A little white boy is dragged to death by a black man, a black man goes on a killing spree shooting white people loudly proclaiming his intentions of seeking out white people to murder, and a black boy murders a white girl at school. But there is no outrage on the part of black leaders against these criminal acts. Why is it that Jesse Jackson, Al Sharpton, Louis Farrakhan, and Alan Keyes are not denouncing these criminal acts of blacks against whites and asking for demonstrations against such racism on the part of black people?

It should be patently obvious that this is a rhetorical question. It is politically correct to denounce and demonstrate against white racism, but not black or Hispanic racism. And all the evidence, which is quite substantial, of racism on the part of white people does not excuse its parallel on the part of non-whites.

As I have pointed out to these black leaders, they do their own people a great disservice and cause grave harm to their own cause by not denouncing and demonstrating against such things in their own ranks. There is a monumental loss of credibility as a result. You simply do not denounce unfairness and injustice on the part of one group without attacking these things with equal fervor among your own and rightly expect to be taken seriously.

Religion, Race, and Politics are the predominant causes of an increasingly dangerous and demon-haunted world. Even as I write, the tensions between China and Taiwan, between India and Pakistan grow increasingly dangerous. North Korea seems determined on a nuclear arsenal. The conflicts in Ireland and Africa show no signs of abating. And in each of these cases, the propaganda of political correctness holds sway, and is often rooted in religious prejudices such as those of India and Pakistan. And in Israel, moderate politics is threatened by religious fanaticism, which finds its match in the abominably cruel and totally uncivilized fanaticism of the Moslem Taleban.

Just recently Bill Bradley in his concession speech quoted Vince Lombardi: Winning isn't everything, it is the only thing! And for fanatics, this is absolutely true! And whether the fanaticism of race, religion or politics, winning is the only thing! But far too many people supposing themselves to be good people don't get the message. And that message is very direct and eminently logical:

Evil can only be overcome by the good when the good confronts the evil with equal determination to win!

It is politically correct to attack gun owners and incorrect to support the rights of law-abiding citizens to protect themselves against criminals who abuse the use of guns. It is politically correct to attack legitimate, law-abiding gun owners instead of making the criminal abuse of guns the legitimate goal of prosecution.

It is politically correct to make the use of marijuana a crime and continue to leave tobacco and alcohol legal drugs. And in all reason we must ask why alcohol has not been attacked with the same fervor as tobacco? We need only look to the drunks in Congress to answer that one. Why is the drug war one that the leadership continues to pursue yet knows cannot be won? Here, as usual, follow the money is part of the answer. I say part because the rest has to do with power over the people and influence in the major drug-supplying countries like Mexico and Colombia.

Why is it politically incorrect to address the extreme abuse of law and taxpayer expense of illegal aliens when it is patently obvious that no other nation in the world puts up with this insanity, when logic dictates that no nation that cannot control its borders can survive? Follow the money; and the building of political agendas and empires. And how did it become politically correct to refer to these criminals as <u>immigrants</u> instead of what they are in fact: criminal illegal aliens? As with the bullying propaganda tactics used by perverts to advance their cause, call all those racists who oppose illegal, and by definition criminal, aliens entering America.

Why is making English the national language politically incorrect? Again: Money and political power.

It continues to be politically correct to arrest and prosecute women as prostitutes but not the men who hire them. But what makes people like J.F. Kennedy and W.J. Clinton exempt from treating women like prostitutes and jail women for prostitution? What kind of message does this send everyone, children as well as adults? No, I'm not that naïve, but I know it still isn't right. Anymore than it makes me naïve to know we have a justice system that is one of how much justice you can afford.

Why isn't the murder of a child of equal gravity to that of a politician or policeman? Why is molestation not treated as a crime of the very gravest consequences to the whole of society? And why is it that the black leadership never addresses this issue that is pandemic in black communities and leads to the early puberty of black children? Talk about politically incorrect!

With over a quarter-million accidents a year caused by those who run red lights, who disagrees that cameras which record these drivers and enables a system that sends them a ticket is not a good idea? It won't be those whose cars, even lives, are destroyed by these law-breakers. Too many of whom are not even licensed or insured! Will anyone disagree who has had to bury a child killed by these law-breakers?

As politicians wring their hands and posture with endless rhetoric over the murder of a child by another child, where are their concerns properly directed at an entire society of their making which has exhibited little but indifference toward children? The history of lip service by politicians that is only given for the reasons of an election or staying in office, not out of true concern for children, is evident to all.

I would be the last to say that addressing the real evils in society is an easy task. But I would also be the last to say that we have an elected leadership capable of addressing these evils.

But I won't let average citizens off the hook either. If you are not politically knowledgeable and active, you are a part of the problem as well. We get the kind of leadership we actively support!

Reform in education is impossible when the very people who created the problems are asked for solutions. But these people who created the problems in education are the very same who will say a six year old boy does not know what he is doing when he shoots another child to death. I would ask the reasonable question of these people: At what age does a child become aware that shooting another child to death is wrong? The so-called experts have no answer to this. But they are very quick to say it isn't six years old.

I totally disagree. I have known children this age that are fully aware of their actions. But such things are generally seen in their cruelty to animals and later acted out toward people. In such cases, where are the responsible adults who should be held accountable for their children?

But the experts in the schools, law, psychology will make every excuse to keep from being held accountable when the cruelty and bullying behavior of some children results in the murder of another child. Why do we not hold these experts accountable for their developing a system that creates victims in our schools and never holds the victimizer accountable or their parents?

Then we come back to the origins of an evil that has done so much to destroy families, and then deny any culpability for the consequences. It is truly an insane system, which continues to create victims, and does nothing to effectively remove the bullying predators of whatever age or for whatever reason they are so.

But there is one inescapable fact that the great majority of thinking people accept: No child, regardless of environment, genetics, or whatever, who bullies and threatens other children should be allowed to put other children at risk. The family and the schools should be held responsible for not allowing these kinds of children to put other children at risk!

Though written in 1951, to understand the failure of our schools, our system of education in America, one needs to understand the following comments by Robert Maynard Hutchins, Editor In Chief of The Great Books of the Western World:

You can set no store by your education in childhood and youth, no matter how good it was. Childhood and youth are no time to get an education. They are the time to get ready to get an education. The most that we can hope for from these uninteresting and chaotic periods of life is that during them we shall be set on the right path, the path of realizing our human possibilities through intellectual effort and aesthetic appreciation. The great issues, now issues of life and death for civilization, call for mature minds... To read great books, if we read them at all, in childhood and youth and never read them again is never to understand them.

The phrase "intellectual effort and aesthetic appreciation" in the above quote is the damning indictment of what is fundamentally flawed in our present system of education.

Oath

Just how harmful is it to swear an oath on the Bible? The question has a lot of merit.

Since my doctorate is in human behavior, such questions pique my curiosity. Just how has swearing an oath on a Bible affected history? And how does it still do so?

In my critique of To Kill A Mockingbird, I point out how neither Mayella nor her father had any reluctance to swearing to tell the truth in court, with their hands on a Bible, and then lied knowing their false testimony would send another human being to his death. Apart from Harper Lee's Pulitzer-winning novel, history is replete with actual cases of this nature, and the practice continues to this day.

We still hold to the hoary tradition of swearing in leaders to elected office with the oath of office taken by such leaders placing their hands on a Bible. William Clinton took such an oath, as have many others.

That many such people place no credence in such oaths and do not feel bound by them may have something to do with their knowing the Bible is a book of myths and fables, and therefore not to be taken seriously. And under such circumstances, neither is their oath of office or such an oath in a court of law.

There are millions such as the Ewells of TKM who will tell you they believe the Bible to be the very word of God. And then lie with their hands on the book. We may reasonably ask whether such people do, in fact, believe the book to be the very word of God. Which gave rise to the expression: I wouldn't believe him with his hand on a stack of Bibles!

While this use, and abuse, of the Bible has had a grave import in history, I do wonder if such a historical superstition and mythology continues to have an impact on our present day systems of judicial and government affairs?

That people like President Clinton, and the Ewells of TKM, do not feel bound to tell the truth under an oath in such circumstances, one should not discount the fact, and should consider it, that such people will defend the Bible as being the word of God, a holy book, the Holy Scriptures.

Then how to account for the discrepancy in fact by such people failing to practice what they say they believe?

We are keenly aware of the parental admonition, if not always spoken at least believed: Do as I say, not as I do.

It would be a mistake to take swearing an oath with hand on the Bible as simple hypocrisy, or even cynicism. It is far more than that. And it is far more than the formality of ceremonial tradition.

Many people believe, or would like to believe, that God has provided an instruction manual for humanity in the form of the Bible. Some believe the Koran to be such a manual.

There is a strong element of the need to believe which is implicit in such things. It is a most seductive thought, that God has literally given instructions to humanity, has actually spoken to men and women, and that these instructions and words of His are to be found in a book.

But underlying this need to believe, there is a strong element of doubt about such things, even among those who profess to believe. And there is also a large element of superstition, which treats of such writings much as a talisman, a charm or rabbit's foot. Believing in things like luck and various mechanisms to enhance chance, belief in astrology, all such things are in the same category as belief in books like the Bible and Koran.

With this exception: Charms, etc. are not usually treated with the fervor of religious fanaticism, as so closely related to divinity and deity.

When a person declares: God said! God told me! God says in his word! The Bible says! These declarations by people are much different than superstitions such as beliefs in lucky charms and amulets.

But a superstition of thousands of year's duration that has been proven to be without any foundation in fact and is still found relevant to a nation's leadership cannot be discounted as being detrimental to that nation's functioning.

It is, therefore, a legitimate source of inquiry as to the extent of the Bible's influence for evil in our system of law and leadership.

To a rational mind, the very idea that the Bible is, in fact, the word of God is repugnant. Still, the rational mind has to deal with the fact that multiplied millions in our society still hold the book to be, if not holy or sacred, venerated in some fashion.

Chapter Six

The Bodfish Philosophical Society

The greatest of philosophical searches may be said the seeking of absolute harmony in which there are no discrepancies, no difficulties or argument with definitions of love, truth, and beauty, where the cognitive is in full agreement with the imagination and recognized and acknowledged by all, and this in turn leads to a coalescing with natural laws in which physics and spiritual physics come together and meld as whole and complete, the two becoming one with the capacity to reach the stars and making the origin of all things comprehensible.

Since it is at this point that infinity, immortality, eternity, become comprehensible terms, it is obvious that the direction in which brain growth and function should be encouraged by increasing intellectual stimulation as well as imagination be acknowledged and acted upon. But the imagination must be tempered, and nourished, by the cognitive; hence the necessity of the progress of both the physics of nature and the physics of the soul or spirit. The cognitive makes it possible to recognize the flower or rainbow, but the imagination gives them meaning of beauty. As beings filled with intimations of immortality and fired with the spark of divinity, we would not want to have one without the other.

This reminds me of a letter I recently sent a lovely lady:

Toward the end of the 30s Nelson Eddy and Jeanette MacDonald were heralded the King and Queen of Hollywood… and rightly so. And Wanting You remains, to me, the most beautiful love song ever done. And no one has ever been able to duplicate the music or screen romance of Eddy and MacDonald.

The sheer beauty of the combination of the two that sends the spirit soaring and promises hope in the face of hopelessness is that "something" lost to the last couple of generations. But I am determined that it will not die with me. I want this for my children, for all children. The very majesty of such a thing must be preserved.

The tragedy of it all is that so many know this, but the cynicism of the age prevents them from reaching out to the stars. The stars are still there regardless the cynicism. And if heaven does not hold promise of this, it is a cheat!

***

It may be that the best of philosophical thinking comes with age. If so, and I believe this to be the case, it isn't any wonder that such thinking depended not only on a developing science, but longevity as well. To be a philosopher, there is the need to experience life and carry out actions requiring much time. The needed study, and reflection on what is studied, by itself requires many years. In such a case, we would not expect to find much in the way of excellent philosophical thought among races, particularly ancient ones like that of the Egyptians, that suffered high infant mortality rates and died in their thirties as adults. Nor would we expect to find developed philosophies among cultures without a pronounced and developed science. These factors alone would account for the very slow development of any truly well reasoned philosophical thought in time past, particularly the flaw of omitting women from philosophy.

It is quite probable and understandable that ancient peoples lacking in science and facing death at an early age would be caught up in mythologies and religions concentrating on life after death… the Egyptians epitomizing this in their religious beliefs and concentration on preparations for the hereafter. It would help explain why even Neandertal buried their dead with ceremony.

It would take a science that could promote longevity and stimulate the resulting intellectual brain activity for brain function to increase at the rate it did in the nineteenth and twentieth centuries, most especially the latter.

An enigma presents itself in regard to Cro-Magnon that developed a mastery of art (cave paintings in France) that did not appear again until the fifteenth century A.D. Now why was this not developed in some of the great civilizations of Egypt and Greece? Renowned for work in stone, these great civilizations lacked the Cro-Magnon mastery of painting. Very puzzling.

It would seem Cro-Magnon had the brain capacity, measuring larger than modern Homo sapiens, to engage in artistic expression, but lacking the intellectual stimulation of a developed science could not carry this further.

Perhaps the short lifespan of ancient cultures leading to a preoccupation with thoughts of death and hope of something better in an afterlife led to working in stone and the building of monoliths, this material having a sense of permanence, rather than more perishable materials.

It has generally required "patrons" to encourage and subsidize the arts. And many have pointed out the necessity of a leisure class in order for the arts to flourish. But once there were means and incentive separated from religious strictures to encourage scientific discovery and exploration, this aided considerably in stimulating intellectual activity that, in turn, appears to have encouraged a wider exploration and experimentation with various art forms, particularly in literature.

With the modern advent of film, there was a quantum leap of artistic experimentation, the exponential impact of which may have been more profound on intellectual stimulation than is generally recognized.

In its way, film provided a media of monumental importance, much like the invention of movable type together with a suitable written language that made the mass production of books and newspapers possible. It was the increasing availability of books, more than any other factor, which gave the impetus to widespread reading and writing, the dissemination of information, so crucial to the kind of intellectual stimulation that would usher in an age of scientific enlightenment and invention.

The "monuments" of humanity began to be books, rather than stones. The printed word would have an impact of far greater significance and lasting value than any number of pyramids or other stone artifacts. Some may think the pyramids speak of immortality, but nothing speaks more eloquently, nor bears a truer mark of what may be called the immortality of divinity in humankind comparable to the stars better than Shakespeare, Lincoln's Gettysburg Address, and Samuel Clemens who was born and departed with Halley's Comet.

But a difficulty for this monument of the highest achievement of Emerson's "Man Thinking," the written word, has arisen with the advent of television; and while films of the past involved going to a theater, TV brought films to the living room, encouraging a sedentary lifestyle. The reading of books was increasingly losing out to a media that did not require the skills and mental activity leading to intellectual stimulation as that of reading.

And books generally, but certainly not always, have some intellectual or artistic merit in order to be successful. TV is not held to this standard. Most importantly, TV as a passive medium does not require the active participation of the mind (hence the appellation "mindless entertainment"), of the imagination, that books do… and lacking such, does not provide the kind of stimulation that is so conducive to intellectual brain growth and function.

What's Wrong?

March 7, 2001

The recent school shooting in Santee, California, like the one at Columbine in Colorado is provoking all the same, and utterly ineffectual responses and hand wringing. I was a teacher at David Starr Jordan High in the Watts District in the sixties; this was "ground zero" for what was happening with our young people in America.

My experience in the ghetto and barrio schools had much to do with my doctoral dissertation on accountability in education. But no publisher at the time would touch the study. It was far too controversial. It still is.

Well, my writing hasn't changed over the years; it still remains far too controversial for the mainstream and I realize that much of it is not very palatable; it just doesn't go down or digest very well. The "cultivated palate" of society and politicians, and most especially for those in education, find my "dishes" not to their taste.

It reminds me of the wise advice concerning the ingredients of sausage, wieners, and hamburger: Don't ask; enjoy!

In my critique of To Kill A Mockingbird, for example, I point out the root cause of such things as school shootings. It is summed up in one word: Indifference! We have evolved a society that is indifferent to children. And children know this. Little Dill didn't run away from home because his parents mistreated him, they were simply indifferent to him. They bought him all the toys and then told him: Go away and play and leave us alone!

As adults, we have bought our children all the toys and have told them: Go away and play and leave us alone!

We are not only indifferent to the needs of children as proved by the constant stream of permissive sex, violence, lying, cheating, stealing on the part of a leadership that should provide guidance and role models, we are telling children we simply do not give a damn about providing them anything better!

I recall the boy at Jordan that came into the office one morning and wanted to leave his gun there and pick it up after school. It was common for the pupils and teachers to be armed and we had armed security on campus. The boy needed the gun to protect him going to and from school. He simply could not understand why his reasonable request was refused?

Now this young fellow had the determination to try to attend school. Under the circumstances, he certainly could be given credit for this when there were so many things that militated against any of these young people getting a real education at this school.

I was popular at the school because I taught metal and wood shop. And I was able to dispose of many a dangerous weapon, Saturday Night Specials, so poorly made that they might well blow up in the shooter's hand.

My first week at this school, a girl from my homeroom knifed another girl to death over a boyfriend. Things like this were a common occurrence, but you didn't read about them in the LA Times. This was the ghetto and no one outside the ghetto gave a damn!

The attitude of both white and black leadership was: Let'em kill each other, let'em do the drugs, crime and time as long as they keep it in Watts (or Harlem, etc. Not unlike the mafia leader's attitude about dealing drugs in The Godfather).

But I knew what was happening in this ghetto would eventually spill over into the "lily white" and affluent schools; it was only a matter of time. And now, it is happening and people are asking: What is wrong?

What is wrong is just what Atticus Finch pointed out and warned of; and the bill is coming due!

Retarded Child

***

With every new influx of light comes new darkness to confront and overcome; with every step of progress comes new difficulties that challenge.

The threat of nuclear annihilation looms as Nobel-winning physicist Michio Kaku and others warn. And the FBI traitor Robert Philip Hanssen was correct in his assessment of America that the U.S. is a powerfully built but retarded child.

What else can you make of a nation that rewards illegitimate births, irresponsibility and a lack of self discipline, accountability, and refuses to close its borders to illegal aliens, that continues to advocate policies and laws that place a premium on ignorance rather than encourage the best and the brightest?

Even now we continue to live with the embarrassment of an ex-president and his wife that made us a laughingstock to the world and continues to shame us and defies pejorative adjectives but the word "tawdry" keeps coming to mind.

Even now we face an energy crisis in this country. But our leaders are willing to spend billions to protect nations that are dedicated to their own wealth, and making the traitors here at home wealthy. "Retarded child" is a charitable phrase under the circumstances.

The Founding Fathers would weep and hang their heads in shame!

***

Well folks, I decided to write about our conversations, especially those we have as I lie in bed at night. I think there is only the thinnest veil between life and death, and that is why I believe we have actual conversations in which you all speak your minds to me. It may be that you all continue to live through me in some fashion.

I believe you are all with me throughout the day and especially as I write. I think many of the ideas I have are from you.

Mother and Father God? It may be that you speak to me as well, that the folks are all joined with you also. Ideas from you? I believe the idea for the amendment was from you, like the compulsion to start that wall of names for the children and most of the writing I do, particularly in regard to children, families, politics and religion.

I've thought that you may all know my most shameful acts and thoughts, that everything is completely open to you. But what kind of life would we all have together if all of our shameful acts and thoughts were laid bare and we had to live with these things in eternity? There must be, I hope, some way of all these things being done away.

The knowledge of any subject is no substitute for wisdom.

Last night I talked to you about whether you folks are "where" or "what;" just where are you and what are you? What really happens when we die, what is it that changes? Does particle physics hold the answer? Is there a sea of consciousness and/or a universal lyre? That thing of Edison thinking he could build a device in order to contact those passed on?

For some reason I think the veil is thin between you folks and me, but what does even such a veil consist of?

Newton and Einstein made the claim that they could see so far because they had stood on the shoulders of some who had gone before them. Is it possible that I do see so far, things like the amendment and equation, seeing the need of the equal value of women, seeing the absence of women in philosophy, because I not only stand on the shoulders of others, but that they and you folks are active in helping me to see these things?

It's good to have a mission, I suppose; so many people do seem to live lives of quiet desperation to no discernable purpose. Still wonder about this "mission" for the children, whether it's of you folks and Father and Mother God?

But I do wish I would get some feedback to encourage my own heart and mind. How much, if anything, that goes on in our minds contributes to life hereafter? How much contributes to the making of our own heaven or hell?

Just had a thought; those that wish me evil seem determined to do what they can to hurt me. But those that wish me well too often do nothing. Like letters to the editor in our local paper; many write against me but none write on my behalf in spite of their telling me they like what I am saying.

I've made the point so many times that it will take equal determination by the good to overcome evil. Perhaps this example from my own battle against evil is a case in point. Extrapolated to a larger view, it may prove the point. Too many people thinking themselves to be good prove not to be good in fact by doing nothing to confront and overcome evil. They won't even write a letter in my support. They won't even write a letter to their legislator.

Haven't thought about it in a very long time, but today (11-5-2k) it came to me. When I was a boy living on the mining claim, I had a dream about the moon striking the earth. The very next day, there was a newspaper story about the moon falling into the earth including a picture- More than a coincidence?

11-16-2k. I just watched a show about volcanic action in the past. Super-volcanic action is posited as nearly making humanity extinct 70 or 80 thousand years ago. Called a "bottleneck" event this eliminated many strains of mitochondria DNA in the genes by the near decimation of all hominid species, leaving only a few thousand survivors. These few passed on a very limited and narrow strain that would account for the great similarity of DNA in all races today.

Question: With so many different types of hominids going back estimated millions of years, with Homo sapiens estimated at 125,000 years, was this God's trial and error method of creating creatures close to His and Her image? And was volcanism used to eliminate inferior creations? Yet there are those early hominids that buried their dead with ceremony.

Brings to mind the stories like that of Genesis of the destruction of the world and starting over; still, in the creation of the universe by whatever method, if there was intelligence such as God at work, was life a result of the method of trial and error requiring a "pruning" process to achieve a desired end like Homo sapiens? Or, could the processes of creation, once set in motion, be beyond the control of God? If a process of trial and error, possibly ... But such a process would seem to indicate some control at some point in time in order to perfect what was discovered and learned in the process of creation. "Let's try this and see what happens" is very much a part of human thinking and action. Curiosity and imagination may be God-like qualities. But if curiosity is such, I ask how God could be curious unless He and She are limited in knowledge?

***

F. Scott Fitzgerald on Lindberg: "Show me a hero and I'll write you a tragedy."

***

The Hereafter

It has been a nagging problem for years but I think I understand it now. Most of us feel some communication with those, especially loved ones, gone on before us. But the problem is that of how to dispense with the bad things and emphasize only the good because even in the closest and most loving relationships things are said and done that need to be forgotten. And in prayer when conversing with a group of such people, as I often do, the problem is one of how you speak of things not exactly complimentary to someone when everyone else is part of the conversation.

It came to me that this might work like a computer program. I did something to my brother or he did something to me that neither of us wants to remember. He has gone on before me but I'm talking about it to my grandmother. The "program" does not let/allow my brother to know or hear even though he is there and is a part of the "system."

As we learn more about brain function, atomic structure and particle physics this becomes ever more a plausible explanation of how we will "remember" things when we pass on. The good things will remain but the bad things will be programmed out where necessary, even in group discussion and sharing with one another.

This kind of "program" is especially necessary if when we pass on there will be another life, a higher life of learning and actual work filled with the promise of ever growing and doing. And if such a higher life is based on the learning and experiences of this life, it becomes even more needful that only those good experiences and relationships, the good work done in this life be the basis of our future life devoid of the memory of bad things that even good people do to one another. Or, it may be that in this higher life even the bad things good people do to one another will be programmed for a useful, rather than hurtful, purpose. Things, even bad things, may be "remembered" in a productive way, particularly if the relationship with these others was based on love for each other.

But philosophically I believe in the necessity of being able to remember and communicate even the bad things my brother and I did to each other. Also, I think the experience of evil in this life is necessary to the building of a better world or worlds in the hereafter.

To this extent most of the best of philosophical thought agrees, that any higher, future life would have to exclude those ugly things like envy, prejudice and hatred that consume so many in this life. Therefore I believe only those relationships based on love will "inherit" that higher life.

It is obvious that love has not ruled in this world, but my belief is that the operant principle in the higher life to which we may be called will be that of love for one another, that no evil of any kind will have a place. I think we will be called on to participate with God (Him and Her I believe) in the ongoing creative process, in which God as well as we have learned and are learning, making use of the knowledge gained by our experiences, the good and right as well as the errors, in this life.

Chapter seven

The Weedpatch Cracker Barrel

February 24, 2001

I guess it all started when I found I had used my last quart of Grecian Formula and Junky Jerry was too cheap to give me some of the Shinola he uses on his hair.

As a result, I was feeling my age and the need to take a break from the writing of an adventure/survivor book entitled My Quest for the Perfect Squid so I was trying to choose between watching TV and reading.

There were the usual TV choices such as *I Was A Sex Slave For Doctor Kavorkian*, I Spit On Your Grave! Survivors Learning To Live With Our Wild Friends In Nature: Snakes, Alligators, Tigers, In-laws And The Winos Next Door, and I Was An Alien Abductee Spy For Amazons From The Planet Playtex In The Victoria's Secret Galaxy.

Well, in spite of that last one having some artistic merit, perhaps a good book instead. They were beginning to stack up, books that were languishing while I had been writing. As a bachelor and always looking for easy cooking hints, one I really had meant to get to was a collaborative effort: Our Favorite Recipes by Jeffrey Dahmer and Anthony Hopkins. A medical science expose clamored for my attention: Guinea Pig Cured of Alzheimer's And Biting His Nails!

But, alas, the National Enquirer won out. Being a real political buff, the screaming headlines of this worthy example of high-class journalism won the day.

Bill Clinton's legacy as President is assured. It will be defined by two words and one wise dictum: The words are "Sordid" and "Tawdry." The wise dictum is: You can't make a silk purse out of a sow's ear. And you know what they say about successful men and the women that made them what they are.

Now that Hillary is using the "I" word instead of the "We" word, the mind reels since she has shown herself more than willing to top her husband's record ... Hillary wanted the silverware, Bill wanted the interns. Hillary has shown she has the "chutzpah" to pull off upstaging her (to be ex?) husband and she's off to a running start.

Born of the "good ol' boy" politics of Arkansas where the bodies of political "embarrassments and indiscretions" really are buried and the phrase is not a metaphor, and well trained to lie, steal, and cheat with the best of any backwater, third world nation, I find it somewhat amusing that Hillary is a senator for a state that thought itself sophisticated.

Well, it's about time New York got its comeuppance. Can you see Hillary on the cover of The New Yorker? Boggles the mind! Mad Magazine, maybe. Ah, if only Al Capp were still here to use her in Li'l Abner's Dogpatch. Now that would be appropriate. I can easily visualize Hillary and Mammy Yokum involved in many cultural pursuits of common interest and on the same level of sophistication.

But "sophistication" is not a word to be associated with either of the Clintons… or their relatives- Nor is the word "civilized." Though I thought it decidedly inappropriate for some pundit to say if he saw one more picture of Hillary's brother swinging a golf club he would puke! Or for another to say he didn't think the guy had ever availed himself of a salad!

As to Bill's brother Roger, well, I once had to bail my grandad out of jail in Redondo Beach. That's right next door to Hermosa. Cost me fifty bucks. He and some other senior citizens were busted for playing penny-ante poker. You don't have to tell me those South Bay cops are tough! But bubba Roger trying to imitate Elvis, well, that reminds me of what that pundit said about Hillary's brother Hugh and the golf club.

But to be fair, I think the thing about Hillary and her Jewish "constituency" was simply due to her watching Exodus, Fiddler on the Roof, and The Ten Commandments a few too many times. Maybe she just hadn't seen The Message or read the Koran?

And to be even fairer, I did a little straw poll here in the Valley on the question of the Clinton's credibility. Well, I tried to do a straw poll but I no sooner asked the question and no one could stop laughing long enough to give me an answer. Déjà vu all over again; as Sam Clemens so eloquently said: Judas Iscariot was only a premature congressman and an honest politician is one that hasn't had time to sell out.

THE WEEDPATCH CRACKER BARREL

MARCH 1, 2001

Forget the SAT; it is woefully out of date. If we really want to be fair to all pupils with aspirations for a college education, we should not be testing for reading, writing, arithmetic, literature, geography or science; we should be testing for knowledge of television, rock and sports stars, and electronic games… you know, things truly representative of the American home and schools, of the real academic level and intellectual life in America.

In a nation where less than six per cent read a book of any substantive literary or intellectual value last year, just how realistic is it to test for real educational achievement as a predictor of potential success in college? Especially when the colleges themselves are the source of encouragement for the lowest common denominator academically and intellectually? It isn't like the colleges and universities require graduating teachers that are literate. Why expect the same thing of incoming freshmen?

Why aren't the schools and colleges becoming more realistic in graduating people that can make it on Oprah and Jerry Springer? They are far more successful in graduating people more likely to make it on COPS or as illiterate teachers. Why aren't the universities granting more Ph.D.s in The Dance? I recently read a very good article in a newspaper, The Bakersfield Californian, by a woman with such a degree that has sat on a number of doctoral committees. The relevance to real life in America is unmistakable.

It should be obvious that a nation that can not catch a spy in the highest ranking position of the FBI, that cannot protect its most sensitive technology secrets, that will spend billions protecting nations that have no interest but their own wealth, that will not effectively control its borders, that is filled with unproductive people who believe reproductive rights belong to welfare parents that have no intention of ever providing for their offspring, a nation that continues to be shamed by the ilk of the Clintons, has no right to require such an unrealistic test as the SAT.

The Weedpatch Cracker Barrel

March 3, 2001

I wish Emerson were here to give us his thoughts on such grand accomplishments like the space station, the great advances in medicine and subatomic particle research, the mapping of the human genome. Then, he could look at the Taleban in Afghanistan, Israel and the Palestinians, India and Pakistan, where people are still waging "holy wars" in the name of God.

Even as I write on this date of March 3, 2001, the Taleban are in the process of destroying ancient sculptures of Buddha and the United Nations is trying to intercede on behalf of these ancient works. The rest of the world looks on and rightly recognizes these acts of religious fanaticism for the barbaric thing it is. Uncivilized! Yes, thoroughly uncivilized, and scandalously so.

Still, the Taleban have only to witness the constant stream through the media of the "worship" of sports, rock stars, drugs, sex, and violence on the part of the West in order to justify in their minds their own brand of barbarism. And how many have given God the "credit" for winning an Oscar or a football game?

But though civilized people agree that the Taleban are totally lacking in civilized behavior, that they are guilty of the most ignorant of religious beliefs, hatreds, and barbaric practices more suitable to some sub species of humankind, the minds and motives of their Islamic fundamentalism is little different except in degree than the "sophisticated" fanaticism that still believes the writings of men are to be held as the "holy word of God" in books like the Christian Bible and the Jewish Torah. The fanaticism of worshipping men like Moses, Jesus, and Mohammad is still a holdover of the dark minds of a nearly primeval past.

As long as "holy" books and "holy" men or women are reverenced and worshipped they are no less idols than the statues of Buddha the Taleban are set on destroying. But such is the darkness of the minds of multiplied millions that refuse the light of knowledge and wisdom, so it is that the mutilation of babies through the barbarism of circumcision as a religious act, the worship of persons and books as idols, so it is that such darkened minds make their contribution to a continuing demon-haunted world, a world that knows nothing of the wisdom of peace.

Whether the Taleban, a judge that wants the Ten Commandments on the walls of public buildings and prayer in the schools, whether beliefs in so-called "holy" persons and books, the mutilation of babies through circumcision, the waging of war in the name of God, it is God himself that remains on trial and we have made no substantive progress in civilization toward the goal of world peace since the infamous Monkey Trial or in spite of the Space Station and mapping the human genome.

The Great Wall of China stands as a memorial of an attempt to stem the hoards of "barbarians." The Berlin Wall was an infamous act of barbarism. But the wall of religious hatreds and prejudices remains more intractable and impervious to reason than any man-made structures, and a "wall" more shameful both to God and to humankind than any made by hands.

The Weedpatch Cracker Barrel

March 7, 2001

A House Divided

While America is the nation that attracts more illegal aliens than any other (and the politicians that have a vested interest in allowing this let them in), it should be pointed out that as a nation we have become a House Divided. The politicians are pretty well polarized between those that support the poor and ignorant have-not non-producers that have become their political base against the other half comprised of those that do produce and try to hold on to what they earn.

Given such evenly divided government, it isn't any wonder that Congress can find little on which to agree. As those black leaders pointed out to Lincoln, they had "theirs" so why should they give it up for their so-called "brethren"? Those black leaders were smart. It had taken a lot for them to earn their way, and they weren't about to give it up on the basis of some kind of ethereal idealism. Such is human nature.

Well, you can argue idealism until it is reliably reported from unimpeachable sources that Hell has indeed frozen over, but the bottom line remains the bottom line: People that earn by the sweat of their brow resent being forced to give it away… and to give it away by force of laws they never approved! Talk about "Taxation Without Representation!"

It was that "other half" of politicians that built their power base on welfare and illegal aliens that I happen to resent. It was this other half of politicians that seem to believe America can "buy friends" with my tax money, that depend on welfare parents and all those getting a free ride on the backs of producers to keep them in office; even if that "office" is one of pulpits and TV evangelism.

I further resent the politicians of any stripe that use tax money to support nations that are clearly interested in their welfare, not that of America. The government is "for sale" it seems regardless of who is in office. It is clear to our young people that the system is one of how much justice you can afford; it is one of whoever has the money makes the rules.

And until we have the kind of elected leadership that will confront this evil system for what it is, things cannot become any better. But that would require an "Enlightened Electorate." And that half of Congress that depends on "dependents" will continue to fight against such an enlightened electorate by continuing to build its power base on poverty and ignorance.

PsychoSearch, Inc.

Since it is now common knowledge on the stock market, I admit to starting PsychoSearch some years ago.

With my background in both science and the social sciences, especially psychology with an emphasis on the paranormal, I realized that regression to past lives held the promise of regression to lives that might have been lived.

With the rapid progress of computers, this great dream of mine was finally realized. The classic study of Arnie Schmartzkoptfer is well known.

Arnie's case seemed ideal to me to test my hypothesis that a person cannot only be regressed like Shirley McClain to past lives, but with the computer power now available, could be regressed in such a manner as to predict what that person's life might have been had circumstances been different.

The cause of Arnie becoming a mass murderer, killing over seven hundred elderly people in various nursing homes before being apprehended, was well publicized.

A few harping critics wondered how it took so long for Arnie to be apprehended. This was explained very satisfactorily when it became known that the homes in which Arnie was employed used the same methods and criteria for determining qualifications as those of Social Services, particularly Child Protective Services.

As Arnie's trial dragged on with great publicity attached, it became clear to me that something had happened to Arnie as a child that caused him to act out this kind of antisocial behavior toward the elderly.

Having honed my hypothesis with the customary rats, guinea pigs, and grad students, I was ready for Arnie.

My reputation was sufficient to gain me entrance to the poor fellow while in prison (the jury had found him guilty of mass murder but innocent by reason of insanity). Of course, the conditions for testing were ideal since he was confined to the psychiatric ward of the prison.

After days of testing, I discovered Arnie had come to this sad pass because of chalk dust. Or, rather say the lack of chalk dust.

Arnie's first grade teacher, a Miss Granola, was quite elderly and well past retirement. But she used dustless chalk for writing on the blackboard.

During Arnie's regression to that point of his life, I discovered that had Miss Granola not used dust free chalk, Arnie would have been chosen to shake out the erasers.

Deprived of this special privilege of responsibility, Arnie had subconsciously known he was being cheated; and cheated by an elderly person.

What Arnie did not understand was that he was being cheated of the life he might have lived had he been able to shake out those erasers.

With these facts in hand, it was no trouble at all for me to convince a fine lawyer to undertake for Arnie. A new jury acquitted him on the basis of my findings and an excellent defense of this fine lawyer.

So it is that PsychoSearch came into being and is now available to all that have been unjustly incarcerated for having been deprived of the lives they should have lived had they not been cheated by those like Miss Granola and dust free chalk.

***

First I want to thank our fine local paper, the Kern Valley Sun, for bringing my noble efforts in freeing that poor misunderstood and tortured soul and mass murderer, Arnie Schmartzkoptfer, to the public's attention. Where but in America would such a triumph of justice have prevailed?

But being the sensitive soul that I am, I was grieved to the quick that some few would misunderstand and misconstrue the noble efforts of myself through PsychoSearch to the point of suggesting that I am a few feathers short of a full duck. Some even suggested, benighted souls they, that Arnie did not deserve to be set free. Fortunately for Arnie, cooler, and may I say more sensitive, heads prevailed.

I notice that the willow flycatcher here locally is being subjected to the same abuse as I have been by misguided people who think they are more important than birds.

It is too easy to get caught up in emotions, trivia and peripheral issues and miss the larger picture. After all, were it not for fine legislators, a Supreme Court that cares about America, and my friends like those of the ACLU, caring, knowledgeable and sensitive people just like myself, where would America be today? Would neo-Nazis be free to march, publish, broadcast, and exercise their Constitutional rights as citizens of our free nation? Would the entertainment industry be free to tell children that perversion, gratuitous sex and violence are perfectly acceptable in our great society? Would our teachers be told to teach our children that homosexuality is a perfectly acceptable alternative to normal sexual behavior?

When well meaning but misguided adults and parents try to keep such things away from children, don't they understand that children know they are being cheated, deprived of the total experiences and realities of life? Such things will always lead to warped psyches and the poor Arnie's that engage in anti-social behavior.

Granted that a few eggs are broken in making an omelet, like the 700 plus elderly that Arnie dispatched (mercifully, by the way), how can it fail to grieve sensitive people that the real blame was that of a society that simplistically, even callously, failed to take his feelings into consideration? What can you say of a system that would fail poor Arnie in such a manner? This was a miscarriage of justice that cried out for amelioration!

Fortunately, most of the response to my being instrumental in freeing Arnie was quite positive. Not a few commented on the constructive action of his making so many beds available (which are becoming a premium) in nursing homes, savings in Medicare, SSI, etc. In fact, not a few suggested... but I digress.

I only regret that PsychoSearch and my services were not available for another poor misunderstood victim of society, Jeffery Dahmer. How that cruelly tormented man must have suffered! No one seemed to take his side. Imagine if you will, suffering the addiction of cannibalism. You develop a sweet tooth for something like this and few trouble themselves to understand the control it has over your life. But where was the compassionate understanding of our justice system in his case? Conspicuous by its absence!

In correspondence with George Bush, I have made it clear to this fine presidential candidate that he needs to take another look at the death penalty. Far too many in Texas are being executed, innocent victims like Arnie, that if my talents and PsychoSearch were put to use, would be found to be stellar citizens if society had not failed them in the way it failed poor Arnie and Jeffrey.

But how many are inclined to think of such people as victims? We should beware of the labels given such people, labels like mass murderer, rapist, serial killer, labels that are strictly detrimental to justice and mental health, labels that deny the merits of the individuals and beat down their self-esteem. How can clear-headed people fail to see how this produces victims like Arnie?

Would space allow, I would take up the case of the LAPD and police brutality in general, how many otherwise fine upstanding citizens... but alas.

Regardless the slings and arrows of the misguided, PsychoSearch (with the continued help of the ACLU, Supreme Court, Alec Baldwin and Hollywood in general, and People for the American Way) will carry on in the cause of fair play and justice for all.

***

Y' know, I really don't understand my detractors. If Alzheimer's is an excuse for running over a young girl and killing her, if a prescription is the excuse for killing your own infant daughter, if alcohol and drugs are the defenses for countless murders, if an underprivileged childhood is the rationale accepted by courts to excuse crime in so many cases, why are people upset with my defending people like poor Arnie for mercifully practicing group euthanasia on the elderly and poor Jeffrey for developing a sweet tooth for eating people? But then, there were many that took Jonathan Swift's Modest Proposal seriously. And if we look to the political scene, nobody is responsible or to be held accountable for anything.

***

Well, it seems there are many people being persecuted and prosecuted for crimes that are not really their fault. Some poor misunderstood boy runs down a bunch of people in Santa Barbara and immediately a lynch mob wants him… a poor commentary on our society. Now I ask you in all fairness, can this poor boy really be held accountable for his genetic predisposition for running down people and killing them?

In the rush to judgment, it is probable that a persecuted couple, Bill and Hillary Clinton, will continue to be hounded by the media and heartless Republicans for doing things like lying, cheating, stealing and having relatives somewhat between dinosaur coprolites and Sister Angelica and Howard Stern. But is this poor misunderstood couple really responsible for criminal behavior, nepotism and cronyism, when it is in their genes to treat the White House and the American people like doo doo?

As the founder of PsychoSearch, I believe it my sacred duty to confront these miscarriages of justice by defending those unfortunates whose genes lead them to actions that are beyond their control, actions for which reasonable people would not think of holding them accountable!

With Mr. Clinton's permission and his well-known cooperation in seeking justice at any price, I was able to regress him to the point where his genes and circumstances proved that in the life he should have lived he would either have been the Pope or another Billy Graham. And Hillary having been gracious enough to submit to my testing proved she would have been another Mother Teresa!

Such is the loss when genes and circumstances lead people, against their will, to lives other than what they would have been had not nature given them a raw deal.

PsychoSearch will continue to do its duty regardless the slings and arrows of those less civilized that believe people should be held accountable for their actions in flagrant disregard of the circumstances and genetic factors that force these poor unfortunates, against their will, to lie, cheat, steal, commit murder, and an addiction to Bay Watch!

PsychoSearch Inc.

July 9, 2001

We at PsychoSearch have delved into heretofore-unexplored territory for our organization. At the request of the Federal Government, based on our outstanding, groundbreaking work in retrogressing people like serial killers back to the lives they might have lived had not circumstances and people (like Miss Granola in the case of Arnie Schmartzkoptfer who had killed over 700 elderly patients in rest homes) betrayed them and cheated them of the lives they would have lived, has requested our organization take a look at the War On Poverty with special attention to President Bush's Compassionate Conservatism and Faith-based government assistance.

The challenge of such a task was irresistible to me as the founder and leader of PsychoSearch. Here was a problem of socially monumental proportions worthy of the genius of my co-workers and myself. Just one example to prove that my use of the word "genius" is well deserved and not self-aggrandizing: People are poor because they haven't enough money and unemployment results when there are large numbers of people out of work.

We were not without resources in undertaking this huge challenge. There was the Carnegie Institute, for example, that helped with the research in Mr. Carnegie's philosophy that the rich are ordained of God to govern the poor. But of truly great help in our research there was the Ayn Rand Institute. Those at this venerable Institute were crucial in helping us to understand that money is the root of all happiness and helped us appreciate the philosophy contained in Ms. Rand's essay: "America's Persecuted Minority: Big Business."

Another source must be cited, one closely affiliated with the institute, Gary Hull who wrote: "The Virtue of Profit," and "Philosophy: The Ultimate CEO" (though this latter must be understood as the philosophy of having enough money to be happy).

Since the details of the research resulting in our suggestions to those in the Federal Government and President Bush will be published in the various academic media, at this time I will only mention one key element for the benefit of the general readership.

One very strong and unanimous recommendation was that homes be provided for single, unwed expectant mothers. These would be gated and fenced institutions with no men allowed, either as staff or as visitors. Once the baby is born, the girls would be sterilized and serve for a period of five years in vocational training doing useful and productive work before being released to various religious institutions of their choice, their sustenance and care for their children being guaranteed by government subsidies to these admirable faith-based organizations.

The fathers of the illegitimate children, whenever they can be found, will be taken into similar homes staffed by men only and have the advantage of being released on the same terms, including sterilization, as the mothers.

We at PsychoSearch decry the uncharitable phrase "Concentration Camps" which some callous individuals have hurled our direction and await the action of Congress and the President as a result of our recommendations. We at PSI are truly and humbly grateful to serve our country in such a fashion as to do our bit in the War on Poverty. We depend on equally compassionate fellow Americans to follow suit.

Samuel D. G. Heath, Ph. D.
Founder and CEO: PsychoSearch, Inc.

Chapter Eight

May 9, 2001

December 23, 2000

President Elect George W. Bush
Number 411
603 West 13th Street, Suite 1A
Austin, Texas 78701-1795

Dear Sir:

As a California State Advisor to the National Republican Senatorial Committee I have an obligation to inform you of a major concern of mine. More than this, I feel it a duty and responsibility as an American Citizen to make this concern known to you as my next President

It is my most sincere hope that as our President you will not lend yourself to the kind of religious propaganda that makes for such a dangerous and demon-haunted world as Carl Sagan warned of.

It was enough that William Clinton disgraced our nation and made us a laughingstock, but the lighting of a "National Menorah" I find thoroughly repugnant to me as an American.

Make no mistake, I would find the lighting of a "National Cross" equally repugnant. And all the religious propaganda aside, the Menorah is as distinctive to the Jewish religion as the Star of David and the world recognizes this.

A major concern of mine as an American is the message this sends to those Arab nations in particular that America has taken the side of Israel in spite of the killing of Palestinians and the refusal of Israel on religious grounds to be reasonable in the peace process.

While I fully recognize the religious hatreds and prejudices on both sides, America cannot hope to lead in the peace process by engaging in such through taking sides on the basis of a religion, whether Jewish, Christian, or Islamic.

I am taking the liberty of sending a copy of this letter to a number of other people, including my congressman and senators, as well as some of the leaders of other nations. As an American citizen, I do not want other nations to think that I give my approval as an American to any religious superstition or prejudice.

The myths, superstitions, and prejudices of religion continue to make the world a dangerous and demon-haunted place. But the very idea of America approving a "National Menorah" is not only an affront to me as an American, it has to be an affront to other nations as well and just one more reason for the distrust of America on the part of other nations. Further, this has to be a "Line in the sand" that those like Saddam Hussein and Osama bin Laden will use to their propaganda advantage against America.

In all fairness and justice, America cannot be represented as a nation that favors one religion over another. And the separation between Church and State, as our Founding Fathers clearly and wisely perceived, must be rigidly enforced. As a nation, and for the sake of world peace, we cannot engage in the kind of national prejudice and hypocrisy that a "National Menorah" signifies.

Respectfully;

Samuel D. G. Heath, Ph. D.

***

Being a very well educated and literate man I am oft times given to dedicating my genius to attempting to solve some of the major problems that confront humanity. For example, there are the problems of world peace, why some drivers have never learned how to use turn signals, and why the pockets of many pants, pajamas, etc. turn inside out in the washing machine?

Another problem of at least equal magnitude to these mentioned recently caught my attention: Mother's Day.

Now that private school in New York that has banned Mother's Day has a very real basis in logic for doing this. One can only hope that public schools will get the message and follow suit. If this gets the national attention and cooperation it deserves, both Mother and Father's Days will be banned in the schools.

Since the argument on the part of this private school is that they teach "diversity" rather than the quaint and antiquated values of the traditional home of a mother and father, may I suggest that we write President Bush encouraging him to announce another day in the place of Mother and Father's Day. I would humbly suggest he call such a day: National Perverts Day. Given the moral climate of America, this should please everyone but a very few carping critics that are never satisfied no matter what.

***

When I ran for state senate on a platform of education reform, people kept telling me: It's the economy,

Stupid! My point that the economy was ultimately based on education was lost on the electorate.

In discussion with then state senator Don Rogers, the political realities led me to withdraw and give my support to Phil Wyman. But I knew in discussion with Wyman that education would continue to be a losing proposition in Sacramento.

When Pete Wilson was governor, I kept hammering away on the desperate need of meaningful education reform. I have continued to do so with Gray Davis. Raising standards makes good political rhetoric, but unless the tools are there, it remains nothing but rhetoric.

Basic to such tools are a society that cares about children, colleges that produce literate, educated teachers that sincerely want to work with children and have the skills to do so, state and local boards of education filled by people who really know about education rather than being nothing but rubber stamps for those who created this failed system of which I began to say: We couldn't have better designed a system for failure had we done so intentionally.

Now that we have two presidential candidates trying to convince the electorate they care about education reform, wouldn't it be appropriate to reveal the causes of this failed system they are promising to correct?

Neither candidate nor Gray Davis is talking about the root causes of our failed systems of education. None seems to know the real mechanisms at work in the universities and the schools. Throwing more money at the problems is not going to work. But where do we see the honesty to address the real issues?

Appalling as it is, politicians seem to be clueless to the real issues involved.

Years ago, I confronted the state board of education and legislators in Sacramento with the utter nonsense of attempting raised standards without the necessary tools mentioned. All this would accomplish, I told them, would be a deepening, festering problem. And so it has proved to be.

KVSun 2-20

The myth of God supposedly telling human kind to subdue the earth has real merit, but every Dominion Theology following, being religious, has never been able to overcome the fatal flaw of dualistic thinking that makes God responsible for both good and evil. Hawthorne and Melville, despite their genius, both made shipwreck on this paradoxical rock.

But the fable of the Garden included Adam and Eve being vegetarians and the shedding of the blood of animals being the result of disobedience to the will of God. Our teeth, for example, are far better designed for the masticating of cereals, fruits, and vegetables than that of predators for the tearing and rending of flesh.

Indeed we should subdue the earth and have dominion over it. We are capable of doing so, we are capable of eliminating the weeds and thistles, the beasts of prey, of an agriculture that would be more than sufficient for our needs once problems like birth control, both human and animal, are acknowledged, confronted and overcome.

And it isn't just the argument that it takes eight pounds of grain to produce one pound of meat that is at issue; particularly when you factor in the issue of unproductive mouths, an issue that does have to be considered necessitating birth control. What is needed is an entirely new way, a new philosophy if you will, of thinking about diet that incorporates all the logical factors impinging on health. Logically it makes no sense for any culture to encourage non-productive welfare births, for example, which have little chance at success, but on the contrary are more likely to sap the resources of a society and enlarge a criminal population, a distasteful fact, but still a fact.

But rather than address such an inflammatory fact, responsible people and the leadership lack the will to confront it, blaming instead institutions such as the schools and social services for not performing miracles. I am not a friend of the way our schools and social services do business. But in all fairness, they are asked to do the impossible under the circumstances.

Such a thing as the failure of responsible birth control measures is patently and inherently unhealthy for any culture or society. Any discussion of "human rights" must begin to take into account those that have no regard for personal responsibility for their actions or the rights and property of others. Here in America we are encouraging hoards of barbarians and vandals by insanely encouraging irresponsibility and a lack of accountability on the part of individuals, the media, and on the part of the leaders of our institutions and government.

It would be legitimate for those being forced to pay the bill for welfare to ask this question: Who made the decision that welfare as a way of life should include reproductive rights without hope of being able to support the resulting children?

***

A vegetarian world of people and beasts... In all logic, what's wrong with the idea? I do believe a generation born and raised in such a manner would consider the previous generations of animal killers and eaters savage and barbaric! But, then, just looking at the violence now so graphically portrayed in films, "games," and TV would quickly convince them of that. Not to mention that people considering themselves "civilized" are still killing one another in the name of God because of their religious prejudices, and over something some call a "Holy Land."

KV SUN 3-28

It was kind; even gracious on the part of C. C. Kelly to stick up for me concerning my remarks about the need to keep religion out of public institutions, particularly the schools; but lest any misunderstand, and I'm sure Kelly didn't intend this, I'm not anti-God but I am anti-religion, whether that of the Jews, Christians, Moslems, etc. I have a sign in my home, in fact, stating: God (both Him and Her) is welcome. Religion is not!

Kelly is certainly correct, as were Voltaire and Paine, about the horrendous and unspeakable atrocities committed in the name of God throughout human history and still on-going. But as the stock in trade of professional religionists and politicians, we will continue to be harangued by such "well-intentioned" charlatans until, and if, the world is civilized enough to act on the principle Confucius stated long before the time of Jesus that each of us should treat others as we wish to be treated.

Having been ordained as a Christian minister and serving as a pastor and having a strong theological background, I am "blessed" with having confronted the religious superstitions and myths I was taught as a child, and overcame these beliefs that I had confused with knowledge.

Having "been there, done that" I understand the religious mind. And I have no illusions about the difficulties in overcoming such. But no real progress toward truly civilized thinking can be claimed on the basis of those things that are solely the basis of beliefs when these beliefs are touted as facts, even to the point of using violence to enforce such beliefs.

My greatest concern is that religious people (as I once was) really believe they do the will of God by trying to force their beliefs on others, whether by law or the sword. I find the only difference between the barbaric Taleban of

Afghanistan and Jews and Christians in America to be one of degree, not of kind.

KV Sun 4-11

Having reached, quite unexpectedly by the way, the exalted status of "Senior Citizen" and enjoying what are euphemistically called the "Golden Years," I was still somewhat surprised by the recent letter in the Sun according me the title of "Bodfish Oracle."

Now, being of an age that I can also enjoy scratching where it itches, not just where it looks the best (Thank you, Claudette Colbert), I would like to comment on the reference by the writer to my "rare avian status."

Those that know me well also know of my shy, retiring, and afraid of women character (which, for some strange reason, didn't prevent my marrying five times). But I have always been peripatetic and as a writer and loving the outdoors, I often spend time walking in my yard, far preferring the beauty of our Valley from the outside of my house rather than the inside. I have written quite a bit about the unusual benefits of creation we in the Valley enjoy and sometimes take for granted. The old song: Don't Fence Me In could have been written for me.

A few months ago, a letter in the paper implied that I might have slighted the elderly. That was since rectified and it did prompt some thoughts about those of us that have lived long enough to look back far enough and be able to say: Been there, done that.

In conversation the other day with Junky Jerry (now before you say anything, I know you don't have "conversations" with Jerry), the point did come out that most of us that have lived long enough to beat the alternative (though since I haven't died I can't say for sure, and certainly can't say "been there, done that" in this respect yet), have a legitimate concern for our children and grandchildren concerning retirement.

Most of us oldsters that have chosen the Valley for our declining years would probably agree that we didn't take retirement very seriously when we were younger. When I first came to the Valley in 1948 to live on the mining claim with my grandparents, I most certainly wasn't thinking in terms of retirement here. One thing that did have my interest at the time was where I could make a dollar an hour for hard labor. A dollar an hour in those days was real riches.

But it seemed in no time at all I was on my own with a family to support. When the lake went in, I found myself in 1954 an apprentice machinist at North American next to LAX making a dollar and fifteen cents an hour. I was working with older men that had spent the whole of WWII in this factory at sixty to ninety-five cents an hour.

Did I give any thought to retirement then? Of course not… and neither did these older men. But they thought they had it made, especially when you could buy a house for less than $5,000 and a new car for less than $1,500. I rented an apartment in Hermosa Beach with an ocean view and a short walk to the beach for $35 a month, a loaf of bread and a gallon of gas were fifteen cents each.

So, looking back do I worry about my children and grandchildren? You bet I do! Having lived long enough to "been there, done that" I worry constantly about the young people that have not "been there, done that!"

I also know that there wasn't any way people my age could have foreseen the kind of world we live in today. The old saying "If I'd known I'd live this long I'd have taken better care of myself" is all too true. But for those of us that grew up in an era when a dollar was significant and a penny on the ground was well worth picking up, how could we know that the dollar an hour we earned way back then would mean so little today?

But my generation still believed in the future of America. Can we say the same for young people today? Sadly, even fearfully, the answer is a resounding NO!

KV Sun 6-20

Reading of Amanda Rossback's "Outstanding Girl of the Year" award by Woodrow Wallace Middle School was a real delight to me. Amanda and her family have every right to be very proud of her and she certainly has my congratulations.

This caused me to haul out the 8th grade graduation picture I have of our graduation class of 1950 from Old Kernville Elementary when "Woody" Wallace was our 7th and 8th grade teacher as well as the principal of the school. I have Mr. Wallace to thank for my becoming the first "Junior Custodian" for the school at the princely sum of $35.00 a month under the supervision of Guy Schultz, the custodian, bus driver, and whatever else he was needed for.

As part of our graduation exercises, some of the kids (primarily the girls, of course) decided it would be fun to have "prophecy" skits depicting what was believed to be the future prospects of the graduates. But unlike Amanda, my accomplishments in the school resulted in my being depicted as a hobo (they stuck Jimmy Maxwell with me, but I could never figure out why?).

Looking back over the years, it wasn't an altogether inappropriate guess as to my future; and I certainly applaud little Amanda for fairing much better… though I still don't understand what the kids had against Jimmy?

***

Belridge places blame. Filed: 06/28/2001. By STEVEN MAYER, Californian staff writer. BELRIDGE -- Dina Alldredge lay awake well into the night Tuesday trying to get her mind around a disturbing image.

"I was thinking, in a few months, this house isn't going to be here anymore," Alldredge said Wednesday. "It's hard to believe."

The home that provides shelter and a sense of place for Alldredge and her husband, their three children, two cats, one dog and a tame raven named Joey, will be reduced to rubble in a matter of months. In fact, all 41 homes that make up the tiny western Kern County community of Belridge will be demolished sometime after September by Aera Energy LLC, the owner of the one-time company town that was doomed by a business decision made public by Aera Tuesday night.

That was when Aera representatives announced the company's plan to close the Belridge housing complex Sept. 30, giving residents about three months to move out. Aera promised to provide unspecified relocation expenses for the tenants, but that did little to soften the blow for some.

At a meeting of the Belridge Elementary School District board Wednesday afternoon, the emotions of a few residents bubbled to the surface as they spoke about the impending death of their community -- and those they hold responsible.

"They had a calculated plan," Belridge resident Kathy Weaver said of Aera officials, her face set in anger and her voice breaking with the strain. "The lies on top of lies on top of lies ..."

Weaver suggested Aera's decision to close the housing complex was a direct result of the strained relationship between Aera Energy and Belridge School District Superintendent Steve Wentland.

Aera and Paramount Farming Co., which together own about 85 percent of the property-tax base in the district, sued Belridge last year after the district placed on the ballot a $30 million bond issue to fund unspecified "improvements" to the school.

The bond was defeated by 78 percent of voters in the district, but the showdown between Aera and Belridge over the bond set the stage for a simmering feud that some say continues to this day.

Wentland declined to be interviewed for this story, but several actions taken by him during the past two years have been harshly criticized by Aera officials and many others.

Last fall, for example, Wentland and the three-member board spent thousands of dollars in school funds to hire private investigators to look into alleged health and safety violations by Aera. No serious violations were ever reported.

But the investigation launched by the Belridge district was just one in a long string of controversial actions taken by Wentland and the school board -- beginning in 1999 with the district's adoption of an evangelical Christian-oriented curriculum and continuing last year with the board's approval of a plan to pay up to $43,000 for Wentland's doctoral education. These and other actions did not go unnoticed.

In a scathing report released last month, the Kern County grand jury charged the superintendent with improper and wasteful use of public money, a pattern of harassment and intimidation of parents and staff and "deliberate and knowing violation of California and federal law."

The grand jury report followed more than 18 months of investigative reporting of Belridge School District by The Californian.

Aera Vice President Greg Hill and company spokeswoman Susan Hersberger said, for five years, Aera has been studying and evaluating the fate of the housing complex that was built by the now-defunct Belridge Oil Co. in the 1970s.

Aera's ownership of the rentals has resulted in a net loss to the company, Hill said. And maintaining the homes would require an ever-increasing level of investment. For example, a proposed program to replace water lines to the houses would cost as much as $500,000, Hill said.

The decision to close the housing was simply a business decision, Hill said.

But Oliver Sprenger, a former school board member who lives in the Belridge neighborhood with his wife and family, said Aera should have made it clear that tenants could be subject to forced removal.

"We were not told this was going to happen," Sprenger said during the board meeting's public comment period. "Yet they tell us this has been in the works for five years.

"It's a very hard thing for people here," he added. "People in the community are really hurting."

Situated more than a dozen miles northwest of McKittrick, the tiny residential enclave of Belridge has no gas station, no grocery store and virtually no violent crime.

What it does have is 41 nearly identical single-family homes with perfectly manicured lawns, a 65-student school with amenities many educators would envy. and a community park with swimming pool, tennis courts and a rope swing hanging from a tree.

Many residents say the neighborhood is much like an extended family, with neighbor willing to help neighbor whenever the need arises.

"Sometimes business decisions are very difficult, and this is clearly one of those times," Aera's Hersberger said Wednesday. "We are very concerned about the impact on people and families, and that's why we're putting together the relocation assistance ... for all of the families, whether they are employees or not."

In response to criticism about Aera waiting too long to inform residents of the possibility that the rental houses could one day be closed, Hersberger noted that Belridge trustee Lee Varnado met with Aera Chief Executive Gene Boiland in February, and one of the topics discussed was the future of the Belridge housing complex.

"At that time, Gene communicated to Lee that a final decision regarding the future of the houses hadn't been made, but that it was indeed under review," Hersberger said. "So, I think the community has been aware for some time that this has been under review."

In the coming weeks, Belridge school board members may need to work fast to appoint their own replacements before September. While most of the pupils in the district come from the Paramount housing tract miles away on Lerdo Highway, two of the three current board members -- Varnado and Gary Lumpkins -- live in the condemned complex adjacent to the school. Chances are, they will be forced to move to a town outside the district, and that would require their resignations.

For Belridge resident Alldredge, who is already searching for a new town and a new home in which to live, the impending move represents a transition back to the "real world," away from the small-town benefits Belridge offers -- and away from the bizarre actions of school's superintendent.

"There's a lot he does that I don't agree with," she said shaking her head in amazement. "I believe the Wentland situation played a part in what is happening to us.

"We are the losers, while Steve Wentland and Aera get to stay."

To the Bakersfield Californian

June 28, 2001

Samuel D. G. Heath, Ph. D.

As a reader and friend of The Californian, having expressed my appreciation for the paper on a number of occasions, I often send comments that I feel will be helpful rather than for print. This is one such instance.

The continuing disgrace of Belridge School District's Superintendent is symptomatic of some of the problems of education as a whole. Now Aera will dispossess all these families and in spite of the reasons given I have no doubt the company is reacting to the "Caesar" complex of Wentland and his puppet board.

I spent a year as a Resource Specialist for Stanislaus County. I was in charge of the Special Education programs for five, rural school districts, some of these schools smaller than Belridge. I witnessed and experienced first hand the dictatorial fashion of these small districts in operation because of the endemic lack of accountability on the part of education as a whole where nepotism and cronyism, the lack of accountability are a way of life. So it was that I commented that those at Belridge would continue doing "business as usual" no matter what the Grand Jury or the Californian had to say on the subject.

I made comment some time back that one of the problems news personnel have in covering stories involving education is that reporters are seldom qualified to ask the right questions; after all how many reporters have made an extensive career in education before becoming journalists? My justifiable criticism of some reporters is that they assume an expertise and knowledge they do not possess.

For example, how many in the news business know that you get rid of a bad school administrator in the same manner that hospitals get rid of bad doctors? How many know that the one real and ultimate sacred cow of America is its universities? How many know the number of school personnel in California and are able to look at the number of actual firings that took place last year and ask the question: What's wrong with this picture?

Granting that we have become the most litigious country in the world and in history, no one can reasonably look at the figures and say that such a large labor pool had so few workers that needed to be fired.

I taught a course for Chapman University in Teaching Strategies for a class of graduate pupils, fresh BAs in hand, that needed the class to fulfill requirements for their teaching credentials. These college graduates, these prospective teachers, could not write a paper worthy of a college freshman. Yet, in all their four years of college not a single professor had challenged these graduates on their inability to write.

Obviously I could go on at great length, and have in voluminous writing on the subject throughout the years, but my point in writing at this time is to try to help those at the Californian to understand the magnitude of the problem, a problem that the Belridge tragedy and disaster so well illustrates. Since the paper is so key to the people and life in Kern County, and I believe in California, I believe those at the paper want to do a responsible job of reporting knowledgeably on such a key factor to our lives as that of education. And I would be remiss if I did not point out to you the fact that Belridge illustrates the need of understanding a problem of immense complexity beyond the usual scope of experience and knowledge of those reporting on the subject.

Sincerely and respectfully,

Samuel D. G. Heath, Ph.D.

***

Community Voices / Samuel D.G. Heath: Schools can obscure truth. Filed: 06/30/2001. By SAMUEL D. G. HEATH: *Americans for Constitutional Protection of Children*

Reading the comments about Californian reporters not being able to get answers about the Rosedale school fiasco prompts a few comments.

When I mentioned not long ago that the Belridge School district disgrace would result in nothing more than continuing "doing business as usual" it was with knowledge and experience of how the education system operates. So my heart went out to reporters who are frustrated when attempting to get questions answered by school personnel.

You must have an administrative credential to become a school principal or superintendent. Part of the course work for this credential is the study of California laws applying to education.

One of many problems resulting in poor education systems is the fact that there are no such requirements for becoming a school board member. The typical school board calls for a superintendent and expects this person to be knowledgeable of laws determining the running of a school district. In effect, this most often results in the school board becoming a rubber stamp for the superintendent.

Unless a "personality conflict" arises, the superintendent is pretty well left alone to run things as he or she sees fit. This, in effect, makes the school district a "fiefdom" of the superintendent.

A further problem is created by the lack of uniformity throughout California regarding fiscal accountability. This encourages poor behavior by unscrupulous personnel. Together with a lack of knowledgeable oversight by school boards is the voluminous paperwork required by local, state and federal laws. It is impossible, given the type of curriculum offered in schools of education on university campuses, to find qualified personnel for the job of business accounting in local schools.

In doing research for my doctoral dissertation on accountability in education, it became apparent to me that the major obstacle to real accountability is the lack of realistic teacher education, together with an utter lack of qualified personnel throughout the entire spectrum of education -- including school board members.

To solve any problem requires expertise in knowing the right questions to ask. When it is said that a proper phrasing of a question in identifying the problem is half the solution, it is assumed that the questioner knows something of the problem itself. In the case of newspaper reporters, this is seldom true regarding education.

As with the series The Californian did on "Loss of Innocence," it was naive in the extreme to expect honest and forthright answers from personnel within Child Protective Services; so, too, with the system of education.

Rosedale and Belridge are symptomatic of the larger issues concerning the problems plaguing education. To someone like myself with specialized knowledge of this system, I can only wish reporters the best as they try to do a job that is doomed to fail from the start.

But I am ever grateful for those who at least try to get answers to their questions and provide a forum through the one medium that I believe remains the best in America: the local newspaper.

Samuel D. G. Heath, Ph. D., of Bodfish: Americans for Constitutional Protection of Children.

***

July 4, 2001

Dear Folks at the Californian,

Please believe that I am not being critical of you folks as you try to keep the public informed about Belridge School District. But as I said, the system of education in general does not admit "outsiders." As a principal once told me: "We do our own dirty laundry." This reminded me of something the then Downey Chief of Police said to me during an interview shortly after the Watts Riot: "We are not here to help people; we are here to slam the door on them!"

That same "door" is one that reporters, and others, face in trying to get facts about the system of education. School boards and superintendents can act with impunity since they are a "law unto themselves." They are used to this and do not want anyone to rock the boat. And while the police have come under ever-greater scrutiny, the system of education has not. And throwing ever-greater amounts of money at the problem is not going to give us better schools (or police).

Given the virtual dictatorial power of school boards and superintendents, the State Department of Education going along with this, and rife with nepotism and cronyism ever as much as any other branch of politics, I came to realize that "public" schools are anything but.

We have become an illiterate nation, filled with people that don't even know what a liberal education is supposed to do for children in preparing them for life. For those that wish to know, and are willing to admit of their own ignorance, they would do well to read the comments of Robert M. Hutchins "The Great Conversation. The Substance of a Liberal Education." Though written in 1951, Hutchins even then saw the demise of education and his comments more than most cut through the cant of the universities and gave us fair warning.

Implausible as it seems, we knew in 1954 that the bottom 15% of college graduates were going into education as a profession. The universities did nothing to change this and we live with the results.

My thanks again to you folks at the Californian for continuing the battle on behalf of children; they have no voice of their own and are the real victims in all of this.

Sincerely,

Samuel D. G. Heath, Ph. D.

July 11, 2001

To the Californian

I'm gratified to read the response to my article about education by board member Gary Lumpkins. But Mr. Lumpkins makes the all too common mistake of believing that good intentions take the place of real knowledge and experience when it comes to improving education. He met the requirements to become a school board member. Just what do those requirements "require" when it comes to the business of leading a school district? Virtually nothing but good intentions and what is often euphemistically called "community involvement."

Yes, it is commendable that citizens want to do something to help their communities. But god help us from the kind of "help" most school board members give their respective communities, help that is based on good intentions (or too often, overweening egos and further political ambition) rather than meaningful knowledge and experience.

If I'm tough, and I am, on those in education it is because I know that America has had two generations of virtual illiteracy and cannot possibly survive further decline. As to school boards, just how, exactly, did Mr. Lumpkins expect to make "positive changes" when he says the requirements for being a school board member are unrelated to the requirements for being a superintendent? It is just this kind of naïve ignorance that dooms many school board members from being able to be anything other than rubber stamps for superintendents, even tyrants like Wentland.

When it comes to our children, there should not be any politically sectarian boundaries. And whether you agree with my proposed amendment for the protection of children or not, I know you will agree that our children are suffering from a failed system of public education.

It was in another life it seems that I sat with California State Senator Ed Davis in his office in Sacramento. We had established a warm correspondence when he was LAPD Chief of Police and I was a fledgling freshman teacher at David Starr Jordan in the Watts district of South Central Los Angeles.

By the time of this meeting, I was no longer the naive young man who thought the problems in education would be relatively easy to fix. The travesty of the sixties in education such as Innovative Designs in Learning, which cast out the things that had worked and instituted the things that made no sense whatsoever, had done their dirty work. Children were going to pay the price of the adult abrogation of responsibility for their education.

The sacred cows remain the same, the universities that produced a failed system of public education which were untouchable then and are equally untouchable today in spite of the damning indictment of them through research and writing like that of Professor Reginald G. Damerell and so many others including myself.

I focused on Accountability in Education in my own Ph.D. dissertation only to discover it was such a hot button no publisher would touch it. Only one Ed. publisher at the time was honest enough to tell me that the material in my dissertation was such an indictment of the schools he didn't dare publish it!

I discovered that the school systems from the universities on down are so rife with corruption and such cronyism and nepotism as to be inbred to the point of impotence. Then I discovered that legislators were dedicated to asking the very people who created the problems in education for answers to the very problems they had created! Insane on the face of it!

And while I would never accuse the educational hierarchy of the purposeful destruction of public education, I do say they could not have better designed a system for failure had they done so intentionally!

I found that schools are not held fiscally accountable because of such creative bookkeeping it is impossible to audit them and the money is embezzled at will in the amount of countless hundreds of millions of dollars every year throughout California alone. The fox that guards the henhouse, the State Department of Education, has its reasons for not wanting this publicized, not the least of these being the public outcry it would cause together with the potential loss of so much federal funding.

I discovered first hand how tenure was abused to the point that the worst teachers who wouldn't have been allowed to continue to work a week in the private sector were guaranteed jobs for life in education, especially in the universities, and children and college students paid the price for such incompetence and lack of accountability throughout the entire system of public education.

I was at ground zero when Special Education began to be the cash cow for schools, a blank check no one questioned as empire building at its very worst became the norm in the public schools. Had I not personally witnessed what I have in this system alone, I don't think anyone could fictionalize the enormous boondoggle of this single education bureaucracy!

I began to try to tell parents and legislators like Ed Davis and Gary Hart, governors like Pete Wilson and Gray Davis, that the problems for children in education were not as bad as they thought, they were far, far worse!

I saw our classrooms being filled with teachers, products of the universities, who could not spell or do arithmetic and no one dared say anything about it! Why not? Because virtually every leader throughout society is a university graduate and would never criticize the institutions on which their own academic credibility and future success were based!

And teachers such as me with industry backgrounds knew the Ivory Tower mind-set was incapable of preparing children for real life. And most teachers who witnessed the terrible destruction of education would not speak out for fear of losing their jobs or becoming pariahs.

It has become the stock in trade of politicians to talk about educational reform. But politics being the trade of generalities does not deal with specifics and politicians always evade answering in specifics because they do not have any specifics when it comes to educational reform (or a host of other problems)! But no one knows better than I the enormity of the problems in education and the enormity of what will be required to fix them.

But as long as our children are defrauded of an education because politicians refuse to deal with the specifics, or even worse, have no idea of what the specifics are, I will continue to be a voice raised against the tragedy of ignorance that has invaded America and become the legacy of so-called educators and their crony political quislings passed on to our children.

Governor Gray Davis saw fit to thank me personally and pass my critique of To Kill A Mockingbird on to State Senator Gary Hart, the head of California's Education Committee. Senator Hart sent me a personal Thank You note.

Politicians have always been very gracious in thanking me for my concerns about our children and their education. But not a single one has ever followed through by doing the hard things my own research and experience proves need to be done. One school board president who tried to institute just a couple of the needed reforms I had suggested lost in the next election because of this.

In spite of my cautionary words, he didn't believe the furor this would cause among teachers who actively campaigned (illegally of course) against him in their very classrooms, even sending home with their pupils flyers produced in the school audio/visual department and taking out ads in the local paper against this man's re-election.

Of course, things were made pretty hot for me as well. I was betraying my kind and biting the hand that fed me.

It is easy to do the trend-forecast of where the present concerns about the latest enormously expensive and tragic boondoggle of education, that of Special Education, will lead. Nowhere. Once the noise dies down, it will be back to business as usual. The educational hierarchy from the universities on down depends on this.

Oh yes, audits there will be. A few arrests may even be made for blatant offenses and thefts that cannot be hidden no matter the creative book- and record-keeping. The lawsuits will proliferate and taxpayers will foot the bill as usual while the guilty in the schools from the universities on down will wring their hands and refuse to accept any responsibility.

But as in the case of the I.R.S. and California's Social Services, particularly Child Protective Services, the enormity of the task will make any meaningful audits virtually impossible. The educational hierarchy knows and depends on this to, as one principal told me, do their own dirty laundry and not expose it to the public.

His refreshing, albeit self-serving, candor reminded me of that of a Downey Chief of Police who told me in an interview: We're not here to help people; we're here to slam the door on them!

Like expressed concern about child abuse, the problems in the Evil Empire of Special Education will sell papers and make for News at Eleven and political rhetoric for a while. And then, quietly fade away until someone sees a way of making headlines and political hay of it once more.

Harper Lee addressed the failure of the schools in Thirties' Alabama. I witnessed it as a teacher in Sixties' California. And not just during my tenure in the war zones of the ghetto of Watts and the barrio of East San Jose, but places like lily-white Castro Valley and throughout Stanislaus County; and, of course, my home county of Kern, the target of Edward Humes' Pulitzer-winning book.

It was in my home County of Kern that a group of high school seniors applauded me for telling them: Any real education you get here will be because you earnestly desire and work for it, not because this school is really prepared and dedicated to giving you an education.

These seniors knew the truth of what I was telling them. Their applause was for my being the only adult school authority to make to them such a bald and honest confession of the failure of the school system to provide them the opportunity for an education, to have in fact defrauded them of an education.

The applause caught the attention of teachers and administrators. When they discovered the reason for it, I was not invited back. But I knew that would be the result. I have always been known as a high roller on behalf of the kids against the system. It is one reason I have worked in so many different school systems in spite of reaching tenure in two of them.

Tragically for our children and young people, my words to that group of seniors would apply with equal truth in schools across America. And while young people like the class of seniors mentioned know the truth, and will applaud me for telling it like it is, it doesn't win me any friends among adult authorities who should be my friends for my honesty.

The enormous fraud of Special Education has succeeded because those outside the system have no idea of what it is really all about. To understand how this is possible, you must understand that the field of education as a whole has its own manufactured language, a foreign language if you will, that admits of no outsiders learning it.

There is an incredible amount of paranoia in both Social Services and the schools. While working in Child Protective Services, I'll never forget my visits to the schools. Because of my experience in Special Ed. I knew the language and what to ask for concerning things like Individual Education Plans (IEPs). There was an absolute look of horror on one principal's face when he realized I was knowledgeable of such things. He was used to being able to dance around other CPS personnel who didn't know what questions to ask.

But CPS workers seldom visit the schools and don't know the system. And the schools rely on this kind of ignorance on the part of Social Services and the general public as well as parents and politicians. It is this kind of ignorance that enables the schools to continue to perpetrate this enormously successful con game of Special Education.

The con would not be so successful if parents and politicians were knowledgeable enough to ask the hard questions and demand answers. But they aren't. And I'm often in the position of asking myself: Does anybody really care?

But ignorance can be a real killer. When Robert Duvall made the picture The Apostle, I pointed out the weakness of the film was in his having never been raised a true believer in the charismatic religion. As a result, he simply was not believable in the role. He didn't really know the language and manners of the charismatic Christian.

But this did not prevent his being able to fool those like Siskel and Ebert who gave the film two thumbs up. Thus displaying their own ignorance of charismatic Christianity.

Even the genius of Sinclair Lewis in Elmer Gantry could not succeed in fooling those born and raised as true believers. And while the lessons in both

Duvall's film and Lewis' novel are universal and as such well worthwhile, the believability in their works falls short because of the lack of real experience.

It is this lack of real experience that dooms the efforts of parents and politicians who would genuinely like to make a contribution to reform in education.

Such people are unaware that unlike true academic subjects, education is itself lacking any empirical body of knowledge and has borrowed wholesale from legitimate disciplines in an attempt to legitimize itself. The resulting language of education is to be compared with a corrupt kind of pidgin, a virtual gobbledygook best compared with meaningless psycho-babble and its own kind of fraternal understandings available only to members of the club.

The system of Special Ed. particularly is a Byzantine labyrinthine monstrosity of nonsense within a larger system of nonsense. The language of Special Ed. is representative of the whole Alice in Wonderland field of education that reflects the language of the Jabberwocky. But unlike that delightful children's piece, the nonsensical words and phrases of Special Ed. make the pretense of sensibility.

In no other field of education is this smoke screen of pretended expertise of knowing what you are talking about when you do not through an invention of the imagination so evident as in Special Ed.

If things are ever going to take a turn for the better in education, they will only do so when political leaders take on the responsibility for confronting this enormous fraud and call it what it is: An Enormous Fraud!

The entire system of education must be called to account and held accountable. But it will take leaders of rare courage and a genuine concern for the welfare of America's children to bring this to pass. If I did not believe there were a few leaders of whom this is true, I would not have burdened them with my concerns.

It was known in 1954 that the bottom 15 per cent of college graduates were going into the field of education and nothing was done to correct this. Those responsible in the universities did nothing to change this and encourage the best and brightest to enter our classrooms. Today, we live with the result of this failure of the universities to act and be responsible. Not to mention the failure of the political leadership; which should have known and done better.

I expect better of those who have a genuine concern for children than I do of the amoral and literally silly - to use the most charitable word - leadership in the universities which gave us this failed system of public education and has even helped to perpetuate the enormously expensive and counter-productive continuing fraud of Special Education.

Only leaders who are genuinely concerned for the future of America, our children, are going to be able to confront this tragedy for our children and our nation and change things for the better. But elected leaders choose this political vocation and are elected for this very purpose.

Samuel D. G. Heath, Ph. D.

Americans for Constitutional Protection of Children

***

KV Sun 7-4

As a self-professed genius and the founder of The Bodfish Philosophical Society and PsychoSearch (modesty alone prevents my declaring my credentials as a genius in reality) part of my obligation is corresponding with noted columnists. One with whom I share a special rapport is Arianna Huffington whose columns are rife with wit.

Her column of June 4, 2001 satirized President Bush's tax rebate and pointed out that the top 1 per cent will receive $690 billion of this and the poor will net about $66 per year over the decade. A focus of her column was Barbara Ehrenreich's book "Nickel and Dimed" which is supposed to provide an inside look at the plight of the working poor. I say, "supposed" because Ms. Ehrenreich makes the usual mistake as that of those that think they understand what is wrong with the educational system and have never spent 20 years in eight different school districts listening to teachers in the coffee lounges.

Arianna contrasts this plight of the working poor with the plight of that top 1 per cent (which correlates with the group to which I belong regarding genius) of the wealthy that have their own difficulties, difficulties that few people seem to take into account but President Bush and those in Congress obviously had in mind by voting for the tax cut. Carnegie knew that God had ordained the rich to take care of the poor. President Bush and those in Congress are simply following the divine plan, something Arianna should have pointed out.

Arianna ends her column by asking "...who can really put a price tag on human suffering?" In my reply to her I said: "I can. It comes to $1.76 per person." But it takes real genius to understand the equation I used in arriving at this sum... and to quote Einstein when asked if anyone understood his Theory of Relativity answered: "Yes, there are two people; but I don't know who the other person is."

Sam Heath

***

KV Sun 7-18

Nuclear Plant for the Kern Valley

When I threw my hat in the ring for state senate some years ago it was on a platform of education reform. "It's the economy, stupid!" people kept telling me. I had the naïve idea that without a good education for children there wouldn't be a viable work force to support the economy. Being a (sometimes) practical man and at the behest of then state senator Don Rogers I bowed out and lent my support to Phil Wyman with his personal assurance he would work for needed education reform.

You can imagine my relief at all the great education reforms that have taken place without my being in the state legislature trying to make the education hierarchy accountable, which would make for better schools. I need only point to recent events in San Francisco's "Diversity Program" and Rosedale and Belridge right here in Kern County as justification... and the much-needed new construction for South Fork.

But now I realize that our elected leaders have no interest in holding the schools accountable. So, I have decided to take on a battle that is comparatively winnable, that is winnable in comparison to real accountability in education.

The energy crisis is a reality regardless of who is to blame for it, regardless of who is profiting by it. I lived with a woodstove and kerosene lamps for years and greatly prefer cooking and heating with propane and flicking a switch for light. It has been deucedly inconvenient to be suddenly "blacked out" after I learned to live with electricity not long after being sold on it by Thomas Edison.

Here's my proposition: Let's bring a nuclear power plant to the Kern River Valley.

Now there are people that will say my dream is too big, that such a thing can never be done. But I beg to differ. Given the things the government has already helped Americans to accomplish, the great attention our elected leaders pay to the American Dream, I think the idea would find any number of supporters in our legislature and in Congress- I know it will be treated with favor by our governor Gray Davis who has already proven how energy-smart he is. Shoot (strike that as politically incorrect. Make it Golly), if taxpayers are properly educated to the wisdom of such a thing it makes perfect sense and will be greeted with enthusiasm... especially by my neighbors right here in the Valley.

Just imagine the mighty Kern being harnessed to provide cooling for a nuclear power plant, taking that wastewater down to Bakersfield where it wouldn't be noticed and would fit with the sludge from LA and the ambience of polluted air in town. Why, I doubt if the citizens of Bakersfield would even notice the addition of a little radioactive waste. With just a little imagination, the Board of Supervisors will find some way of using the water to hose down the planned mega-dairies. As I understand it, the wastewater would be guaranteed to kill bacteria (and I would think we that live here in the Valley would get a terrific break on our power bills).

Think for a moment what this would do for full employment right here in "Welfare Valley." We would be the envy of all California... and why should illegal aliens be excluded from the American Dream? Politicians want to invite them in wholesale anyway. Why relegate them to stoop labor when they can have jobs with a real future?

Solid waste? Not to worry. Moslem nations and friendly countries like Mexico and North Korea would start a bidding war for this.

When you really stop to think about it with so many benefits accruing, just who with an ounce of common sense would dare voice any opposition? Why, the concrete towers of the plant would put Split Mountain and the Watts Towers to shame! With such monuments and cheap, unlimited power for the Valley, I would imagine the Chambers of Commerce and local business people will be falling all over themselves to get this grand plan off the ground!

Mad? Me? Not if you really think about it. If the people of New York can get nuclear submarines parked off the Atlantic coast to provide them power, why not go them one better and have our very own reactor in Kern County? Truly, this is an idea whose time has come. President Bush would be proud of us.

Chapter Nine

Death of a Beagle

Mr. Cavendish was very anxious to pick up his pet beagle, Merl, from obedience school. It wasn't that Merl was really disobedient, but he had acquired a few bad habits and Mr. Cavendish, being such a gentle person, just couldn't bring himself to properly discipline his little friend. So, enrolling him in obedience school seemed the best solution.

Entering the school's office he was greeted by the headmaster, Doctor Diabole.

With a warm handshake, the good Doctor bid Mr. Cavendish welcome and invited him to have a seat while he sat down behind his desk.

"Well, now, Mr. Cavendish; how very kind of you to drop in. I assume you're here to inquire about Merl?"

"Why yes, of course, Doctor Diabole. I know I should have called before coming by, but I have been very anxious to see Merl and I had hoped he would be ready by now for me to take home. It has been very lonely for me without him and I'm certain he misses me as well."

With a polite cough Doctor Diabole cleared his throat, and averting his eyes from Mr. Cavendish slowly folded his hands on his desk and with bowed head as though reluctant to speak replied, "Ah, my dear Mr. Cavendish I'm afraid I have some unfortunate news."

"What is it Doctor, Merl isn't sick is he?"

"No, no, nothing of the sort. As a matter of fact Merl is dead."

Mr. Cavendish was stunned!

What? Merl dead? How did it happen? He couldn't believe what he was hearing. Merl dead?

Attempting to comprehend what he had just heard, Mr. Cavendish began to cry and took out his handkerchief to wipe the tears from his eyes ... His Merl, dead? It simply could not be true! He could not be hearing Doctor Diabole correctly! There must be some terrible mistake!

Doctor Diabole arose, and stepping out from behind his desk he went over and put a comforting arm around the shoulders of the sobbing Mr. Cavendish.

"My dear sir, I'm sorry to have to tell you this but Merl proved incorrigible. In fact, he consistently failed an essential course on properly piddling. You know, of course, how a rolled up newspaper is used to gently correct a dog?"

"Yes, I know," Mr. Cavendish replied with an effort past the lump in his throat all the while wiping his eyes with his handkerchief.

"Well," Doctor Diabole continued, "Merl just didn't respond well to such a training technique utilizing a newspaper. So I was forced to apply sterner measures with a whip. But even this proved insufficient and finally left me no choice but to beat him with a baseball bat."

"WHAT!" Mr. Cavendish roared, jerking up from his chair.

"Now, now, Mr. Cavendish, I understand your concern, I truly do, but really, we simply cannot have dogs piddling just anywhere, now can we?"

"But, but, beating Merl to death with a baseball bat! You can't possibly be serious! This is some kind of sick joke, right?"

"Not at all, sir. But you do have the option of having Merl stuffed and mounted quite attractively in a pose of your choosing, or we can simply give you his pelt."

"Stuff Merl! Give me his pelt! Are you insane?"

"Please calm yourself Mr. Cavendish. We here at the Kind and Gentle School of Obedience are not savages; we are not insensitive to owners such as you. But surely you must realize that the school's reputation is at stake. We simply cannot be viewed as not taking our responsibility seriously. Nor, may I be so candid as to suggest that you, as Merl's owner, would surely not wish it to be known you owned a dog that was so cloddish he couldn't learn to piddle properly, now would you?

"You! You! ...!"

"Please now Mr. Cavendish, I do urge you again to calm yourself and try to put yourself in my position. Now beating Merl to death has to be put in its proper perspective. I'm sure you will, upon calm reflection, come to see the wisdom of my action. Your agitation is understandable, but do be civilized my dear man. After all, didn't your parents beat you when they were lovingly trying to teach you to piddle properly?"

"No! They most certainly did not!" Mr. Cavendish shouted.

"Come, come now, my dear Mr. Cavendish it's perfectly permissible and quite understandable to indulge in some fantasy, but for the sake of sound mental health it does no good to continue in denial and pretend such a thing didn't happen. After all, I came to see the beatings my parents gave me were out of their purest love for me. Denial is very harmful, damage to the psyche and all that, you know. It would be far better to simply admit the truth of the matter rather than continue in such denial. Most harmful, you know, to a well-adjusted and healthy mind toward such things."

"You sadistic fiend! My parents never beat me to get me to piddle properly and how dare you even suggest such a thing!"

"Oh, dear, I simply cannot deal with you about this issue if you continue in this hysterical vein, Mr. Cavendish. Perhaps it would be better if you simply left Merl's final disposition to me. The choice of the pelt in your case, I would imagine. Yes, that would be best, I'm quite certain. I assure you that once you have Merl's pelt in your hands you'll feel much, much better and be able to put all this in its proper perspective. In time you'll come to appreciate the wisdom of my action and the fortuitousness of no longer having to bear the disgrace of being the owner of such a shameless and incorrigible animal. Now my professional recommendation is a nice hot tub, a cup of tea and a good book. You'll feel much, much better, I can assure you."

Now being struck dumb and utterly incapacitated by his profound grief, without another word Mr. Cavendish allowed Doctor Diabole to quietly and gently usher him out the door of the Doctor's office.

Postscript: Oakland, California: A man, Damon Valrey, 25, was charged with murder for beating a toddler, Dante Jones, 2, to death because the boy was having problems with potty training. The little boy's body showed signs of previous abuse including burns from scalding water.

Samuel D. G. Heath, Ph. D.

Americans for Constitutional Protection of Children

***

When asked who the first two Apostles were, Tom Sawyer replied: Adam and Eve? We may laugh at Tom's desperate answer but it reminds me of many a similar answer to Bible questions. My great-grandma was fond of showing off my Bible knowledge as a child to others. She would ask: What was Noah's Ark made out of? And I would dutifully reply: Gopher wood.

Now my grandparents, my great-grandma and I had no idea that the Hebrew word translated Gopher wood was an uncertain translation. In the NIV it is given as Cypress. But we knew our King James Bible was God's Word and would defend Gopher wood to the death. I don't think anyone in Little Oklahoma knew there were any other versions or translations of God's Word and we would have branded anyone a heretic and blasphemer who suggested such a thing. The Old Time Religion was good for Paul and Silas and it was good enough for all of us. And anyone that had a lick of sense or cared anything for God knew Paul and Silas used the King James Bible!

But while ignorance and superstitions were rampant among us dumb Okies, we did have one advantage over many educated people, and we believed what God said. We didn't understand a lot of it but we believed it. If God said He destroyed the world by a flood, we didn't doubt it. If He said the sun stood still for Joshua that was that. Jesus was virgin born and cast out demons and no one better say otherwise. There are some plain advantages in just simply believing and taking God at His Word.

As I, often, reach back in my memory to that simple time of my childhood among simple and honest folks, the women in flour sack dresses and us boys in our bib overalls and barefoot, I long for the plainness and openness of our dirt-poor community in old, Southeast Bakersfield. A time before drugs and a collapse of morality destroyed our nation. A time when the bad guys really did wear black and the good guys wore white and, sensibly, kissed the horse instead of the girl (I know, but the aberration of Hopalong Cassidy didn't count. Maybe he was the forerunner of the anti-hero, in attire at least. But I'd hate to hang that on Hopalong. In any event, there was never any question about his being a good guy and our hero).

But, by the end of WWII, there was a quick change of culture in our nation. The boys came back from overseas where so many had gained a cosmopolitan outlook and that, together with the nation having become the preeminent world power, an industrial giant, the Atomic Bomb, women working at men's jobs, the abandoning of the simple, agricultural way of life, so many, many changes. Gone forever, the way of life we knew as children.

I have lived long enough to look back far enough. I grieve for the loss of so much for our children. In my simple Okie way, it seems a tragedy that young people know more about the local Mall than an animal trail along some shimmering, singing, mountain stream or a clear, night sky, bejeweled by countless stars, that their ears are accustomed to the noise of Metallica as opposed to the hoot of an owl.

It is incredible, thoroughly implausible, that a Dust bowl, Weedpatch, Little Oklahoma Okie like me should one day be sitting at a computer, a Ph.D. hanging on the end of his name and reaching back to such a simple time of life in order to make sense of it all. It's all a little fantastic and, maybe, a little silly. It does bring to mind the statement in the Bible that God uses the foolish things of this world to confound the wise.

I just got back from a hike in Fay Canyon. The recent snow and rain has been sufficient to cause the streams in the area to be running nicely. This is a particularly beautiful area and I was reminded of the time I lived there with my youngest son in an attempt to turn him around. He was having a dreadful time with his mother and sisters. He was bombing out in school and this was a desperate try at getting him on track. It was also an attempt to encourage the people I knew in Lancaster by my being able to visit them more frequently.

But, as with my many other failures, this was a doomed effort as well. The folks in Lancaster were too busy with other things and Michael, my son, soon made a bad reputation for himself in the local school. I ran out of resources and went back to San Jose to face his mother's I told you so! And more failures like starting private schools (But, happily, the one in Colorado is still going strong).

While walking through the forest, I lived again some of the fun Michael and I did have there, and, while I did not succeed, I am sure that someday he will treasure the memory of the time just as I do.

As I walked along one of the streams, my eye caught a glimpse of a piece of obsidian. Sure enough, it was part of an arrowhead. This area has a lot of game and, judging from the shape and size of the fragment, I'm sure some Indian had shot at something, probably a rabbit or squirrel or even a deer and this was the remains of his attempt at dinner.

A couple of hours later when I was returning to my car I came across a place where it was obvious some folks had been cutting trees for firewood. I spied some shell casings, .45 auto. Being a re-loader from many years' back, I have a habit of picking up brass. Someone must have emptied a clip from the number I found. As I was gathering the cases, I found a 1985-penny. I'm gray and my eyes are growing dimmer but I still see obsidian, shell casings and money on the ground.

I sat on a granite boulder beneath a big, old Digger pine beside the stream and, with my ubiquitous and some say, disparagingly, disreputable cup of coffee and a cigarette, examined my artifacts.

It must be my Cherokee blood that responds so to such an environment. I could well imagine the Indian and what he had to contend with in living off the land. My thoughts ran to what it must have been like here before the intrusion of the White-Eyes. Then I looked at the .45 casings and the penny. The Indian could never have imagined the culture that would produce such marvels. What a difference between that arrowhead and the .45 and his wampum and the penny with the technology that produced such things.

And I thought about some dumb Okie, (me) who has taken it upon himself to question the teachings of the great scholars of the Bible. But I also thought about what that Indian understood in his own culture and environment. His knowledge was certainly extremely limited compared with what European nations possessed. But he functioned well enough in the world he knew. And, as in the allegory of the cave, thought he knew a great deal.

But the Indian's knowledge and expertise were to prove no match for the superior learning and technology of more advanced cultures. An arrow is no match for a .45 auto. But imagine if you will, the tremendous difference between the time and the world that existed for both the Indian that shot his arrow and the person that stood in the same place firing that .45! Who do you suppose God holds more accountable for knowing what is best?

While I long for a simpler way I once knew as a child, while I know that much of what I was blessed with as a child was denied my own children, I, like the Indian, will learn and adapt or perish.

The Indian may well have had a profound belief in The Great Spirit but it did not save him or his way of life when opposed by a greater power. That he was ignorant of things like systematic theology, having his own equivalent in his own system of superstitions and beliefs, was to prove no match for the great learning and better ways of his conquerors.

I was impressed once more by the seeming accident of birth that made me the beneficiary of being a citizen of the United States, and that I was born in a time of such vast advances in the sciences.

And so it is that so many things twist and turn through our lives that bring us to moments of decision that can so thoroughly change things for good or evil. So it is that I began to question so many of the things that I had simply accepted as Articles of Faith that had no sound basis in fact or reason.

I do not have any longer the excuse of the Indian or, even, a simple product of Little Oklahoma for my ignorance. I got educated. More, I have a wealth of experience for which I am both responsible before God; and from which, I am to draw for examples of my own blind orthodoxy and childishness. I can envy my Indian ancestor for his freedom from technology, for his escaping having to pay a mortgage and fight traffic. But I cannot envy his ignorance and superstitions. I loved my grandparents dearly but I cannot envy their own ignorance and superstitions.

I do believe, however, that, as with the Indian, had they known better they would have done better. They did the best they could on the basis of what they had and they were honest in those things. I hope I can do as well.

***

Fishing as a religious experience

Over the years, I've noticed some differences between men and women. Now some will applaud the sagacity and profundity of that statement while others, those without a sense of humor or lacking Attic Wit, will say: It's about time!

Even an Okie poet like myself needs the guidance of the Little Woman in matters like dress. For instance, when I think my outfit of chartreuse shirt, brown, plaid pants and two-toned, perforated shoes with argyle socks appropriate for dinner at Burger King, it takes the little woman to notice the possible clash in my sartorial choices.

It's true that men and women have many, different priorities and notice different things. That's often a good thing. If only they could cooperate rather than making such things a chip on the shoulder or a line in the dirt where each dares the other one to cross.

I've also noticed that when it comes to fishing, men and women simply don't communicate on the same level. The real importance of fishing is lost to most women but is obvious to men. That's why no amount of explanation to a woman will suffice.

Now I know some women who like to fish. But they don't seem to comprehend the religious significance, the true worship of the devout angler. The ritual of adorning one's self with the liturgical vestments and equipment of Holy Office is, mostly, nonsense to a woman.

I have asked women if they have something as peculiar to their sex as fishing is to men. So far, none have been able to come up with anything. If you have any ideas on the subject, please let me know. It seems quite a conundrum at the present. I believe we could all profit from a thorough research of the question.

If women do have something of a like nature that speaks to their souls, as fishing does to men, it seems an elusive thing for the time being. Remember one thing; if such a thing exists only women, as with men and fishing, will be able to understand it. If it does not, I have to wonder why?

In conversation with the few women who still speak to me, it is admitted that fear is one, legitimate concern that deprives women of the wilderness experience. It may be, that, while the peculiar distinction between men and women that results in men being the real romantics, explorers, artists, inventors, risk-takers, etc. exists, it cannot be denied that women have every reason to be afraid to wander in the wild. Imagine what must go through a woman's mind if she finds herself alone at some distant stream and three, strange men approach.

While in today's evil society even men must be on guard against one another, it is women who bear the brunt of having to be constantly vigilant against the depredations of two-legged animals. And this has been the case throughout history. It goes a long way toward explaining the resentment, animosity and need that women have toward, and for, men.

Now a man seems to have an instinct for what is acceptable worship when embarking on Pilgrimage to the trout stream. He knows that to enter the Holy of Holies, the Cathedral of the wilderness, requires the proper sacrifices and attitude of worship or God will not bless his quest.

The first, and most important, sacrifice is time. It takes real grit and determination, real honesty and integrity, to make the time available from his busy schedule, for the true believer to "go to church." He must do this at the possible risk of incurring the wrath of those less devout, like the little woman. She may think it more important to clean the garage or cut the grass.

Heresy! But the true believer will not let such inconsequential things stay him from his course.

It's unfortunate that women don't seem to understand the significance of having a man who loves to fish. If they knew that the time he spends at the lake, river or stream might be the one thing that makes him different from a man who would punch her lights out, she might be properly grateful.

If you are a woman with a man who loves to fish, it would help you to accept the fact that, like a woman with PMS, he will suffer the same symptoms when deprived of his soul's need of the supply of a pool of trout or catfish. When that time comes upon him, you'd better let him go or be prepared to suffer the headaches, crabbiness, lethargy and other complaints common to the malady. And, of course, nothing you say or do, during such a time, will be right.

Keep in mind the fact, that, if a man denies the spirit and does not go fishing when it is his clear duty to do so, it will only create a "situation" at home. His inner battle will result in all kinds of inharmonious behavior; he will wander aimlessly and listlessly, he will seem to be distant and not hear when spoken to (Some women will say I have just described their man whether he loves to fish or not).

In some of the worst cases, he may resort to watching football or basketball on TV. If he takes up golf or watching bowling on TV, the situation is irreversible... terminal. You have lost him… a word to the wise.

Now we all know that there is a difference between the true believer and the fanatic. When I first received the call to fish, I was a small boy equipped with cane pole, string and rusty hook. A hapless angleworm dangled from the end. But the Damascus light struck with my first fish off the muddy bank of the old, Kern River. I say the "old" Kern because that sacred spot is now under the waters of Lake Isabella. Sacrilege.

It was a marvelously sunny, warm summer day. My granddad and grandmother had taken me to the river soon after we moved to the old mining claim in Boulder Gulch. The river, its surface mirror-like between the rapids, glistening in the sunlight, moving slowly around large, granite boulders, its banks shaded by rows of leafy, old Cottonwoods, looked and smelled like heaven on earth. The good, warm, honest mud and grasses of the riverbank squirmed up between my toes… heavenly. The water was crystal clear, the bottoms of the pools with their rock-strewn and sandy terrain easily visible. Fish could be seen moving about… Electric excitement!

I don't recall that granddad had given me any specific instruction in the art of angling, but being an honest Okie and half Choctaw Cherokee he probably knew it was in my genes. His own equipment and dress were little different than my own.

That first fish and I were both hooked irretrievably. Even though my tackle was the most rudimentary imaginable, even though I was barefoot, shirtless and had on bib overalls, I was doing the best I could with the light I had and The Lord rewarded me accordingly. Even though that first fish was the lowliest of the low, a seemingly, worthless mud cat, it had done its task; the dew of "The Chosen" sprinkled my feverish brow. It remained for time to do its work in establishing a systematic theology, a doctrine of belief and acceptable Worship and Service of Devotion.

But, for the sacred moment, holding aloft my wriggling treasure of the deep, the sun sparkling, glistening from its smooth skin, Isaak Walton, split-bamboo rods and Royal Coachmen, hand-tied, were yet future unknowns. I had much to learn, was ignorant of so much, but I had entered upon the Pilgrimage and my calling and election were sure.

Time has passed and, while the spring has long gone from my steps and my pilgrimages to Mecca (the trout stream) are, now, less frequent, my memories serve to take me there whenever I choose. Pity those who know nothing about such things and have no such memories.

***

Santa

Two of the most endearing qualities of a child are trust and imagination. They will believe in magic, they thrill to stories of fairies and enchanted lands. Christmas, Santa Claus, the Easter Bunny, stories of birds and animals, enchanted islands and forests, these are the domain of childhood.

We don't forsake these things in adulthood. We continue to want our Merlins, Camelots, and enchanted glades. As parents, we enjoy making things like Santa and his elves and reindeer real to our children. All too quickly, we grow up and learn of the fantasies of childhood but the intent of parents in wanting their children exposed to the myths is the innocence of goodness.

Santa is the ultimate angel to a child. There isn't the slightest trace of evil connected to Santa; he could never do anything wrong or anything to hurt a child. Santa believes in children, in the innocence of childhood.

Our desire, as adults, to believe in angels follows the same pattern. We grow up and have to leave the myth of Santa, but we desperately want to continue to hold on to what he represents.

The history of Santa Claus is interesting. He is generally thought to derive from Saint Nicholas, the bishop of Myra about the end of the 4th or beginning of the 5th century. But no written document attests of this.

Legends surround the bishop who became the patron saint of children and sailors. These legends and devotion to the saint penetrated into every part of the world.

Early Protestant Dutch settlers in what was to become New York replaced St. Nicholas (Sinter Claes in Dutch) with Santa Claus. The change to Father Christmas began in Germany and extended into other countries through the Reformed Churches.

No other saint of the church has the popularity of St. Nicholas when it comes to children. And none other made the transition through the Reformation to acceptability in Protestantism, though not, of course, in the tradition of Catholicism. But it would be of interest to pursue the question of why both systems of religion find Santa acceptable?

The emphasis of Santa relating to children is the basis of his enduring popularity. He personifies the love of children and the best of childhood as no other figure, historical or mythological.

Yes, Virginia, there is a Santa Claus. Who will forget these words to a little girl written by Francis Church for the New York Sun in 1897?

His concluding words to little Virginia:

Alas! How dreary would be the world if there were no Santa Claus. It would be as dreary as if there were no Virginias. There would be no childlike faith then, no poetry, no romance, to make tolerable this existence...the eternal light with which childhood fills the world would be extinguished...The most real things in the world are those that neither children or men can see.

Did you ever see fairies dancing on the lawn? Of course not, but that's no proof that they are not there. Nobody can conceive or imagine all the wonders there are unseen and unseeable in the world.

Thank God! He lives, and he lives forever. A thousand years from now, Virginia, nay, ten times ten thousand years from now, he will continue to make glad the heart of childhood.

Do I believe in Santa Claus? Of course! I couldn't be a poet otherwise; I would lose the best part of the man that makes me so, the child within.

The Christmas season with the distinctive music and decorations, the buying of gifts, the celebration of the hope of peace on earth, is something none of us would like to see disappear.

Singing Jingle Bells, Santa Claus is Coming to Town and reading "Twas the Night Before Christmas celebrate the season. Children write letters to Santa and hang stockings with care and we watch A Christmas Carol, It's a Wonderful Life and Miracle on 34th Street. We have added The Grinch to the story of Scrooge, there is now a Charlie Brown Christmas, Frosty the Snowman, The Little Drummer Boy, Rudolph and so many more with all the innocence, charm and fantasy of childhood.

The story of the North Pole, Santa's home and the workshop of elves, the magic of Santa's being able to visit every home with a child in a single night, going down chimneys, his Ho, Ho, Ho, children leaving cookies and milk for him and, very important, Santa knows if you have been bad or good, naughty or nice.

Believing in Santa is as natural to a child as faith and prayer. George Beverly Shea sings a beautiful song: If I Could Pray as a Child Again. How many of us, as adults, haven't wished for this?

Childhood is of so very short duration, such a short time in which to teach and encourage children in the things that will prepare them for adulthood. The whole concept of Santa is one of the things that will do this. We know that all too soon our children will face the realities of the denouement of Santa. But the lesson of goodness and the memory of the magic and innocence of childhood, like the healing power of a mother's kiss, should remain.

Of the greatest importance is the fact that Santa loves all children no matter the physical or mental differences, the race, religion or geography. This is what children learn from Santa.

The non-Christian world recognizes the jolly old elf, separating him from sectarian religious beliefs. He is welcome in Turkey, China, Cuba and even Iraq!

And unlike the cruel religious wars of Christianity, Judaism and Islam, none have ever been fought over Santa Claus.

To my Christian friends I would say Santa is not the enemy of Christ. Quite the contrary. Santa epitomizes the very essence of the Gospel. How I wish the emphasis of Santa on children was practiced in the churches!

One Christmas, a store displayed Santa hanging on a cross. Many people were outraged but the storeowner said he was only trying to make people aware of how commercialized the season had become.

The philosophical aspect of this revolves around the substitution of Santa for Christ. People would yawn over a crucifix, but Santa? Perhaps, I say to myself, this may be the result of the virtually non-controversial universality of the goodness of Santa versus an image that separates people and one that has been steeped in controversy and bloodshed for nearly two thousand years and is still on going?

Some of you will remember a song, Green Christmas, by Stan Frieberg years ago that satirized the season. Many radio stations would not play it. But Frieberg was only following Charles Dickens' A Christmas Carol that made the name Scrooge a household word. But many religious people reviled Dickens because the emphasis of the story, as with Frieberg's song, was on the spirit of human goodness rather than Christ. The larger view of an entire humanity to which the Gospel makes a universal appeal is lost to such people.

It would be interesting indeed to know the thoughts of that early Bishop of Myra about this turn of events. But, of course, Santa turned out to be an expression of goodness, hope and belief that transcends all sectarianism chiefly because he is the champion of children and childhood.

Children are the basis upon which the peoples of the world can come together and coalesce for the common good of humanity… once children are made the proper priority of humanity.

It is far past time that humanity grew out of and overcame sectarian hatreds. Santa represents what the attitude of all adults should be toward children and childhood devoid of any evil.

Henry Adams said: Politics, as a practice, has always been the systematic organization of hatreds. Had it not been for the time frame, I think Adams would have included religion in the statement. But only a poet or a child would point to Santa as another direction for humanity.

***

I will never undervalue the effects of my wilderness experiences in the forming of my own character, the way I perceive life and the values I maintain. I have written much on this theme. But it is in living life with others that gives the "voice" to our character. For example, as Thoreau pointed out, if you are not sharing the things that delight your own soul with others, there is a missing dimension in your life; the real joy is not there.

Too many people today fail to find that sharing of mutual delights in their own lives. There has to be someone who gives the color and scent to the flowers, who will make the music meaningful, the moon and stars shine brightly, who makes life a living experience and redeems it from mere existence. The single most important thing to come from such a relationship is the learning to live for the benefit of others rather than selfishly.

The family is supposed to be the ultimate expression of this kind of love. Obviously the color and scent of the flowers is there whether you notice them or not. But it is love that causes you to notice them in all their glory that gives real meaning and value to them.

Since I communicate with National Review, I found it odd to read Anthony Lejeune following up my essays (with no comment on them) in his article of 3/29 entitled: More Enchanted Evenings. But rather than chaff under the slight, I soundly applaud the excellent article which gave a much broader voice to my own thoughts on the subject of what I consider, with Lejeune, the greatest American art form of the twentieth century; the musical play.

He, as me, pays homage to the genius of such great artists as Jerome Kern, Sigmund Romberg, Rudolf Friml, Victor Herbert, Rodgers and Hammerstein and mourns their passing. "The musical-comedy lyric" mused

Wodehouse, "an interesting survival of the days, long since departed, when poets worked."

But for the great Broadway musicals like Showboat and Oklahoma with their emphasis on True Love conquering all to survive required a national Ethos, which, with the betrayal of our nation by the evil leadership of an increasingly evil system of government, fell into dark decline. There remains no more ...bright, golden haze on the meadow. To have traded I Walk Alone and Younger Than Springtime for A Tear In My Beer, Ice T, VH1 and Madonna borders, to me, on sacrilege and speaks volumes for the conditions our young people face and the tragedy of their betrayal and loss.

But poets and philosophers do not flourish in ideological hatreds, in systems of evil where the value of the individual is sacrificed to the vulgar, common cry for unearned bread, in systems where slavery to such evil punishes all efforts to live responsibly and cheats a man of his manhood, victimizes a woman of her womanhood and children of their childhood.

It takes a common culture to produce the great works of art, of love and romance, which the great Musicals exemplified. It requires the genius of that culture to produce hope of the ideals of commitment and fidelity being fulfilled, of a family being able to work with the hope that they are building a future for their children.

No one is more opposed to men taking advantage of women than I am. I have made my position abundantly clear in regard to the abuse of our girls in our schools and society. But I have not lost sight of the fact that society must accept the obvious that as long as our girls and women are encouraged to invite lust by the way they act, talk and dress, unless reasonable approaches to these things are faced and dealt with, such things will continue to provoke violence against them.

One of the most devastating things we have to confront as a society is the proliferation of pornography in the guise of "free speech." Whether it is the pornography of destructive trash like Playboy or the sex and violence of TV, so-called "music," videos and movies, if a society and its leadership is going to force a mode of inviting and inciting the violence and lust of human nature in men on women by promoting such things, as long as girls and women buy into such a thing and lend themselves to the encouragement of inviting and inciting such attacks, by selling themselves so cheaply to the animalistic urges of boys and men, there will only be an escalation of such things no matter how many laws are passed!

Face it; if girls and women talk, dress and act like prostitutes, they are going to be treated as such no matter how they and the liberals howl against the very abuse they are, in fact, subjecting themselves to. Our young girls are deceived and encouraged into dressing immodestly and "displaying their wares" long before they have the maturity to handle the power of their sex.

Then, when the situation gets out of hand, when the boys take advantage and respond according to their own nature, both may become victims (the girl most surely, the boy?) and, in too many cases, a baby (and society, in the form of ruined lives, welfare and disease) has to pay the price for that society's wicked lack of morality and its hypocritical double standard.

***

Grandad, the Indian, the deer, and me

It was a dark, but not stormy, night. It was, actually, a beautiful and balmy, summer evening when the Indian and grandad decided it would be a good time to jacklight some deer. The Indian was visiting us on our mining claim and had a brand new Hudson and was anxious to show what it could do. Grandad, with a mischievous twinkle in his eyes and a surreptitious wink at me, suggested we take Jack Ranch Road up into Wagy Flat where the deer were plentiful. This sounded good to the Indian (who was unfamiliar with the area). I would go along as spotter in the back seat, my eyes being exceptionally sharp and well-suited, almost cat-like, to night vision.

Loading various weapons for the nefarious purpose into the Indian's new car, we were off in a cloud of night-dust. For some reason the only gun I had in the back seat was an H&R .22 nine-shot revolver. I suppose it was for killing a rattler if we spotted one in the road.

For those unaccustomed to the delights of Jack Ranch Road, suffice it to say the Hudson was in for a workout. A dirt track with sudden switchbacks, numerous pot holes and sundry rocks, steep hills, trees that grew close enough to scratch fenders, the road is not to be dignified with the label, rather one should call it a glorified animal track. The Indian was soon cursing a merry tune in his unique dialect (a few Anglo-Saxon, four letter words were easily distinguishable) and wondering at what insanity had brought him to this sorry pass in his new car.

The right, front wheel slammed into a hole and we were treated to the caressing sound of the dirt track screeching against the bottom of the car and impacting with the differential as the rear end was bounced, forcefully, into the air jolting the joints of the occupants. My head hit the roof of the car. The Indian added a couple of lyrics to his tune. Some fun.

Coming around a curve in the track, the headlights picked up a small herd of about half-a-dozen deer lying down against the side of the hill. There was some confusion with the occupants of the front seat trying to stop the car and get one of the guns unlimbered. Not so in the back seat. Its occupant had the window down and was already cracking away with the .22 H&R.

Having made the deer dance to the music of the .22, the deer were scattering all over the hill. One jumped into the road and started up it in some obvious distress from the .22. The Indian began to give chase but grandad still didn't have his gun operating for some reason. It was then that grandad's genius for improvisation came to the fore.

Having a small piece of rope with him, he quickly fashioned a loop at the end. As the Indian pulled alongside the deer, a young forked horn, grandad was able to get the noose of the rope around his horns. Yanking the deer against the side of the Indian's new Hudson, the deer, understandably, began to tap-dance, beating a smartly executed, staccato tattoo with his small, very sharp hooves, against the side of the car. The Indian, adding new lyrics to his music, understandably, expressed some concern about the obvious damage being done by the deer beating the tar out of the side of his new car with its horns and hooves. I have to admit it was considerable noisy and exciting.

Grandad, in some pique at the Indian's lack of sense of humor and good sportsmanship, drew his hunting knife, reached out the window and cut the critter's throat so as to end the spirited exchange between the hapless source of our Bambi Burgers and the hide of the Hudson. A profuse amount of blood erupted and sprayed all about and into the car, satisfactorily baptizing the front seat occupants and, incidentally, the Indian's new upholstery. He slammed on the brakes. New lyrics were added. With feeling.

Bailing out of the car, we surveyed the gore and damage. I marveled that the hapless creature could have done so much alteration of the sheet metal and paint with his small hooves and horns. But, alas, such was the case. The Indian was adding a hunting dance to his music, obviously one of the native customs to show his gratitude to the Great Spirit for a successful hunt; though his tone of voice might have been easily misinterpreted by someone not well tutored in the lore of his tribe. In fact, to the unschooled in such ritual, his language and dance might even be misunderstood or misconstrued as anger about the damage to his, used to be, new Hudson. Fortunately, grandad and I knew better and were duly appreciative of the Indian's performance in propitiation of the hunting gods.

The carcass was loaded and transported back to the claim without further incident and the venison was excellent. All's well that ends well. Oddly, the Indian did not volunteer his car for future excursions after meat for our lodges. The ways of our Native American neighbors are indeed somewhat strange and inscrutable to us at times.

Chapter Ten

WEEDPATCH UNIVERSITY

A clinical study by researchers at Weedpatch University has concluded that the caloric heat of a 300-pound man or woman is sufficient to run five refrigerators. Since porkers are epidemic in America, these dedicated scientists at W.U. are to be congratulated for seeking means to use all this lard to some beneficial effect. An added benefit of the research was the discovery that the average opening of a refrigerator door by fatsos was sixty-two and one-half times a day (and night) and during the very hot Weedpatch Summers, this meant a decrease in air-conditioning use of almost 10%, a significant savings on electrical use if the refrigerator was run by the caloric heat of the lardo. Another benefit is to the environment through such a decrease of electrical usage.

Further good news for tubbies is the university's considering a correspondence course in liposuction. This came about from the discovery that one of the professors was successfully marketing a do-it-yourself kit for fatties. The professor is on administrative leave pending a hearing to determine why he wasn't sharing the profits with the university.

On another serious note, Dean Mordacai Culpepper expressed his displeasure at the members of Phi Delta fraternity standing outside the science building chanting: Hefty hefty hefty, oink oink! calling such a display in very poor taste and reflecting badly on the university. The Phi Delts have been given a stern warning against further such juvenile antics.

Encouraged by the scientific progress of my old alma mater, I'm considering letting the university in on a piece of the action for my home embalming kits which would allow the budding young mortician to begin early with the family goldfish and progress from the family hamster, cat or pooch to the grand finale for married adults: The Mother- or Father-in-Law Special (subject, of course, to local health codes). For those who would be too quick to admire the sheer genius of such a scheme, I must honestly and in all humility give credit to my childhood correspondence course in taxidermy and, later, to Anthony Perkins.

***

Being naturally incensed by my old hometown, Bakersfield, coming in last of mid-size cities desirable in which to live, I did some research. And much to my chagrin, I think I've gotten onto something; apart from the city not having a consistently good music radio station.

I wanted a new meerschaum pipe. So I went to a tobacconist shop in one of the most upscale shopping malls in the city. In all the array of tobaccos, cigars, cigarettes and pipes, not a single meerschaum was to be found. Corncob pipes, yes.

To add insult to injury to the reputation of Bakersfield, when I queried the clerk, she didn't even know what meerschaum was!

Hopefully, some degree of sophistication will be brought to Bodfish, at least, by the new web site for my books. The address is - http://solo.abac.com/sdghacpc/mb.htm

But Bakersfield is trying harder. The X-Files movie features Mulder and Scully running through a cornfield just outside town. Of course, it had to be corn. How else would the sophistication of Bakersfield having corncob pipes instead of meerschaum be upheld?

There is a bright side. Mulder and Scully felt right at home in an environment that boasts Weedpatch University (Fox Mulder is an old acquaintance of Doctor Smedly Tiffany Smyth, head of the science department). And when it comes to just flat plain and simple weirdness of all varieties, my old alma mater is right there on the cutting edge every time!

Few people know, though I'm sure it was one of the reasons Bakersfield was selected by Mulder and Scully, that the genetic work at WU was the cause of the recent headline: Man Electrocuted by Fireflies!

A few of the bugs, which are capable of generating 600 volts of electricity, had escaped the science lab at WU. Some people are trying to say that these super generating fireflies are from Central America. But Mulder, due to his relationship with the head of the WU science department that supplies no small amount of the scientific expertise of the X Files episodes, knew better.

Since the bugs are now out of the jar, so to speak, an X Files sequel is already being considered featuring the little critters. It is anticipated that WU will be featured as well.

Further informative bulletins of this nature as circumstances and events warrant.

In spite of Gone With the Wind placing number four in the list of 100 best films ever made, I'm gratified it still holds the title of the most popular film ever made as evidenced by its still being the number one money-maker. Not too shabby for a sixty year old film.

As to the film voted number 2 of the 100 best films ever made and nearly as old as GWTW, Casablanca, what am I offered for the original Best

Bets column by Mark Hellinger in the December 6, 1942 Pictorial Review section of the Los Angeles Examiner complete with the large picture of Ingrid Bergman?

Some of Mark's prophetic comments concerning this new release headed for theaters in America:

A superb cast in as fascinating a movie as has been turned out by Hollywood in some time. A skillful blending of spy stuff, action melodrama and intelligent romance, Casablanca is guaranteed to bank the box office bell the nation over - and it rates all the praise that will unquestionably be heaped upon it.

Can you imagine what Hellinger would say today of his insights concerning the film?

I find it amusing that there are people who think they know something of films and try to tell me that Casablanca was not very notable at the time of its release. Wrong! Like GWTW it got a running start and never stopped!

The newspaper I have in which this review by Hellinger appears includes the first pictures released to the public of the attack on Pearl Harbor. In addition, my archives include large color Pictorial Review pictures of Carol Lombard, which were released shortly after she was killed together with the news release of Clark Gable's attempt to reach the plane wreckage. One of my relatives on the Caldwell, or maternal, side was involved in the investigation of the crash.

Of real personal interest is the fact quoted in the article that Carol had flipped a coin to decide whether she would take the plane or train to return to Hollywood.

Sorry folks, these items are not really for sale and only escaped the flooding of my house last February due to my superior foresight, skill and cunning. Though some callous, insensitive clods have inferred dumb, blind luck was the actual reason.

I came by these treasures long ago from my mother who was in Pearl Harbor when it was attacked and always had a great interest in show business and always sympathized with the same interest I exhibited.

But I mention GWTW in particular because of recent questions about my old alma mater which I mentioned earlier and so favorably impressed X-Files stars Mulder and Scully, a prestigious institution of rare sophistication and quality education, an institution where the civilities of the genteel South of courtly manners still holds sway: Weedpatch University.

So many have made inquiry about the university that I thought it would be of benefit to supply the following information:

Requirements for entrance to WU are stringent. A grade point average of 3.9 from high school, SAT score in the top 3 percentile, proven social involvement in things like community service, school newspaper and academic clubs, membership in social service organizations while in school, proven leadership qualities while active in such organizations and score in the top 2 percentile on the entrance exam. An exam must also be passed proving ability to speak, read and write fluently in a modern foreign language.

But WU, wishing to give all able and conscientious young people a chance at an education such as that offered by such a highly esteemed university, will allow of a waiver under special circumstances. If the prospective student wishes, he or she may make a special appointment with Dean Mordacai Culpepper to explain any extenuating circumstances (It is advisable to bring a checkbook).

WU is world renowned for many reasons- The Peter Falk Chair of Albanian Studies and its Institute for the Advancement of Frogs (endowed by wealthy Lamont orchardist Benjamin J. Frog) for example. Time Magazine's coverage of the recent astounding success of WU's genetic scientists in cloning a polliwog illustrates the university's high level of scientific achievement.

The school is also well known for avant-garde work in the social sciences as evidenced by its chairs for Yellow Peril and Religious Studies, Psychic Healing, and, I must in all modesty submit, my own position of filling the Chair of Men/Women Relationships. Our most recent symposium covering the very sensitive subject of Why Men Beat the Hell out of Women and Why Women Nag and Scream at Men was held at the extension campus in Oildale and very well attended.

The Bakersfield Californian newspaper and Channel 29 TV accounts of a wild melee during my presentation and involving the Bakersfield SWAT team were quite exaggerated. The natural enthusiasm and spirited exuberance of panel members due to the nature of the subject matter was only to be expected and well within the bounds of propriety in spite of some TV coverage which led to misconceptions of what one commentator uncharitably labeled a slug-fest and an attempt on the part of the university to ape Jerry Springer.

It was further proved that only a single shot was fired during the entire exchange of viewpoints and this solo round hit no one.

The university, naturally, deplored this singular display of incivility and rude over-enthusiasm.

The wide network of extension courses of great diversity is another reason for the university's reputation. For example, a degree may be earned by extension work in such interesting and timely fields as parasite research. It helps if the student has an extended family of in-laws from which to draw for his or her laboratory research in this exciting and most rewarding area of study.

Of course, virtually everyone knows of the WU science departments that have excelled in being on the cutting edge of things like UFOs and abductee research. The Alien Studies Department alone has garnered some of the best specialists in the world in this area of scientific research and possesses the only alien cadaver in existence.

For the benefit of skeptics, the body was found to have a bracelet on one tentacle with the words Space Alien clearly legible on it. As the head of the Alien Studies Department and another close friend of Fox Mulder's, Doctor John Boy Buford, so well says: *Seeing is believing.* It isn't well known that Mr. Mulder gives Doctor Buford credit for his motto: I Want to Believe!

The Missing Link connecting dinosaurs and birds is a triumph of WU's paleoanthropology department. Though The National Geographic Society tried to hog the limelight, it was renowned WU professor and paleoanthropologist Mendell Murky Mendelsohn who first boldly announced: Tyrannosaurus Rex had tail feathers!

The prestigious publication, Nature, admitted it had erred in misquoting Doctor Mendelsohn as saying: The dinosaurs were for the birds! The correct quote was: The dinosaurs were birds!

Nature has yet, however, to give proper credit to professor Mendelsohn for finding the largest T-rex coprolite (dinosaur doo doo) measuring 17 by 6 inches ever found and proving the saurian velociraptor had good table manners and chewed his food.

One suggestion by doctor Mendelsohn is in hot dispute in academia. : His contention that the dinosaurs became extinct by becoming queer. His pointing to the homosexuality of Big Bird and Barney as cases in point has led to one colleague, when asked about the good doctor's hypothesis, uncharitably replying: He's out to lunch!

The WU music department is another reason for the vast and well-deserved reputation of the university. WU was the first to incorporate the indigenous American art forms of music in its marching band utilizing cigar box banjos, oil drums, jugs, saws, washboards, tambourines, bones, combs and spoons.

And having mentioned WU's astounding music department, I cannot fail to mention another department worthy of high praise, that of its performing arts.

Again, with all due modesty of course, I have to mention my role in this fine area of the university's renown. Many well-known celebrities including Walter Matthau and Jack Lemmon have attended my very popular and well-attended on-going seminars on Grumpy Old Men held at the university's other extension campus in Pumpkin Center. My seminars on this popular subject, as the more astute among my readers may already have surmised, gave these worthy gentlemen the idea for their movies on this theme.

But you will have to look closely to find WU mentioned in the credits of the films, an oversight for which the producers apologized profusely. The apology, accompanied by an appropriate token of good will in the form of a handsome check, was accepted by WU with the university's usual magnanimity. As Dean Culpepper graciously said at the time with his usual and inimitable flair of originality for a well-turned phrase: To err is human, to collect divine.

If you wish more information concerning the university, don't hesitate to write me. I am always willing to share the riches of learning offered by my old school with others who are truly interested in excellence in higher education.

And, of course, my books are readily available; some of which are filled with wit and half-wit just as illuminating as the above anecdotes concerning WU.

***

Speaking of computers, in my on-going crusade to uphold the honor of my old hometown, Bakersfield, I offer the new CompUSA store that recently opened. Just everyone who is anyone attended the grand opening (at least, everyone interested in computers). As many of you know, CompUSA is the largest retailer of computers in the country.

But, alas, it seems Bakersfield just can't seem to do anything right. Immediately following the grand opening, thieves broke into the store and made off with over $80,000 worth of merchandise.

Two things- well, three actually.

One: When the store opened, I decided to test one of its experts. I asked if they had a simple program to accelerate a cursor? No. The guy had no idea. But DOS has such a program. Maybe the guy didn't smell enough money since I didn't have anything further to ask him.

Second: How could such a supposedly smart store fail to have proper security devices? The theft occurred on a Saturday night and wasn't even discovered until the store was opened the next day.

I'm used to seeing this kind of thievery having worked in the schools. But a large, retail, state of the art computer store? I have to assume the guy who didn't know his DOS must have been responsible for security. My little cottage in the country has better security devices.

And thirdly, it is a vile canard impugning Weedpatch University that there was some connection to WU which was, coincidentally at the same time of the burglary, upgrading its computer lab. Dean Mordacai Culpepper would not dignify such an outrageous accusation with a reply. The large number of empty CompUSA cartons discovered in a dumpster on campus was easily explained.

Sensibly, Bakersfield judge Ezekiel Culpepper refused a search warrant based on such flimsy, circumstantial evidence (to add insult to injury, some reporters have tried, unconscionably, to call the decision of the honorable judge Culpepper into question simply on the basis of his being Dean Culpepper's brother).

Dean Culpepper did graciously condescend to make a statement to the press: *Store should've had better security.*

CompUSA has not responded to Dean Culpepper's sage counsel.

But there is little doubt that such evidence of having a better quality of thieves than most other cities has enhanced the image of Bakersfield.

I am proud to say that I, as a tireless worker for WU, have been busy as well in trying to better the image of Bakersfield on behalf of the university.

Given to a sense of culture and refinement, it was due to my tireless efforts and the utilizing of the prestige of the university (modestly, not to mention my own), that I was able to persuade the powers that be to make possible a visit to Bakersfield by the Oscar Mayer Wienermobile. It will proudly be on display at the offices of TV-29 KBAK (let me say there isn't a shred of truth to the vile and vulgar accusation of a kickback to me from the TV station. The other two TV stations, KGET and KERO, in Bakersfield were engaging in the worst form of sour grapes. That KBAK should force some modest token of their appreciation upon me for my high-minded and extraordinary effort to benefit Bakersfield was altogether appropriate and quite within the bounds of propriety. In fact this token was so small I almost refused it. But, being the sensitive man that I am, I didn't want to hurt the feelings of the owners of this fine TV station).

Dean Culpepper together with myself are expecting to be honored by receiving a plaque of recognition and appreciation from the city fathers for achieving this striking accomplishment leading to the enhancement of Bakersfield's cultural image (though I thought my idea of displaying WU's medical lab's tapeworm of truly heroic proportions together with the Wienermobile would have added a deal of panache to the whole ceremony).

And speaking of culture and refinement, WU is inviting input for a new name for its football team. Surrounded as the university is by orchards, cotton fields and vineyards, the main contender is The Fighting Nematodes. But perhaps one of my readers can come up with a better name?

A recent coup of the university was getting Pat Robertson, Jerry Falwell, Kenneth Copeland, Robert Schuller and Jimmy Swaggart to agree on becoming advisory members to WU's outstanding Religious Studies

Department. The head of the department, renowned German theologian Zeno Ignatius Turklheimer (affectionately known as ZIT to his friends), is thrilled beyond words.

With such an array of super luminary theologians, it is expected that WU will be making quite a mark on the advancement of religion in America. To quote Reverend Falwell, for example: Keeping uppity women in their true, Biblical, place will be one of many holy ghost anointed missions of our ministry through the good offices of WU.

This exciting news of religious progress through the unstinting efforts of far-seeing WU trustees together with the recent and widely publicized agreement of Fox Mulder to become the Dean in Absentia for WU's Alien Studies Department makes for quite a feather in the cap of the university. The title was selected and conferred in case Mr. Mulder is abducted and thus, he could legitimately represent WU while among aliens.

This, of course, would enhance WU's stature immeasurably and provide space aliens an inside look at the workings of one of America's most influential universities, one that accurately and truly reflects and represents the marvelous realities of higher education in our nation.

When interviewed about Mr. Mulder's position, Dean Culpepper's personal secretary, Dimples L'amour who is never at a loss to put the activities of WU in the best light, replied: *We are naturally just thrilled to itsy pieces! Fox is such a fox*!

By the by, Reverend Schuller has graciously agreed to moderate the up-coming symposium to be held at the Oildale campus on Pope abusing and nun beating done correctly. The public is invited.

(No, pardon me; my bifocals must need a valve job. I got that one wrong. A visiting professor, Carlos Canteleva who used to be a Sandinista general, will be hosting that symposium. Reverend Schuller will be moderating the symposium in Pumpkin Center on the subject of "Dealing correctly with uppity flight attendants." Again, the public is invited).

For those who would like to attend these fine presentations and have small children, an electrically charged fenced enclosure is provided for their security (knew I'd be able to use that idea concerning Michael somewhere).

Jimmy Swaggart will be giving a lecture at the main campus in Weedpatch for freshman orientation this fall on the subject: Christian Morality: Is it for everyone? Sorry. This will be open to students only.

Pat Robertson will be hosting the Men's Prayer Breakfast and will speak on the subject: Why God has it in for Mickey Mouse.

Kenneth Copeland will do what he does best in the Christian Community with his message to the faculty: Healing hemorrhoids by the laying on of hands and taking up a collection.

I will continue to keep my readers up-dated on the tireless efforts of the many fine people representing WU to bring Bakersfield, Weedpatch, Oildale and Pumpkin Center their due recognition. It is a very exciting time in history for the university and there is virtually no doubt in any body's mind that WU will accurately reflect the progress of civilized decorum and culture of these cities.

***

Want to destroy an ant trail, especially one leading into your house? Bleach is good, especially in the kitchen and bathroom, but where appropriate spray it with WD40. Works every time.

Another handy hint from the laboratory of Weedpatch University: To kill ants, mix molasses and powdered yeast. Then spread the mixture on a strip of cardboard and place it by the anthill or trail. The ants eat this, swell up something fierce like a puff adder full of dried apples and water or a pizened pup and explode. Works like a charm. This is a very agonizing death for ants and might well appeal to some people with just a tad, a mere trace, of sadism.

Just as an aside, I pity those who fail to find the poetry in my on-going saga of my old alma mater, Weedpatch University. Such people just don't get it- Clueless once more.

For example, clearly people simply cannot afford to die. This is the reason Weedpatch University decided to accept the generous offer I made concerning my idea for home embalming kits. Now, you talk about something truly poetic!

During the recent Handicapped Olympics held at WU (the Make Fun of the Handicapped Race being the highlight), tragically one of the participants, one with a prosthetic left leg, fell down dead.

To add to the tragedy, the poor fellow had no relatives or insurance.

The university had already suffered an ugly incident where one fellow claiming handicapped status on the basis of tongue warts was disqualified. And now this!

But, Ah Hah! My embalming kit to the rescue, and In no time at all, the unfortunate runner was suitably eviscerated, stuffed, sewed up, and pumped full of juice and properly interred.

Readers will recall my considering this some time ago when the university and I were so caught up in the plight of frogs, this leading to our speaking up so clearly and courageously, exposing the sordid truth of discrimination against frogs, bringing this dreadful conspiracy against frogs to the attention of the American people through the efforts of myself and the university.

Readers will also recall the conspiracy I mentioned that led to not including frogs among all the critters sent into space on Columbia. But WU researchers have succeeded in levitating frogs right here on earth without the help of NASA- More about this fascinating experiment and its promise in fighting obesity at a later date. Also to be addressed in the future is the research at WU that indicates drinking diet sodas contributes to obesity.

In the on-going struggle of WU and me to put Weedpatch and Bakersfield on the cultural map, we proudly announce the phenomenal success of the musical group KORN. Their most recent album is being hailed as a milestone in Hollywood. We know these fine musicians will give credit to WU's music department for their cultural success.

But I am somewhat disappointed that WU's self-sterilization seminars are not being attended by the numbers the subject warrants; as with the Queer Studies classes, too many are missing a rare opportunity provided by the university for more than the usual education.

***

Some of you are aware of the great progress being made by scientists at Weedpatch University in amphibian research.

No discussion of green things should exclude frogs. And for those who expressed gratitude for my bringing this up in the last issue of TAP, where else but in this publication would you find questions of such burning intensity addressed, questions which undoubtedly involve NASA cover-ups and government conspiracies leading to the omission of frogs from Columbia's last mission? Who is responsible for not taking frogs (or lizards) into space? Fearless as I am, and not to be outdone by Rush Limbaugh, Extra, 20/20 or any others in fearlessness, as a representative of Weedpatch University I am committed to getting answers to such questions no matter where the chips may fall! In my righteous crusade to expose the kind of shameful and blatant discrimination perpetuated against frogs (or lizards), I intend to pursue this flagrant violation of the rights of frogs no matter where it may lead! And in total disregard, I might add, of threats to my own person! I will boldly go where no man has gone before in this holy crusade for justice for frogs (and lizards)!

There are those who feel I am attaching too much importance to the subject of frogs, some nay Sayers who go so far as to disparage me and frogs, who say my attention to the subject is overweening and could be much better directed toward subjects of greater gravity. Such calumny and accusations are vile canards at best and, at worst, attempts to misdirect me from a subject not only dear to my heart but one that should be of consuming interest to all right-thinking individuals with a concern for justice. After all, what kind of world would it be without frogs? Just think about that one for a moment! And we cannot discount among my detractors those with FBI and CIA connections who would remove me from this noble effort, sensing as they do, the threat this poses to such interested parties in their own attempts to bamboozle and flimflam the public.

An excellent example of this is the fact that we hail the bald eagle no longer being on the endangered species list. We have spent vast amounts of money on saving this noble symbol of America. And it was right that we should have done so. But I have to ask myself, as I'm sure any thinking person would, why such interest in bald eagles and none for frogs? An obvious conspiracy more than suggests itself.

Where, I ask, is the same consideration given frogs as the government has given bald eagles? You think being a frog is easy? You think because the lowly frog cannot soar in the heavens he is less worthy of our notice? Or do you despise the poor frog because he hops, has webbed feet, has funny eating habits, a long tongue and is often abused by small boys tucking him in their pockets and using him to surprise mothers and scare little girls and teachers? Or, even most despicable of all, do you despise him because of his color, because he is green? For shame!

Why does the witch turn the handsome prince into a frog? Why not a toadstool? Rank discrimination because only the kiss of a princess will return the prince to his former station! And where the princess who will kiss a frog? Discrimination! And the witch understands this! She knows she has doomed the prince because of this prejudicial attitude of so many princesses toward frogs, an attitude fomented and abetted by secret government agencies and NASA! An even more serious indictment: When has a witch ever turned a frog into a prince? Ah, ha! Never!

When will people become aware and sensitive to their ingratitude for all that frogs have contributed toward civilization and become ashamed of their treatment of frogs? Fearlessly I stand up for these unfortunate creatures and invite all of you to take part in the rally I envision on the steps of the White House itself in defense of these noble amphibians and will, like Gandhi, if necessary, fast until the magnificent, and often sacrificial, contributions of frogs to science, literature, music and art are recognized and frogs are given justice! Let Riddup and Ribbett ring out across America!

By the way, for those who expressed an interest in the bronzed bullfrogs there is still a small quantity available on a first come, first served basis. But you must hurry; supplies are very limited; a real buy at only $29.95 each or two for $65.00 plus tax, shipping and handling. Show you care, buy a frog. Other items such as paperweights, lapel pins, tie bars, earrings and bookends are available also. Write or call for a complete list of I Care About Frogs items.

Or, if you wish, you may purchase these items with the motto: Be A Real Friend with a tasteful picture of a frog appended.

And for those who really care, who want to make a difference and can afford it, don't forget to request information on the Adopt A Pond program. If you could see the living conditions in some of the ponds I have witnessed, it couldn't fail to bring tears to your eyes.

For those of limited means, there are also programs ranging from Adopt A Lilly Pad to an individual polliwog, tadpole (one of my personal favorites), individual adult frogs or even a frog family.

Another program under way is the Equal Rights For Frogs movement. Be sure to inquire about this worthy effort directed toward stamping out discrimination against frogs. Truly inspiring! I envision a new political party, The Green Party which will absorb the present ineffectual one, arising from this.

One last thing, I have written a pamphlet that I'm sure you will want to have if you are interested in the movement. It is titled: Understanding Frogs and Our Enigmatic Toads. Just ask for this by the initials: UFOET.

For that small number of readers who believe I've finally taken leave of my senses, this soul-stirring plea for justice for frogs on the part of Weedpatch University and myself, as a representative of this prestigious university, ought to restore my credibility.

***

Hillary to Bill: But dearest, he was having sex, not me.

Of course, Bill's defense was Alzheimer's since he couldn't remember anything during his grand jury testimony and for quite some time he has forgotten he's married.

Under such a circumstance, perhaps the suggestion of a $50 fine and a stern lecture from Judge Judy might have had merit.

Those of us who are native to Kern County, and Bakersfield in particular, have news of world-shaking import that makes us prouder than a purple pig!

Buck Owens' radio station KUZZ has just been named Country Western station of the year and the music group KORN is making the Bakersfield sound equally famous. This in spite of some uncharitable souls and carping critics saying this Bakersfield sound should be equated with hog calling and Budweiser frogs belching.

But, in an attempt at fairness to such critics, another Bakersfield band, Big House, has a book entitled Chicken Soup for the Country Soul in which the author states: Do what you love and the money will follow, to which I can only reply: I'm doing what I love but...

Still, critics should be hanging their heads in shame if for no other reason than the fact that musical and literary triumphs as the above should be acknowledged for the degree of culture they represent on behalf of the fair city of Bakersfield.

And still more! We now have a Buck Owens Boulevard. It runs right in front of Buck Owens' Crystal Palace.

Together with these exceptional achievements and accolades of acknowledgment of the city's ever-growing cultural refinement heaped upon Bakersfield, the Oscar Meyer Wienermobile has made another appearance. There seems no end to the cultural advances of my old hometown. And no institution or agency has been more influential in bringing this to pass than Weedpatch University.

But too many people are unaware of the university's influence in such things. For example, when Disney utilized the expertise of the university's fine cinema resources for the making of George of the Jungle, Disney failed to give proper credit to the institution.

And when critics hailed this outstanding film as refreshingly ... well ... Dumb! the Disney studio took all the credit. For shame, Disney!

And speaking of the truly macho and *haute kultur* (yes, I know that's French and German), the Kern River Valley is having its annual Rubber Ducky Race.

There are days when I feel like my rubber ducky came in last. And there are mornings when I get up feeling my shelf life has expired. But I do have my finer moments. Just the other morning in one of my usual flashes of brilliance, occasioned undoubtedly, by a generous helping of Mauna Loa chocolate covered macadamia nuts, Bakersfield's Trader Joe's Black-Eyed Pea Dip accompanied with Trader Joe's Famous Pinto Bean Chips, I was considering a monumental question of human behavior, a question of the nature that comes to all of true, intellectual genius:

When I lay out my bib and tucker, slick up my spats and prepare for an evening on the town (like going to Slugger's Saloon and shooting pool), I put on both socks then both shoes (or, in the case of Slugger's, my boots). But what about people who put on one sock, and then one shoe (or boot)? Then the other sock and the other shoe (or boot). These are truly weird people (and you probably were thinking this revelation was related to some other less desirable effects of those nuts, black-eyed peas and pinto bean chips. Sorry about that).

If a study were done on this subject it might go a long way toward explaining Hillary and the Stock Market! It might even explain why Winnie the Pooh tooth art is becoming so fashionable! But, then again, it might not. Explain the Stock Market, that is.

Another great idea! Why isn't anyone doing a study concerning the effects on the psyche of watching a sleeping cat and the equivalent effect of staring at an aquarium?

Speaking of the finer things and civilized culture, does anyone out there remember a once famous Barber Shop Quartet song that was sung in a Maggie and Jiggs movie? All I remember is the line: As the mush rushed down my father's vest, and settled gently on his chest... Your cooperation in finding the rest of the lyrics to this fine piece of music and sending them to me will be deeply appreciated. And speaking of fine music, I would greatly appreciate someone sending me the lyrics of The Dooky Bird Song also.

Those who know me well know I don't always frequent establishments where a clean pair of bib overalls and a pair of socks that match is being overdressed. On the contrary, I sometimes frequent establishments that are even worse.

But enough about my country bumpkin ways and pretensions to mendacity and high-toned, high-falutin' appreciation for the finer things in life; seriously folks, it is my great pleasure to announce great news that is bound to bring glory, honor, and further prestige to Weedpatch University's School of Archaeology!

Doctor Isaiah P. Shovell has concluded from a recent dig in Israel that the Dome of the Rock is, in fact, built upon the site of an ancient Hebrew brothel!

It is to be admitted, however, that this has caused some consternation in the Religious Studies Department of the university. The head of the department, Zeno Ignatius Turklheimer (Zit to his friends), together with the members of the advisory board to the department: Pat Robertson, Jerry Falwell, Kenneth Copeland, Robert Schuller and Jimmy Swaggart, these great theologians and Bible scholars, are arguing doctor Shovell's findings.

Lest any misunderstand, the spirit of inquiry and debate is very much alive and encouraged in the university. The Bakersfield Californian and KBAK-TV were much in error in reporting that, at one point during the spirited, academic debate, Jerry Falwell struck doctor Shovell in the nose.

However, it cannot be denied that at another point during the discussion the Reverend Kenneth Copeland engaged in language unbefitting a Bible scholar and clergyman. Still, being the fine gentleman he is, he later apologized for the phrase *Dirty little Jew anti-Christ hole-digger* that he directed at doctor Shovell and admitted the language was not in the best of taste and might be misconstrued by some few people as an insult.

Doctor Hashish ben Soloman, Dean of the School of Astrology, being a Moslem did, however, raise the objection on behalf of Moslems that such a discovery might create an international incident should it be widely publicized. Not a few Jews and Christians, he added in an admirable spirit of ecumenicism, might be offended as well.

But doctor Shovell, with the staunch backing of the Dean of the University, Doctor Mordacai Culpepper, stood his ground on the basis of truth and academic freedom.

And on behalf of the university, both the Californian and KBAK-TV did admit that it took only about three hours for the Bakersfield Swat team and county deputy sheriffs to disperse the crowd outside the hall where the debate was going on and no charges had been actually filed against the Reverend Falwell. Only about a dozen protesters had to be arrested of which only two or three were armed.

At this point it is well for me to make it clear that the meeting was advertised for students only. Apparently some of the less desirable elements of the neighboring communities of Taft, Arvin and Lamont decided to take it upon themselves to come on campus and cause this disturbance. Many claimed fellowship in various churches but local pastors have disclaimed rumors to the effect that the ministers actually encouraged this demonstration on the part of parishioners.

And with a single voice, they all disclaimed there being any truth to comments about encouraging members of their respective congregations to take their guns with them together with the vicious rumor that they had put a price on doctor Shovell's head.

And, while on the subject of religion and its marvelous influence for good and civilized behavior in our communities, Doctor Turklheimer has introduced a truly trend-setting innovation to his department: Virtual Religion. As this renowned theologian said: Who needs peyote or a bad piece of cheese for visions and prophecies and to get close to God when we have such marvelously miraculous technologies available?

Thus, a new course offering entitled High-tech Religion will be introduced next semester (together with the usual notices sent out by the university to the various peace-keeping police agencies throughout Kern County). This, it is certain, will be a feather in the cap of WU. Stephen Spielberg, Stephen King and Tom Clancy have already approached the university with film and book offers based on the concept.

But doctor Turklheimer and Dean Culpepper, evidencing the integrity one naturally expects of men of their stature, are firm in their refusal to allow the commercialization of God.

As Dean Culpepper so wisely pointed out:

If anyone is going to make a movie or write a book about doctor Turklheimer's innovative approach to God via High-tech Religion, it will be done under the wise guidance of the university and not by a bunch of

Johnnies-come-lately chasing a buck (it should be noted, however, that rumors of negotiations with Fox Mulder, a close friend of the university and doctor Turklheimer and Dean Culpepper in particular, have not been entirely discounted).

When quizzed by reporters about the potential for disturbances over this new course offering of the nature of that which accompanied doctor Shovell's announcement of his amazing, recent discovery, Dean Culpepper replied in his inimitable fashion and with his usual genius for the coining of original phrases:

You can't make an omelet without breaking a few eggs!

I get so many inquiries about the university that it occurred to me I should provide readers some background on its Dean and faculty. Let me say at the outset that there is such a stellar array of scholars, scientists and artists on the faculty, I hardly know where to begin.

But it is probably most appropriate that the history of Dean of the University, Doctor Mordacai Jedidiah Culpepper, is the most logical place to start.

Dean Culpepper's American ancestry can be traced to the earliest beginnings of Colonial plantations in the South in the early 1500s. In fact, there is some relation by marriage to Captain John Smith.

While Dean Culpepper's heritage is deeply rooted in the civilized and genteel manners of the Southern traditions, few are aware of the many famous writers and scientists he can boast in his family tree.

It was Colonel Jeremiah Elihu Culpepper that anticipated Benjamin Franklin's famous kite and key experiment by over 30 years. But instead of a kite and key, Col. Culpepper had one of his Negro houseboys stand in an open field while holding a branding iron aloft during a thunderstorm.

The Culpeppers, notwithstanding their well-deserved reputation in the arts, were, as the mentioned example proves, much given to science as well. In fact, long before our present experiments in space, one Amazah Jedidiah Culpepper sent a dog into orbit around the earth in 1873.

Having earned a degree in science from Georgia University and having devoured Newton's Principia in the process, Amazah was fascinated by the idea of space exploration. With a solid background in mathematics, he reasoned that the earth being a sphere, one only had to propel an object at a speed necessary to overcome earth's gravity in order for it to achieve an orbit around the planet- Solid, scientific thinking.

His first attempt using gunpowder to launch a subject, in this case a pig, was first thought to be successful until word came to him some days later of a peculiar story circulating in a town some miles distant about a pig falling from the sky and crashing through a farmer's roof. To add mystery to the improbable story, the farmer even claimed the pig was cooked on arrival at his domicile.

Nothing daunted and having further considered Newton's Principia, Amazah determined that acceleration by force of an explosive charge to overcome gravity had certain disadvantages. One being that such a method might indeed cook the subject projectile. Another being that it was doubtful any living creature could survive such instant acceleration.

Though lacking certain knowledge of whether it was the cooking, shot or fall that had killed the pig, Amazah, scientist that he was, felt there had to be another way by which he could accomplish his purpose without the undesirable side effects.

Amazah was determined to launch a living creature successfully into orbit, an inanimate object being far too mundane and plebeian for his aristocratic sensibilities. And being somewhat sensitive to causing undue pain or injury to living creatures, he was not going to again risk another subject to the possibility of such by use of an explosive accelerant.

Giving much thought to factors of overcoming the cooking problem and instant acceleration by use of an explosive charge, he calculated instead of an explosive, a massive rubber band of sufficient length, about 50 yards, attached to a stout oak tree with sturdy, forked limbs of the correct configuration of a sling shot would accomplish the purpose.

This ingenious device required an elaborate design of a number of ropes and pulleys to stretch the rubber sufficiently. The first subject chosen for an orbiting trajectory using this marvelous work of genius was a turkey. Amazah's reasoning being, indicating the powerful scientific mind of the creator of such an apparatus, that a solid, heavy, winged fowl would have an additional flight advantage should it fall a little short of orbit.

However, he met with failure again as the large bird was completely denuded of feathers when shot out of the powerful sling. While the bird was not recovered, the feathers, though covering a wide area, were.

But in spite of such disappointments, he heeded the maxim that perseverance alone is omnipotent and his next attempt using one of his favorite fox hounds, Ol' Beller (since no human volunteer of sufficient courage and scientific curiosity was to be had), met with success- The proof of this being the fact that the dog was shot out of sight and never recovered. Therefore, logical scientific reason declares it must have successfully established an orbit around the earth.

Because of such an illustrious and venerable history, much of Dean Culpepper's ancestry has been recorded by a family biographer, Mrs. Catalpa Culpepper of Pumpkin Center, and entitled The Culpepper Chronicles in which many stories of the spirit of scientific inquiry that imbued the family may be found.

A particular instance of this surrounds an ancestor, one Archibald Culpepper, when, as a child, his scientific precocity evidenced itself very early.

One example of this precociousness took place as described by biographer Catalpa Culpepper when Archibald, a winning child but with a somewhat disconcerting habit of teasing other children, at the age of nine tied a cat to a neighbor's child, one Samantha Noglesby.

This in itself wouldn't have been so bad but he proceeded to squirt a liberal dose of turpentine on the cat's posterior causing it to shred the poor little girl's clothes, skin and hair. According to the record of this event, the Noglesbys were some upset about the whole affair and it was rumored that little Samantha suffered an adverse and life-long fear of cats and little boys thereafter.

On another occasion, he had the rest of the children in the neighborhood believing an evil spell had been cast on them by the town witch (a harmless old crone who only wanted to be left alone) and the children, repeating the story to their parents, resulted in the tarring and feathering of the poor old creature.

Also described is an incident where he had shown some proclivity for becoming a future inventor by an experiment using the family cotton gin in an attempt to find out if it would pluck chickens and de-hair the neighbor's small dog.

The results, ghastly and messy, were somewhat of a disappointment. Particularly to the neighbors who were quite attached to the dog; overly so in Archibald's opinion. As Archibald later wrote in his memoirs, some people, he had discovered, simply didn't appreciate the encouraging of natural, scientific curiosity in children.

The family archives contain another sample of Archibald's instinct as a child for scientific investigation.

An Aunt, Begonia Culpepper, wrote of the time Archibald was visiting and had, in childish curiosity, mixed gunpowder in her husband's pipe tobacco to see what would happen. It chanced that she had witnessed the extraordinary event.

Her husband, Major Mordacai Culpepper (for whom Dean Culpepper is named), had just come into the house of an evening and, as was his custom, charged his pipe, a large meerschaum with a carved figure of a lion on the front. Settling comfortably into his favorite chair, he touched a match to the tobacco.

It should be pointed out in Archibald's defense that he probably had no idea of the proper amount of gunpowder to use. So, being motivated by scientific curiosity, he was generous.

Begonia would never forget the scene, she wrote. The sudden flash, the whooshing sound of the blast of flame and the shriek of the Major all happened so suddenly.

The Major's face finally materialized through the smoke and fire. His small beard, mustache and eyebrows had totally disappeared in the combustion. His hair was still blazing nicely though as he raced for the kitchen and the water bucket with which to quench the conflagration.

Having been wounded in the war, which had crippled him, it was pitiful, Begonia wrote, to watch his attempt to hasten in his crab-wise, lurching strides.

In describing the event, Begonia wrote that in her imagination she could still smell the noxious odor like that of singed chicken that had lingered for quite some time afterward. It was weeks she wrote further, before the Major's skin resumed its normal color and his hair, beard and mustache grew back.

Begonia Culpepper did not write of any punishment meted out to little Archibald; an indication, perhaps, of the Culpepper's fine tradition of encouraging and supporting scientific curiosity and experimentation in their offspring.

Thus the spirit of scientific inquiry was manifested to a large degree very early in the life and character of Archibald who went on to contribute much to scientific research before the turn of the century in many and widely diverse fields such as those of explosives, anesthesia and hybridization. His experiments in these areas using chickens, frogs, and Albanians, are legendary. Much of this material may be found in WU's fine and extensive library.

That Archibald Culpepper was exceptional and had quite an extraordinary childhood may be inferred from the fact that one Samuel Langhorne Clemens (a family acquaintance) used many of the incidents from Archibald's childhood in a book he entitled The Adventures of Huckleberry Finn. Though, to Mr. Clemens' discredit, he made no mention of this fact.

As a well-known historical researcher in my own right and a representative of WU, it became incumbent upon me to try to correct one possible inaccuracy in Catalpa Culpepper's Chronicles.

Begonia Culpepper's account that her husband, Major Culpepper, had been wounded in the war, this accounting for his mentioned disability, has been called into question.

I chanced on a letter written by a schoolteacher of the time, Miss Cothilda Buxley, who lived and taught school in the Culpepper's town of Chickymogum, Alabama.

According to this teacher who was a frequent visitor to the Culpepper's plantation, the Major's disability occurred in the following manner, which I quote verbatim from Miss Buxley's written account, and, if I might say so, is quite poetic:

As she sat out on the veranda of the spacious manor, a minor chord of nuisance from the backyard privy wafted in on the magnolia and honeysuckle-scented noon breeze. She was reminded of the time the Major had exploded when he had been taken in by some traveling physician.

The Major had hemorrhoids something fierce and no doctor had been able to alleviate the problem. The quack had made him up a concoction of gunpowder, soda, onion, garlic, black-eyed pea and bean juice extract which he guaranteed would cause a gas bubble of such force that it would blow the varmints to smithereens.

Such a heroic cure appealed to the Major's brave nature. Besides, he was in such pain he was willing to try anything.

It must be admitted that it took great fortitude to swallow the vile-tasting potion. Once administered, though, its influence was quickly appreciated. The Major had barely enough time to make it to the sanctuary of the outhouse.

As he related the incident to a few intimates, the single, instant explosive expulsion of that huge volume of flatulence lifted him bodily off the seat of the privy and loosened the sideboards of the structure; it even rattled the windows of the house. The Major did not admit to suffering any ill effects of this sudden assault on his bowels and rectum but he, forever afterward, walked in a crab-wise, halting gait that made many wonder if it were not due to war wounds.

The Major did not disavow such speculation. But he did keep a shotgun loaded and handy if the traveling doctor should ever be incautious enough to make another appearance in the town.

Thus it can be seen from the differing accounts, how very important it is for historians to have all the facts. However, biographer Catalpa Culpepper has told me that family tradition has it that Miss Buxley was given to some whimsy in her writing and probably had the facts of the case confused with events concerning a hired hand.

It seems Begonia Culpepper had a sister who had gone quite mad as a result of her husband being decapitated (his head being shot off by a cannonball) during the war. The graphic description of her husband, Captain Ashley Montague of the Alabama Montagues, valiantly dancing around without his head and squirting blood like a stuck hog before falling on the field of valor was too much for the fair Cornelia's fine and sensitive sensibilities to accommodate, resulting in her, in the words of her sister, going loony.

This sister, Cornelia, stark naked and brandishing the Major's sword, had once chased a hired hand down the road threatening to carve him into chittlins (chitterlings). This incident had been precipitated, as described by biographer Catalpa, by the hired hand making sport of the Major's disability and calling the account of his wounds into question.

One thing that lends credence to this account is the fact that it is a matter of court records that the hired hand, one Joe Bob Cunningham, had been caught red-handed and arrested for committing unspeakably vile and unnatural acts with a neighbor's German shepherd.

But, alas, once more, in regard to the real cause of the Major's disability, I have to bow to the unfortunate circumstances that place such a burden on the honest researcher when dealing with such discrepancies that often cast doubt and are at variance concerning events of history.

No one who has studied the records of The Battle of Monongahela can fail to appreciate the difficulty of such labors on the part of the honest historian.

Due to discrepancies of this nature impinging on the history of the Culpeppers, and on Dean Culpepper in particular, and in an attempt at historical veracity, I promise readers more in the future about the truly amazing background of this fascinating and influential family.

(And a word to critics: Just try using your spellcheck on this stuff!)

Modesty alone has prevented my accepting the many attempts to honor me in respect to the effort I have put forth on behalf of Weedpatch University, Bakersfield and Kern County. But since I was born in Weedpatch, one suggestion may be of possible merit.

It was suggested that there should be a monument of some kind in Weedpatch. Perhaps a statue or a mausoleum, somewhat like that of Lenin's tomb complete with hermetically sealed glass casket, where worshipers can come to satisfy their need to acknowledge the monumental accomplishment of yours truly in putting my place of nativity on the cultural map.

For this reason, I have let it be known to my children that I should not be cremated. I understand the need of worthy people to have such a monument with my intact remains available to them when they make their pilgrimage to the Mecca of Weedpatch in the future.

I felt I should make this known since so very many have expressed concern about my well-known, self-effacing humility and diffidence toward personal honors. In fact, a faculty member just the other day remarked on this saying I had the most enormous, wholly untapped capacity for humility and modesty he had ever encountered. For this reason, these good people have expressed the fear that I would pass on without giving any assent to their wishes in respect to even this small token in remembrance of me.

At the urging of those who want to build this memorial, I have decided to let readers know of the special fund being set up for people who wish to honor the university in this tasteful fashion and make donations. Keep in mind that the money is for the memorial; not, heaven forbid, for me!

Chapter eleven

Bullies!

August

It is true that I have become what I have through my work, particularly my work for the amendment for the protection of children. It is this work that has changed me so drastically, especially in regard to my opposition to corporal punishment of children and the death penalty, and in the process I often recall the words of Henry Thoreau:

My life has been the poem I would have writ,

But I could not both live and utter it.

With debates going on concerning things like corporal punishment of children,. the death penalty, abortion, stem cell research, and so much more, there is a desperate need for clear and civilized thinking. I hope the reader will stay with me as I approach these concerns in a rather different way than the usual.

Being an academic, I fully appreciate the traditional methodologies of historians and scientists. But to get to the truth of a matter often puts one in a position of risk if the stakes are high… and if getting to the truth demands risk of a higher order, such risks can only be taken by those with nothing to lose, no empire or reputation to protect. So it is that much truth remains undiscovered because in such cases it takes "mad" men or women of the mold of Boo Radley in *To Kill A Mockingbird* to bring such truth to light.

Such truths are of the nature of why women and children are not considered to be of equal value to men? The fact until women have earned their place in philosophy, the King of all disciplines, this will never happen is not a truth that people, particularly women, want to hear. The truth that until this happens women will never have an equal place in the decisions that guide the course of history and nations is not a truth easy to acknowledge. Even the Ayn Rand Institute and many women in positions of leadership do not want to hear this truth; but refusing to acknowledge truth, like the truth that you cannot expose children to a constant barrage of violence and not raise them to be violent, does not change the truth.

The following is from a larger work in progress in the hope of explaining a peculiar chapter in my life, a "mad" chapter if you will, that had so much to do with the proposed amendment and the course of my life on behalf of children thereafter. In my novel *Donnie and Jean, an angel's story* the boy has occasion to question his sanity. As readers get into the following account, they will have ample occasion to question my own. You may well ask why any sane person would do what I have done? The question answers itself.

With so many asking me what is to be done about "bullies on the playground" I am compelled to offer the following excerpt from this larger work that rightfully calls my sanity into question.

But to be charitable, I would ask the reader to keep in mind that the world itself seems bent on suicide rather than the progress of civilization. With that seeming outrageous statement, permit me to explain how I have come to such a conclusion. Further, you will be able to decide for yourself whether the risk on my part for the sake of truth was worth it.

We rightly deplore the violence in the Middle East. But few Westerners are knowledgeable of the intense religious hatreds that fuel and drive the violence and continue to make for a demon-haunted world. And few of our leaders are willing to confront this religious hatred for what it is. It has nothing to do with politics and will never admit of a civilized, political solution. In essence, it points up the problem of bullying on a global scale, much like the bullying tactics of the Taliban in Afghanistan and the Jews in Israel.

The most dangerous situation presents itself to the West, particularly to America, which is being asked to step in and take a more active role in resolving the problem. But this is a religious problem, one of thousands of year's duration. As such, what America is being asked to do is to take a religious position, favoring Judaism over Muslimism. And make no mistake; neither side, Jew nor Moslem, will settle for anything short of dominance of the so-called "Holy City" of Jerusalem.

Yet the most "enlightened" have no more claim to a knowledge of God than the most heathen and pagan practitioners of religion. But no political leader anywhere in the world is going to take a stand and point out the fact that the Albert Schweitzer's and Mother Teresa's have never changed the world for the better on the basis of religious beliefs regardless of personal sacrifice on the basis of such beliefs.

America is already seen in too many instances as the "Bully of the world." What would it take on the part of America to intercede in the Middle East and not contribute further to this image of bullying?

It took the work of Upton Sinclair's *The Jungle* to bring about radical and needed social changes. The power of the pen was exemplified by Sinclair as few other things have done. But as with *Uncle Tom's Cabin*, there was a needed "flash point of history" for Sinclair's book to be so monumentally successful in bringing about needed social change. And as Harriet Beecher Stowe proved, it does not take a great writer to accomplish the purpose when that flash point of history is met.

Harper Lee's To Kill A Mockingbird was a real masterpiece. But the needed flash point of history was lacking in order for it to accomplish its purpose. But neither Stowe nor Lee set out to change the world.

Nevertheless, the message in Ms. Lee's Pulitzer-winning novel was one that directly impacts on this thing of bullying. My proposed amendment is directed at the most cowardly and heinous of all bullies, the child molester. But to take the broadest view of this thing of bullies, one needs a *Weltanschauung*, a world-view of the problem.

Was Harper Lee anti-Semitic when she grouped little Scout's teacher, a Jew (and calling special attention to this), among those that considered black people inferior, that was incensed that a black man would feel sorry for a white woman? The people responsible for awarding Harper Lee the Pulitzer apparently didn't think so.

Some years ago, I engaged in perpetrating a fraud against myself, a Swiftian parody much like his "Modest Proposal," along the lines of Dolphus Raymond in Harper Lee's To Kill A Mockingbird that enraged people toward me. But these were people guilty of the same kind of ignorant prejudice that made Scout's teacher, who had made such a fuss about anti-Semitism in her classroom, and the others that condemned an innocent man just because of his color and felt they were justified on the basis of their own self-righteousness. In the same way that Tom Robinson felt sorry for Mayella Ewell, I felt sorry for those like people in the John Birch Society and the churches that felt, so very self-righteously, that they are the "saviors" of America, and all the while so very ignorant of their own need of "salvation" from their own fears and ignorance, their own prejudices.

I will grant that by choosing to dance with the devil, in choosing him as a partner through the mechanism of my intimate knowledge of various hate groups, I invited the attacks of those like the people who condemned Tom Robinson. But I did so in an attempt to expose, among other things, the very same kind of ignorant prejudice that afflicted those in Harper Lee's masterpiece, the same kind of people that loved the applause of others by being "on the side of the angels" just as those "good Christians" that horse-whipped Frank Shallard in *Elmer Gantry*. Sinclair Lewis understood the hypocrisy of self-righteousness "on the side of the angels."

There were other reasons for this fraud against myself. Why, I asked myself, should any one be excluded from seeking help of their own elected representatives solely on the basis of their belonging to some group no matter what it might be? The very hypocrisy of Congress as so well exemplified by the Clinton/Condit affairs makes this attitude of not wanting to "soil" themselves that much more repugnant!

But no one would have suspected my motives in doing so. I had taken the basis of Harper Lee's masterpiece and turned it around, I had chosen the devil for a dance partner in order to learn what it would be like to be hated for all the wrong reasons, just as I had learned similar lessons by my teaching in Watts and having to confront racial prejudice in many different forms. But this time I would not, most assuredly, be perceived as being "on the side of the angels."

"It is beautiful when prosperity is present with intellect, and when sailing as it were with a prosperous wind, actions are performed looking to virtue; just as a pilot looks to the motions of the stars." Iamblichus, *Life of Pythagoras.*

Would that the actions of those in Congress, since they have both the prosperity and the intellect, were performed looking to virtue. But because they choose to look to political expedience rather than either virtue or the stars, this is seldom the case... and I could hardly expect people like this to understand my own motives, let alone ascribe anything of virtue in making the choice that I did in dancing with the devil.

The media and others are quick to condemn police that shoot unarmed black people. And well they should be condemned for doing so. But what the media and these others ignore, or are ignorant of, is that there is a similar mentality at work in the minds of both police and lawbreakers. As a result, it is well known that virtually a third of those in police work are unfit for the job (a similar ratio to those in education). The Downey Chief of Police that candidly told me the police weren't there to help people but to slam the doors on them was quite accurate in his appraisal of the "cop mentality." After all, what can you expect of personnel that are attracted to a job that naturally appeals to those that like to be bullies, carrying a gun and club, thumping heads behind the protection of a badge of authority?

The job description alone for police work does not appeal to those with any kind of altruistic attitude of "helping people," quite the contrary. It is the kind of job that appeals to the very worst of human nature. I have often said the number of bad people in police work does not surprise me; the number of good people surprises me.

As one LAPD officer told me, the job of a policeman is a "garbage job." The longer you associate with the "garbage" of humanity, the more like it you become, the more of a "us vs. them" mentality you acquire, both toward criminals and law abiding citizens, and before long the only "friends" you have are other police officers. "Serve and Protect?" About as much as politicians think their job is to serve the citizenry rather than elected office being a license to steal.

In researching my *Birds With Broken Wings* book, I tell the reader that I purposely went out in the bars and consorted with prostitutes and many on welfare in order to really understand what I was writing about. I associated with drug addicts and alcoholics, with people that had HIV and some that were dieing of AIDS in order to know what I was writing about. As a teacher I took jobs in the ghetto and barrio in order to learn and understand things about education and race relations that could not possibly be learned and understood in any other environments.

Is there any kind of morality that should apply to police work? Or should the morality of Congress be our guide?

Once in a while I watch Hardball with Chris Matthews. Just recently while the Condit/Levy case was being discussed, a woman made the astounding statement that going after Clinton and Condit were examples of "Sexualizing Morality!" She did not respond to the question whether the "Everybody does it" excuse applied in her case.

That phrase really hit me: Sexualizing Morality! Especially being used by a woman. Was she trying to excuse herself, as with the "everybody does it" comment, or her own husband? I had to wonder.

Then another thought struck me. Why did this amazing statement impact me so peculiarly because it was used by a woman, or maybe because such a self-serving statement would more commonly be used by men?

Well, so much for wishful thinking about "Mom and apple pie."

But "Sexualizing Morality;" if infidelity is not immoral, if a sexual relationship has nothing of morality to it, what constitutes immorality to people who agree with this woman?

Then another thing came to mind. Here's Congress, filled with such immorality and corruption so mirroring this woman's comment, discussing making the flag an object of religious veneration (as the term "desecrate" is defined), haggling over a religious and sexist article like the Decalogue, whether it should be granted the "Divine blessing" of that august body, in spite of its religious and sexist nature, and the Clintons and Condits continue to get away with rubbing our faces in their own immorality!

Well, maybe this woman is right. If marriage vows have become quaint anachronisms, perhaps we have finally attained that high plateau of civilization where sex no longer has any moral connotations attached? Perhaps we should allow a Congress and people like the Clintons to dictate a whole new set of rules concerning morality? Perhaps the hypocrisy of a Congress discussing the merits of making the flag a religious symbol of veneration and the Decalogue a showpiece of morality in spite of its obvious sectarian religiosity and purely sexist view stand for a new morality approved by Congress is the wave of the future? An old Roman Senator was succinct when he said that publicly he believed in all the gods, but privately in none of them. Human nature, especially in politics, hasn't really changed much in this regard.

As a nation we seem dedicated to glorifying sex and violence on an escalating scale. Perhaps this woman sees the situation more clearly than I do. I always thought faithfulness and fidelity were somehow moral things, things to be honored.

And with all the bullies in our institutions, with all the violence and corruption our children are fed on a daily basis through cop shows, WWF, MTV and the political arena, we are going to do something constructive about reform in education and bullies on the playground?

Will Condit get away with it just as Clinton did… and continues to do?

As I was writing the novel Donnie and Jean, an angel's story that focuses on Bakersfield during the summer of 1948, it became ever more clear that confronting the evil on so many fronts that is consuming our children has to become a national priority. But given the ingrained religious and political hatreds endemic to humankind, just where will we find the kind of honorable leadership that is so desperately needed?

People often wonder why I am so hard on the educational establishment together with those like politicians and those in the media that profess some knowledge of the educational system. The fact is that very few "outsiders" know anything substantive about how the system of education operates. To know this, you must have been an "insider." More, you must have worked in many areas of education in several school districts plus spending a few years in teacher lounges listening to the conversations. My own experiences in education eventually led me to do my doctoral study about accountability in education.

In other words, to be considered a primary source of knowledge and information, you must have the experience and the credentials. Less than this makes a person (as with too many politicians and media people) like the men that "know" what it is to be pregnant and give birth. I have met many such people, and in few areas of life are they so abundant as they are in any discussion of education. But I have found them abundant in other areas as well, as I will explain.

Before going further, I need to point out that only one intimate friend, Nelson Hussey, knew the facts of what I was doing. Not even those like then state senator Don Rogers knew. I purposely kept the facts from others, including my own children, for their sake. Tragically, Nelson committed suicide shortly after these things took place. I was surprised that Brett Bradigan, then editor for the Kern Valley Sun ran my article on Nelson, a full half page in the paper. I told Brett to edit it as he saw fit but to my surprise he replied that he wouldn't consider changing a single word even though it took up that full, half page.

I will say first that as a human behaviorist there are certain things that are of deep interest to me. Why do people do some of the things that they do, often to their own detriment? Why are we generally so intensely interested in war, the dark and macabre things out of Stephen King novels and slasher films, why do we want to stop and view accidents and find ourselves glued to the TV screen when great calamities of nature (or otherwise) are being shown? This often reminds me of Thoreau's describing the men that after napping immediately want to know upon waking: What's the news?

There is a very morbid aspect of human nature that feeds on death and destruction. Some people can't seem to get enough of such things. Very much like rabbis, priests, ministers that act like vultures and love funerals all the while feigning piety.

So I confess that my interest in perpetrating this fraud against myself was fomented, at least in part, by some kind of "need to know." At the level of cultural anthropology and as a qualified behaviorist I had a need to know in respect to this organization that so quickly catches the imagination of people. What qualified scholar and historian wouldn't want to sit down with and personally interview Attila the Hun or Hitler?

But, then, not many would take a job as a white teacher in the middle of Watts, as I did. The experience I gathered during my tenure in this community about racial hatreds, black and white, and the failure of education in such schools was to prove invaluable to me in my further work and writings. So it was no surprise to me that columnist William Raspberry showed intense interest in my writing until he found out I was white.

In the beginning of my research into the organization I quickly learned that the Ku Klux Klan had something that every politician and actor or actress would kill or sacrifice their firstborn to have, to use the aphorisms: Name Recognition. Charlie Chaplin once said very proudly that people in many parts of the world had heard of him that had never heard of Jesus Christ. The same might be said of the KKK.

Another thing I learned very quickly in the beginning of my research was that regardless of whether anyone really knew anything about the organization or not, virtually everyone had an opinion about it... but, curiously, very, very few, even among those that professed "credentials" had any certain knowledge of the organization and even less of its real history as so ably presented by historian Claude G. Bowers in his book The Tragic Era.

Another curious thing I discovered was that the most gullible and naïve about the Klan were among the most educated people, people in the schools, politics, and the media. It seemed that these people were willing to believe virtually anything they were told about the organization without any facts or proof. I attribute this to those involved with these institutions being, after all, really just people like anyone else with a Fox Mulder mindset: "I want to believe!" Just as there are multiplied millions willing to believe just about anything about anything of which they have a strong bias, it is easy to understand this kind of gullibility. It is particularly found among the religious and conspiracy buffs. The human behavior aspect of such a thing is obviously of great interest to those like me that are specialists in the field.

In my critique of the masterful novel To Kill A Mockingbird by (Nelle) Harper Lee, you read of a man, Mr. Dolphus Raymond, who has purposely perpetrated a fraud against himself about his drinking and his relationship with colored people. Little Scout wonders why he would do such a thing and asks why he has shared this secret with her, Jem, and Dill? His reply: Because you're children and you can understand it.

In the words of Atticus Finch "Seems only children weep over injustice." This was the meaning of Mr. Raymond's reply to little Scout, though he was specific about the injustice in the way white people treated colored people without ever seeming to take into consideration that they were people also.

It takes a lot of effort to properly research organizations like these. The FBI never has been able to do so because no one has ever been able to successfully infiltrate to the very top of such organizations… but I did.

The story of how I accomplished this (and most of all why?) is the stuff of nightmares and underlines the cautionary word that the difference between reality and fiction is that fiction has to make sense as well as the fact that the truth is, indeed, often stranger than fiction. In the case of my involvement with the Klan (though there is no such thing as "The Klan"), the story makes a book, a book that is still in process since there is so much material to cover.

This is something missing from all the stories people in the media believe about such organizations because in their rush to I Want To Believe they miss the most elemental thing of all: Primary Sources. But, as I said, such primary sources do not welcome people in the media or government. It took someone with my "special qualifications" to gain the primary source material in my possession, material that is in some cases very dangerous.

In the musical Paint Your Wagon a fellow says: I don't care how a man prays, there'll be room enough in hell for all of us! As I moved among people in these organizations and the various militia groups I would often be reminded of this. Still, this was little different than the situation I found myself in while teaching at a high school in Watts during the sixties when the FBI wanted me to be an informant. In retrospect, I now know I was in far greater danger during this episode of my life than I was while gathering facts about the KKK or Aryan Nations.

I can laugh about it now but the two white agents that walked onto that black campus in South Central LA and met with me might as well have been wearing jackets with the words FBI clearly stenciled on them instead of their hats, ties, three piece suits and carrying the ubiquitous attaché cases. The embarrassing (and sometimes deadly) problems the FBI has encountered of late are not surprising to me; nor was Ruby Ridge and Waco.

Not long ago the Kern Valley Sun ran an article of mine about a fictional company I claimed to have started called PsychoSearch. In the article I claimed I had been able to get a new trial for a mass murderer and he was acquitted since it was proved he had committed these murders because of his deprived childhood. The point being, as per the killings in places like Columbine and Santee, the murders committed by "children" and the lies and corruption of politicians like the Clintons and Condits, that "no one is personally responsible or to be held accountable for anything!"

A few readers were outraged and took me to task, not realizing that the whole thing of PsychoSearch was a contrived Swiftian parody along the line of that great writer's A Modest Proposal. Years ago I had accomplished the same thing with a story entitled "An Apologetic To My Critics Regarding The Iguana Ranches." This won me a literary award from The Writers of Kern for humor.

My many years of working with children in education, my years as a minister, my own education and experiences of life led me the path that culminated with my proposed amendment to the U.S. Constitution for the protection of children from molesters. But those years also led me to hate bullies and hypocrites, to despise those that abused their positions of power and authority. And, yes, those years led me to suspect the motives of most that claimed: Our children are our most important priority!

That mother that was shot at Ruby Ridge, those children that died in Waco, where was justice to be found when those with the authority like Janet Reno abused that authority and like Pilate, simply washed their hands declaring themselves to be "innocent of blood."

As Americans, used to unprecedented freedom, the thinking person knows such things as occurred at Ruby Ridge and Waco have nothing to do with whether Randy Weaver or David Koresh were nut cases, it has everything to do with whether the progress of civilization can only be had on the basis of people being able to express their views, to live differently, without fear of persecution or murder in the name of the State.

I've seen too much of this kind of thing. So it was that I carried out the charade of being on the side of the KKK and only now because of the continuing heinousness of those like the Clintons and the Condits and so many others, continuing to "get away with it" am I willing to expose myself.

The children continue to suffer because of scoundrels in positions of authority without any in positions of trust and authority proving by their actions that they are people of honor worthy of being called "Role Models."

One thing is certain. If those in the media think they can accomplish any substantive good for children and remain ignorant of the inner workings of the schools and organizations like Child Protective Services they are wrong.

During this brief episode of my life and learning, I was denounced by the Birchers, religious groups, and many individuals... and understandably so. But the essential message was lost to such groups and individuals.

Not the Pope, the Birch Society, Jews, Christians, Moslems, Buddhists, Hindus, Republicans nor Democrats are the saviors of the world. Quite the contrary, as long as blacks kill blacks, whites kill whites, blacks and whites continue to kill each other in the name of God or political ideologies, as long as there is no moral, civilized leadership in any of these groups it will continue to be a demon-haunted world dedicated to suicide rather than peace.

I exposed a very dark side of humanity during this episode of my life as well as gathering a wealth of knowledge and material for my writing about prejudice and ignorance on the part of those that should have known better. I can only hope the lessons learned and taught will yet prove to be of value.

Do you recall the Jewish judge in Tehachapi, California that said the greatest crime Hitler committed was not the killing of Jews, but his making it impossible thereafter to discuss race distinctions in academia? This man caught hell for his comment. But as an academic myself, I know the truth of his statement, and the truth of it continues to play itself out in wars still on-going on the basis of religious and racial hatreds. Not so easily seen or understood is how such a thing plays itself out in the failures of the media and the most essential institutions of our society.

I will continue to oppose the bullying tactics of those individuals and organizations that think they alone are the "saviors" of America, of the charlatans that take advantage for the sake of their egos and empire-building of which Special Education and Child Protective Services are worst case scenarios. And I will especially oppose the bullying tactics of those in authority, especially in government, that give lip service only to the plight of our children.

And there is no doubt that Americans, including children, have no need of pundits when they can easily see through, and are sickened by, the hypocrisy of a Congress that dares not bring accusations of "breach of ethics" against members of the "Club" since so few can withstand a like scrutiny, the "pot calling the kettle black," of their own dirty laundry. And how many of us in California do not feel revulsion when it is patently clear that energy companies, protected by political leadership at the highest level, caused great harm to our state by an engineered so-called "energy crisis?"

We are sickened by the Clintonesque evasions from honest replies to honest questions, of the continued defrauding of the electorate by those for whom the phrase "voting their conscience" on the part of politicians fills us with revulsion, particularly so as the gap continues to widen at an accelerating rate between the "haves" and the "have-nots" both materially and educationally.

In spite of the melodramatic phrasing, it is sometimes essential to "dance with the devil" and invite calumny to get at the truth. But until the truth is exposed we cannot expect to rid ourselves of bullies on the playground until we can rid ourselves of the bullies against children in their homes and religious and political scoundrels, hypocrites, and bullies like the Clintons, Condits, political and religious leaders here and abroad. The best we can expect or do otherwise is to continue to build more prisons, sentence more children as adults and wonder where society went wrong when even a child can recognize we live with a system where children are bought the "toys" and told by adults "Now go away and play and leave us alone!" and "How much justice can you afford?"

Nature red in tooth and claw! But has the human species achieved a higher end? No… nor will it until fundamental changes leading to civilized behavior come about. These changes will only come about when humanity decides they must, and is willing to make the necessary sacrifices and do the necessary work such as women earning their place in philosophy.

In my novel, *Donnie and Jean, an angel's story*, the boy soliloquizes about the subject of the relationship between humans and animals. He asks himself whether the way people treat animals relates to the way they treat each other? He asks if animals can really talk to each other? He posits the following: If animals could talk to humans, would people still kill and eat them?

I was recently taken to task by a woman, who claimed to be compassionate toward all creatures, for my admitting of shooting blue jays and ground squirrels.

This set me off and I sent her the following note:

Yesterday I was in a mood. As the temp went past the 100 mark I opened my doors and drapes and just reveled in the heat and brilliant sunshine, closing my eyes and imagining I had finally made it and moved to the middle of Death Valley. Like Donnie in my novel, I dream of being somewhere far removed from all signs of human habitation.

You ask how could I shoot jays and ground squirrels? Easy. I'm still a pretty good shot.

Knowing this is not what you meant by your criticism, allow me to elaborate.

I was talking to the animals long before Dr. Doolittle. I would explain to the rabbits, chickens, hogs, goats, and deer why I was killing them and butchering them for food. As I grew older, I had to learn the language of reptiles in order to carry on my political activities.

It was difficult for the animals I killed to understand why the cats and dogs were getting a free ride? I tried to explain that people related better to cats and dogs than they did to bunnies and chickens, just the luck of the draw and their karma to be born to be butchered and eaten by a "higher" species like humans, lions and tigers.

Understandably some of the animals I killed and butchered had a little difficulty understanding the distinction. I recall one conversation with a hog especially just before I pulled the trigger on a .32-20 between its eyes (much more humane than the sledge hammer used in slaughter houses). Had another such conversation with a goat as I straddled it, pulled its head back and cut its throat (as per my grandad's instructions).

With all the animals I have killed, butchered and eaten, including a fair amount of Bambi Burgers, there has always been this understanding between the animals and me; if the human species prefers cowburger to cat or dogburger, who am I to try to change society?

Well, there is hope. The Chinese are breeding St. Bernard's for food; now, if I could only get my hands on some of these molesters and send them to some our sanitized abattoirs to end up so nicely packaged as the meat at Vons.

The blue jays, ground squirrels, rattlesnakes and black widows remain on my kill list. Come to think of it, where's the compassion for spiders? I'm reminded of ol' Merl, the lobster my boy saved for me live. No "Aunty Em" before he went into the pot.

I wouldn't want to go back to the farm. It's hard for me to think about picking up that bunny by the hind legs, giving it a rabbit punch to the back of the neck, hanging it by the legs on those hooks, cutting off its head, ripping off its hide and gutting it for fresh meat. Nope. Don't want to go back to that. Don't even want to wring the head off a chicken anymore. In its way, that preparation was ideal for the work I do now in respect to those that abuse and murder children and a diet of mostly rice and beans.

The larger question my reply to this woman opens is that of Donnie's: Does the way we treat animals reflect on the way we treat each other as human beings? Most would say it does. But that larger question contains the elements of fundamental changes in ourselves as human beings, changes to which we would not readily acquiesce. Still, as with leaving the corporal punishment of children, the death penalty, abortion, those things that promote violence rather than civilized progress, it usually comes down to a human nature not willing to acquiesce to such change.

The novel contains the question of whether the lack of angels like the little girl, Jean, has to do with the way boys are raised to think of girls, that some things like girls becoming doctors or liking to build a model airplane are not fitting for girls?

Unquestionably, if boys are raised to think of girls as "things" rather than human beings of equal value, there are a multitude of things not "fitting" for girls. And as girls are raised to use their sex to achieve their ends, there are a multitude of things not "fitting" for them.

No problems of such historic dimensions as political and religious hatreds, of prejudices based on race or gender, admit of easy solutions. It makes me angry when I get letters asking for such solutions from people that think there are easy solutions.

I can only hope that what I have done, and continue to do, in my madness will open the door of realization to people that there will be no answers forthcoming to these problems until people are willing to make fundamental changes in their own thinking and actions, the changes that Donnie had to confront when a little angel came in to his life and demanded simply on the basis of her being an angel that these changes be made.

In respect to the death penalty as one of these changes that is needed in America, no one that knows me well or has knowledge of my past stand on this issue could ever confuse me with those that are typically opposed to capital punishment; I supported capital punishment most of my life and am still, personally, of the same mind I have always been that the beasts in the form of humans that torture and murder do not deserve to live.

What changed my thinking about the death penalty was the realization that the progress of civilization cannot be enhanced by violence done in the name of the State. Further, not even the strongest proponent of capital punishment can logically deny that this most serious action of the State cannot in any way be called "justice" unless there exists absolute universal agreement and uniformity, nation-wide, in its application.

The purpose of my proposed amendment for the protection of children from molesters is to bring this kind of uniformity to bear on this heinous crime against the most innocent of all victims, a uniformity that is practically non-existent on a state-to-state basis. Would a rational and fair mind deny the need of such uniformity? I don't believe so. To think otherwise would be to say that the value and welfare of children is dependent on geography, that people in Texas, for example, have a different set of values pertaining to children than those in California.

You cannot logically and reasonably separate fairness from justice. Had there been such uniformity of fairness in law concerning the death penalty during the trial of Tom Robinson, can you imagine his being sentenced to death? No. It is on this basis of the need of fairness in order to meet the criteria of justice that cries out for a uniform system of law respecting what are considered capital crimes be established and not left to the too often arbitrary state-to-state systems. The very same argument holds for crimes against children. There is a desperate need of national standards, national agreement on such crimes and their penalties.

There is no question in my mind that murderers and the monsters that prey on children must be permanently removed from civilized society. And while I continue to resent the fact that such monsters would continue to live, and be kept alive, at the expense of taxpayers, if the goal is a progress of civilized thought and behavior for society there is no other rational course but imprisonment without the possibility of parole for these monsters rather than violence, particularly the present arbitrary violence, done in the name of the State.

***

The following is from a larger work in progress in the hope of explaining a peculiar chapter in my life, a chapter that had so much to do with the proposed amendment and the course of my life on behalf of children thereafter:

In respect to "dancing with the devil," I turned the central issue of To Kill A Mockingbird around and perpetrated a fraud against myself, and made myself, like Dolphus Raymond, an object of scorn and calumny, the target of equally ignorant and prejudiced people like those that condemned him and Tom Robinson. But was Harper Lee anti-Semitic when she grouped little Scout's teacher, a Jew (and calling special attention to this), among those that considered black people inferior, that was incensed that a black man would feel sorry for a white woman? The people responsible for awarding Harper Lee the Pulitzer apparently didn't think so.

It wasn't the KKK that enraged people toward me, it was the same kind of ignorant prejudice that made Scout's teacher, who had made such a fuss about anti-Semitism in her classroom, and the others that condemned an innocent man just because of his color and felt they were justified on the basis of their own self-righteousness that caused this rage toward me. In the same way that Tom Robinson felt sorry for Mayella Ewell, I felt sorry for those like people in the John Birch Society and the churches that felt, so very self-righteously, that they are the "saviors" of America, and all the while so very ignorant of their own need of "salvation" from their own fears and ignorance, their own prejudices.

The New American, the official publication of the Birch Society, was guilty of the very worst of "Yellow Journalism" respecting Ruby Ridge but the Birchers were taken in because of their own blind "need to believe" in their own cause. A local Birch Society leader, Jim Fahnestock, even went so far as to lie in print that I had made application to join the Birchers and been refused on the basis of my "Klan membership." I challenged him to produce such an application but, of course, he couldn't, any more than anyone could have produced an application from me to join the Aryan Nations, NAAWP, or KKK. But such a thing does call to mind the wish of Thoreau that he could find a document he could sign that would absolve him from all organizations, especially those of church and government, to which he had not made application. And in this instance of the claim of Fahnestock, those at the paper, the Kern Valley Sun, didn't bother to ask me about the truth of this self-righteous hypocrite's claim… another media failure to go to primary sources.

I will grant that by choosing to dance with the devil, in choosing him as a partner through the mechanism of my intimate knowledge of the KKK, I invited the attacks of those like Mr. Fahnestock and others. But I did so in an attempt to expose, among other things, the very same kind of ignorant prejudice that afflicted those in Harper Lee's masterpiece, the same kind of people that loved the applause of others by being "on the side of the angels" just as those "good Christians" that horse-whipped Frank Shallard in *Elmer Gantry.* Sinclair Lewis understood the hypocrisy of self-righteousness "on the side of the angels."

There were other reasons for this fraud against myself. Why, I asked myself, should any one be excluded from seeking help of their own elected representatives, as J. W. Farrands was, solely on the basis of their belonging to some group no matter what it might be? The very hypocrisy of Congress as so well exemplified by the Clinton/Condit affairs makes this attitude of not wanting to "soil" themselves that much more repugnant! As I got the whole picture by personally becoming involved, it was me that had to make the call to U. S. Senator Jesse Helm's office in order to find a constitutional lawyer that would intercede for Farrands against the suit by Morris Dees.

But no one would have suspected my motives in doing so. I had taken the basis of Harper Lee's masterpiece and turned it around, I had chosen the devil for a dance partner in order to learn what it would be like to be hated for all the wrong reasons, just as I had learned similar lessons by my teaching in Watts and having to confront racial prejudice in many different forms.

But this time I would not, most assuredly, be perceived as being "on the side of the angels."

"It is beautiful when prosperity is present with intellect, and when sailing as it were with a prosperous wind, actions are performed looking to virtue; just as a pilot looks to the motions of the stars." Iamblichus, *Life of Pythagoras.*

Would that the actions of those in Congress, since they have both the prosperity and the intellect, were performed looking to virtue. But because they choose to look to political expedience rather than either virtue or the stars, this is seldom the case… and I could hardly expect people like this to understand my own motives, let alone ascribe anything of virtue in making the choice that I did in dancing with the devil.

Farrands was no more a hater of colored people than I was. But he had chosen to be the leader of an organization that was hated, not because of a racial prejudice, but because of a shared hatred of what Big Brother Government was doing in all our lives in America.

The suit by Morris Dees had no merit; it was harassment, hypocritical bullying.

The media and others are quick to condemn police that shoot unarmed black people. And well they should be condemned for doing so. But what the media and these others ignore, or are ignorant of, is that there is a similar mentality at work in the minds of both police and lawbreakers. As a result, it is well known that virtually a third of those in police work are unfit for the job (a similar ratio to those in education). The Downey Chief of Police that candidly told me the police weren't there to help people but to slam the doors on them was quite accurate in his appraisal of the "cop mentality." After all, what can you expect of personnel that are attracted to a job that naturally appeals to those that like to be bullies, carrying a gun and club, thumping heads behind the protection of a badge of authority?

The job description alone for police work does not appeal to those with any kind of altruistic attitude of "helping people," quite the contrary. It is the kind of job that appeals to the very worst of human nature. I have often said the number of bad people in police work does not surprise me; the number of good people surprises me.

As one LAPD officer told me, the job of a policeman is a "garbage job." The longer you associate with the "garbage" of humanity, the more like it you become, the more of a "us vs. them" mentality you acquire, both toward criminals and law abiding citizens, and before long the only "friends" you have are other police officers. "Serve and Protect?" About as much as politicians think their job is to serve the citizenry rather than elected office being a license to steal.

In researching my *Birds With Broken Wings* book, I tell the reader that I purposely went out in the bars and consorted with prostitutes and many on welfare in order to really understand what I was writing about. I associated with drug addicts and alcoholics, with people that had HIV and some that were dieing of AIDS in order to know what I was writing about. As a teacher I took jobs in the ghetto and barrio in order to learn and understand things about education and race relations that could not possibly be learned and understood in any other environments.

Is there any kind of morality that should apply to police work? Or should the morality of Congress be our guide?

Once in a while I watch Hardball with Chris Matthews. Just recently while the Condit/Levy case was being discussed, a woman made the astounding statement that going after Clinton and Condit were examples of "Sexualizing Morality!" She did not respond to the question whether the "Everybody does it" excuse applied in her case.

That phrase really hit me: Sexualizing Morality! Especially being used by a woman. Was she trying to excuse herself, as with the "everybody does it" comment, or her own husband? I had to wonder.

Then another thought struck me. Why did this amazing statement impact me so peculiarly because it was used by a woman, or maybe because such a self-serving statement would more commonly be used by men?

Well, so much for wishful thinking about "Mom and apple pie."

But "Sexualizing Morality;" if infidelity is not immoral, if a sexual relationship has nothing of morality to it, what constitutes immorality to people who agree with this woman?

Then another thing came to mind. Here's Congress, filled with such immorality and corruption so mirroring this woman's comment, discussing making the flag an object of religious veneration (as the term "desecrate" is defined), haggling over a religious and sexist article like the Decalogue, whether it should be granted the "Divine blessing" of that august body, in spite of its religious and sexist nature, and the Clintons and Condits continue to get away with rubbing our faces in their own immorality!

Well, maybe this woman is right. If marriage vows have become quaint anachronisms, perhaps we have finally attained that high plateau of civilization where sex no longer has any moral connotations attached? Perhaps we should allow a Congress and people like the Clintons to dictate a whole new set of rules concerning morality? Perhaps the hypocrisy of a Congress discussing the merits of making the flag a religious symbol of veneration and the Decalogue a showpiece of morality in spite of its obvious sectarian religiosity and purely sexist view stand for a new morality approved by Congress is the wave of the future? An old Roman Senator was succinct when he said that publicly he believed in all the gods, but privately in none of them. Human nature, especially in politics, hasn't really changed much in this regard.

As a nation we seem dedicated to glorifying sex and violence on an escalating scale. Perhaps this woman sees the situation more clearly than I do. I always thought faithfulness and fidelity were somehow moral things, things to be honored.

And with all the bullies in our institutions, with all the violence and corruption our children are fed on a daily basis through cop shows, MTV and the political arena, we are going to do something constructive about reform in education and bullies on the playground?

Chapter Twelve

September

An open letter to the elected leaders in America from a concerned citizen:

I have some concerns and questions for which I and many other American citizens would like honest and forthright answers.

Why are the babies of illegal aliens, criminals, given citizenship?

Why are such criminals eligible for welfare and education at the expense of lawful citizens in America?

Why isn't contraception a mandatory part of welfare?

If farmers in this country need labor, why aren't welfare recipients doing this work instead of illegal aliens?

Why aren't those in government listening to We the People in respect to the legalization of marijuana, an obvious and sensible choice in clearing our courts, jails, and prisons? No law is any better than its enforcement.

As an American, I am vitally concerned for my children and grandchildren as to their future in my America. Why are we being made to look like fools to the rest of the world because our leaders will not control our borders or institute meaningful welfare reform? Why do we have an "Ethics Committee" in our Congress when its members flaunt ethics with impunity? Why has our nation become known as one in which "Justice" is defined by "How much justice can you afford?" and one in which there is no real accountability on the part of elected leaders?

The concerns for Social Security and Medicare, the uncertain economy that has led many to question whether there will be any future security for those now working, these concerns have their foundation in the betrayal of America by the leadership that lack either the integrity or the will to confront the issues I have baldly stated.

Am I to tell my children that they should buy a $20,000 shack just to keep a roof over their heads because when they retire they will not be able to afford the taxes on a suitable home? The leadership of America is fast selling out any prospects of a future for my children and grandchildren by not dealing honestly and forthrightly with the issues that are bankrupting the future for honest, hardworking and taxpaying citizens.

I hope the political recipients of the questions I have posited will understand the justifiable anger I feel as an American, an American that feels betrayed by the leadership of this nation!

August 26, 2001

Legalized Extortion!

In March of 1997 the Bakersfield Californian ran an article of mine in Community Voices concerning divorce. Since that time, more than a thousand studies and books have been published on the subject together with seemingly endless debates on talk shows and the consensus is that children do better in a two-parent home. Surprise!

Life is unfair. God (should He/She be there) made some really stupid mistakes in creating people the way they are. In a perfect creation every woman would be attractive and every man handsome, none of us would grow old and wrinkled, there would be no genetic injustices. In a perfect creation the sex drive wouldn't come upon us before we were able to handle a job and a mortgage. And, of course, in a perfect world there would be no racial or religious hatreds and prejudices, and women would be of equal value to men.

But life is unfair; we are imperfect people living in a far from perfect world. God(s) really blew it and like earthly parents undoubtedly wishes He/She had done a better job.

No one ever asked me if I wanted to be held responsible for someone else's child, if I wanted to make child support payments for someone else's baby. But thanks to Big Brother Welfare, for many decades now I have had to support other people's children. Big Brother has made certain that I will be the one put in prison if I don't make these legalized blackmail payments through taxation, a tax where I was never given any choice as to how this extorted money was to be spent.

When I complained that the mothers and fathers of these other babies should be held accountable, not me, Big Brother either threatened or ignored me. When I suggested that contraception should be a condition of welfare, a judge said: Oh, we do not interfere with the "Reproductive Rights" of people in America!

Reproductive Rights? I wondered where that was guaranteed in the Constitution? Perhaps it is with the same section or article that says people can get divorced and if they have children, they become my responsibility to care for instead of the parents, it is my responsibility to provide child care for these other people's children, it is my responsibility to provide food and shelter for these other parents that decided they didn't want to be married any longer, or hadn't even been married to begin with?

To add insult to injury, there are some that preach I should be held accountable for slavery in this country, that further extortion by Big Brother, Caesar, should be legalized to make blackmail payments to those that want a free ride on my sweat! I would ask those that preach such a hellish doctrine to clean up their own mess of crime, drugs, and alcohol, molestation and rutting like barnyard animals with no thought for the future of the resulting children!

I don't think we are going to see Al Sharpton run for President on such a "reform" platform. But given the likes of "leaders" like the Clintons/Condits, why should he? And why play Lotto when Big Brother pays off with far better odds?

Life is unfair. Perhaps I should have been born in Mexico and have become an illegal alien. Big Brother would have given me "victim" status like those crying for reparations, like those that have babies and extort the money from me to support them.

But I find myself, inexplicably, in a different kind of victim status: that of a person that lived responsibly without Big Brother handouts, never "Caesar's dog" feeding at his table, that got an education at his own expense and supported a family and raised children with no thought that they should be someone else's responsibility. As a "victim" I thought this was what America was all about: Personal freedom with personal responsibility. But America's "leadership" has shown me the error of such thinking.

August 16, 2001

Are the Ramsey's responsible for the murder of little JonBenet? Witnessing the travesty of a so-called "investigation" at the time, I wrote then Governor Roy Romer expressing my concern that power and influence were at the bottom of this travesty. Two things were needed: A thorough and independent autopsy and a DNA test to establish paternity.

Governor Romer never responded and these things were never done. And to my astonishment, no one to date has even brought up the point that one of JonBenet's parents may not be the biological parent… something that would have a direct bearing on her murder.

But Roy Romer has gone on to bigger and better things. He now fills the ideal position for any one that does not want to be accountable: A Superintendent of Schools! And at that, the second largest school district in America, the LA City Schools! How about an "attaboy" for the "honorable" ex governor? When I mentioned this to the LA teacher's union, they had no comment.

Given the success of Roy Romer and William Clinton, I expect Gary Condit has his eye on bigger and better as well, something like Hillary Clinton playing the game of loving spouse while eyeing the White House. But, then, I knew from the beginning that this was her game when she wasn't interested in the job of Vice President. Ms. Clinton isn't exactly cut out for being second honcho. As I wrote a couple of years ago, I could imagine hearing the loving Hillary early on saying: " I know I can do a lot better job of running this country than that sonofabitch!" Of course, this would be her attitude if God Himself were running the country.

Y' know, there just seems to be a common thread running through people like the Romers, Clintons, Condits, people without any conscience or scruples that gets them elected (or becoming school district superintendents like Romer in LA and Wentland of Kern County, Belridge infamy). You don't suppose this says anything about the electorate in America, do you?

Some have made the utterly asinine comment that the attorneys for Anne Marie should have filed in Washington, DC! Don't we remember how Janet Reno handled "justice" for Ruby Ridge, Waco, and the Clinton debacle? Don't we remember how those in power thwarted every attempt to bring Clinton and his "loving spouse" to justice in several instances? You might as well trust "DC justice" to handle Clinton's pardons! The so-called "Ethics Committee" in Congress revolts most Americans! When will they ever know anything about ethics when something like the behavior of the Clintons and Condits is called morally reprehensible but not criminally liable?

If all those politicians that are mouthing concern for Chandra Levy put their money where their mouth is, they will support this attempt of Anne Marie's to get this despicable sorry excuse for a man in a proper forum where he will have to answer questions concerning his affair and her disappearance.

Is the local DA biased? In my opinion yes; but I am ever so grateful that a process has been initiated where We the People may eventually bring one very dirty, if not sociopathic, politician to justice.

August 29, 2001

Judas?

When Sam Clemens called Judas Iscariot a "premature congressman" he must have had Gary Condit in mind. And when Sam said he was opposed to women getting the franchise because it would reduce them to the level of Negroes and men (keep the time frame in mind) because politics was such a dirty business, I think of Mrs. Clinton and Mrs. Condit. You make your deal with the devil and he remains your partner as any reader of Machiavelli or Goethe knows.

Now our governor Gray Davis wishes to distance himself from sleazeball and possible (probable, in my opinion) murderer Condit. Surprise! The "poor" children? They made their deal when they opted for the cronyism and nepotism of politics... luck of the draw. Anyone that has had to deal with the dark and sleazy side of politics has to know that real ethics had to go by the way on the way up. Cynical? What American isn't by now? And we are doing a bang-up job passing this cynicism on to our children.

I received a letter from a lady decrying the "media frenzy" over Condit. My reply to her was that the media looks to ratings. But I admit to a certain uneasy feeling when I see commercials. If I didn't know (i.e. Believe) better, I would think God purposely made so many genetic defects because He had shares in the diet, Bowflex, and cosmetics industries, that He delighted in appealing to the lowest common denominator when brains were passed out.

But my real uneasiness from the commercials (apart from what they say of the "intellectual" level of Americans) comes from the knowledge of how the world perceives us from this venue. This, even more than dirty politicians like the Clintons and Condit, causes me real concern. My real concern is that we are no longer a book-loving and literate society. We have failed miserably to educate our young, making the great ideas and heritage of learning of our past important to our children.

If the world perceives us as hedonistic, ignorant bullies that can do no better than the Clintons and Condits as leaders, it is because we have failed to pass on to our children the heritage of those things that made America a truly great nation. Speaking of Judas...

The Weedpatch Cracker Barrel

September 8, 2001

Clintons/Condit/ and the hoards of Barbarians and Vandals at (and already through) the gate.

Why is Mexico's President Fox so eager to get rid of hundreds of millions of his own hard working, law-abiding, stellar citizens? Simple. As a fifth column movement, these hundreds of millions will enable more hundreds of millions to cross the border. In no time at all, California becomes Mexifornia and people in Iowa will be helping to fund all those welfare checks, and paying for a disabled infrastructure that cannot keep pace with the need of schools, police, medical, housing (not to mention the huge number of new toilets that will be needed and made in Mexico), water, sewers, etc. As to housing, have you asked yourself how this is to be accomplished in the highest priced geography in the world? Can we reasonably expect an enormous increase in gangs, muggings, shootings, home invasion robberies and carjackings? Of course.

But the Roman Catholic Church won't object for the same reason Jerry Brown won't: Building their power and economic base. The RC Church has never objected to, let's say, members that are less than well educated or those with the sterling character of Mafiosi.

***

Having buried my daughter Diana because of a motorcycle accident and enduring a son, Michael, being missing for over two and one half years now, the reader will understand I have a great deal more than the casual interest of many about what happened to the Levy's daughter, Chandra. You never stop grieving the loss of a loved one, especially a child, and the hell never ends of not knowing the whereabouts of a missing loved one, especially a child no matter the age.

Now to shift gears and take on the reptilian scoundrels, thieves and liars affectionately otherwise known as politicians of whom Sam Clemens said Judas Iscariot was only a premature congressman. It took three drafts after submitting this to my secretary, Frau Blaucher, her kindly suggesting that words and phrases like Tax-fattened hyenas, filthy scumbags that think elected office is a license to steal and pick up interns, should be somewhat tempered.

Being a college graduate, I know both of the Clintons and Condit had to take a course in Semantic Differential Techniques otherwise known as to how to evade questions, lie your head off, and not get caught doing it. Unfortunately, I think these three fell asleep in class during the lecture on how to accomplish this without making yourself look like the stupidest kind of moron while doing so, as in trying to redefine "is" and "relationship." Or, in the case of Hillary, taking a page from her husband's "playbook:" But Bill, dearest, he was having sex, not me. I wonder if our own Congressman, William Thomas, tried that one on his wife?

Ok, so humor makes the medicine go down, but there has never been any humor to me about anyone betraying the most solemn oath in our society, the marriage oath. And I will never understand why anyone would ever again trust such a person? The time-honored custom of lying with your hand on a Bible is one that we have come to accept and no one takes that seriously, least of all God. Yet these bottom feeders keep getting elected and make the "Ethics Committee" in Congress a cruel mockery as We the People are lied to, duped, and stolen from hand over fist and expected to take it? Well, if God didn't love stupid suckers he wouldn't have made so many of them of a mind to elect these vermin. And among the stupidest throughout history and the nations today, are those who have a religion that teaches them not to expect justice now, but in the Sweet, By and By (thanks Emerson).

Since I have no empire or position to protect, I can afford to say the things the pundits wish they could say. For example, didn't you wish you could reach into that TV and slap the smirk off the fat face of that lying scumbag Clinton while he was redefining "is?" And didn't you wish you could reach into the TV and shake Condit until his teeth rattled when he gave his cold-blooded interview with Connie Chung? And when "Mr. Peepers," Condit's top aide was on Larry King along with that whole disgusting bunch of sycophantic liars, didn't you feel the same way?

What in the ever-lovin'-blue-eyed world was God(s) thinking when he/she made it possible for eleven year old girls to get pregnant? Now I know there had to have been a few heavenly spats over stupid mistakes like this.

I was raised to slaughter animals for food and did a lot of hunting. So I came to vegetarianism late in life. I found, as Thoreau pointed out, that like the Death Penalty, the raising of animals to slaughter and eat seemed uncivilized and "inconvenient to my imagination."

And while I'm convinced we must save the whales, I've killed a great number of rattlesnakes, blue jays and verminous ground squirrels, the ones that carry the diseased fleas and kill trees by burrowing into the roots, and dig holes for horses and cows to break their legs.

I only mention this to call attention to Condit's eyes. They are those of predator and scavenger, cold as a snake or a blue jay's. I look at those eyes and easily tell myself: Yep, he did it! Some have been so uncharitable as to suggest Condit is without emotion. Not so: He has all the emotion of a Mojave Green rattlesnake.

Of course, he certainly has the ego, like that of the Clintons, to believe he can get away with anything, including murder. Being on the House Intelligence Committee would acquaint him with some pretty clandestine stuff.

The Barbarians and Vandals. Y' know, sometimes our hearts just have to go out to some politicians. Take Jerry Brown, the mayor of Oakland, affectionately known as The Flake and Moonbeam, who, when he doesn't believe he is God, believes he is Moses. When he doesn't make me feel like puking up my toenails, I find he only makes me mildly nauseous or queasy. Willie Brown, the mayor of San Francisco and the black Moses... Oddly, Willie has always been an honest thief in my book. If the money is just there, as in school districts and the Department of Education, why just take it.

Now why on earth should I feel any sympathy for either of these scoundrels? Because both face the problem of building their political base on

Welfare... both would like to invite the criminals that have come, and are coming, across our borders for their own evil purposes of fiefdoms built on those welfare checks.

But Willie's problem is one of his political base being welfare and, at the same time, keeping "those people in their place" while placating the peacock feather, wine and Brie crowd; a not inconsiderable juggling act.

The Weedpatch Cracker Barrel

September 10, 2001

I couldn't understand Mexico's President Vicente Fox being willing to give us so many millions of his educated, hard working, law abiding, upstanding, stellar citizens; you know, the kind of people Castro in a similar spirit of largesse gave us (though I think it was in very poor taste for Al Picino refusing to share with Fidel a part of the enormous proceeds from the resulting film Scarface). But now I think I've got a "handle" on it.

It isn't widely known that President Fox is a major shareholder in Mexico's toilet industry, which makes most of the toilets for export to America. An interesting sidelight was discovering Fox is called "The Big Flush" by his friends, or sometimes "The Four-Flusher," not just because of any chicanery, but because of the heroic size of his... but titillating details of this puerile nature leading to some crass individuals saying "Vinny is really full of it, a natural born politician" are better left to the Enquirer than family newspapers.

President Fox having a vested interest in toilet exports, the more Mexicans here... Of course, locating all these additional millions of people in the most expensive geography in the world and needing the water to flush all those additional toilets poses some problems. But I'm confident George Bush, Gray Davis, Jerry Brown and Willie Brown will figure them out. Willie's will be the greater difficulty since he will have to satisfy his welfare society political base, the same as Jerry's, but the peacock feather, wine and Brie crowd as well.

The larger problem President Fox faces is dealing with the thoroughgoing, top to bottom corruption of government at every level in Mexico. But he knows that to deal with this effectively, he must make himself a target and make his speeches to the sound of cocking pistols in his audience. I just don't see his taking on this role of "reformer." Yet he is asking us to trust him!

Just the mere hint of "Berlin Wall" is political suicide, it seems. But the Israelis are taking it seriously, why shouldn't we?

But having mentioned being "really full of it" the U. N. Conference on Racism was really a religious matter (apart from Jesse Jackson doing his usual stick it to whitey routine). When you spend centuries telling other people that God likes you but they are doodoo to Him, the ignorant and ultra-prejudiced Chosen People Syndrome, whether Hindu, Jew, Buddhist, Christian, Moslem, you don't need the sniff test to understand why you offend civilized and intelligent people. Or even some of those not so civilized or intelligent.

I admit to some difficulty thinking of God as being religious or a Jew, Christian, Moslem, Hindu, etc., favoring any one group of people over another no matter how many candles are lit or incantations from magic scrolls or books purporting to be the Word of God. With friends like these, God has never needed any enemies.

Solving the world's problems:

Take the eye of a newt, a dried toadstool and batwings, one dead cat…

Chapter Thirteen

August 28, 2001

I Wonder?

I wonder if God is more human than religion gives Him credit? While writing the novel Donnie and Jean, an angel's story, this thought came to me in a different way than it has usually suggested itself, it didn't come to me by the usual way of such thoughts. Having heard a sermon by Jean's dad, Donnie does think Pastor Samuels was talking about God in a way that seemed to make God more human, more friendly and understanding of the human condition.

As I lay in bed one night, I thought again as I have many times that there seems no way of our understanding where God came from, the monumental questions of the How? and the Why? of the origin of the universe still remain elusive. Perhaps there is another kind of "dimension" beyond what we are able to determine and the physical universe within which we live precludes our being able to understand these things. It may be that we enter into this other dimension after death; that we enter into, perhaps are "born" into, another phase of life that will enable us to know these things. It is well said in astronomy that there are not only things beyond our imagination in the universe; there are things beyond our ability or capacity to imagine!

Now I don't know about you, but I have a pretty good imagination. It takes a real stretch of the mind to even consider that there are things beyond my ability or capacity to imagine. And yet, I do believe this to be true. Given this, there may well be explanations for things like the How? and the Why? of the origin of the universe presently unexplained, things such as the origin of God that would seem to be unexplainable. Anomalies, paradoxes do exist. So it isn't beyond either reason or speculation that these things may yet be explained.

But be that as it may, over the years, it has become more sensible to me in the realm of philosophical speculation to think of God as Mr. and Mrs. God, our heavenly parents.

Allow me to say at the outset that I do not purposely engage in the misty seeming profundities by which mechanism fools attempt to appear wise.

Much as I love Henry Thoreau and others like him, his statement, for example, that there seems to be something in the lapse of time by which time recovers itself, poetical as it is, as much as I might feel that there is something of merit to such a thought, does not tell me anything of fact.

But there are facts connected with poetical thought and expression, there are facts of what are called the heart, which as the poets say reason knows nothing of. I would be the last to denigrate or attempt to minimize the import of such things. However, the muse in many instances do not answer the legitimate questions I often have about physical, material things, particularly the detrimental things like disease and so much more that have such a great impact on us as imperfect human beings living in a far from perfect world.

Why nature red in tooth and claw? Why the dinosaurs? Why those that love war, why the monsters without any semblance of conscience who murder others and prey on children? It has never "computed" in the context of a loving, sentient, and perfect, all-powerful "Creator." Most certainly the insanity or, charitably, neurosis of religious beliefs and superstitions has never offered a satisfactory explanation. And being insane, without reason, how can they ever do so? Not even the most "enlightened" have any more claim to a factual knowledge of God than the most heathen and pagan practitioners of religion.

So, I wondered? What if God is more human than religion gives Him/Her credit? Suppose, if you will, that God has been, and still is, subject to the very same weaknesses of human beings, that He/She made a mistake with the dinosaurs, with predators that live on the killing of other creatures, that in an effort of creation mistakes were made that resulted in these and beings like serial killers, for example?

If so, does God feel any of the pain or remorse that many parents do of believing He/She should have done better? Even as I write there is a group of religious fanatics in Afghanistan threatening to murder another small group that have a different belief in God simply on the basis of such a difference, and the civilized world seems helpless, powerless to prevent such murders in the name of God. The situation in the Middle East, past and present, seems to give the lie to any ability on the part of God to intervene on His own behalf. Why, I wonder, did God ever allow murder in His/Her name to begin with... unless He (They) is in fact powerless to intervene?

It has been my own failures and selfishness in too many instances, as a man, a husband and father that led me to wondering if our heavenly parents (should there be such) do not condemn themselves for not having been better parents?

Did ancient writers have some thoughts like this? For example the writer in Genesis that says God was sorry, grieved, He made man and had decided to destroy him from the face of the earth. But according to the fable, how very human God seems in changing His mind and sparing humankind because of Noah. But the first part of Genesis does have the pronoun "Us" being used of God and perhaps there was a family dispute involved, particularly regarding the decision to kick Adam and Eve out of the Garden for being disobedient children. Sounds like family trouble to me; not a few parents have wondered where they went wrong in such a fashion.

This idea of God being sorry for having made mistakes, of changing His mind, of even being angry with Himself, of having the human attributes of anger, love, and hate has a tradition in many myths and mythologies; it is particularly a part of that of the Greek mythologies as well as Egyptian and Hebrew, virtually no religion is without such a thing. As to "family planning," that there could be any kind of "divine plan" resulting in such monumental suffering and death of creatures, animal and human, seems to stretch credulity to the breaking point for any thinking person dealing in facts, rather than beliefs, unless some latitude is granted for the making of mistakes in such a plan despite divinity. But the "consolations of religion" too often get in the way of the facts, the result being what I call "blind orthodoxy," something that believers in religion call "faith."

So-called "providence" or the euphemism "grace of God" quickly falls to the wayside when the facts of life are weighed without religious bias. Far more sensible to reason, if a belief in God is to be maintained devoid of religious bias, is that God, both Him and Her, has made the kinds of errors that human parents commonly make, the kinds of errors that torture and torment them as they become aware of such errors.

But granting, philosophically, the power of creation, especially the creation of life that God is accorded, there is no putting the omelet back in the shells when disastrous errors are made, even the "errors of love."

I often think of the ignorance and prejudices that parents commonly pass on to their children. Such things may be done out of love, but the fact that ignorance and prejudices are the result does not mitigate the consequences. If our heavenly parents have been guilty of making such errors, no amount of love on their part mitigates the consequences.

As a mere mortal, I have done stupid things only to wind up saying: How could I have done such a stupid thing? Especially when it seemed like a good idea at the time. I taught my own children many ignorant, prejudicial and hurtful things, many that I had been taught as a child by those that loved me and meant me no harm, only to later learn better. But my learning better at a later time didn't undo the harm I did to my children, harm that had been done them in love, and as they grow older, I can only hope that they will learn better just as I have.

This need to learn better might account for the errors on the part of God(s) and would explain the mistakes of the dinosaurs, the mistakes that resulted in nature red in tooth and claw, the mistakes resulting in murderers, war and hatreds. God (or Gods, Him and Her, as understood throughout) did some stupid things, and I wonder if He/She does not feel the pain of having made such mistakes, just as I do? The very magnitude of so many suffering children throughout the world would seem to indicate a very cavalier attitude on the part of God toward such a thing. Either that or a monumentally stupid mistake!

"Let's try this and see what happens?" Could God, just like us humans, have this kind of curiosity? Perhaps so, but if in the process of creativity and curiosity the whole thing blows up in your face… As I said, you can't put the omelet back in the shells.

Life is unfair. As Tevye so well puts it in Fiddler On The Roof "Would it upset some great, divine plan if I had been born rich?" Apart from a similar and very human complaint on the part of most of us, it does seem to me that a huge error of creation exists in regard to sex. There are many people who are simply ugly. A fat, bald, man with terminal acne doesn't have much of a chance. Neither does a fat, hirsute woman plagued with cellulite. And few would dispute the fact that the sex drive comes upon us far too early to be able to meet the concomitant responsibilities. Certainly in the far distant past of cave dwelling this may not have posed a problem when creatures could rut like barnyard animals without concern for employment, mortgages, and child support payments. But couldn't God foresee the immense problems such a thing would create later on in a more civilized and technological future? Didn't God know the problems that would arise, problems in Wordsworth's Intimations of Immortality so eloquently portrayed by "Splendor In The Grass" directed by Elia Kazan? Why would a loving Creator design things in such a fashion that would lead to so much unhappiness and tragedy through no fault of our own?

Pretty poor planning if you ask me… equally poor in my opinion is the fact that even though we may be blessed with being beautiful or handsome in our youth, we grow old and wrinkled but that sex drive does not diminish. And let's be candid; who wants an old man or woman for sex? No one that watches Baywatch or pours over Playboy. Couldn't God foresee MTV?

I find myself asking why God couldn't foresee a future for our species that took into account so many unattractive fat people and Bowflex advertisements? I wouldn't want to accuse God of being on the side of the exercise, cosmetics, and diet industries, but why didn't He do a better job of circumventing the need of such? Where was the planning when God overlooked varicose veins, etc.… and the question still remains of why God didn't do a better job of creation that would have prevented religious and racial hatreds, not just physical and genetic injustices?

I virtually never think, or write of such things that I am not reminded of Transcendentalism and Margaret Fuller. Here was a woman with an extraordinarily beautiful mind, trapped, by her own admission, in an extremely ugly body; but even Emerson and Thoreau, as well as many others, paid homage to her mind. Life is unfair.

But in regard to sex, it would seem obvious that monogamy, a lifetime of faithfulness to a marriage partner based on equal value and honoring the compatibility of differences and a close-knit extended family would solve most of the problems that arise from infidelity and promiscuousness. However, we are not going that direction in America, quite the opposite. And as to religious and racial hatreds, there is little light at the end of that tunnel. Genetics? Time will tell concerning this. But I can't help but believe a strong family unit, based on faithfulness and equal value and rejecting the superstitions of religion, would carry us a long way toward truly civilized behavior.

Quite some time ago, it came to me that while God cannot do some things, as seems obvious to me, He might be able to influence our thoughts and thereby motivate some people to take a certain course of action. I say only "some" people because there are people over whom it seems God has no influence.

If this were the case, it would explain some of my own behaviors. I have wondered, for example, where the compulsion comes from for the proposed amendment for the protection of children from molesters, for my Memorial Wall with the names of murdered children, for much of the writing I have done, and continue to do as with this present effort? Perhaps such things are the influence of God in my life, or even including the influence of loved ones and friends now gone on ahead of me? I don't know; separating belief from knowledge, I most certainly do not have a better claim to knowledge of such things than anyone else. And if you are like me in this regard, you find such a thing enormously frustrating! It's as though God is playing at hide-and-seek with us.

But not wishing to think or believe God purposely engages in childish or cruel behavior, it leaves me with only the frustration of not knowing. Yet, there is no discounting the compulsive "need to know" on the part of those of us who delve into philosophy, who are given, for whatever reason, to a life of questioning so many things that are not amenable to testing in a laboratory.

Still, as with empirical observation and testing leading to great scientific advancement, the philosopher and poet is no less interested in such discoveries and knowledge. The very physics of a Newton and Einstein, philosophers themselves, is essential to inquiries of a metaphysical nature.

From the earliest times, even pre Homo sapiens times, there seems to have been a belief in God or Gods. And it may be that as we progressed in knowledge and science these views of God, a Supreme Being, Creator, or whatever, have become better defined. However, being in the realm of speculative philosophy and lacking empirical evidence, such ideas remain just that: speculative.

There is in theology that which is called "progress of doctrine," though the word progress is an oxymoron applied to any system of such narrow exclusivity as that of religious systems. Still, a kind of progress of ideas concerning the nature of God(s) may be taking place with the advancement of civilized thought and behavior. In considering some of my own views of years past, I can readily see where I have made progress in my own thinking. As a writer, I have the advantage of being able to reread my essays and books of the past and can readily see how my thoughts and opinions have changed in many instances.

There is something to be said for maturing with age; as the years pass we should be able to take a broader view of things, to become more tolerant and capable of changing our minds rather than becoming more rigid. Unhappily, this is not always the case. And given the decline of literacy in America, the failures of the homes, schools, and universities to promote the reading and study of the great literature of the past, the failure of new generations to learn from this great heritage, does not bode well for the future.

There is the potential for advancement in civilized thinking and action, but only if real learning is taking place. It was only after writing was invented that complex ideas and philosophies could be passed from one generation to the next and an age of science could be ushered in. With the advent of the printing press, ideas could be shared with the general population and literacy could become the foundation for true civilization. But with the modern decline of literacy, by supplanting this with entertainment, a dark foreboding clouds the future. And I can't help but wonder if the "age of accountability" for children isn't tied to this as we witness an increasing need of treating, and trying, children as adults for horrendous crimes? Unquestionably very young children are committing these monstrous acts, and civilized society is going to have to deal with this on an increasing scale. To my mind, there are going to have to be fundamental changes in society, in people's thinking and behavior, in activities like sports, and violence in the name of "entertainment" before any progress can be made in meeting such a challenge as this "age of accountability."

I except, exclude, religious views as contributing to civilized thought and behavior as long as people continue to persecute others and commit murder in the name of God. Truly rational, civilized people do not as a matter of course drink urine or take urine baths, bathe in highly contaminated water in the name of religion and commit murder in the name of God, yet there are people in cultures where these things are commonplace and these people would take great offense at anyone calling their behavior "uncivilized." But none, regardless of what in too many cases is only the veneer of civilized thought and behavior, have a claim to truly civilized and rational thought who believe and teach that only belonging to their peculiar group whether Jew, Christian, Moslem, Hindu, etc., guarantees them a place of joy and happiness in the "hereafter" to the exclusion of all others.

There are cultures, predominately religious cultures, where beheading, decapitation, is the form of capital punishment, where "heresy" is a capital crime. But no truly civilized culture can truly call itself such where violence done in the name of the State, by whatever definition and whether a theocracy or democracy, is still practiced. Violence done to children such as circumcision, abortion, corporal punishment, cannot be practiced, condoned, on the basis of a progress of civilized thought and behavior. And most certainly war itself is the most uncivilized act of any culture or nation.

But even as I write of this, I recall the words of the German soldier after WWII that said: Under Hitler, I really lived for twelve years and I haven't lived since. This man reflected the thoughts and feelings of multiplied millions of men that love war. It is well said that Woman is the antithesis of war, that men make war, not women, that women do not bear children to sacrifice them upon the altar of the wars of men. Ideally, I believe the compatibility of differences between men and women would be an amalgam of hardness and softness, the two forming a proper alloy neither too hard nor too soft, each complimenting the other. But while there are examples of this, we have yet to see this in any society as a whole. Nor can we reasonably expect to see such a thing until women have earned their place in philosophy.

It is the existence of such things as disease and a love of war, the failure to put aside religious and racial prejudices among societies and nations that has caused me to wonder, and make my own speculations lead to consider whether a Father and Mother God may not have had their own disputes leading to some degree of at the very least seeming disorder in creation, and in some instances downright chaos. The whole area of sex, as well as religion, is, to me, in this category. One could legitimately say that if we are the "children of God," there is much of family disorder and chaos representative concerning this point of view of the "humanity" of God among people.

I have written much about the need of honoring the compatibility of differences in order for men and women to get along together, to value each other equally. Since this has never been the case throughout history, I can't help wondering if it isn't a struggle in heaven itself?

I doubt the family has ever existed where men and women have not faulted each other for some decision, if there has ever been a family where a mother or father has not blamed the other at some point for the failure of offspring to meet expectations. But, of course, in a perfect creation there would be perfect families and no genetic defects, no "children of the devil" lacking a conscience.

It is most likely to me that our Creator(s) set things in motion, not being certain of the outcome, unable to forecast every possibility, much as earthly parents.

But there is this thing of "hope" that is most peculiar and so very human, and most certainly, I believe, an attribute of God(s) that we reflect as humans of a heavenly parentage. We often do things in hope without any idea of the eventual outcome.

While much of the universe, of creation, seems to reflect a "let's try this and see what happens" attitude, this idea of the possibility of "divine hope" has much, in my opinion, to commend it.

Good vs. Evil is the most common theme of humanity. The single greatest difficulty we face as human beings in accepting the idea of God(s) just like us with all the human characteristics including mistakes and failures is the enormous personal responsibility we would have to accept for the triumph of good over evil.

If there are things impossible of our heavenly parents, things that are the responsibility of us as the children of God(s) just as there are things that are impossible for us as earthly parents to do for our children, it is a fearful idea that we are to be held responsible and accountable for doing all we can in confronting and overcoming evil. And just as our children must eventually learn to accept responsibility for themselves, and in so doing remove themselves from the decision making processes of the parents, so we may well be in the same position relative to our heavenly parents, admittedly not a very comfortable idea… and not one very amenable to religious views.

Most of what is called "prayer" is a blaming of God by people who are not willing to accept their responsibility for being responsible. This led Thoreau to accuse those in the churches of "blaspheming God in song, prayer, and sermon," of "enduring" God rather than worshipping Him. In my own considerable experience in the churches, I have found Henry to be correct in his dismal assessment.

One would think such outrageous hypocrisy would be readily apparent to those professing a belief in God, but when it comes to facing such a thing, most such people seem no more able to do so than those in To Kill A Mockingbird who condemned a black man to death solely on the basis of his color after white people lied with their hands on a Bible.

Whatever one's view of God(s), it cannot be denied that as long as people use their beliefs to cover and excuse hypocrisy, as long as religion remains a mechanism by which horrible crimes, even murders, are said to be justified because of religious beliefs, so long will it remain a demon-haunted world in need of civilization, a world that has little regard for children, the future of humanity.

The Moslem suicide bombers believe they will be immediately transported to Paradise where they will have 70 beautiful virgins for their reward. While the Jewish and Christian Bibles and religions express a very low opinion of women, it is the Koran that teaches that men are so far superior to women that the latter don't even have a soul equivalent to that of men; that the position of women in the scheme of God is to satisfy men. But the fable of the creation in Genesis has Eve made of Adam's rib, and both the Jewish and Christian religions teach the subservient position of women to men.

It is surprising how women allow themselves to be dominated by men through the mechanism of religion, even failing to see how chauvinistic the Decalogue is. But this device of men using religion to "keep women in their place" will likely continue to be successful until women earn their place in philosophy.

Men like this keeping of women in their place, meaning a place subservient and of lesser value to men. But men are the war-lovers, and as such resist the attempts on the part of women to be included in the King of all disciplines: Philosophy.

The best of philosophical thought is directed at attempting to understand creation and humankind's place in that creation, toward peace and harmony by properly interacting with creation and with one another as a species. But since men have dominated philosophy, very little of philosophical thought has been given to the place of women in the scheme of things.

But as the brawn of men is of no account in philosophy, neither is the sex of women. Neither can earn a place in philosophy, nor make a contribution on the basis of anything but the ability to engage in the Great Conversation through the processes of ideas. As essential as it is for the compatibility of differences to be emphasized in order for a complete philosophy to evolve, neither men nor women can earn a place in philosophy by bluster, deviousness, or by bashing one another. It is the equal value of both men and women that must be emphasized, each making their contribution to a whole and complete philosophy on the basis of the compatibility of differences, each honoring those differences.

Knowledge plus Wisdom equals Peace. But wisdom, and by logical extension, peace, is unattainable as long as a full half of humanity is excluded from philosophy. The shortsightedness of humanity as a whole is exemplified by this exclusion.

It was my hope that the proposed amendment would be a first step toward opening the door for women to come forward and begin the process of earning their place in philosophy. Women, much more than men, are child-oriented. Since children are the future of humanity, they must become the priority of nations. This has never been the case in history and I believe it will take women earning their place in philosophy to bring this to pass.

I have devoted time to a discussion of religion, a sharing of my thoughts on the subject, because of the inordinate power of religion in the world for evil. The superstitions and prejudices of religion, as with racial hatreds, keep the world a demon-haunted and dangerous place.

As such, the power of religion needs to be confronted, even though many might consider the subject silly. But as long as it holds so much power to divide people and cause such suffering and conflict, it needs discussion, it needs to be confronted for the evil it actually is. It especially needs to be confronted as the evil mechanism it is in being used to make women appear inferior to men.

You women would do well to consider this, to confront it and refuse to any longer subscribe to systems of religious thought and practice that have no other view but that of making you a subservient half of humanity of less value than men.

As the King of disciplines, philosophy brooks no pretenders. Only the genuine have a place in this unique area of human endeavor that guides the course of history and nations. It will take women of extraordinary intelligence and character to both understand and make a contribution. It will take such rare women to even understand the need.

And as long as politicians, especially, use religion (along with their professed "concern" for children) as their stock in trade, it needs to be confronted. Don't you feel the same revulsion I do when the Clintons and Gary Condit, et al use a "God bless you and God bless America?" As if God didn't have enough to handle, there are these hypocrites as well as those in thousands of pulpits of every description throughout the world! It is a wonder that "heavenly vomit" isn't spewed out on such hypocritical charlatans! As long as religion remains the mechanism by which scoundrels and murderers attempt to justify their heinous actions, it is far from a "silly" subject. Would that it were simply "silly!"

Somehow, many people have the mistaken idea that the poet's calling is to deal with rainbows and butterflies. The poet true to his or her calling deals with life. And life is unfair. The poet/philosopher is acutely aware of this and is compelled to confront ignorance and injustice. But first, you have to get the mule's attention.

Chapter Fourteen

I Wonder?

Part two

With the advent of TV, the literacy rate of America has fallen to an abysmal low that should be cause for alarm throughout our nation. Fewer than six percent of people read a book of any consequence last year. So many factors, especially TV, are involved in our becoming a society given to instant gratification (which impinges so detrimentally on real learning and literacy) that books and talk shows are given to the subject. TV, unlike radio shows that required imagination has had a most profound, dark influence on learning and literacy. This influence has degraded literacy and real education, continuing to drag these things down to the point where it becomes difficult to engage people in meaningful, knowledgeable discussions of ideas. As a result, philosophy has fallen on hard times as people become increasingly unable to hold a sustained thought while either reading or speaking. It is nothing short of a stark tragedy in America to consider how few today could follow the writings of Goethe or Emerson in a sustained thought.

In the "good old days," a parent would tell a child: Look it up in the dictionary. Now, there are too many homes without a dictionary, let alone an encyclopedia or subscription to National Geographic. And far too many suffer the delusion that Internet access to these things, provided the home has such equipment, will ever take the place of actual books. Further, as the gap continues to widen between the haves and have-nots, materially and educationally, it is less and less likely that the rosy scenario forecast for "Internet learning," as valuable a tool as it is, will take place.

"Virtual" learning is not what most children use Internet access for and to the disgrace of America the pornography sites are the most popular in all age groups. As to "virtual reality," as useful as this can be in some applications, one might reasonably compare the difference between the computer fishing games to actually being in a pristine wilderness, casting a fly of your own creation onto the water of a magnificent trout stream. And as a pilot myself, I can tell you that no simulator or game will take the place of the real thing where you don't usually walk away from a catastrophic accident, just as no web site can take the place of holding that physical book in your hands. I have never, and never likely will, fallen asleep as I often do with a good book that has become a good friend with a palm or laptop computer in my hands.

Few would dispute the fact that the epidemic of obesity in America is another "contribution" of television to our society, together with so many people, most especially the poor, living vicariously, "virtual living," through entertainment rather than expending the effort to make their own lives meaningful through education and the reading of great literature that has the power to move minds to take meaningful action.

Unlike television, a book of real value and consequence challenges the thinking processes particularly critical thinking. This is the reason philosophy became known as the King of Disciplines. It is in the disciplined sharing of ideas and knowledge that humankind was able to progress, each generation building upon the ideas, the learning and knowledge of the generation past. Once writing was available, such a sharing of ideas and knowledge could be passed from one generation to the next with far greater faithfulness and exactitude than with that of pictographs and oral histories and traditions. With the invention of the printing press ideas and knowledge could be made known to the general populace, as literacy became a hallmark of civilization.

The decline of literacy, and by that I mean not just the decline in being able to read but the decline of reading material of real value that challenges the intellect and contributes to civilized thought and advancement, therefore, cannot help but contribute to a decline in civilization.

In America, Emerson remains unsurpassed in his ability to think in civilized ways. His, as one commentator puts it, was a "Mind on Fire." While we rightly look to Shakespeare for the superlative epitome of the beauty of the English language, we look to Emerson for the beauty of the expression of ideas. It took a man of Emerson's rare and unique mind to inspire those like Thoreau. Anyone who reads Emerson's "Nature" and "Friendship," for example, will discover a use of language in a way that provokes the best of our own thought processes.

Those who are well acquainted with Emerson's writings are well aware of the, sometimes, pompous arrogance, the pedagogic, didactic, pontificating personality of the man and the expression of such things in his works. But great ideas need all the room they can get for expression, including room to exercise what would be damning in a lesser mind given to smaller issues. A large degree of latitude must of necessity be granted towering intellect and genius, even to the often eccentricities of a far from average mind though it may sometimes display itself in pugnaciousness and dogmatism, especially in not suffering the pretensions of fools. Such room should be granted, as well, to the ability of such a mind to both change and accommodate such changes with growth and maturity, growth and maturity that is a natural result of the stimulation through honest inquiry and the "need to know" common to true philosophers and poets, such that are compelled and self disciplined, accepting their "calling" and responsibility to all of humanity to be what they are... not for material reward or the plaudits of others.

Having said these things, I would ask the reader to exercise some compassion toward those like Emerson on the basis of their often having to pass through the "Slough of Despond," confronting and striving to overcome their own prejudices and hypocrisies on their journey toward knowledge and in the attempt to gain wisdom. But even the most dull and obtuse would, I believe, be willing to admit that there can be little of real value in the words of those that have no real depth of experience in tragedy and suffering else the "well" would never be deep enough from which to draw the "water of life." And without the necessary tools of a disciplined, civilized and educated mind, the "rope and bucket" if you will, no amount of effort would avail in drawing the water.

The true philosopher/poet is not of the vulgar class of "elitists," but is compelled on his or her course regardless the outcome or how others perceive them, not out of vulgar and egotistical disdain for lesser minds but actually helpless to be other than what they are, which is all too often to become the "conscience" of an unworthy and thankless, if not persecuting, society that will neither know or understand nor wish to know or understand, those "sluggish minds of the masses, slow to the incursion of reason" with which the history of humankind has been cursed throughout and continues on today without let in far too many cases.

I am in the debt of Henry Thoreau for his legacies of "Walden" and "Civil Disobedience." But "The Man of Concord" as Emerson called his disciple did not reach the zenith of his life to me for a night in the Concord jail, but for the faithful hoeing of his bean field. For, as he said, why should one kind of success be exaggerated over that of another? And while it can legitimately be argued that one kind of success is of greater benefit to humankind than another, while Thoreau's writings are of more benefit to me than his work in his bean field, whether one's employment be cleaning the gutters of earth of their vile filth or dusting stars and sweeping the golden streets of heaven with a silver broom, all work a person does faithfully as a calling is of a kind and differs only in degree.

Still, I am constantly reminded from my own failures that there is no work of whatever nobility or goodness that I cannot make shipwreck of by my own ego or selfishness, even my ignorance and prejudices, my own hypocrisies and failure to be responsible or desire to be held accountable in too many cases. And there are far too many examples in my life where even some of my most well intended efforts were ill advised and too much the result of my own selfishness, ignorance, and prejudice.

But if the "hoards of Vandals and Barbarians" are at the gates in too many instances, who are we in the supposedly enlightened and civilized society of America that should know better to blame if not ourselves? I recall one episode while working for Child Protective Services when a black man came up to me outside the courthouse and asked: What gives you people the power to come into my home and take my children away from me? I asked him in turn if he knew the name of his local legislator? He did not. I asked if he was even registered to vote? He was not.

The point, as I make clear in my critique of To Kill A Mockingbird, is that there are far too many people who may be good people but they are not good citizens. And it brooks no argument that if one is too busy to be a good citizen they are too busy to be free! And even though parents may buy their children all the "toys," if the parents are too busy for the children and tell them to "go away and play and leave us alone (or commonly: Go watch TV)," an entire society is doomed through such selfish and hedonistic indifference to children! And if a government is fixed on a course of holding parents less and less responsible for the actions of their children, if a government is fixed on a course of ever more accepting the responsibility (at an ever increasing cost to taxpayers) for the unwanted children of unwed, largely uneducated, irresponsible and undisciplined mothers and fathers, and so on. Utopian Socialism is a consistent failure, consistently failing on the precept that one will long work to support either another or a government that will not provide like effort or service.

We often have latent ideas that require someone like Emerson to bring to fruition. The analogy is that of "iron sharpening iron," the sharing of thoughts and ideas that stimulates and results in progress of such thinking.

Last night as I was once more reading Emerson's small essay on Friendship, I recalled what I had written about death possibly leading to being reborn into another stage of life, one where we cast the slough of these "vile bodies" subject to disease and decay and emerge beautiful and immortal? It is the magnificence of a magnificent mind such as Emerson's that my own thinking is stimulated, causing me to explore new ways of looking at things. Perhaps, I thought, this life is only the larval stage of humankind; perhaps we die only to emerge, metamorphose as beautiful butterflies on the other side?

The question comes to mind whether the "butterfly" recalls its previous existence as a caterpillar? Does it recall the larval form of its previous existence? I have often thought that if we are reunited with loved ones and friends gone on before us that there would have to be a lot of "forgetting" wrongs of commission or omission for such an existence to be anything like "heaven."

And, too, there are those whose very virtue, character, rises far above the crowd, who are in fact the conscience of a culture or society. Are they to have a special place of significance in the "hereafter," are they to be more beautiful butterflies than others?

It has been a nagging problem for years. Most of us feel some communication with those, especially loved ones, gone on before us. But the problem is that of how to dispense with the bad things and emphasize only the good because even in the closest and most loving relationships things are said and done that need to be forgotten. And in conversing, some might call it "prayer," with a group of such people, as I often do, the problem is one of how you speak of things not exactly complimentary to someone when everyone else is part of the conversation.

It came to me that this might work like a computer program. I did something to my brother or he did something to me that neither of us wants to remember. He has gone on before me but I'm talking about it to my grandmother. The "program" does not let/allow my brother to know or hear even though he is there and is a part of the "system."

As we learn more about brain function, atomic structure and particle physics this becomes ever more a possible explanation of how we might "remember" things when we pass on. The good things will remain but the bad things will be programmed out where necessary, even in group discussion and sharing with one another.

This kind of "program" is especially necessary if when we pass on there will be another life, a higher life of learning and actual work filled with the promise of ever growing and doing. And if such a higher life is based on the learning and experiences of this life, it becomes even more needful that only those good experiences and relationships, the good work done in this life be the basis of our future life devoid of the memory of bad things that even good people do to one another. Or, it may be that in this higher life even the bad things good people do to one another will be programmed for a useful, rather than hurtful, purpose. Things, even bad things, may be "remembered" in a productive way, particularly if the relationship with these others was based on love for each other.

But philosophically I believe in the necessity of being able to remember and communicate even the bad things my brother and I did to each other. Also, I think the experience of evil in this life may be necessary to the building of a better world or worlds in the hereafter.

To this extent most of the best of philosophical thought agrees, that any higher, future life would have to exclude those ugly things like envy, prejudice and hatred that consume so many in this life. Therefore I believe only those relationships based on love will "inherit" that higher life.

It is obvious that love has not ruled in this world, but my belief is that the operant principle in the higher life to which we may be called will be that of love for one another, that no evil of any kind will have a place. I think we will be called on to participate with God (Him and Her I believe) in the ongoing creative process, in which God as well as we have learned and are learning, making use of the knowledge gained by our experiences, the good and right as well as the errors, in this life.

It may be that the place to stop thinking about a subject is at that point where the person finds contentment and satisfaction: If ignorance be bliss, 'tis folly to be wise has a lot to commend it. In some ways, when I find myself considering things like the Why? and the How? of God(s) and the universe, the origin of evil, I would like to stop at that point where the idea of the larval stage becoming the chrysalis, death, from which emerges the beautiful butterfly for humankind has precedence over other considerations. I find this a point of contentment, and further exploration of the idea leads into areas where I must leave a "comfort zone" of presumed safety and sail uncharted waters where there be monsters and dragons lying in wait.

In my ignorance of what may lie beyond the grave, my own bliss in such ignorance allows me the benefit, even the comfort, not only of thinking of emerging beyond death as the immortal butterfly, or reborn as a god in my own right with works of on-going creation to be accomplished as a child of God(s), but of thinking that perhaps my loved ones, friends, and people like Emerson, Thoreau, Sam Clemens, and so many others who have gone on before me now know in full the things about which I can only hope, guess, or believe, are helping me along the way I seem compelled to follow in my thoughts and writing, are helping me in those solitary times of communion with them in which I find myself more often wishing that my occupation were that of a child's, to play rather than struggle with the imponderables of the universe, of life and what lies beyond.

But as William Hazlitt so well pointed out, an inch of pasteboard on a wooden globe may represent China, but it is far from the actuality of China itself: "Things near us are seen of the size of life: things at a distance are diminished to the size of the understanding. We measure the universe by ourselves, and even comprehend the texture of our own being only piecemeal."

So, whether there be monsters and dragons ahead, I can't help wanting to go beyond that "inch of pasteboard" in order to expand my understanding, believing the frontier of the mind at least as worthy and exciting as the exploration of the universe promises.

While the world of ideas, of philosophy, is a largely solitary one, it is a not quite lonely one in the company of Nature. And longevity is not measured in time when Nature is at her best, when just the right combination of sun or moon, light filtering through the branches and leaves of the trees, upon a grassy swale or in a forest glade, even the wide vistas of the great deserts or oceans, the very universe set forth in the stars of a crystal clear night sky sets the mood of contemplation and satisfaction. There are so many things of this kind that move us, sounds or no sound, hot or cold, sunshine, moonshine, or a thunderstorm, summer, winter, spring, fall, all have their enchantments and their contributions to make to the mind and soul. In such instances time really is relative and the exquisitely indelible rapture of a moment, like the singing and laughter of children at play, may last throughout one's life.

The birds and other creatures make their contributions as well… not only to the philosopher but to all. One does not have to be a philosopher to feel joy and take inspiration from the first snowfall of winter or the first promise of spring, the flight of a bird or butterfly, the blossoms of flowers, the scampering antics and scolding bark of the squirrels or the call of quail and wild geese.

The very colors, whether of sun, clouds, rainbow, plants or animals, of the trees and rocks, the very earth itself, at certain times may move our very souls. The scent of freshly mown grass or the whole of Nature, resplendent and sweet-scented after a refreshing rain shower may move us as well… and in combination with other factors such as the light and climate of the day may result in a poem that springs unbidden to mind, or the actual creation of a new thought set to the lyrical language of prose and poetry, though for the true philosopher/poet such expression is all too often the result of the darkness having become their closest friend through their suffering or the suffering of others, rather than the gladsome dawning light of a newborn day that makes merry the heart.

The most untutored, even loutish or cloddish, mind can revel to some degree in such magnificence and the mysteries of Nature and their impact on the senses especially. But as Mortimer Adler warned, the Great Books expressive of the greatest of literature and ideas, the disciplined liberal education in the best sense of this phrase leading to enlightened minds of intelligent and sensitive persons truly desiring to be educated are requisite to both the knowing and the understanding leading to further inquiry and contributions that will be of benefit to the whole of humankind.

When I consider all these things, it is at such a time that I realize how very destructive to all of humanity such things as the prejudices and hatreds engendered by religion and racism are. When I consider To Kill A Mockingbird as poetry, the lesson is clear since no truly civilized mind can justify condemning another on the basis of either religion or race. Neither can such a civilized mind take what is only a belief and attempt to substitute it for factual knowledge. I can know the redolent beautiful scent of a rose, but I can believe a skunk or feces equally or even more delightful.

The brutish among us, the uncivilized like the "musket worshippers" will have none of this. The brutish mind will always hold fast to its prejudices and hatreds. The present conference on Racism evidences this. Where there is an agenda based on race and/or religion, there the brutish mind finds its true home. Sadly, and tragically, there is no meeting of minds as long as these factors of religion and race hold sway.

Even now some judge wants to force the Decalogue, a religious and sexist symbol, on everyone else simply because he believes a certain way. He is using his bullying power of position and authority to force such a thing on those that do not believe his way. There is no crime so heinous or despicable that cannot be justified against an individual or group, even the whole of humanity in the mind of the fanatic on the basis of his or her beliefs.

But this judge, solely on the basis of ignorant, prejudicial, religious belief, thinks everyone that does not believe his way is wrong… and so with the present U. N. conference on racism. Too many of those in attendance want others to be forced into submission to their beliefs, choosing to ignore their own hatreds and prejudices, their own ignorant and uncivilized ways of thinking.

The fact that no one has any legitimate claim to knowledge of God above that of others seems to escape those at the conference; as does the fact that no one race is superior (the Chosen People Syndrome) to another on the basis of such claims. And the insanity of asking for "reparations" in the face of facts and rational thought to the contrary, not to mention the utterly thoroughgoing hypocrisy of such a thing, ignoring the historical fact of African chiefs selling their own people to Arab slave traders, the continuing dealing in slavery today in some of these nations, the continued murders in the name of God in Arab nations, in Africa, India, and elsewhere absolutely dooms any attempt at an impartial and objective goal being met, of any lasting good being accomplished.

Further, the sheer insanity, for that is what it is, of thinking anything "sacred" or "holy" that makes such a contribution to human suffering as does religion and its various objects of veneration whether Vatican, Ganges, Mecca or Jerusalem, Vedas, Torah, Bible or Koran, is beyond the civilized mind; is in fact repugnant to and an insult to civilized reason and the whole of civilized humanity!

While poets wax eloquent about Nature, and rightfully so, my argument with God(s) is why there should be the venomous spiders, reptiles, insects, and predators, both animal and human, that rob one of the joy of simply being able to lie down on a bed of pine needles without a foxtail or any poison ivy or oak in sight, possible errors of creation like the dinosaurs, alongside some beautiful, pristine lake or stream without any concern for such things? Why should a beautiful girl like my daughter be denied the wilderness experience on her own because of predatory men? As with those attending the U.N. Conference on Racism, were there errors in Creation on the part of God(s), if such there be, which led to such dangers in the wilderness, such hatreds, and prejudices on the part of some people at the conference?

So it is that I wonder? Perhaps there are genetic factors involved with such behavior by some people, and unquestionably there are the factors of environment and of people teaching their children to hate those that are different or have a different religious system of belief. The song in South Pacific, Carefully Taught is on the point.

But to call attention once more to the fact that real education devoid of hatred and prejudice is the responsibility of those that know such education is needed and able to supply it, that each generation must learn those things of the one past, that it is the responsibility of the past generation to teach the next, the failure to pass on those things of value like the great literature and ideas of our heritage has doomed American literacy and real education. In such an ignorant environment, one that is still ongoing in many parts of the world leading to the religious hatreds and hypocrisies exemplified at the U.N. conference, one cannot hope to make real progress in civilized thought and behavior. And because those like Emerson are considered by too many in the universities to be "hobbies for antiquarians," there is little to hope for from the universities, which for far too long have become amoral institutions in which there are no absolutes of moral and civilized behavior.

If our government in America has degenerated into a "Bread and Circuses" mentality, we must look to the electorate for the cause. Enlightened self-interest and an enlightened and responsible electorate is our best hope. A New Way, a New Path, is needed and it is my belief that by making children the priority of nations devoid of religious, racial, and political hatreds such a new way will be found.

The proposed amendment is something no nation in history has ever incorporated into its foundational charter of government. For that matter, no nation has ever included children as a priority in any fashion by its foundational charter of government. The amendment points the way for a new path because there is one thing all peoples in all nations have in common: Parents' love for their children. By making children a priority in America through the amendment we will have taken the first step upon this new path, we will have opened a door for a dialogue on the basis of something all peoples of all nations have in common: Children and their future.

I never fail to be entertained when I recall a story from the meeting between the great American evangelist Dwight Lyman Moody and that great orator of the Metropolitan Tabernacle in England, Charles Haddon Spurgeon. Immediately after dinner, Spurgeon lit one of his famous cigars. Moody was aghast! "My dear brother Spurgeon" he remonstrated, "Don't you know that is a sin!" Spurgeon reached over and poked his finger into Moody's quite ample and generous belly (for it is well said that the much loved and famed evangelist dug his own and early grave with a fork and it must have taken a gaggle of angels to bear him to his reward) and jocularly replied: "No, my dear brother Moody; that is a sin."

While pictures of Spurgeon don't indicate that he ever missed a meal either, his point is well taken. Here were two men with religious differences. But those differences, unlike the Protestants and Catholics of Ireland, did not require nor motivate either to consign the other to the flames of hell and the outer reaches of perdition on the basis of such differences.

Granting that both professed the Protestant Fundamentalist Christian religion, they did not allow differences of opinion on some issues divide them or separate them from each other's friendship; would that all religious people were of the same mind. Unhappily, often tragically, this is not the case.

It takes an issue of far greater import, one upon which none would disagree, to bring such a diversity of humanity as presently exists together in common cause. It is my firm belief that the welfare of children, the very future of humankind, is that issue and that cause.

Both Emerson and Thoreau delighted in the Oriental philosophies, particularly that of Confucius. In his brief comment on his visit to Stonehenge, Emerson relates the story of the boy asking Confucius "how many stars in the sky?" Confucius replied, "he minded things near him:" then said the boy, " how many hairs are there in your eyebrows?" Confucius replied, " he didn't know and didn't care."

The point is obvious: When it comes to the welfare of the children of the world and what to do about their future, many will talk about the stars, which they can do nothing about, but when it comes to those things that they can do, those things near them, "they don't know and they don't care." Realizing that this was not the point Confucius was making, that he meant those things near him that were of real consequence, not hairs in his eyebrows, were of concern to him, it is close enough to draw attention to the fact that the welfare of the children of the world is the responsibility of adults that should both know and do better. The amendment offers an opportunity for all of us to do better in concert, apart from our biases and prejudices.

It was only appropriate that Emerson deliver Thoreau's eulogy. But Emerson was aggravated by his disciple's lack of ambition to be other than what he thought Henry should have been. While Emerson's was the much greater intellect, the far more disciplined and far better organized mind, he felt a keen love for Thoreau and was disappointed in his seemingly squandering his talents, content to be the "Captain of a huckleberry-party" rather than "... engineering for all of America."

Emerson appreciated the work of Thoreau in caring for his bean field, but as Emerson pointed out: "Pounding beans is good to the end of pounding empires one of these days; but if, at the end of years, it is still only beans!"

Because of the success of Walden and Civil Disobedience in later years, Emerson has been criticized for his just criticism of Thoreau. But Henry had in his lifetime earned the opprobrium of Lowell that there was no basis for his unbounded egotism.

Still, as Thoreau pointed out neither Poor Richard nor the Bible truly met the needs of humanity. Henry intuited, more than he knew; that a new way and path for humanity was needed. Yet it was Emerson, more than Thoreau, who gave a voice to such a need.

As a free spirit and wanting a "large margin" to my own life I can hardly fault Thoreau on this basis. At his best, when he is not being insufferably pompous and egotistical, we find Henry more likable than Emerson. Walden occupies, along with To Kill A Mockingbird, an honored place on my nightstand. I still think, apart from his legacy of Walden and Civil Disobedience, Thoreau's bean field the zenith of his life. The noble work of one's hands in the soil is my thought along with that of the Greek and Roman philosophers, the thought of Thomas Jefferson and others. It is no wonder that gardening is so popular, that a potted geranium is needed in the meanest of circumstances for the poor tenement or ghetto dweller before we inherit our own "peck of dirt."

And I am indebted to Thoreau for his thoughts on vegetarianism; that the eating of animals had become uncivilized and "inconvenient to his imagination," just as occurred later in life for me, proving that even I can eventually come around to a more civilized frame of mind in some instances and I freely confess that my favorite Star Trek film is The Journey Home.

But since it is true that neither Poor Richard nor the Bible answers to the need of humanity for a new way and path neither does Emerson or Thoreau answer to this need. What they do, and the reason I have constant resort to both, is to enliven my mind and soul, to enrich me in such a way that I pick up where they showed the trail. I find within both a kinship that I find with few others. I find a similar kinship with Samuel Clemens, who with his great intellect and talent so ably pointed out the weaknesses and foibles of human nature in such an admirably unique fashion.

I suppose that in sum what I am attempting to do here is to point out the essential necessity of being able, through education, to take advantage of the best of our own very great heritage of literature and ideas to the end that a truly enlightened humanity will evolve from these. It is also my hope that the reader will realize and understand the essential need of education, real and disciplined education, in order for us to maintain any hope for true progress in civilization, for any hope of peace in the world.

I further hope that the reader will accept that the reason I so often question the wisdom of others is the fact that I so often question my own. Still, I credit myself with enough intelligence and education to know the problems that civilized, thinking and educated people face when confronting the "sluggish minds of the masses" and attempting to slay sacred cows and gore another's ox.

Because of this reality of human nature, I more often receive criticism than praise, which is only to be expected when one intrudes onto "hallowed ground" without removing one's shoes. But if one chooses to dance with the devil, attempting to beat him at his own game and dance him to death, it is only sensible to expect that he will try to call the tune and is generally well prepared with his very vocal advocates ready at hand as his choir and orchestra, though beneath their costumes and behind their masks they are discovered to be nothing more than Samuel Johnson's "Screech-owls" and the mules whose attention, no matter the size of the stick, cannot be gained.

It is the most difficult of tasks to separate belief from knowledge, particularly those beliefs into which one is born and taught from childhood by those that love you. The "consolations of religion" are particularly powerful to those that have little hope of their earthly conditions holding much promise of improvement or happiness. Early on, the wealthy and those in authority recognized the power of religion to keep the poor from killing the rich. And, as Emerson pointed out, religion with its message of eventual justice and reward after death prevents the seeking of justice now in far too many cases.

When extreme poverty and ignorance hold sway as in Afghanistan, for example, the rise of a group like the Taliban can be expected, suicide bombers can be expected. You do not find many martyrs among the rich and powerful or among the well-educated classes. Religion as the "opiate of the people" has a well-deserved reputation for holding masses of people in check.

Martin Luther King's appeal was largely enhanced by the religious fervor of the evangelist, his message delivered from a pulpit. The promise was that of a Moses, sent to deliver slaves from bondage. But like all messianic messages filled with the promise of something for nothing, there were some glaring omissions, like the equal value of women to men, there was the glaring error of confusing equal rights with equal value, the fact that education had to be earned, that there has never been any royal path to learning. And, of course, there has never been a "free lunch."

All such messianic preaching fails because it removes personal responsibility and accountability for one's own condition and destiny in the name of God.

And if people in America continue to believe they can have moral leaders with true integrity without their being involved in the political process, if people believe they are too busy to be involved, the outcome is easily predictable.

Chapter Fifteen

September 15, 2001

A New War!

When asked for my thoughts about the Attack on America of September 11, I replied that words were totally inadequate, pitiful things by which to attempt to express my feelings for the magnitude of such barbaric horror, that I felt ashamed to make any such an attempt. I've lived long enough, a part of that "Great Generation" that lived through WWII to understand why some returning veterans of that war could not talk about it. The horrors were too great, the magnitude of the evil so monumental; that mere words could never convey the reality of such malevolence, such evil that was beyond the scope of any civilized mind, that any attempt to verbalize it could only profane by the failure to be adequate in the process of such an attempt.

But without realizing it, I had begun the attempt when I began to write my philosophical treatises on the origin and practice of evil, a subject that I could only adequately address on the basis of a detached philosophical exercise in which logic and reason, not the emotions, were the tools with which I worked.

A large part of this was my becoming involved in child advocacy, my attempting to understand the monumental and historic evil perpetrated against the most innocent of all victims: Children.

I realized that in order to confront and overcome such monumental and historic evil, one must have an understanding of it. But very few qualified people are drawn to such a study, and understandably so, requiring as it does that one "dance with the devil," so to speak, in order to do so.

Now that this evil has declared itself so openly in an attack on America resulting in the murder of so many innocent people, it may be that Americans will be willing and able to finally confront it for what it is: An attack on civilization and the inherent goodness of America.

In confronting the evil done against children, I had come to the logical conclusion that the good will never prevail against the evil until the good confronts the evil with equal determination to prevail. Now, Americans have the choice to meet the evil with such determination. The question is whether we will do so? And it is a question fraught with many complex issues that will have to be resolved if we are to do so.

Some years ago when asked what she thought the greatest threat to America to be, Marilyn vos Savant replied: The hyphenated American.

While shouted down by the political correctness of the universities and their products of judges, politicians, etc., Marilyn had it right.

Some time before the attack, I had been writing something that caused me to pause, get up and look out my back door to my little piece of wilderness of trees and rocks, the birds and critters, and reflect on the question of America. I recall thinking to myself that this was not "My America," it was not the America I had known as a child, as a young man. That America had fought a great war, after which we had helped Europe and Japan, China and other nations to rebuild. Ours had been an America that had shown itself magnanimous beyond belief both to its former enemies as well as its friends and allies.

As a child, I recalled the many sacrifices that Americans had made in order to prosecute and win the war against the Axis powers. I recalled the blue and tragically gold stars in the windows of homes, the scrap metal and rubber drives, the rationing, the daily news of battles fought, the accounts of the rising total of dead and maimed in the fight against tyrants and despots, the enemies of democracy.

I still remember the attack on Pearl Harbor, my mother being there at the time of the attack. I remember the radio address of our president, Franklin D. Roosevelt and his words: A Day of Infamy!

And now, when America should be the better America those of my generation sacrificed and fought for, wanted for our children, I find my children facing their own Day of Infamy just as I did as a child, one that should never have happened.

But it happened because America, the America I knew as a child, had been betrayed by its leadership, a leadership that had betrayed all that was won by those that sacrificed and gave their lives for that better America that should have been the inheritance of my children.

Now the generation of my children is going to be asked to make the necessary sacrifices to win another war, a war against an enemy that should never have been allowed the means and opportunity to commit the recent atrocity against America. But it was my generation and its leaders that enabled this enemy to arise and become the power against civilization it represents.

We knew this was coming when we allowed political correctness to encourage this enemy in our very midst, when we allowed the enemies of democracy in the high-sounding rhetoric of "equality and fairness" to eviscerate the means of combating this enemy, when we allowed political leaders that had only their own selfish interests in mind, their own political ends of a welfare, socialistic power base when refusing to properly control our national borders to out-shout reason.

We knew this was coming when we lacked the kind of leadership that would call those like the Clintons and Renos to account for their crimes against America. We knew this was coming when we allowed our intelligence and police agencies to be made impotent eunuchs in the name of "profiling" and "invasion of privacy."

Political and economic greed is at the basis of the lack of control of our borders, for the failure of real reform in welfare and education. These are the things that invited the attack on America and made it possible. At a time when the Israelis are beginning to speak of a "Berlin Wall" in order to protect itself as a nation, where is the political leadership in our nation that has the integrity to admit such a wall is necessary for the protection of America, has in fact been necessary for decades?

President George Bush and Colin Powell are making it known that those that are not with America, are against America in this new war. The enemies of America are clearly identified by the willingness of such to encourage and help those dedicated to our destruction in the "Name of God!"

My reaction to this war declared against America in the name of God is one of hatred toward those that are obviously enemies of both God and civilized peoples. But my hatred is also directed toward those here in our own nation that have betrayed us as a nation and allowed America to fall into such moral decline as to justify, in far too many cases, the accusations against America that we are a selfish and hedonistic nation dedicated to wealth and ease, rather than real justice and fairness, to the principles that made America a beacon of hope for true democracy to the nations of the world.

As the present leadership calls upon Americans to make the necessary sacrifices to prosecute and win this latest war against tyrants attempting to, once more, enforce their will on others, I want us to hold these leaders to account, to be held accountable for the sacrifices they are requiring of us as Americans! It cannot be the America representative of those like the infamous Clintons and Renos, the Condits and others like him, that we are being called on to sacrifice for, it has to be the America I knew as a child, the one that far better men and women died to protect and pass on to me to hold in trust for my children and the children of the world, it cannot be a nation of "hyphenated Americans."

As an American that knows what that term really means, I also know that the only good rattlesnake is a dead rattlesnake. Those that argue the contrary under the high-flown rhetoric of "environment" and "balance of nature" are either the enemies of civilization or know nothing of rattlesnakes.

We are a nation aroused to deep and righteous anger against the attack of rattlesnakes under the guise of "holy war." There are already many voices of the rattlesnakes in this country trying to shout "moderation" in the face of this monumental evil perpetrated against America. But as a real American, I know a rattlesnake when I see one, whether in Afghanistan or right here at home. And if war is to be prosecuted successfully against these snakes, it must be a war against them all, both at home and abroad!

And I would repeat to the leaders of America, don't you dare ask for the necessary sacrifices unless this war is one that will be prosecuted against the evils both at home and abroad, the evils and evil people that have betrayed My America!

September 18, 2001

Wanted Dead or Alive!

Most of those I have heard from applaud President Bush's statement concerning Osama bin Laden. The problem those of us among the "great unwashed" have with such statements coming from our leadership is that we don't believe them.

Why don't we believe them; because the appropriate response to the Attack on America would have been to have immediately launched a cruise missile with a tactical nuclear warhead on Kabul. I say an appropriate response not only because of what most Americans feel about the attack on our nation, but the fact that the most powerful nation in the history of the world had an opportunity to once and for all show the world that such barbarism against civilization supported by rogue nations would be met with a force they cannot survive.

One can reasonably ask what the thoughts of those over 6,500 victims of this sneak attack on America would be in respect to an appropriate answer to such religious terrorism that took their lives? But their voices are stilled forever, just as those over Lockerbie and others are. Are the victims of religious terrorism convinced by political rhetoric that they will ever be avenged or civilized people made safer, that a "Sleeping Giant" has been aroused by the posturing of appeasement and rhetoric any more than Hitler was?

And while it is wonderful to see so many displaying the flag, if the national anthem and God Bless America are to be played and sung, do it straight without the stylizing of personal, self-aggrandizement. These are national treasures and not for the shameless display of personal egos.

I can say the things on behalf of the multiplied millions of Americans I represent, the millions that feel just as I do, that the politicians and pundits cannot say because I have no job or empire to protect, I do not have to grovel before the throne of "political correctness," I can say these things because I am an American and feel no shame in denouncing the enemies of my country without apology. I can point out that religion is no friend of democracy and I don't believe any American wants religion in any form to dominate our freedom as Americans, even the freedom to denounce any religion that believes it should be the exception to democracy, particularly a religion such as Islam that actually teaches that women are not of equal value to men, that all are infidels that do not believe in their Prophet and Koran.

No one disputes the fact that the good will never overcome the evil unless the good confronts the evil with equal determination to prevail. Our leadership missed this opportunity for an immediate response to terrorism that would have made the will of civilized nations unmistakably clear, an opportunity that would have been timely and cannot be reclaimed, and we are now mired in the usual political rhetoric of those that believe religious fanaticism will ever respond to reason.

Those of us that recall the attack on Pearl Harbor, that remember Franklin D. Roosevelt's Day of Infamy speech have no doubt of what America's response would have been to Japan had such weapons as we now possess been available to us. It would have been a short war; just as this would have been had our leadership not lacked the will of an immediate and appropriate response to this new Day of Infamy.

Now we hear, too long after the attack, that many measures are being taken to protect us from further attacks. We hear that orders have been given to shoot down airliners that stray off course, that air marshals will be provided, wire taps easier to obtain, some racial profiling will now be acceptable, etc. We hear that crocodile tears are being shed by the nations supporting terrorism; that the leaders of such nations "sympathize" with our loss here in America.

I watched with disgust as our President took off his shoes in order to give a talk about bigotry in an Islamic Mosque, as though he didn't know that the two most bigoted religions in the world are Judaism and Islam, as though he was not aware that the Attack on America has its roots in an interpretation of the Koran by the Taliban with which many Muslims here in America agree, that the Attack on America could never have succeeded without a "Fifth Column" of such believers entrenched in our nation.

Make no mistake, the enemies of democracy, of America, are well entrenched right here in our country. They worship a god of war, they believe in a religion of the sword all the while crying out how "peaceful" the religion of Islam is, denying their own history of warfare in the name of their "Prophet."

One only has to recognize how willing the nations of Islam are to open their borders to those of another religion to realize how bigoted Muslims are in fact. The religion does not change with American citizenship; it is a religion that does not recognize, and is no friend of democracy.

As an American, and not a "hyphenated American," I confess I have little confidence in a leadership that lacks the will to prosecute a war against terrorism, a leadership that failed to respond immediately with force to this Day of Infamy, a leadership that is proving to be unwilling to properly control our borders, a leadership that is still committed to welfare socialism as a basis of political power, a leadership that will commit untold billions of dollars of taxpayer's money to the blackmail of nations that are no friends of democracy. I sincerely and fervently hope that events will prove me wrong in my dismal assessment.

September 21, 2001

The evening of September 11, I watched the news as an attack on Kabul was taking place. My first reaction was "Wonderful, fantastic, at last Americans are showing that we will not be bullied and terrorized without immediately striking back at our enemies!" I was literally ecstatic that our leaders had made the decision to respond immediately with force, the only thing fanatics understand, to the horrific Day of Infamy against thousands of helpless civilians here in America!

I think most of you can understand how deflated my spirits were to learn that the attack on Kabul was by the Afghanis of the North, not by us. I felt nearly betrayed as an American that the attack had not been ordered by our own leadership.

Those of us that remember Pearl Harbor have no doubt how we would have responded to that Day of Infamy in 1941 had we the weapons America now possesses. One cruise missile with a tactical nuclear warhead would have made it a very short war, saving countless lives in the process.

Now, because America did not respond in such a way, we are in for how many years of conflict? And how many lives of Americans will be lost in addition to those whose voices have been stilled forever, especially those in that airliner that sacrificed their lives against the terrorists?

President Bush gave a marvelous speech and I am grateful America has the kind of leadership it has. As an American, I will do all I can to support my country, just as we did in those long years of WWII.

But it gives me real cause for concern to realize something that our leaders, and the citizens and pundits of America, seem not to understand. This war is one that will be waged because of religion. And religion, by definition as I have pointed out and history proves, is no friend of civilization or democracy.

During the Russian attempt to subdue Afghanistan, a reporter wrote of the Afghanis taking a couple of Russian soldiers prisoner. The prisoners were taken over a hill and the reporter heard shots. When the Afghanis returned without their prisoners, the reporter asked what had happened to them? The Afghanis replied that they had been shot.

Why? The reporter asked. The Afghanis replied: Because they were not Moslems.

This, fellow Americans, is something we do not understand. But this is the kind of war we are facing; this is why I believe that cruise missile would have been the best and most appropriate response to religious terrorism, that such a response would have made for a very short war.

CHAPTER SIXTEEN

SEPTEMBER 26, 2001

President George W. Bush
The White House
Washington, DC 20502

Mr. President,

It has been a privilege for me to have enjoyed our personal correspondence since I first encouraged you to run for President while you were the governor of Texas. Your letters have always evidenced a sincerity and forthrightness that is, sad to say, too often lacking on the part of those that win elected office and I have always been encouraged by your honesty in answering my questions, as well as those of all Americans.

Because of the warm and high regard in which I hold you and the First Lady, I take the liberty of sharing some concerns that have come to the fore as a result of the Attack on America, concerns that I know are shared by multiplied millions of Americans that seem not to have a voice in the media.

Permit me to begin by saying that a copy of this letter is going to be sent to several elected officials like our own governor in California, Gray Davis, as well as many others in state and federal government, media personalities, and various organizations because they, as well as you, need to know of the concerns I am expressing on the part of so many Americans that have no voice or are fearful for a number of reasons, some quite legitimate, to express these concerns in person.

The evening of September 11, I watched the news as an attack on Kabul was taking place. My first reaction was "Wonderful, fantastic, at last Americans are showing that we will not be bullied and terrorized without immediately striking back at our enemies!" I was literally ecstatic that our leaders had made the decision to respond immediately with force, the only thing fanatics understand, to the horrific Day of Infamy against thousands of helpless civilians here in America!

I think most can understand how deflated my spirits were to learn that the attack on Kabul was by the Afghanis of the North, not by us. I felt nearly betrayed as an American that the attack had not been ordered by our own leadership.

Those of us that remember Pearl Harbor have no doubt how we would have responded to that Day of Infamy in 1941 had we the weapons America now possesses. One cruise missile with a tactical nuclear warhead would have made it a very short war, saving countless lives in the process.

I am far from being a warmonger and I have an intense hatred of bullies as my proposed amendment for the protection of children from molesters, the most cowardly and heinous bullies of all proves.

But it has been estimated that since Japan, led of fanatics like the Taliban, would have fought to the last man, woman, and child in protecting the homeland from an invasion, an estimated 2,000,000 lives were saved by the decision to drop the bombs on Hiroshima and Nagasaki.

Now, because America did not respond in such a way as we did in ending the war with Japan, we are in for how many years of conflict? And how many lives of Americans will be lost in addition to those whose voices have been stilled forever, especially those in that airliner that sacrificed their lives against the terrorists? What do you believe these whose voices have been stilled would consider being an "appropriate" response?

Mr. President, you gave a marvelous speech and I am grateful America has the kind of leadership it has. As an American, I will do all I can to support my country, just as we did in those long years of WWII.

But it gives me real cause for concern to realize something that our leaders, and the citizens and pundits of America, seem not to understand. This war is one that will be waged because of religion. And religion, by definition as I have pointed out many times, and history proves, is no friend of civilization or democracy.

During the Russian attempt to subdue Afghanistan, a reporter wrote of the Afghanis taking a couple of Russian soldiers prisoner. The prisoners were taken over a hill and the reporter heard shots. When the Afghanis returned without their prisoners, the reporter asked what had happened to them? The Afghanis replied that they had been shot.

Why? The reporter asked. The Afghanis replied: Because they were not Moslems.

This is something Americans do not understand. But this is the kind of war we are facing; this is why I believe that cruise missile would have been the best and most appropriate response to religious terrorism, that such a response would have made for a very short war.

Was the reluctance to respond to this Attack on America as we did in ending the war with Japan the result of decades of "political correctness" that robbed the leadership of America of the courage and the will to prosecute an appropriate retaliatory strike against Afghanistan, a nation notorious for encouraging and training terrorists throughout the world?

Now I have a legitimate concern about how this present war is to be prosecuted? Will we be forced to pay for the "friendship" and "cooperation" of nations that hate us, the nations of Islam especially? Are we going to be blackmailed into paying for the millions of refugees resulting from this war, refugees that have no love for America but still hold their allegiance to Islam and from whom more terrorists can rightly be expected to come? Are my children and grandchildren going to be forced to pay such blackmail and sacrifice and do without in order for politicians to keep their bloated and cushy jobs?

Speaking for the multiplied millions of Americans that have no voice in the decisions of leadership, that have for too long been subject to "bought offices" without any meaningful campaign reforms and a legal system of "how much justice can you afford," I ask whether the lack of an appropriate response to the horror visited on innocent civilians in America was the result of too many in Congress and state legislatures gaining and holding their positions on the basis of a welfare/socialist platform, a basis of political power that takes from workers and rewards things like illegitimate births without accountability, that has for too long rewarded our universities for their incompetence, their failure to provide for meaningful reforms in education and have for decades taught that there are no moral absolutes or personal accountability?

Here are some concerns and questions for which I and many other American citizens would like honest and forthright answers, questions I am at liberty to ask since I have no job or empire to protect and do not have to bow before the throne of political correctness or even exercise polite tact and diplomacy:

Why are the babies of illegal aliens, criminals, given citizenship?

Why are such criminals eligible for welfare and education at the expense of lawful citizens in America?

Why isn't contraception a mandatory part of welfare?

If farmers in this country need labor, why aren't welfare recipients doing this work instead of illegal aliens?

As an American, I am vitally concerned for my children and grandchildren as to their future in my America. Why are we being made to look like fools to the rest of the world because our leaders will not control our borders or institute meaningful welfare reform? Why do we have an "Ethics Committee" in our Congress when its members flaunt ethics with impunity? Why has our nation become known as one in which "Justice" is defined by "How much justice can you afford?" and one in which there is no real accountability on the part of elected leaders?

The concerns for Social Security and Medicare, the uncertain economy that has led many to question whether there will be any future security for those now working, these concerns have their foundation in the betrayal of America by the leadership that lack either the integrity or the will to confront the issues I have baldly stated.

Am I to tell my children that they should buy a trailer or $20,000 shack just to keep a roof over their heads because when they retire they will not be able to afford the taxes on a suitable home? The leadership of America is fast selling out any prospects of a future for my children and grandchildren by not dealing honestly and forthrightly with the issues that are bankrupting the future for honest, hardworking and taxpaying citizens.

The following is an article I posted on my web site, as this present correspondence will be, and sent to a large number of columnists. I hope the political recipients of the questions I have posited will understand the justifiable anger I feel as an American, an American that feels betrayed by the leadership of this nation, while reading it:

Legalized Extortion!

In March of 1997 the Bakersfield Californian ran an article of mine in Community Voices concerning divorce. Since that time, more than a thousand studies and books have been published on the subject together with seemingly endless debates on talk shows and the consensus is that children do better in a two-parent home. Surprise!

No one ever asked me if I wanted to be held responsible for someone else's child, if I wanted to make child support payments for someone else's baby. But thanks to Big Brother Welfare, for many decades now I have had to support other people's children. Big Brother has made certain that I will be the one put in prison if I don't make these legalized blackmail payments through taxation, a tax where I was never given any choice as to how this extorted money was to be spent.

When I complained that the mothers and fathers of these other babies should be held accountable, not me, Big Brother either threatened or ignored me. When I suggested that contraception should be a condition of welfare, a judge said: Oh, we do not interfere with the "Reproductive Rights" of people in America!

Reproductive Rights? I wondered where that was guaranteed in the Constitution? Perhaps it is with the same section or article that says people can get divorced and if they have children, they become my responsibility to care for instead of the parents, it is my responsibility to provide child care for these other people's children, it is my responsibility to provide food and shelter for these other parents that decided they didn't want to be married any longer, or hadn't even been married to begin with?

To add insult to injury, there are some that preach I should be held accountable for slavery in this country, that further extortion by Big Brother, Caesar, should be legalized to make blackmail payments to those that want a free ride on my sweat! I would ask those that preach such a hellish doctrine to clean up their own mess of crime, drugs, and alcohol, molestation and rutting like barnyard animals with no thought for the future of the resulting children!

I don't think we are going to see Al Sharpton run for President on such a "reform" platform. But given the likes of "leaders" like the Clintons/Condits, why should he? And why play Lotto when Big Brother pays off with far better odds?

Life is unfair. Perhaps I should have been born in Mexico and have become an illegal alien. Big Brother would have given me "victim" status like those crying for reparations, like those that have babies and extort the money from me to support them.

But I find myself, inexplicably, in a different kind of victim status: that of a person that lived responsibly without Big Brother handouts, never "Caesar's dog" feeding at his table, that got an education at his own expense and supported a family and raised children with no thought that they should be someone else's responsibility. As a "victim" I thought this was what America was all about: Personal freedom with personal responsibility. But America's "leadership" has shown me the error of such thinking.

When asked for my thoughts about the Attack on America of September 11, I replied that words were totally inadequate, pitiful things by which to attempt to express my feelings for the magnitude of such barbaric horror, that I felt ashamed to make any such an attempt. I've lived long enough, a part of that "Great Generation" that lived through WWII to understand why some returning veterans of that war could not talk about it. The horrors were too great, the magnitude of the evil so monumental, that mere words could never convey the reality of such malevolence, such evil that was beyond the scope of any civilized mind, that any attempt to verbalize it could only profane by the failure to be adequate in the process of such an attempt.

But without realizing it, I had begun the attempt when I began to write my philosophical treatises on the origin and practice of evil, a subject that I could only adequately address on the basis of a detached philosophical exercise in which logic and reason, not the emotions, were the tools with which I worked.

A large part of this was my becoming involved in child advocacy, my attempting to understand the monumental and historic evil perpetrated against the most innocent of all victims: Children.

I realized that in order to confront and overcome such monumental and historic evil, one must have an understanding of it. But very few qualified people are drawn to such a study, and understandably so, requiring as it does that one "dance with the devil," so to speak, in order to do so.

Now that this evil has declared itself so openly in an attack on America resulting in the murder of so many innocent people, it may be that Americans will be willing and able to finally confront it for what it is: An attack on civilization and the inherent goodness of America.

In confronting the evil done against children, I had come to the logical conclusion that the good will never prevail against the evil until the good confronts the evil with equal determination to prevail. Now, Americans have the choice to meet the evil with such determination. The question is whether we will do so? And it is a question fraught with many complex issues that will have to be resolved if we are to do so.

Some years ago when asked what she thought the greatest threat to America to be, Marilyn vos Savant replied: The hyphenated American.

While shouted down by the political correctness of the universities and their products of judges, politicians, etc., Marilyn had it right.

Some time before the attack, I had been writing something that caused me to pause, get up and look out my back door to my little piece of wilderness of trees and rocks, the birds and critters, and reflect on the question of America. I recall thinking to myself that this was not "My America," it was not the America I had known as a child, as a young man. That America had fought a great war, after which we had helped Europe and Japan, China and other nations to rebuild. Ours had been an America that had shown itself magnanimous beyond belief both to its former enemies as well as its friends and allies.

As a child, I recalled the many sacrifices that Americans had made in order to prosecute and win the war against the Axis powers. I recalled the blue and tragically gold stars in the windows of homes, the scrap metal and rubber drives, the rationing, the daily news of battles fought, the accounts of the rising total of dead and maimed in the fight against tyrants and despots, the enemies of democracy.

I still remember the attack on Pearl Harbor, my mother being there at the time of the attack. I remember the radio address of our president, Franklin D. Roosevelt and his words: A Day of Infamy!

And now, when America should be the better America those of my generation sacrificed and fought for, wanted for our children, I find my children facing their own Day of Infamy just as I did as a child, one that should never have happened.

But it happened because America, the America I knew as a child, had been betrayed by its leadership, a leadership that had betrayed all that was won by those that sacrificed and gave their lives for that better America that should have been the inheritance of my children.

Now the generation of my children is going to be asked to make the necessary sacrifices to win another war, a war against an enemy that should never have been allowed the means and opportunity to commit the recent atrocity against America. But it was my generation and its leaders that enabled this enemy to arise and become the power against civilization it represents.

We knew this was coming when we allowed political correctness to encourage this enemy in our very midst, when we allowed the enemies of democracy in the high-sounding rhetoric of "equality and fairness" to eviscerate the means of combating this enemy, when we allowed political leaders that had only their own selfish interests in mind, their own political ends of a welfare, socialistic power base when refusing to properly control our national borders to out-shout reason.

We knew this was coming when we lacked the kind of leadership that would call those like the Clintons and Renos to account for their crimes against America. We knew this was coming when we allowed our intelligence and police agencies to be made impotent eunuchs in the name of "profiling" and "invasion of privacy."

Political and economic greed is at the basis of the lack of control of our borders, for the failure of real reform in welfare and education. These are the things that invited the attack on America and made it possible. At a time when the Israelis are beginning to speak of a "Berlin Wall" in order to protect itself as a nation, where is the political leadership in our nation that has the integrity to admit such a wall is necessary for the protection of America, has in fact been necessary for decades?

Mr. President, you and Colin Powell are making it known that those that are not with America, are against America in this new war. The enemies of America are clearly identified by the willingness of such to encourage and help those dedicated to our destruction in the "Name of God!"

My reaction to this war declared against America in the name of God is one of hatred toward those that are obviously enemies of both God and civilized peoples. But my hatred is also directed toward those here in our own nation that have betrayed us as a nation and allowed America to fall into such moral decline as to justify, in far too many cases, the accusations against America that we are a selfish and hedonistic nation dedicated to wealth and ease, rather than real justice and fairness, to the principles that made America a beacon of hope for true democracy to the nations of the world.

As the present leadership calls upon Americans to make the necessary sacrifices to prosecute and win this latest war against tyrants attempting to, once more, enforce their will on others, I want us to hold these leaders to account, to be held accountable for the sacrifices they are requiring of us as Americans! It cannot be the America representative of those like the infamous Clintons and Renos, the Condits and others like him, that we are being called on to sacrifice for, it has to be the America I knew as a child, the one that far better men and women died to protect and pass on to me to hold in trust for my children and the children of the world, it cannot be a nation of "hyphenated Americans."

As an American that knows what that term really means, I also know that the only good rattlesnake is a dead rattlesnake. Those that argue the contrary under the high-flown rhetoric of "environment" and "balance of nature" are either the enemies of civilization or know nothing of rattlesnakes.

We are a nation aroused to deep and righteous anger against the attack of rattlesnakes under the guise of "holy war." There are already many voices of the rattlesnakes in this country trying to shout "moderation" in the face of this monumental evil perpetrated against America. But as a real American, I know a rattlesnake when I see one, whether in Afghanistan or right here at home. And if war is to be prosecuted successfully against these snakes, it must be a war against them all, both at home and abroad!

And I would repeat to the leaders of America, don't you dare ask for the necessary sacrifices unless this war is one that will be prosecuted against the evils both at home and abroad, the evils and evil people that have betrayed My America, the America I want for my children and grandchildren!

Mr. President, I have taken great liberty in making my thoughts and concerns known to you and others in such bold and impolitic words. I can only hope that you, and they, will not take offense but rather consider what I have said in the light of the extreme seriousness of world conditions, conditions in which religion, as Carl Sagan and others have warned, makes for a demon-haunted world. I will conclude by saying that it would, in my opinion, be a grave error if the civilized nations do not take this fully into account as civilized peoples attempt to prosecute this war against civilized freedom on behalf of the progress of civilization.

Samuel D. G. Heath, Ph. D.
Americans for Constitutional Protection of Children
Sent as email

September 29, 2001

I've written an open letter to President Bush and sent a copy to several others like California Governor Davis and senators Feinstein and Boxer in justification of my view that our immediate response to the Attack on America should have been a cruise missile with a tactical nuclear warhead launched on Kabul. In sum, being a part of the "Great Generation" that lived through WWII (my mother being in Pearl Harbor when it was attacked) I have no doubt of how our leadership would have responded to that Day of Infamy had we the weapons America now possesses.

But our present leaders did not respond immediately to this Day of Infamy as they should have, and by failing to do so we are promised a war of years' duration, more attacks of terrorism, and the killing of many more Americans here and in battle abroad. And where will the money come from to prosecute this war of many years' duration? The cost will be the future of my children and grandchildren.

But we do not have the kind of America or the leadership that existed in 1941, and while I am deeply gratified to see so many displaying the flag, the obscenity of the smirking faces of America's shame, Mr. and Mrs. Clinton, the ilk of a Janet Reno seeking a governor's position, and Jesse Jackson trying to make political hay of America's tragedy take the bloom off the rose for me as an American.

I also see our leaders and the pundits ignoring the plain fact that we are facing a religious war, refusing to acknowledge that Islam particularly is a threat to the whole world, that the followers of the Koran and Mohammad pose a growing threat right here in America! Make no mistake; Moslems in America are loyal to Mohammad, not America! And our leaders are going to make "friends" of such religious fanatics abroad by extorting taxes from American citizens in order to pay blackmail in the form of taking responsibility for the refugees, from whom more terrorists can rightly be expected to come, resulting from the fanaticism of Islam!

Can our own leadership and the pundits be that stupid that they do not recognize the power of religion at work in Islamic nations to keep the poor from killing the rich? No matter the poverty in places like Iraq, Iran, and the Sudan, the leaders build palaces while their own people suffer. And our leaders suffer the delusion that such leaders in Islamic nations are going to cooperate with America! Who believes the leadership in Pakistan is willing to "cooperate" with America unless we pay blackmail to such a corrupt, theocratic regime?

Our lives here in America have been changed forever for the worst because of the attack by religious terrorists and our leaders and the pundits seem stupid enough to believe that the followers of Islam can ever be trusted, either here or abroad, that by paying blackmail extorted from American citizens in the form of aid to refugees when the leaders of Islamic nations refuse to take any responsibility for the suffering of their own people will make friends for America! The whole idea is repugnant to civilized reason!

The following is an excerpt from my letter to President Bush:

We are a nation aroused to deep and righteous anger against the attack of rattlesnakes under the guise of "holy war." There are already many voices of the rattlesnakes in this country trying to shout "moderation" in the face of this monumental evil perpetrated against America. But as a real American, I know a rattlesnake when I see one, whether in Afghanistan or right here at home. And if war is to be prosecuted successfully against these snakes, it must be a war against them all, both at home and abroad!

And I would repeat to the leaders of America, don't you dare ask for the necessary sacrifices on the part of American citizens unless this war is one that will be prosecuted against the evils both at home and abroad, the evils and evil people that have betrayed My America, the America I want for my children and grandchildren!

Mr. President, I have taken great liberty in making my thoughts and concerns known to you and others in such bold and impolitic words. I can only hope that you, and they, will not take offense but rather consider what I have said in the light of the extreme seriousness of world conditions, conditions in which religion, as Carl Sagan and others have warned, makes for a demon-haunted world. I will conclude by saying that it would, in my opinion, be a grave error if the civilized nations do not take this fully into account as civilized peoples attempt to prosecute this war against civilized freedom on behalf of the progress of civilization.

The whole text of this letter may be read on my web site: http://solo.abac.com/sdghacpc/tap.htm

Samuel D. G. Heath, Ph. D.

Americans for Constitutional Protection of Children

Chapter Seventeen

The Bakersfield Californian

September 24, 2001

Most of those I have heard from applaud President Bush's statement concerning Osama bin Laden. The problem those of us among the "great unwashed" have with such statements coming from our leadership is that we don't believe them.

Why don't we believe them? Because the appropriate response to the attack on America would have been to immediately launch a cruise missile with a tactical nuclear warhead on Kabul, Afghanistan. I say an appropriate response not only because of what most Americans feel about the attack on our nation, but the fact that the most powerful nation in the history of the world had an opportunity to once and for all show the world that such barbarism against civilization supported by rogue nations would be met with a force they cannot survive.

I watched with disgust as President Bush took off his shoes in order to give a talk about bigotry in an Islamic mosque, as though he didn't know that the two most bigoted religions in the world are Judaism and Islam. It was as though he was not aware that the attack on America has its roots in an interpretation of the Koran by the Taliban with which many Muslims here in America agree and that the attack could never have succeeded without a "Fifth Column" of such believers entrenched in our nation.

The enemies of democracy, of America, are well entrenched in our country. They worship a god of war, they believe in a religion of the sword all the while crying out how "peaceful" the religion of Islam is, denying their own history of warfare in the name of their prophet.

***

October 3, 2001

Prime Minister Tony Blair
Number 10 Downing Street
London, England

Dear Sir;

I want to express my deep appreciation to you for your unequivocal stand against terrorism, and especially for your no-nonsense approach to solving the problem. At a time when politics seems to stymie direct action, you have shown what I consider to be extraordinary courage in speaking logically and directly to the point.

My own roots are deep in England, as my name testifies, and I have always been of the mind of Emerson who so eloquently pointed out what the term "Englishman" means.

Enclosed you will find a copy of a letter I sent President Bush. I want you to be aware of the fact that there are millions of Americans that feel as I do and have no voice in the mainstream media. But some of us do try to articulate our views despite this handicap.

The world has suddenly become a very dangerous place for civilized people. It is my fervent hope that more leaders will take your stand against the enemies of civilization.

With my most profound gratitude for you and for England,

Samuel D. G. Heath, Ph. D.
Americans for Constitutional Protection of Children
P.O. Box 82
Bodfish, CA 93205-0082
U.S.A.

***

OCTOBER 6, 2001

THE BAKERSFIELD CALIFORNIAN

Being grateful that America is still the land of free speech, so far, and being most grateful of all for a free press that is the one greatest bastion of freedom in America, I take the liberty of responding to detractors of my views by pointing out that I am quite expert in religion and history. One of my most prized possessions is an autographed copy (by Dr. Charles Lee Feinberg of Talbot Seminary) of the pilot edition of the New American Standard Bible published by the Lockman Foundation.

Having served as a pastor for a number of years, I know the Christian religion very well and certainly did not mean to exclude Christianity (or Hinduism) from being any less bigoted as a religion than either Judaism or Muslimism.

But with advancing years and learning, I have come to the conclusion along with Thomas Paine and Carl Sagan that religion is no friend of civilization or democracy, that religion does indeed make for a "demon-haunted world."

I'm very well acquainted with the fanaticism of fundamentalism, whether that of Christian, Jew or Moslem. And rather than spending all their time in their various Bibles, I would suggest religious people spend some time with those like Paine, Emerson, Sinclair Lewis and others in order to get a real education, rather than a religious one that has put the entire world at risk.

I stand by my view, one that I have made clear to President Bush and posted on my web site, that a cruise missile with a tactical nuclear warhead on Kabul would have made for a short war saving countless lives in the process, just as the dropping of the bombs on Hiroshima and Nagasaki did in ending the war with Japan.

Samuel D. G. Heath, Ph. D.
Americans for Constitutional Protection of Children

***

THE FEAR FACTOR

There is no question America is a nation in fear, and because of the tyranny of religion leading to the September 11th Attack on America our lives henceforth will not be the same either in our nation or anywhere else in the world.

Some have accused me, and quite understandably so, of being extreme in my view of what would have been an appropriate response to the heinous Attack on America of religious terrorism, that of a cruise missile with a tactical nuclear warhead launched immediately on Kabul. To such I say that the fear in America and the world would have been considerably lessened had our leaders responded in such a fashion.

Being grateful that America is still the land of free speech, so far, and being most grateful of all for a free press that is the one greatest bastion of freedom in America, the second being our right to bear arms, I take the liberty of responding to detractors of my views by pointing out that I am quite expert in religion and history. One of my most prized possessions is an autographed copy (by Dr. Charles Lee Feinberg of Talbot Seminary who was head of the translating committee) of the pilot edition of the New American Standard Bible published by the Lockman Foundation.

Having served as a pastor for a number of years, I know the Christian religion very well and certainly do not exclude Christianism (or Hinduism) from being any less bigoted as a religion than either Judaism or Muslimism.

With advancing years and learning, I have come to the conclusion along with Thomas Paine and Carl Sagan that religion is no friend of civilization or democracy, that religion does indeed make for a "demon-haunted world."

I'm very well acquainted with the fanaticism of fundamentalism, whether that of Christian, Jew, Hindu, or Moslem. And rather than spending all their time in their various "Bibles," I would suggest religious people spend some time with those like Paine, Emerson, Sinclair Lewis and others in order to get a real education, rather than a religious one that has put the entire world at risk.

I stand by my view, one that I have made clear to President Bush and posted on my web site that a cruise missile with a tactical nuclear warhead on Kabul would have made for a short war saving countless lives in the process, just as the dropping of the bombs on Hiroshima and Nagasaki did in ending the war with Japan.

Having failed to respond to terror tactics appropriately and immediately, we are being promised a war that may extend beyond the lifetime of many of us, a war in which the civilized nations are going to be at continued risk from those willing to murder and die in the name of God. But the civilized mind should realize, since it is a matter of speculation alone, that no one has any legitimate claim to knowledge of God or Gods above that of anyone else.

Having said this, I come to the issue at hand: The Fear Factor.

One of the things that have brought this forcefully to mind is the fact that another form of "political correctness" seems to be emerging. Now that Americans are beginning to find their misplaced patriotism busy buying and waving flags everywhere, it seems some of the pundits and politicians are becoming fearful of raising a dissenting voice in the midst of such patriotic fervor.

Unquestionably it serves no good purpose to engage in tasteless, so-called humor at the expense of something as tragic as the Attack on America. Unquestionably Americans are going to have to get used to increasing restrictions on their lives and more government/police intrusion in order to make our nation safe. But far too many of the "freedoms" Americans have taken for granted are not the freedoms our Founding Fathers had in mind, they are for the most part so-called freedoms muddy-minded legislators and judges have bartered out of greed and for political advantage, things that led to a loss of control of our borders and the invasion of criminals from many nations, they are "freedoms" to live on welfare without any responsibility, the "freedoms" of having a hundred different ballots for voting because of so many in America not knowing what ought to be, according to reason and a needed Supreme Court decision, the national language of English.

As an "un-hyphenated" American, I should be able to go to a doctor and understand him/her, I should be able to call a government office, a public utility, etc., and be able to talk to whoever answers the phone without having to ask them to repeat themselves numerous times because it is obvious that person does not know and cannot speak English. An accent is one thing; indecipherable gibberish is another.

America has become in too many cases a "polyglot" nation, filled with foreigners, millions illegally, and making it all too easy for terrorists to infiltrate. Imagine if you will the basis of any protest on the part of foreign students, of the FBI examining their backgrounds and visas?

Because of decades of failure on the part of America's leaders in government and the judiciary to properly secure our borders, the failure to legislate according to reason, the failure to maintain a proper intelligence system in the face of an increasingly dangerous world, the failure of the universities that produce the leaders of America to be accountable for the huge role they play both in education and in America's safety, the price is going to be a heavy one for all of us.

***

October 10, 2001

Kern Valley Sun

In reference to Mayf Nutter's letter in the paper, November 29 of last year the Sun ran an article of mine entitled *The Sounds of Music* in which I pointed out how important the music programs of old Kernville Elementary and the high school were to all of us in the Valley in those days, especially to those of us that played in the orchestra (I played clarinet and tenor sax).

I can only reiterate what I said then as to the importance of learning to play a musical instrument in relationship to brain function as per the studies mentioned in Nutter's letter and the books written such as The Mozart Effect. When I became a teacher, it was obvious to me which pupils were involved with band and orchestra because they were vastly disproportionately the better students, in behavior and academics.

The enormous differential in self discipline required to master an instrument, the great boost in self esteem in doing so, are the benefits, benefits lost to the schools and children that have been denied the opportunity others and I enjoyed in the past.

The leadership in government and education, most especially the universities, is not comprised of those that had the benefit of mastering a musical instrument. Such leadership was thus very shortsighted in removing music programs from school curriculum.

This points up a larger issue, one I have written extensively about, the issue of attempts at education reform. Lacking experienced and knowledgeable leaders in both government and education, such attempts are inevitably doomed. The presumed metaphor is obvious: These leaders never learned to play the clarinet.

Samuel D. G. Heath, Ph. D.

***

October 16, 2001

Tyranny of Religion

Last night I found myself thinking that perhaps science lacks the vocabulary of literature and poetry since there are many scientists and physicists who are obviously of a poetic nature though seemingly unable to express themselves in such a way. But, then, poets and writers need the knowledge of science in order to make the best of their most sensitive insights into nature and human behavior.

Admittedly it is not a new thought and much has been written on the theme, so why did it come to me as a new thought? Knowing myself as well as I do, the only explanation was that some unconscious item of information, perhaps some not quite conscious but new insight, was causing me to look at the problem. This often happens when I have read something, some book or article, something in the news that percolates in my mind, perhaps even while asleep.

It might have been the result of conversations I have been having with those who, like me, are searching for answers to the How? and the Why? of the universe, of what actually lies beyond the "veil" when we pass on? I've written so much on this theme, I am always searching for new thoughts, new speculations with which to expand on this subject that consumes so many minds and results in so many books being written about it. Among the religious, it is a consuming thing leading to so many books about angels, for example. The entire field of theology, once known as the "Queen of the Sciences," came into being about the subject. The King of Disciplines being Philosophy.

I often think of Einstein's phrase "Spooky communication at a distance" in reference to the ability of some of the smaller parts of the atom, tachyons, instantly communicating with each other across a relative universe of distance. How do they do this seemingly impossible thing? I think of it in terms of the speed of thought or imagination.

In this respect, on a much smaller scale, what if I had a loved one or friend in China with whom I could instantly, mentally communicate by way of our minds, telepathic communication if you will? If these small atomic particles can do such a thing, why can't we? There are many instances of such things seeming to happen, particularly in the animal kingdom, the whole field of Psi is dedicated to such research.

Perhaps there are other dimensions to the universe than length, breadth, and height? The universe is composed of and exists on the basis of Time, Space, and Matter. But within these there are anomalies, things without an explanation at present, things like Einstein's Spooky Communication at a Distance.

Have some actually seen ghosts? Are there things that "go bump in the night?" Have some of us experienced other planes of existence? Are there further planes of existence ahead for us? all grounds of fascinating speculation, the very "stuff" of books on metaphysics, angels, and the nature of God or Gods.

Perhaps it is a step-by-step process, further planes of existence, to know and understand God? I can frame the question: How did God or Gods come to be? But it is a question impossible of an answer in my present plane of existence.

Given other states of matter, other characteristics of the universe that are for the present anomalies, things that we presently characterize as Psi, it may require these other planes of existence for us to grow into understanding. It may be that we "metamorphose" not unlike the caterpillar into the butterfly. The question that comes to my mind in such a case is what the butterfly may recall of its former existence, if anything? I like to think my loved ones and friends gone on before me will be there to receive me… that I, in turn, will be there to greet those like my children and grandchildren.

We seem to be religious by nature, using that term in a behavioral sense of it being natural to think of God and a hereafter by whatever definitions; it seems natural to pray, in whatever manner, to call out to God especially *in extremis*. Even the most hardened skeptic seems to realize the sense of intelligence behind the creation and order of the universe. I can't help thinking of Father and Mother God while gazing at the stars or a beautiful sky with brilliantly white clouds tinted by the sun. The very longings of immortality seem to reside within us, this refusal to accept physical death as the end of our being. Nihilistic philosophies are very unwelcome, even abhorred with fright by most people.

But even the most pure of heart cannot escape the vile thoughts that are engendered by our present lives and intrude themselves into the mind, those legions of demons so common to this present existence no matter how carefully we guard our behavior. Even the most loving relationships have elements of things needing forgiveness, and perhaps will need to be utterly forgotten in a higher plane of existence.

Because of this, I find it sensible to entertain the thought within the realm of philosophical speculation that another plane of existence is needed in which evil cannot find a place, where evil is thoroughly banished and all the ideals of this life are at last realized and love and peace are finally triumphant.

But if we call such an existence "Heaven" or "Paradise" it could hardly be such without the challenges and learning that make our present existence meaningful, without those things that presently add so much meaning to our lives. This higher plane may require our learning things in this life that will be of importance to us then. It may be that evil will never be vanquished in this world, but must wait upon that to come?

The present world crisis engendered by religion gives me pause and does make me wonder if peace is possible before we destroy ourselves? Perhaps, as Nobel-winning physicist Michio Kaku and others have theorized, if there had been other civilizations in other worlds throughout the universe, they destroyed themselves for the same reasons, particularly after reaching that plateau of atomic energy that makes such self-destruction possible, perhaps even probable?

Does our present existence have such importance as to prepare us for a better, to become as "gods" entering into a plane where we ourselves will have the power of creation and take part in some kind of plan of on-going creation? Will my present delight in the charm of nature find fulfillment in being able to, myself, create such things of beauty as that of the wings of a butterfly or a creature like a hummingbird or the flowers and trees that presently delight my eyes, or being able to bring a new snow, or rains on another planet given into my care that presently delight my senses when fallen fresh upon the grass?

There is that within many of us as human beings that feels a need to love, to do and build, even create, which I believe might be of divinity, the "thing" that enables us to love even sacrificially and gives us pleasure in nature and human companionship.

It is in the writing of such things that I wonder if God(s) needs a voice based on the progress of civilization, rather than the cacophony of voices purporting to speak for Him/Them on the basis of so-called "scriptures" and "prophets?"

It may even be that those loved ones and friends gone on before me that I believe are now the experts in things about which I can only guess are helping me and lending their thoughts, their voices to what I write? My *mantra* having become I Don't Know, I don't know? But I do wonder. Still, as per the "IT" girl of silent film stardom Clara Bow: "Why can't we know?" Her legitimate question remains unanswered.

CHAPTER EIGHTEEN

OCTOBER 22, 2001

HITLER STILL RELEVANT

My novel Donnie and Jean, an angel's story, answers a need for people to not only satisfy a reaching back to a simpler time of simple verities in many instances, it also has the effect of challenging those ideas that have made for Carl Sagan's "Demon-haunted world." So it is timely in two major respects: It will cause people to think about what civilization is facing and what must be done if we are to avoid the nuclear Armageddon Nobel-winning physicist Michio Kaku and others have warned of.

This present "war" has all the earmarks of a failure on the part of America's leadership to properly propagandize our cause. Toward the end of WWI a German commander, knowing the war was lost, blamed it on the failure of Germany's leaders to recognize the supreme value of propaganda. It had been too easy to demonize the "Hun" and this commander realized Germany had not recognized that the Allies on the basis of ideas that they had successfully propagandized were fighting the war.

Hitler did realize this and with his peculiar genius for understanding the mood of an age took full advantage, coming to power on the basis of successful propaganda. His success is summed up in the words of a German soldier decades after the war: Under Hitler, I really lived for twelve years! I haven't lived since.

So it is that Hitler's ideas, even his persona, continue to have a relevance to multiplied millions of people worldwide. The Jewish judge in Tehachapi, California who made the observation that he considered Hitler's greatest crime to be that of making it impossible to discuss racial distinctives in academia made a telling point (though he caught hell for doing so).

I'm a pretty good historian of Hitler's Germany and having lived WWII I'm a pretty good historian of America during this period. I know how enormously important it was for us to demonize Germany and Japan through propaganda including the comic books, funny papers, and cartoons of the age as well as the adult media, particularly film, and things like scrap metal and rubber drives, the rationing, etc.

Now the civilized world is facing a war of ideas, ideas held by terrorist fanatics. But civilized nations are not doing a very good job of propagandizing the cause of civilization or democracy against these ideas. There are no leaders, apparently, that seem to realize this or have the backbone to confront it. So it makes it too easy for the enemies of civilization and democracy to demonize our cause, just as Hitler found "easy pickings" in doing so against Jews and others in his rise to power.

Unless terror is to be met and overcome by greater terror, as per Hitler's observation, civilized nations are going to have to come up with better propaganda, a "better idea." And while civilized nations focus on economics as opposed to religion, which is, admittedly, no friend of civilization or democracy, "conspicuous consumption" is not that better idea that lends itself to successful propagandizing against religious fanaticism.

October 23, 2001

Lord Charnwood in his biography of Lincoln (1916) wrote: It may perhaps be said that American public opinion has in the past been very timid in facing clear-cut issues. But ... an apt phrase crystallising the unspoken thought of many is even more readily caught up in America than anywhere else....

Thanks to my mother I have an original LA Examiner of December 21, 1941 with the headline in large, red, block letters: REMEMBER PEARL HARBOR!, U.S. PACIFIC WAR SLOGAN

Now here's the problem. That slogan like REMEMBER THE ALAMO! and REMEMBER THE MAINE! was one that really caught on. But somehow REMEMBER THE WORLD TRADE CENTER! is too much like REMEMBER CONSPICUOUS CONSUMPTION!- admittedly a hard sell to quicken patriotic hearts, let alone one that would endear America to any other nation.

We're going to have to do better.

October 25, 2001

Most people are aware of the thought that even if people believed the devil did not exist we would have had to invent him. This has been a ploy from antiquity to attempt to excuse evil on the part of humankind.

"If the Jew did not exist," Hitler said, "we would have had to invent him. A visible enemy, not just an invisible one, is what is needed."

Creating the personalized concept of an evil that you can demonize is the idea behind successful propaganda. If we indulge the notion that simply because our cause is just and right it will prevail, this will be foolish indeed. "We will bring evil-doers to justice" simply does not suffice.

In WWII we demonized the "Rotten Japs" and "Stinking Knocksies." Media of every kind successfully caricatured the enemies of democracy and even Bugs Bunny and other cartoon characters were brought into the fray. The "funny papers" and comic books were enormously useful tools of propaganda.

But since WWII, apart from editorializing cartoons, civilized nations have progressed beyond the use of such obvious and crude mechanisms of propaganda. Still, the same problem presents itself: How to put a personal face on the "devil" civilized nations must confront in this war? That such a personal face is needed is beyond contradiction because Hitler was absolutely correct! Our leaders during WWII were absolutely correct in demonizing the enemies of democracy! The fact, in spite of civilized progress on the part of civilized nations, is that evil will never be overcome of good until that evil is met with equal determination to win!

It is bad enough that our leadership seems too much like "Frick and Frack" in stumbling and bumbling toward uncertain goals using uncertain methods. Even those in the Pentagon are asking input from the public for ideas about combating terrorism, not something that inspires confidence in the military. They all seem to be overlooking the lesson from the past that this is a war of ideas ever as much as WWI and WWII. Yet the better idea "Democracy" seems to be lagging behind "Death To The Infidel!" Why? Because the leaders of democracy have failed to properly propagandize its cause. And worse, seem to lack the essential backbone to do so!

I ask myself why the leaders of civilized nations are so timorous? Who are they afraid of alienating by "telling it like it is?" Are we, the great unwashed, to be chided if we claim to "detect the smell of oil" among other things, behind this lack of telling it like it is? Are we to be upbraided because there seems to be too much of the stench of politics still at work in spite of this dreadful attack on America?

But what American wasn't ashamed to see the members of Congress scurrying to safety at the hint of anthrax, getting their Cipro immediately and only as an obvious afterthought taking care for menial postal workers?

Perhaps some soul-searching is required on the part of all Americans in an attempt to understand why a "REMEMBER PEARL HARBOR" is so difficult to come by in this present crisis, why it seems so difficult to properly propagandize the cause of democracy as the "better idea?"

If the "coalition against terrorism" seems to be losing steam, don't Americans have a right to ask why? If it is obvious to the great unwashed that Islam is no friend of democracy, if we see billions going to benefit those that could care less for the welfare of Americans, don't we have a right to ask why? My Medicare payments are guaranteed to increase, but we are spending billions to pacify nations that would applaud America's demise or on those that are flaunting our laws in order to take advantage of our stupid immigration and welfare laws such as the insanity of granting instant citizenship to the babies born of criminals as long as American taxpayers remain to give them a free ride. I have a right as an American to ask why?

As a result of these legitimate questions that most Americans have and continue to go unanswered, are we to be blamed for crying out that the stench of politics has reached the point where that, not anthrax, is the reason we are becoming increasingly fearful and we cannot properly propagandize the cause of democracy?

***

OCTOBER 26, 2001

I just learned that the government has asked the help of Hollywood in producing some propaganda. I like to think that I have had a hand in this. But recalling those like Ronald Reagan and Clark Gable doing some propaganda films for the military during WWII, just whom does Hollywood have of like stature to a Clark Gable of that era? Elton John? Ludicrous as such a thing is, it is the "Elton Johns" that have provided much of the material for successful propaganda on the part of our enemies against us. The very immorality that has reigned in Hollywood and government is against our being able to properly propagandize the cause of Democracy.

***

INSTINCT

OCTOBER 27, 2001

Using the analogy of the caterpillar that metamorphoses into the butterfly, it may be that we believe in God (or the plural of a Mother and Father God understood throughout) by instinct, that such belief, the universality of calling out to God *in extremis*, the very natural instinct for prayer, the thing that causes us to believe that death is not our terminus, the thing that drives us to seek out answers through the mechanisms of philosophy and religion, all these may be in fact driven by instinct. In spite of all our scientific advances, the essence of what life really is eludes us, just as there are things, anomalies for example, in our physical universe that we cannot explain.

Continued studies in particle physics, brain function, astronomy and many other areas of science offer hints and open doors of understanding. But the greatest questions of the How? and the Why? of the universe, of life itself, are still beyond us.

But just as the caterpillar has no idea, we assume, where it came from or where it is going, continues to live by the rules, the instinct built into its very being, prepares the cocoon from which it will emerge as a butterfly, so we may very well live by such an instinct for believing in God and immortality, that there is intelligent reason and purpose for our lives and the universe.

The caterpillar has no idea of where it came from or where it is going. Neither do we. We may find nothing wrong in our questioning such things, we do strive for answers to these questions and like the "IT" girl, Clara Bow ask the question "Why can't we know?" we seem no closer to answers than the most ancient of our ancestors.

I can't help but smile at the question Clara Bow in her interview with Liberty Magazine phrased so succinctly and eloquently, the haunting question from time immemorial, so seemingly ingenuously. No philosopher or theologian has ever phrased it better or more honestly.

Religion and its varied monuments, artifacts and methods of worship and the King of Disciplines, Philosophy, do not provide us any certain knowledge of where we came from or where we are going. They do not answer Clara Bow's honest question.

But it does seem that we are possessed of an instinct that drives us, just as the caterpillar, in a direction that death is not the end, that life does have purpose, that by whatever form of a "butterfly" we emerge, that purpose will be fulfilled.

There is an instinct of self-preservation and for procreation in all life forms. Perhaps we human beings even have an instinct for love? Why shouldn't there be an instinct for a belief in God, for a belief in purpose in our lives and that death is not the end?

Religion and the biases and prejudices in our lives may be matters of choice or what we have been taught to believe. Such things do not seem to be "instinctive" but depend on such things as others and how they impact our lives, of things like the circumstances of environment and what we are taught. But could it be that we have an "instinct" to believe in God?

It may be that Clara Bow's question cannot be answered while we remain in our present form? It may be that as the caterpillar may not know or recall anything of its larval stage, and the butterfly may not recall either of its previous stages of existence, such "knowing" isn't possible for us at this time, that such things progress on the basis of an unconscious "knowing" that we call instinct?

Like the caterpillar, we may believe in God(s) by instinct, and by that instinct attempt to live our lives in preparation for the hereafter, our instinct in most cases being to emerge the most beautiful butterfly possible at the next stage of life.

We may believe in God, Gods, or Mother and Father God by instinct and by that instinct, in most cases since the majority of people are for the better part good and decent, attempt to live our lives decently and morally in preparation for the hereafter, our instinct being to emerge the most beautiful butterfly possible at the next stage of life.

Though answers to such questions may in fact not be possible at this stage of life, the pursuit of answers, the curiosity that drives people to search for answers continue. It seems that the quest for answers to these questions is just as natural (instinctive?) as that of the caterpillar preparing for its next stage of development.

But the caterpillar, while having the instinct for survival and preparation for becoming a butterfly, has no sense of impending death... and it does not die, but metamorphose.

The quest for answers has much to do with a great deal more than just curiosity. Humankind has the knowledge of death, something the caterpillar does not have. The butterfly? It lays its eggs and dies and that is the end of the cycle of nature for it... but human beings?

This is a great distinction between a lower life form and human beings, self-awareness... the image of God... the children of God? Perhaps; and perhaps also an instinctual knowing resulting in a search for answers and the refusal to accept death as the end of the cycle of nature for humankind,

Religion by definition is no friend of civilization or democracy!

***

A Fight For Civilization

October 27, 2001

I was gratified to hear Hugh Downs make the comment that it distresses him that no national Moslem leader has yet stood up for America in our war against terrorism. Nor has any of national stature here in America done so.

The reason none have done so is patently, and painfully, obvious. Moslem nations are theocracies, and as such are anti-democratic, as are all religions, by their very nature. The religion of Islam is particularly anti-democratic, both here and abroad (one only has to consider the position of women in this religion to understand the point). But even when our own leaders claim God (or Jesus, Jehovah, etc.) to be on the side of America, they have no more legitimate basis to do so than any Taliban leaders have of Allah blessing their efforts.

What leaders from the President on down actually accomplish by bringing God into the equation of war is to justify and harden the position of the enemies of civilization and democracy, who have every legitimate right on the basis of metaphysical apologetics to make such a claim on their own part. The leaders of civilized nations may attempt to make a case of their "God" being the more civilized deity, but such a thing flies in the face of honest reason and logic.

I believe there is a legitimate basis for prosecuting a war against terrorism in the cause of civilized behavior and democracy, for the need of such action on behalf of civilized progress worldwide. But in the process of doing so, it is utterly counterproductive for America's leaders or citizenry to try to make this a war in which God, by whatever definition, is on our side. Lincoln was absolutely right during the Civil War in this nation to point out that "it might well be The Almighty does not agree with either those of the North or South."

By taking the side of Israel, which Moslem nations rightly see as a theocratic state, not a true democracy, on the part of America is another obstacle to any resolution for peace in this war. Here again, as with our leaders invoking God, the battle takes on the characteristic of a "Holy War" rather than a fight for civilization and democracy by their proper definitions.

In pointing these things out, I have had many people, including some well-known columnists and politicians, take me to task in no uncertain terms. I understand their doing so.

But no amount of "righteous indignation," no amount of false claims of America being a "Christian nation," no amount of claims of "God is on our side" will change the facts, reason, or logic of the case. Lincoln was absolutely correct in his assessment and we would do well to accept it.

By failing to take immediate and decisive, unilateral action the very day of the Attack on America, we are now in for a long war. And with a very few notable exceptions, America is going to have to go it alone for the most part unless our cause can be made on the basis of a fight for the progress of civilization and democracy devoid of any religious claims of justification.

***

October 28

Things haven't changed that much since *Innocents Abroad* and *The Ugly American* in spite of the modern age of communications. Americans for the most part still expect the rest of the world to be pretty much as per their view of the world; a parochial world-view due to a lot of factors.

But we can't lose sight of the fact that the world's perception of America is too much one of what is seen on TV and Hollywood productions, which hardly present us in a favorable light and terribly distorts the image of the real American citizenry. If we are ignorant of foreign countries, they are at least as ignorant of ours.

John Toland's masterful work about Japan during the years '36 - '45 is little known outside academia but a major point is one Americans would do well to heed. During the final exchanges between America and Japan before the attack, the word "China" meant including Manchuria to the Japanese. To FDR it did not. The President was perfectly willing to cede Manchuria to Japan, but diplomatic exchanges failed to make this clear. Why? The supreme egos on both sides of the ocean, the diplomats on each side being unwilling to admit they did not understand the language of the other.

So the attack by Japan turned on the misunderstanding of that single word: China.

We face much of the same thing due to similar "diplomats' on both sides in this current crisis.

And the ACLU does have a point, though a self-serving motive drives it, concerning Home front Security measures. But as with Toland's history of Japan, few leaders, apparently, are aware of Claude Bower's definitive work about Reconstruction and the wholesale abrogation of the Constitution during the "*Tragic Era*."

We all know the old saw about "those that do not learn from history..." but I fear we are not being led of a well-educated government and when I consider the wholesale ignorance of our citizenry...

***

November 1, 2001

Truth, Justice, and The American Way

(From the Weedpatch Cracker Barrel)

Well, President Bush has reached out to Hollywood and Madison Avenue in an attempt to propagandize Truth, Justice, and The American Way. Some would say: Better late than never. But I doubt Hollywood or Charlotte Beers will be able to pull it off. They have the universities to confront and overcome in doing so. And the universities, as I have pointed out many times, are the true sacred cows of America, untouchable by any politician or columnist.

In my four-page letter to President Bush immediately following the Attack on America I pointed out several things, all of which the universities would oppose, such as the failure of our leadership to immediately respond that very day by launching a cruise missile with a tactical nuclear warhead on Kabul, which, I wrote, would have made for a very short war. Since this was not done, we know we are in for a very long war, one that the pundits and politicians are loath to call WWIII.

But since no amount of propaganda on our part will make this anything but a religious war to Moslem nations, and since the insanity of our leadership, trained and abetted by the universities, actually inviting the wholesale invasion of our nation by a Fifth Column of illegal aliens and terrorists has been the norm for decades now, we are indeed embarked on WWIII.

Hollywood and Charlotte Beers notwithstanding, too many nations for far too long have seen America portrayed as a nation dedicated to wealth and conspicuous consumption with little regard for Arab nations and too much the "friend" of Israel which they rightly discern as a theocratic state, not a true democracy, and I simply can't see Ms. Beers overcoming what Madison Avenue has already accomplished by advertising that has successfully made Americans look like immoral, hedonistic fools with a like leadership intent on acquiring wealth, stuffing fat faces and buying new luxury cars and SUVs.

Copies of my letter to the President (as I informed him and is posted on my web site at http://solo.abac.com/sdghacpc/tap.htm) went to Prime Minister Tony Blair, California U. S. Senators Dianne Feinstein, Barbara Boxer, and others along with some well-known columnists. I wanted the President and these others to know that there were some Americans, those like me of the Great Generation that had experienced WWII, that knew the history underlying what we are now facing, that knew then President Truman, as columnist Cal Thomas and others have recently pointed out, had made the right decision by using the nuclear option in ending WWII and saving countless lives in the process.

But Cal Thomas has also pointed out that the nuclear option should not be discounted in the war against terrorism. Nor can it be discounted, now that the threat of a "dirty," radiation bomb using conventional explosives set off at LAX or elsewhere in America has become a very real and distinct possibility. Moslem fanatics set on killing "Infidels" and the destruction of America have no concern about making this nation a nuclear wasteland, uninhabitable for thousands of years. Allah and his prophet Mohammad will bless the total destruction of America.

Certainly Sergeant York killed in order to save lives. Certainly President Truman did the same. But we seemed to have been lacking the kind of leadership that knew either history or the enemy we are facing in failing to respond immediately and appropriately to the Attack on America. We might have had a slogan like REMEMBER THE TOWERS! not unlike REMEMBER PEARL HARBOR! But by missing the "flashpoint of history" the very real possibility of WWIII being upon us presents itself.

The universities produced educators, judges, and politicians that opposed the strengthening of our borders, denying illegal aliens and enemies of democracy easy access to America. The universities produced leaders that would make welfare a political base, those like the Clintons that proved they lacked the integrity and character to truly represent the America of our Founding Fathers and our Constitution, the America so many of my generation gave their lives for in the cause of freedom and democracy, not a welfare, socialistic society comprised of a government intent on betraying the ideals for which far better men and women paid the ultimate price and for which my generation made the sacrifices here at home in order to win that war.

The universities will never admit of not only having produced amoral scoundrels and scurrilous leaders in our schools and government, but of making it possible for a Fifth Column numbering in the thousands right here in America ready to strike, and having already done so in the recent anthrax attacks, a Fifth Column that is undoubtedly planning to kill more Americans and to plant that dirty, radiation bomb somewhere.

It is interesting to read a few columnists that are writing of the system of government in Mexico being thoroughly corrupt, a system of government based on bribery. But do we have the kind of leadership that is willing to confront this government (along with Saudi Arabia and others); even though we know that money will buy easy access to America for terrorists? Not as long as we continue to treat illegal aliens, criminals, with a welfare mentality, rewarding these criminals for their criminal activities with things like instant citizenship for their babies, free education, medical services, and food stamps.

We face some extremely hard choices here in America. Neither Hollywood nor Madison Avenue are going to be able to overcome the materialistic view of America, that we are a stupid people as per our welfare society and the failure to control our borders, concerned only for our own comfort and ever growing hedonistic way of life where Sports is King and Entertainment is Queen.

WWIII is a war of ideas, ever as much as that of WWII was. The question confronting America and all civilized nations is whether we have the better ideas? And if so, do we have the will to protect and enforce these better ideas for the sake of civilized progress as opposed to religious fanaticism, both here and abroad?

Halloween was an exciting and fun-filled event when I was a child. Two things marked Halloween 2001: We had a Harvest Moon, not seen for 46 years. And children had to be cautioned about anthrax-contaminated candy. Those of us that recall the America of the Great Generation as children have just cause to fear and weep for our children today.

***

NOVEMBER 2, 2001

THE SLIP OF A LIP MAY SINK A SHIP

Those of us that were growing up during WWII and doing our "bit" for the war effort will remember such slogans, just as we recall the blue, and sometimes, tragically, gold stars on small flags proudly displayed in the windows of the homes across America. A proud nation, imbued with the history of those like our Founding Fathers and Abraham Lincoln we had much to be proud of. Every school day began with the Pledge of Allegiance, we trusted in the righteousness of our cause in the fight for democracy against the Axis powers, we trusted our social and government institutions, we trusted our leaders from our President on down, we trusted those in police authority from the G-Men to the cops on their beat.

We willingly made the sacrifices on the Home Front peeling the foil from empty cigarette packages, participating in scrap metal and rubber drives, kids buying war stamps in the schools and adults buying war bonds. Part of our patriotism was sending Cigarettes to the fighting boys overseas (but this was a time when doctors were recommending their favorite brands).

Because my stepfather was in the Navy and stationed at Pearl Harbor when it was attacked, my mother was there and a shell landed in her kitchen. I still have the original RCA Radiogram from my grandparents asking if she was ok after the attack.

My mother kept a marvelous scrapbook during those years, filled with the memorabilia of the war years and her stay in Hawaii. As a boy, I thoroughly enjoyed going through that scrapbook, asking all kinds of questions about this or that item or picture. Just before mom died, she asked if there was anything special of hers that I would like to have. There was- The scrapbook.

As a boy, the one thing I always turned to was the page where the back of fire-blackened pocket watch was Scotch-taped. It had an inscription that read: *To Joe, with all my love. Joyce* (my mother). I recall when it was given to my mother. It was just after dark one evening when a man in a full dress Navy uniform knocked on our door. I heard him say something to my mother and he handed her a manila envelope. The burned back of the watch was in the envelope when my mother opened it. I remember her crying.

I suppose it is natural enough for an old fellow like me to reminisce about my boyhood, to have a somewhat rose-tinted memory of simple times of simple people and simple verities as I recall them. And certainly growing up in a world at war had its share of excitement; our comic books, funny papers, films and radio shows were all about the world at war. Our toys were cap guns, rubber knives and handcuffs (until the war made such toys, especially cap guns, unavailable) and my brother Ronnie and I were often dressed in diminutive uniforms of sailors or soldiers.

As children, we engaged in fantasies and games of repelling the enemy from our shores, of glorious combat and killing the "Stinkin' Japs" and "Dirty Knocksies!"

Mom saved many clippings about the war from newspapers. Of special interest to me were columns by Edgar Rice Burroughs, who was living in Honolulu at the time. And why wouldn't I be interested? After all, this was the guy that wrote *Tarzan*!

But the columns by Burroughs were filled with humor, which I always thought odd for the man that wrote such wonderful and exciting adventure stories about the life of Tarzan in Darkest Africa.

As I was recently looking at mom's scrapbook, it occurred to me that this present "war" doesn't lend itself to much in the way of humor. I don't believe there will be an Edgar Rice Burroughs poking fun at our foibles and the enemies of democracy this time around; and a Garry Trudeau notwithstanding, I don't see the cartoons of "Willie and Joe" becoming popular in the face of biological and nuclear threat.

I look at my worn copy of "Up Front" by Bill Mauldin and recall when the cartoons of this Pulitzer-winning book were new and fresh, when I was enjoying them as a boy. I thumb through my copy of James Jones' book (author of "From Here To Eternity") simply titled: "WWII." I wish everyone had a copy now and was reading it. Joseph Heller, author of Catch-22 said of it: *The most stirring and lucid account of WWII that I have ever read*. Heller was far from alone in his praise.

It is rightly said that: *Truth is the first casualty of war*. It does take propaganda and slogans to prosecute a war, and propaganda and slogans are not the stuff of truth. That is not their purpose.

As I reflect on what we Americans now face with this new war, I realize the need of propaganda and slogans. After all, slogans like *Death to the infidel*! and the pictures of maimed and dead children, stories about atrocities, should not be the sole purview of our enemies.

But I may be getting old in the head bone. There seems to be some confusion on the part of our leadership about how to prosecute this war. I recall something from childhood days about some grownups talking about a "phony war." When I grew up and studied this period of history, I learned about the phony war these grownups were talking about. But could this have anything to do with the reason I just previously put the word *war* in parenthesis? Is this present war, in fact, a "phony war?"

Chris Matthews of "Hardball" was thoroughly angered at such a suggestion recently. I do wonder at times why people would submit to his egotistical and insultingly abusive lack of good manners unless they simply want to be on TV. But if this war does have the stench of oil interests rather than being "for keeps," I suppose Americans have a legitimate right to know. I'd also like to know why the Mayor of New York thinks illegal aliens are entitled to anything due to the Attack on America, let alone free education, medical, and food stamps? He sounds too much like the Clintons, that disreputable and despicable duo that has shamed America and is unworthy to polish the boots of the men and women that gave their lives for America. Cynical? No. Just the facts as I see them as an American.

We can wave all the flags, we can bring back all the great songs like *God Bless America* (though only Kate Smith could really sing it) and the Sousa marches, but can our present leaders produce the *Rosie the Riveters* and *Willie and Joes*, those that had never so much as had Econ.101 but believed in America and its leaders?

I know those men and women in WWII that hadn't studied economics but paid the ultimate price didn't believe they were giving their lives for fat cats and tax-fattened hyenas otherwise known as politicians, they died for something we used to believe in, they died for America! But it was an America I knew as a boy. It isn't the same America now. And as the years rolled by since WWII, I saw my America being sold out by politicians intent on building their power base by giving away my America, the America better men and women than these politicians and university leaders died to protect and pass on to me and my children.

We had "Vietnam," and then "Desert Storm" where it was quite obviously: *Protect the oil and go no further*! Can our leadership have any cause to wonder if Americans have legitimate questions about this war being "for keeps?" Or, as Rambo put it: *Do we get to win this time sir*?

I wrote President Bush right after the Attack on America. One of the things I pointed out to him was that our leaders better make a good case for this war if they are to make the demands on Americans that were made on us during WWII.

In view of the way this present "war" is being prosecuted, as an American that knows our history I have given the President a most difficult assignment. But as an American, I had every right to do so. As Americans, we all have that right.

As I turn once more to mom's scrapbook, the years fall away and I'm a boy once more, believing in America and the righteousness of our cause during WWII. Will the present leadership, I ask myself, prove worthy of asking what will be required to win WWIII? Or will the decades of Political Correctness taught by the universities and carried as a banner by the enemies of America do us in? Where is the General Patton now for this generation of Americans that said *Don't die for your country, make that other bastard die for his*!

It isn't just nostalgia that makes me fearful for America, for my children and grandchildren and the civilized world as a whole. It is the apparent lack of the will to win this "war" that gives me cause to wonder? It is a fearful and haunting thought at this time and I can only hope I am wrong.

***

NOVEMBER 5, 2001

GUILT!

(FROM THE WEEDPATCH CRACKER BARREL)

Henry Thoreau wrote that if there were a document available for him to sign absolving him from membership in any organization to which he had not personally subscribed, he would willingly sign it. But, alas, no such document existed. Charles Shultz must have had this in mind when he did a strip in which Lucy had such a document, but hers absolved her from all guilt for anything that ever went wrong in the world. Now that, folks, is a document worth having!

When the demons are tormenting me for not having been a better husband, father, citizen, etc., I think a document absolving me from the guilt of World Wars, Global Warming, Ozone Depletion, Ocean Pollution, the Salem Witch Trials, SUVs, Maya Anjalou and really atrocious pretensions to poetry in general, Michael Jackson, Elton John, the Smirking Clintons and Gary Condit, etc., would be a nice thing to have. In fact, a balance sheet of the ills of the world over which I had, and have, no control and for which I am not guilty on one side and the things for which I must take personal responsibility on the other might prove a real comfort to me and would prove, undoubtedly, that I'm not such a bad fellow after all.

Of the ills of the world for which I would be able to disclaim any responsibility would be things like the "Isms" that Emerson, Thoreau, and Carl Sagen would agree make for a demon-haunted world such as Judaism, Christianism, and Islamism. Further, I never owned slaves and didn't invent Welfare or take part in the attack on Custer or the Warsaw Ghetto (well, maybe I wouldn't mind being blamed for the attack on Custer).

But maybe my thoughts about guilt have come to the fore with particular emphasis recently because of this present "war?" Maybe the constant barrage of pictures showing the poor Afghanis next to their bombed out houses or living in ragged tents, the suffering and wounded children in makeshift hospitals are making me feel guilty about the tons of bombs being dropped on "defenseless civilians?" Maybe Americans need to be "treated" to every news broadcast being opened with the pictures of those planes diving into the Towers? I have to admit that this would have a far greater impact on Americans than the "close calls" for Daschle or Brokaw and the constant barrage of the latest anthrax discoveries or how many people are slipping through airline "security."

Propaganda and Slogans: It really comes down to these in any war. One only has to consider the failure of Lyndon Johnson to properly propagandize and sloganize to be aware of the importance of such a thing. The lying hypocrite and egotistical scoundrel simply couldn't compete with *Hell No! We Won't Go*!

It might seem the height of presumption on my part to suggest that our present leaders consider four of the most world-changing men in history and take some lessons in propaganda from them: The Apostle Paul, Thomas Paine, Karl Marx, and Adolph Hitler. I would also advise them to read Harriet Stowe's *Uncle Tom's Cabin* (But my presumption about the leadership is ameliorated by the knowledge of how long it took them to realize that the food packages being dropped on Afghanistan were the same color as bombs. I won't even go into the insanity of dropping both food and bombs).

Of the men mentioned, none still captures the imagination like Hitler. He remains one of the most fascinating characters of history. The countless films, books, and presentations on TV, especially the preoccupation of the History Channel, keeps Hitler very much alive in the minds of people throughout the world. Hitler and the KKK have name recognition that any politician or Hollywood personality would cheerfully sacrifice their first born to have. Now that, folks, is the result of successful propaganda and slogans leading to events of historically world changing proportions.

While these examples point out the truism of the Devil getting the most press, any political or military leader that feels reading Machiavelli is all they need to know of deviousness in spite of it being the bedside reader of Bonito Mussolini had better think again.

I highly recommend to our leadership that they read Joachim Fest's "Hitler." As with Albert Speer, one has to be practiced in getting past any self-serving commentary in Fest. But the biography is one of the best of its kind in pointing out the absolute necessity of successful propaganda and slogans in prosecuting a war.

Does America have a "spirit" to which our leaders can appeal in order to prosecute this war? This is the first and most paramount question for which our leaders must have an answer. If so, the second question is how to make a successful appeal to this spirit of America? Now we are talking propaganda and slogans, ever as much as Paul, Paine, Stowe, Marx, or Hitler did and the very thing the enemies of America are trying for… and doing a much better job.

Fest notes: "The slogans that formulated the 'spiritual' alternatives did far more than the vague economic pledges to lead the disoriented masses toward the Nazi party… Hitler's great trick was to leap over the economic contradictions and offer instead high-sounding principles… his key weapon was his understanding that the behavior of human beings is not motivated exclusively by economic forces or interests. He counted instead on their need to have a suprapersonal reason for living and trusted in the power of an 'alternative culture' to dissolve class limits. This alternative was a 'package of slogans' - an invocation of national honor, national greatness, oaths of loyalty and readiness for sacrifice. He called for dedication without prospect of advantage."

These are the things that made America strong enough, united enough, and filled us with purpose in winning WWII, that enabled us to beat Hitler at his own game. The question is whether these things will be present for WWIII?

The masses, as Hitler rightly understood in a time of distress, wanted a stern and uncomplicated system of order. And this is what he gave them, and so successfully a German soldier decades after the war said, *Under Hitler I really lived! I haven't lived since.*

Obviously we Americans and our leaders have some very tough questions confronting us, legitimate questions that demand an answer if this "war" is to be prosecuted successfully. If this is to be a global war, as appears to be the case, will we find the necessary answers and leadership to commit to such a war?

One of my fears is that with the lack of real education so evidenced in both our citizenry and leaders, many not even knowing the history of our nation any longer thanks to the universities, or such a history at the best being a thoroughly revisionist, politically correct one, that mistakes are being made that will make fighting this war a losing proposition. Even the most fundamental problems of fighting this war are going unsolved, even unaddressed, because the leadership seems ignorant of them, the problems so well outlined by Fest that Hitler was fully aware of and addressed successfully.

Of such is the problem of "Know Your Enemy!" I ask whether the leadership either really knows our enemy or is capable of clearly defining just who the enemy is? The stench of oil interests still lingers about these things for me. Nevertheless, in what may be at least some degree of naiveté I strongly urge our leaders from the President on down to read Fest's biography of Hitler and make some notes. The better minds will read far more into what I have written in such a brief space and will, without offense, take advantage of what is offered by way of advice.

My generation of WWII was indeed a Norman Rockwell world by comparison to what our children and young people face today. It would behoove our leaders, and all Americans, to consider the difference in the decisions that will have to be made in winning this war.

***

November 6, 2001

The Struggle for Our Side of the Story

(From the Weedpatch Cracker Barrel)

I like to begin my day by punching up the Washington Post comic's section. With the particular genius of Thomas Nast having led the way, for the most part, I have found that many cartoonists give me a better slant on politics and life in America than most of our well known pundits like George Will, et al… perhaps because I wasn't born to the TV generation. I particularly liked the way Charles Shultz handled things. Snoopy didn't sweat the small stuff; he left that to Charlie Brown. BC, Hagar the Horrible, Garfield, The Wizard of Id, Barney Google and Snuffy Smith (real bit of childhood nostalgia in this one), and Doonesbury are always good for a laugh at myself when I find I am taking life too seriously.

As a man that often wonders how he could have done so many stupid things in just one short lifetime, comic relief from "life is real, life is earnest" is always welcome and I remain my own favorite source of humor. I probably enjoy poking fun at myself because so many things, stupid things, which I have done, and still do, just strike me as funny. Like the time I had put a can of hominy in a pan of water on the stove to heat it (yes, ladies, bachelors resort to such mechanisms to avoid getting out dishes you have to clean).

But the phone rang and it wasn't until I heard what sounded and felt like a truck had run into the house that I remembered the hominy. It took me two days to clean, patch the hole in the ceiling, and re-paint the kitchen. Just as an interesting scientific sidelight, I learned that exploding hominy has all the properties of Superglue. Reminded me of the time I mistakenly used baking soda for baking powder in the cornbread. The result was fascinating, a vulcanized, yellow Frisbee with the pliable consistency of a hockey puck.

Ok, so it wasn't funny at the time… just as so many things happen in our lives and we tell ourselves that someday we will look back and laugh at them. And, sure enough, time is often kind in such matters.

But like most of us, I do engage in some forms of self-abuse so one of the other sites I call up after reading the "funnies" is CNN. And while this news site isn't generally noted for a lot of yuks, today as I scrolled down something really struck my funny bone. The heading was: The Search for Intelligent Life.

Now don't ask me why, but the first thing that came to my mind was that this was an article about Congress.

I'm pretty knowledgeable in the science department; I knew the article had to do with SETI or something similar. But my doctorate is in Human Behavior. So I wondered; why did that first thought about Congress strike me? Could it have anything to do with my habit of reading the comics before I turned to more serious reading like CNN?

Nope, that wasn't it. As I analyzed the matter, it came to me that my first thought was an appropriate one, especially in respect to the way politicians are acting in this present "war" and "Home Front Security."

But there was something else. Was there intelligent life to be found in America?

Now my mind was definitely working in a serious fashion, there was nothing funny in this question. As a teacher for over twenty years beginning in the mid-sixties, I knew about the intellectual as well as the moral decline in America.

I reflected on the America I knew as a child during WWII. I recalled a moment not long past but before that fateful September 11th when I was standing at my back door, looking out at my wilderness yard of trees, rocks, and a view of the forested hills and saying to myself: This is not my America, this is no longer the America I knew as a child.

It was a very melancholy thought… and it struck me as a very odd thought and I wondered about it? Was it because I knew we had become a polyglot, mongrel nation without a definable national purpose or spirit, or so much as a national language by definition of law? Why, I thought to myself, because of decades of political correctness taught by the universities and Hollywood we don't even have a Congress that can make English the national language! Insane! Too bad, I thought, that the Congress of WWII and FDR hadn't had the foresight to do such a thing when it could have been done so easily and without controversy. But, then, how could they have ever entertained the thought that such a thing would ever be needed by way of legislation any more than our Founding Fathers, that such a thing would ever be a question resulting from the university-taught and thoroughly brainwashed political correctness of present America? As an American of the Great Generation, such a thought would have been silly to me- No longer.

Then too, that Congress and President didn't have to worry about political correctness in the form of Affirmative Action, foreign languages, in keeping our borders secure or having a Supreme Court that made laws instead of upholding the Constitution, thereby making America a socialist nation, creating a Welfare Society on the one hand and supporting the rich on the other. Didn't the Court or Congress eventually see the kind of insanity and potential bankruptcy to which this was leading America? The question of "intelligent life" began to make sense to me. It became less and less funny the more I thought about it.

What group of really intelligent persons would invite illegal aliens into a nation wholesale and even give them free education, medical services and food stamps, let alone driver's licenses and ballots in a foreign language, primarily Spanish? If you come up with any other group than the Supreme Court, Congress, and state legislatures of America please let me know.

I began to wonder about this present war in the light of how other nations, particularly Arab nations, perceive us, given the seeming stupidity of such leadership as our Supreme Court, Congress, and the California and New York governors and legislatures? Most would agree that perception is what it is all about in most cases, especially when America is no longer viewed as the "brightest bulb on the Xmas tree" when it comes to either brains or morality. If anti-American propaganda makes us appear a stupid, violent, drugged-out, immoral, hedonistic, mongrel nation without a national identity or purpose other than thorough-going selfishness with a bullying attitude, one only has to watch TV commercials for a day with brain-in-gear to understand this dismal assessment. We are now too often seen as the "Elmer Gantry" of nations flying the flag everywhere as though people really understood what it used to stand for, which makes it all the harder even for me as an American to stomach "God" being brought into the equation whether by our leaders or anyone else.

To simplify it for our Congress, which obviously needs all the simplification it can get, I'm always reminded of the football team praying that God will help them win. Now what, I reasonably ask myself, does God have against the other team?

While President Bush is saying the words that terrorism is a threat to civilization, he has yet to make the point that this is a religious war in which America and civilized nations are caught up, all of course having recourse to the Almighty like any football team or aspirant for an Oscar or Emmy, in which the historic battle between Judaism and Islamism has predominated and makes, and keeps, the world a dangerous place.

When Pat Buchanan made the comment about Congress being "Israeli occupied territory," no one laughed, and when Dolly Parton and Burt Reynolds commented on the Jewish ownership of Hollywood no one laughed. On the contrary, due to the power of Hollywood, these entertainers were constrained to apologize for their remarks. But what truth there may or not be to such remarks, the facts are not lost on Muslims when it comes to the relationship between America and Israel. And to make things even more dangerous, what leaders in either Israel or Arab nations doubts the true "friendship" of America to any of them is based on anything other than oil as was proved by the shameful hostage crisis in Iran or in "Desert Storm." At least Saddam Hussein knows he is alive because of oil interests in America.

To make a bad situation worse, the university-taught and Hollywood-led practice of aggrandizing homosexuality as per Tom Hanks and too many others isn't lost on Muslims either. No matter how many "benefits" and how much flag-waving Hollywood does, you can't have it both ways, attempting to appear patriotic on one hand and cutting America's throat on the other. The "patriotism" of perverts isn't something that was a part of the America those of the Great Generation died to protect; it isn't the America that had the spirit and identity of a people that made the essential sacrifices to win WWII. If I had to choose to be a Goebbels for America or Muslims for the sake of money as per Madison Avenue, you can easily see which would be the better bet in terms of ease for propaganda.

These things make it perfectly understandable why our leaders and pundits are struggling for appropriate propaganda and slogans in prosecuting the present war. I certainly do not envy Charlotte Beers her assignment for any amount of money.

But what the hey, what does a simple Weedpatcher and bumpkin whose favorite hymn is "Drop Kick Me Jesus Through the Goalposts Of Life" know anyway? Still, I'm smart enough to know why gun sales and requests to carry them are skyrocketing. I wonder if those in Congress know? Do any in Congress recall the history of politics in this nation when speeches were made to the sound of cocking pistols in the audience? Now that I'm thinking about it...

***

November 13, 2001

Anti-Politically Correct Now Chic

(From the Weedpatch Cracker Barrel)

I suppose it was bound to happen. When so many of the pundits begin to make fun of their previous views of political correctness we know the country has taken another fork in the road. But why am I reminded of the ease with which so many Islamic factions change sides depending on who's winning?

But I remind myself that religion has generally proven to be convenient in many ways whether in salving consciences or waging war. If T. S. Elliot could change his mind…

Now, with President Bush reaching out to Hollywood for propaganda I can't help wondering if Universal Studios will withdraw its lawsuit against Romania concerning Dracula? After all, does Hollywood really want the franchise on a creature made famous by his sucking the life's blood of human beings? Well, now that I think about it, why do images of government come immediately to mind in this context? Talk about a symbiotic relationship!

It is somewhat comical when you think about it. There is this thing of both politicians and actors being unabashed groupies in the presence of each other, Kennedy and Clinton, you know.

But it isn't "Houston we have a problem" this time. It is "Hollywood we have a problem."

The problem in a nutshell is one that government and Hollywood, trained and encouraged by the universities, has made for themselves: How to "change sides" at this stage of the game and come out believable? Facing a population that has become too sophisticated in many cases and too cynical in most cases, for the propaganda that worked in WWII it is a daunting task. Both government and Hollywood face the task of replacing those guys in robes carrying the placards reading "The End Is Near!" with believable propaganda that voices optimism in the face of too many people actually believing the end is near. Bible sales, the belief in angels and astrology are at an all time high in America; TV evangelists are experiencing a real comeback as people reach out for comfort and escape from ugly realities.

I recently wrote a lady who worried about so many Middle Eastern mechanics working on our airplanes. I pointed out to her that with the invasion of foreigners taking over so many responsible jobs in America due to the failure of our educational system to produce machinists, mechanics, doctors and nuclear physicists, the "Dumbing Down" of America, you know, mistakes are often made simply on the basis of these foreigners not really knowing the English language.

As I witnessed our vocational programs being gutted in the schools, as the universities would have it since everyone was going to go to college and didn't have to know how to run a lathe or fix an engine anymore, I realized our nation no longer had much interest in teaching kids the practical skills that had made America the richest and most self sufficient nation in history.

I got my first full-blown education in the political correctness of the universities when I did my doctoral dissertation (1975) on accountability in the schools (there isn't any) with an emphasis on vocational education and no one would publish it. The only publisher that was really honest with me was the one that said the study was too much of an indictment against the system of education and too hot to handle (In retrospect I might have had a chance if I had been going for an Ed. D. instead of a Ph.D. No one in true academia takes the work of Ed. Ds. seriously).

It may be that the recent airline disaster will be found to have happened because of a lack of communication. History is replete with disasters of this nature. One only has to look at what happened that triggered the war with Japan, the misunderstanding of the word "China" to appreciate the magnitude of which such things are potentially possible.

Recently I was to get a chest X-ray and blood test. But Medicare being what it is, I had an oriental doctor that didn't have the best command of English. She didn't make it clear that I was to go to one place for the X-ray and a different place for the blood test. Since I am not fluent in Mandarin Chinese (or whatever her native language is), I first went to get the X-ray. Here those at the place that took the X-ray simply looking at my paperwork and shuffling me through for both the X-ray and the blood test compounded the mistake. Apparently they didn't know I was to go to two different facilities either.

It was only when the results of the blood test came back that I was made aware of the problem. The doctor called me and through broken English I was told that because the blood test was done by the wrong facility, Medicare wouldn't pay for it. I got the distinct impression that the doctor was trying to tell me that she wouldn't pay for it either.

Our government and Hollywood have a similar problem. Thanks in large part to the universities, neither government nor Hollywood have personnel that are fluent in English; that is, they lack people that can communicate, those like Phil Harris described in his Darktown Poker Club song: "Talk American, big A, A, A, that's what I can understand!"

Now, folks, Peter Sellers in "Being There" could easily convince all those highly-educated and important people that he was a genius simply on the basis of his keeping his mouth shut in all the right places, or letting them attribute a great degree of intuitive genius to his simple replies to their complex questions.

But neither those in government nor Hollywood are noted for speaking "American" or for succinct and direct answers to direct and legitimate questions. Both are noted, however, for the "art," as per Voltaire and Jefferson's remarks on the subject, of removing money from the middle class of tax-paying Americans and giving it away to groups and nations that can hardly be said to have the best interests of America in mind.

Hollywood certainly wasn't talking "American" when it chose Ellen DeGeneres to represent the institution at the Emmy Awards! What did the world witness and hear by this "foreigner" standing there in the spotlight? They saw and heard an America being represented by perversion! Folks, she most certainly didn't represent me as an American! Nor, do I believe, did she represent the great majority of Americans!

But the normal (yes, the word is still in dictionaries) revulsion that normal people throughout the world have for perversion isn't the stuff of Hollywood. And more and more does it seem that our government doesn't have the "right stuff" either when it comes to perversion. There are still too many Clintons and Gary Condits out there and a Congress unwilling to confront them.

Now Hollywood, and Madison Avenue, is going to attempt to propagandize an America that the world can trust to do what's right? Good luck!

Still, I can feel some sympathy for those in government and Hollywood. In an America that is suffering an epidemic of obesity in the face of so many starving in other parts of the world, as the world watches the Bowflex and diet commercials followed by fast food commercials and advertisements for luxury cars and SUVs the mixed signals are enormous! Among my own "Handy Hints for Bachelors" I recommend that single men do not use an electric can opener and that they buy shoes with laces for the needed exercise.

Well, since there is no vaccination for plutonium or hyphenated Americans, maybe when those old quarantine cards are dusted off and start appearing for smallpox once more We the People just might get our act together.

***

November 18, 2001

Another Hitler Possible?

(From the Weedpatch Cracker Barrel)

What politician really believes they are public servants? None that I have ever known, no more than cops generally really believe they are. From the dogcatcher to the President, from the rookie on the beat to John Ashcroft, there is something about feeding at the public trough that seems to remove people from thinking in terms of either public service or public accountability. Not that the majority of such people don't believe they are, in fact, performing public service since most of them have a very low opinion of the public they "serve."

That those who are being paid through tax dollars are hired like those in our public schools and universities or elected to perform a service is usually obvious, but the thinking of such "hirelings" doesn't follow the same train of thought that punching a clock digging ditches in private industry for an hourly wage does. The not-so-tongue-in-cheek comment of Sam Clemens that an elected office in particular is a license to steal also comes readily to mind in far too many cases, and far too many like the infamous, smirking Clintons actually display contempt for the "little people" and the laws that govern the ordinary citizen, thus continuing the dirty legal tradition of "How much justice you can afford."

In recent articles and editorials, including some of my own, the point is being made that America is losing the philosophical war, and in large part because of the aforementioned items. One must be careful, however, to distinguish this from the propaganda war, though we are losing this as well, and in some cases it is an admittedly fine line in the minds of many, particularly so in view of the fact that philosophy has fallen on hard times in America due to the lack of real education and critical thinking skills requisite to philosophy and the continued exclusion of women from the *King of all Disciplines.*

But to demonize ones enemy and at the same time make your own cause one approved by God and humanity is a requisite of propaganda. The philosophical truth in such a case during wartime must often take a cautious approach, particularly so since philosophically no one can legitimately claim God's approval on one side or the other, as Lincoln so well pointed out.

If in the present state of the world we can make the case philosophically that the progress of civilization depends on factors such as eliminating ignorance, prejudice, and poverty, it would seem to follow that in order to achieve these goals certain courses of action must be pursued, and propaganda to achieve these may be argued as justified.

But the philosophical war is one in which the truth must be emphasized, and the truth (recalling Melville's cynical and too often true comment that it doesn't pay) often finds itself in opposition to propaganda. For example, the philosophical truth of the equal value of men and women is denied by the propaganda as well as the facts of most religions whether that of Hindus, Buddhists, Jews, Christians, or Moslems. For that matter, this truth is usually denied in most political systems, if not in theory, at least in practice, which accounts for the paucity of women being represented in the member nations of the UN. I was particularly keen to this here in America through our last Presidential election in which neither candidate felt they could win if they chose a woman as a running mate in spite of several worthy potential candidates being available for this office (I would not, however, shame such worthy women by suggesting that Hillary Clinton belonged in their group... The KKK and Hitler can't be beat for name recognition but...).

The more civilized nations may win this present round of the war due to better technology, but the "war" against ignorance and poverty so desperately needed that the present phase of this war emphasizes so dramatically will undoubtedly continue for many years to come and can only be won on the basis of a successful philosophy that makes the case for those nations considered the more civilized. But there are certain philosophical requirements still unmet, such as the exclusion of women, among nations considered the more civilized in order for them to successfully make their case on the basis of a promise of the progress of civilization.

Hitler more than any other figure of modern history continues to captivate minds- There are many reasons for this, not the least of which is the fact that scholars still struggle with the mechanisms of his enormous popularity with the people to the point of worship, and his enormous political success. For these reasons, among many others, he continues to be relevant in any discussion of both philosophy and propaganda.

As the "Political Pope" and the "Political Billy Sunday of Germany" Hitler was successful beyond the dreams of most leaders throughout history, either religious or political, in propagandizing, "evangelizing" if you will, an entire nation. But in spite of the advantages of a nation in disarray and appeals to nationalism and racial purity that Hitler enjoyed, a judicious consideration of the philosophy underlying his successful propaganda leads the objective scholar to the conclusion that the intuitive genius rightly ascribed to Hitler included certain philosophical truths in his propaganda.

Among these was the essential need of education that Hitler emphasized, albeit corrupted to the end of the glorification of Nazism that was far more of a religion than a political ideology, it being too contradictory to qualify as such. Contradictions are inherent and accepted in all religions, but political ideologies must incorporate logical analyses.

Also included in Hitler's program was the truth of at least attempting to eliminate class distinctions of the kind that have always plagued democratic governments in which the rich invariably get richer and the poor get poorer. Unfortunately for Hitler, Nazism bred its own class distinctions, as any religion will do, and thus thwarted the ideal of such a truth.

But no objective scholar can discount the enormous success Hitler enjoyed through the kind of propaganda he was able to formulate from basic philosophical truths. And it is these philosophical truths that modern, civilized nations must consider in prosecuting the present war if the outcome is to be a conciliation of nations to the end of meeting the needs of a world in which too many are ignorant and impoverished, here in America as well as elsewhere.

Another philosophical truth Hitler addressed successfully was that of the need of people for a spiritual dimension to their lives in order to give meaning to their lives. In addressing this need, Hitler created a cult of the state in which a cause greater than the individual could be literally worshipped, the purpose and end of all religions. In the case of Hitler, he thus became a religious leader. History makes the point that the German people wanted this more than a political leader, a not uncommon human trait. By recognizing that the role of propaganda was to achieve "an encroachment upon man's freedom of will" Hitler successfully corrupted the philosophical truth of the spiritual need of people to achieve success here as well.

While recognizing these truths, and as Dickens and others have pointed out so eloquently, civilized nations have yet to accept these truths in practice. And no amount of attempts to make a case of "God is on our side" will do other than make a bad situation worse. In all logic I doubt the world distinguishes between an American television "Praise-a-thon" and those repeating nonsense in a temple, mosque, or minaret.

For example (though this doesn't make it so) the use of *In God We Trust* here in America. The very hypocrisy of this slogan, particularly as it appears on our currency and the phrase "under God" in our Pledge of Allegiance are easily construed as hypocrisy throughout the world. So it is that a claim on God becomes counterproductive in the philosophical war in which no nation has a legitimate claim on God above that of any other.

While the "flashpoint of history" can create either a Hitler or a Lincoln, the present world circumstances leave me in doubt of which, if either will arise? And while a *cultus* of the worship of a Caesar, Jesus, or Mohammad that sometimes arises is not unfamiliar, in modern history that of Hitler's is; and few if any would compare in combining all the psychological elements on the scale of Wagnerian Grand Opera including mystical sexuality and orgasmic speeches to the multitudes that bound Hitler and the German people together.

And while the propaganda of both the Allied and Axis powers during WWII would be considered too crude for success by the standard of technology today among nations that are jaded, sophisticated, and cynical, there remain lessons to be learned especially from Hitler's propaganda of the past.

Henry Thoreau declared: I do not mean to prescribe rules to strong and valiant natures, who will mind their own affairs whether in heaven or in hell, and perchance build more magnificently and spend more lavishly than the richest, without ever impoverishing themselves...

But the mass of men (and women) that "lead lives of quiet desperation" are not of the stuff of the strong and valiant natures that mind their own affairs to the end of building and spending more lavishly without impoverishing themselves and in the process contributing to the welfare of others. Few in America take it upon themselves to cultivate a quality of the kind of poverty that leads to a freedom of the mind, rather mistakenly laboring through their lives to attain a material success that the masses consider of greater importance than freedom of their minds.

Further, Hitler recognized the need of the multitudes for a leader, a *Fuhrer*, for order in their lives that guaranteed peace and safety; that guaranteed their not having to think for themselves or be responsible for the wider issues such as geopolitics. But, admittedly, a weakness of Hitler's idealism of National Socialism was not accounting for the acquisitive nature of people, their desire for material success as well.

Americans, while no different than the German people of Hitler's era in their desire for order, peace, and safety, epitomize the mistaken notion of material success being the *sine qua non* of life, and by doing so, to use the poetic phrase, may be said to have *sold their souls* in the process, leading the Russian poets to the accusation that America lacks a soul.

The Faustian Mephistophelean elements are undeniably alive and well in America, even those elements of Machiavelli's *Prince* among its leaders. America is far from alone in these things; they are to be found in virtually all the technological nations. And it can be truthfully said that those nations that have not been successful economically envy those nations with the highest standards of living materially.

Though it is true that the leisure to engage in the arts, the cultivation of minds and manners and the progress of civilization must be bought by a degree of meeting material needs first, it may be argued that the inordinate emphasis on material success by the more technologically advanced nations has caused humanity much grief.

While I may argue the cultivation of that quality of voluntary poverty by comparison to what most construe as "success" as the better choice throughout the world, I am not naïve enough to advance that argument against the panoply of Hollywood and Madison Avenue in this country or any other. It must be sufficient for me without the need of "disciples."

Still, it remains the most difficult task confronting the advanced and materially successful nations to make their case against religious and political ideologies in other nations unless the problems of ignorance and poverty are addressed. The difficulties of conspicuous consumption will have to be overcome in order for America in particular to escape the accusations of hypocrisy in prosecuting the present war against terrorism.

I think it would be well for those that buy their meat in sanitized packages at the supermarkets to read *The Jungle* and visit the *abattoirs* where the animals are butchered. As a metaphor, this serves the purpose of calling attention to the fact that we live in a demon-haunted and dangerous world that is breeding many would be "Hitler's," and unless the problems of ignorance and poverty are addressed, the world will continue so at great risk. The primary risk, in my opinion, that we in America are taking by not doing so is the potential for laying the groundwork for another Hitler.

If the time should come when, as a Roman Senator once warned, we cannot longer endure either the problems or the solutions, it will doubtless be the result of those nations we consider being the more civilized having failed to take heed to the maxims of history and human nature.

Chapter Nineteen

November 25, 2001

GOD DAMN YOU!

(From The Weedpatch Cracker Barrel)

No, not you personally, the attention-getting and blatant phrase seemed to leap to mind after hearing the latest "God Bless You" from President George Bush. And no, the thought was not directed at the President either, and the reader will recognize that the separation of words makes this a statement, not the usual profanity that, along with so many vulgarities, has so corrupted civilized speech making many Americans appear vulgar and ignorant barbarians incapable of civilized speech and manners (not unexpectedly from a culture that has substituted Hollywood and TV for education, good books, and quality literature).

The phrase leaped to mind because it suddenly occurred to me that President George Bush is not a priest, rabbi, or minister. Does his position as President qualify his pronouncement of God's blessing upon me, upon all Americans?

Ok, I know it's just a phrase often prompted by a sneeze and not peculiar to professional religionists like Schuller, Kennedy, Copeland, and other snake oil salesmen. But if a person, even a President, is comfortable using the phrase, why shouldn't he be equally comfortable using the opposite phrase as well? If he feels qualified to pronounce God's blessing upon me, shouldn't he be equally comfortable pronouncing God's anathema upon me as well, if benediction then why not malediction? Maybe I resent this because someone like Saddam Hussein, Osama bin Laden, or some rabbi in Israel feels they can use the same phrase with at least as much legitimacy and authority as George Bush or Billy Graham? Or, maybe I've personally known too many Elmer Gantry's like images of the Clintons marching into church, Bibles in hand and approved of their minister, and see too many of them on TV? Now I'm all for people having fun with and enjoying their religion, but when they start taking it seriously and expect me to do so as well...

I'm reminded of the story passed on to me by my friend Pastor Steiner, a Missouri Synod man, of Billy Graham during his salad days offering to become a good Lutheran if they would give him his own radio show. And if you can't trust good ol' Billy ... But then, that's show biz.

Someone recently took me to task for allowing too much of Weedpatch and not enough of my professional education and literacy into my writing. It reminds me of the history teacher that took it as a personal insult that a man with a Ph.D. would ever teach vocational classes to the "rejects" in high school. So, I'm used to such criticism. But I would never allow myself to be that far removed from Weedpatch that the pretentious veneer of sophistication would ever overcome me any more than Lincoln would allow himself to be removed from his origins. I'll leave the real sophistication to those that wear it comfortably. Besides, and Lincoln evidenced this, it's fun to prick the balloons of pompous asses. Besides again, who wouldn't sacrifice their first born to be able to say: I was born in Weedpatch! I know sour grapes when I hear it.

Speaking of pompous asses ... Now I know that God, like children and education, is the stock in trade of most politicians as well as those that try to make people believe they have the inside track with the Deity by turning their collars backwards and surrounded by the trappings of holy office, pronounce the various incantations and spells from supposed holy books. In some few cases, though an affront to God in my opinion such things make good theater.

The obscenity of the Ewells in To Kill A Mockingbird placing their hands on a Bible and swearing an oath to tell the truth, then lying to send a Negro to his death is matched, in my opinion, by the scene of Clinton and so many others doing the same thing. There is just something about such creatures putting their hands on a Bible and taking an oath that makes the oath an obscenity, not to mention the distrust of such people that immediately comes to mind. After all, just how many people really believe that someone taking an oath with hand on Bible makes them trustworthy?

But in the particular case of George Bush, I find myself feeling uneasy by his use of "God Bless You" as though he were actually pronouncing a benediction. On the lips of the President it is not a meaningless or innocuous phrase and reminds me too much of "My country, right or wrong." Along with this uneasiness is the impression that the President, unlike his predecessor who was laughable in his sheer, outright hypocrisy and not expected to be taken seriously, may actually believe he is qualified to pronounce such a benediction, that he actually believes he has God's special blessing and approval of his decisions, an admittedly uneasy, if not downright fearful thought!

As with too many leaders throughout history, once that leader, like some pope, rabbi, or minister believes he has God's special approval of his decisions, any abomination in the name of God becomes possible. Certainly Hitler believed he had God's special approval and leading in his actions.

So, I'm admittedly uneasy with our President's use of "God Bless You." It makes me a little less trusting of him because unlike the professional religionist or politician we view with a comfortable and legitimate cynicism, George Bush seems to believe there is something peculiarly legitimate and sincere in his use of the phrase, something that uniquely qualifies his use of the phrase. Adding greatly to this uneasiness is the President's surrounding himself with "Bible believers." People like John Ashcroft may be relying on their own "special" relationship with the Deity in making decisions and in providing counsel to the President "in the name of God." The fact that this phrase is used by cons of every description of religion doesn't bother me as much as the possibility that the President and some of his friends take it seriously, that they somehow consider themselves in such positional favor with the Almighty that they, being the better, are correct in blessing the lesser (me, for example) for as the "Scripture" has it in Hebrews 7:7: And without all contradiction the less is blessed of the better.

Make no mistake; this present war is a religious war, made such by the atrocities committed in the name of God. And while civilized people can easily discount the use and abuse of God by those that believe atrocities are approved through their invoking the Deity, the very act of our own leaders invoking the name of God does nothing but harm on behalf of the rightness of the cause of Democracy and too easily devolves into a kind of "My God can lick your God!" Progress of civilization? Not on this basis. Ever! Once you make God the excuse for waging war, once you use God as an excuse for countering war, every conceivable crime against humanity and civilization becomes possible. And just because the President claims to be a Bible believing Christian does not give him any more authority on behalf of God or to speak for God than that of Osma bin Laden, as I am certain Abraham Lincoln would inform George Bush.

When I was a child, I would hear the story of a relative that was very religious and didn't believe in doing any work of any kind on Sunday; "keeping the Sabbath," he called it. But he had chickens that had to be fed daily. So, on Saturday evening, he would place a pan of chicken feed on the top of the gate post to the chicken yard and Sunday mornings he would "accidentally" hit the post with his shoulder knocking the pan of feed into the yard.

Silly? Why of course... but not to that relative, who was very sincere in his beliefs as was Cotton Mather.

This "God" thing that politicians of every stripe, both foreign and domestic, love to use causes a lot of stress when it isn't downright silly. And stress, like ignorance and prejudice, can be a real killer.

It may be that the God thing that is at the basis of this present war has contributed to some stress on the highways. I travel highways 99 and 5 quite a bit. These main roads of California get a lot of traffic, and if you want to witness the "lawlessness" of We the People, just drive these highways (or make your way through the traffic at LAX).

My daughter, son-in-law and grandchildren live in Modesto. Going to see them for this Thanksgiving, I found myself having to drive 80 in a 70mph zone just to keep up with some of the traffic and not get run over. At this, there were people commonly driving 100. The big rigs especially make this a nightmare!

In the 534 miles round trip, I didn't see one single California Highway Patrolman! And I couldn't help wondering: Where are the cops... especially during the most traffic-heavy holiday of the entire year?

Stress. Driving a few hundred miles under these circumstances will do it. But if total disregard for the law, not to mention safety, are a sign of the times you can easily witness this on our roadways. Adding to the problem is knowing that many of these drivers are drunk or high on drugs, are driving without insurance or even valid driver's licenses, especially so in California where so many illegal aliens are on our highways. If you want an exercise in frustration, have your car totaled by an illegal alien. You will discover, as I did, they have more protection by government than a legal citizen in such a case! And, of course, you have no protection by law from illegal aliens or any chance whatsoever of collecting damages.

It was most disconcerting during this recent trip to see how many old vehicles with bad tires, no current registration, and you assume, no insurance since half of California drivers don't have insurance, would go whizzing by at 90 to 100mph; and, of course, the big rigs.

With only two lanes, these behemoths of the road easily block traffic while passing each other. The 55mph limit for these trucks is treated as a bad joke. More lawlessness... and how many of these truck drivers are on drugs?

Now I know truck drivers; I used to work as a mechanic for heavy equipment and met many of them. I even hauled tomatoes in a double trailer rig one summer in the San Joaquin Valley so I've had some experience on the road with this "society."

With this background my uneasiness about one of these rigs coming up on me at 90mph is justified, kind of like my stint in Aerospace and seeing how airplanes are actually put together and maintained making me fearful of getting on a jetliner.

But in an age of political correctness and ever increasing ignorance on the part of most Americans (if you don't believe this, just watch a few TV commercials), it is easier to go along with the stupidity of the kind of "Road

Warrior, Cowboy" and "Outlaw" mentality of too many of these people fabled in bad movies and equally bad Country Western music without calling attention to the fact that maturity, education, intelligence, and lack of a criminal record are not prerequisites for a license that puts you behind the wheel of these lethal monsters of the road.

When you think of how many "societies" within society that exist like truck drivers that consider themselves to be as far above the law as our past President and his wife, most politicians and judges, rock stars, Hollywood celebrities, and evangelists, it isn't any wonder we have some of the problems we do on our roadways. As to those speeding tickets that us poor "civilians" get, they are not only expensive but the average citizen knows his word, even with five witnesses in the car and an attorney, is worthless against that of a single "Chippy" in court (Funny, you never think of the tickets you didn't get but you always remember the ones you got when the officer flat lied! a personal experience of mine on two separate occasions). You would think this would slow people down, but it hasn't.

While the exigencies of war dictate certain police powers superseding civil rights in some cases, my own experiences with the abuses of such power, particularly by those that like to invoke God in the process, are legitimate grounds of concern. And with such a situation, stress increases.

This present war has aggravated the problem of stress phenomenally. I see it to an exaggerated degree in the way people are now driving with a "To hell with it, there is no tomorrow" mentality.

Stress will make good people do bad things. In my own experience as a husband and father, stress has caused me do bad things I wouldn't have done otherwise. In my work in the schools and Child Protective Services, I have witnessed this demon of stress make otherwise good parents abusive parents. My experience in such things has made me an advocate of those that are opposed to striking a child under any circumstances! Logically, I can't see this, along with the violence in films and TV, as anything but provoking and promoting violence in children.

I recall the time my grandfather broke my left elbow with a stick of firewood. It was the closest thing to hand he could find to hit me with. I can't even recall the infraction I had committed but I think it had something to do with my not having done the dishes when I was supposed to.

Now my grandfather was not a bad man, he was an exceptionally good man and he had seldom ever done such a thing. But looking back, I understood the stress he was under with my grandmother being an invalid, his worry about money to pay the bills, our living conditions, all these things came together in an instant that drove him to a sudden loss of his rational mind and made him commit such violence for an inconsequential lapse on my part.

This understanding in no wise excuses what my grandfather or any other may do of such a nature. But it is exactly that: Understanding... though actions do carry consequences, regardless of how much understanding may apply.

For example, there is no mystery about why children suffer substantially more abuse from living in the "homes" of welfare mothers where ignorance and poverty are a way of life. But actions carry consequences regardless of the stress or socioeconomic factors.

Another source of stress today is found in the mixed signals of government. Are we in a war or not? Unlike Korea and Vietnam, if we are in a war now is it a war our leaders are committed to win?

Asking the help of Hollywood for propaganda is just another source of stress. Just how much help of this nature can such a blatantly immoral and hypocritical institution provide? Hollywood, like the universities, is notorious for espousing homosexuality and every other form of perversion and violence and the world at large still views perversion as exactly that: Perversion! No amount of the corruption of language in calling perversion "Gay" will make such people happy, spreading joy and cheer. Nor will it make every pervert a loving, Berkleyite liberal devoted to the arts and peace as per Tom Hanks and Ellen DeGeneres.

In reflecting on this hypocrisy of Hollywood, I'm reminded of the liberal professor I once had that took the "cure" when he rented his house in Beverly Hills to a group of perverts. By the time he had effected the eviction, it cost him well over a hundred thousand dollars in legal fees and repairs. Odd isn't it, how economics dictate so much of "values."

But as with those that espouse a so-called "liberal" attitude toward perversion, it only takes having their own child molested or murdered by such a person for them to take the "cure." Unfortunately for America at this point in history, just what will it take to "cure" the political correctness that has led us into this morass where there are no moral absolutes of civilized behavior? Where is our leadership to look for the moral vindication that gives them the authority to "preach" to other nations?

Whether God Bless You! or God Damn You! it will take moral and civilized leadership devoid of the toxins of perversion and religion to convince me that those that use such invocations on behalf of The Almighty have the right to do so. Until such a time, I will continue to take offense. And worry, because there is such a thing as normal, civilized behavior and water and oil don't mix, nor does faith and oil.

***

November 28, 2001

From The Weedpatch Cracker Barrel

Times change but human nature doesn't. People still do the same things for the same reasons they always have whether of need, greed, jealousy and envy, avarice, the time-honored list goes on. But I'm fond of Henry Thoreau's point concerning fashion that "the head monkey at Paris puts on a traveller's cap, and all the monkeys in America do the same." It would indeed take a "strong press" to squeeze the notions out of some people. Some would suffer physical torture rather than be caught wearing a patch on their "pantaloons" or skirt in our "plastic and styrene throw away society."

Now, what I resent about this fashion slavishness is that I miss my two-tone perforated shoes. Further, I think the Head Monkey that decided men should wear ties and couldn't carry sensible purses with sensible mirrors in them should have been strangled at birth!

But, let's face it; America is now the Head Monkey in many respects including being the land of conspicuous consumption. And many nations hate us for our prosperity that has led us to this kind of society. While I can understand Rhett shooting the pony, it wasn't the fault of the poor animal that his little girl died. If Moslem terrorists believe that "shooting" America will make their lot better, logic dictates otherwise. And in the case of the Attack on America, we had better not allow emotions to overcome reason on our part either.

I'm with Arianna, do our "bit" by dispensing with unnecessary mailings like Xmas cards. But, then, I haven't sent Xmas cards since Currier and Ives went out of business so I'm not exactly sacrificing this to the "war effort." And I'm with Kathleen Parker concerning pacifists; there is no room for them during this crisis any more than we had room for them in WWII. Logic does dictate that when it comes to terrorists it is a kill or be killed proposition. Let's get real folks, there is no pacifying either dictators or religious terrorists. But as Kathleen and many others would agree, there is always a need for dissenting voices or this wouldn't be America. However, we can't afford to take leave of reason in the process; the stakes are far too high for the entire world in this instance!

I like Buckley's point (possibly because I have made the same point many times) that when confronting evil with equal determination to win, the rules of civilized behavior do not apply. I wish we could turn back the clock to pre Sept. 11 but we can't, and we had better accept the fact that we have little choice but to do everything within our means to defeat terror, and the "Fifth Column" of millions of illegal aliens and foreigners here on the basis of fraudulent declarations of their intentions, fraudulent "marriages," etc., had better be caught and shipped out post haste (no criticism of our postal system intended, at least in this instance)!

My sympathy for Moslem or any other religious regimes is non-existent. These people have chosen the tyranny of religion with its concomitant misery over that of reason and human rights for their populations, especially for women, and I will do all in my power to confront and overcome them. I do not believe the world can be safe or make any progress in civilization as long as any theocratic state, including that of Israel or any other kind of dictatorship holds sway in any part of the world.

Well we can certainly hear the opening shots being fired here in the homeland as a result of September 11. A college history professor is facing termination for making the statement to his class on this date of infamy that "anyone that can blow up the Pentagon gets his vote." The case will, of course, go to court. Now, if he had said that Israel is an apartheid state and should be blown up or all Negroes should go back to Africa or all illegal aliens or homosexuals or child molesters should be shot no one would be questioning his termination, but the attack on the Pentagon, that's ok and the professor's hailing this with his blessing should fall into the category of "academic freedom."

There is certainly nothing unusual in a university professor calling for the demise of democracy in America (or the demise of America under any circumstances) and substituting communism or some other form of socialism. There is nothing unusual in any hare-brained pronouncement coming from the Ivory Tower of academia and "blest with a text" along the same line as the most ignorant and prejudiced Bible-thumper. But such pronouncements must be within the politically correct parameters of the time and set by university standards. You can bless terrorists that blow up the Pentagon but don't touch perverts, illegal aliens, or welfare; understandably since most teachers and professors live by a form of welfare called "tenure" like that of most federal jobs that don't even require tenure.

I watched and listened as Tom Tancredo (R-Colorado) tried to make his case for getting tough on illegal aliens. With several million of these now in America it would be a monumental task to track them all down. Now why did it take the attack on the Towers and the Pentagon to make some politicians aware of the fact that a nation that cannot control its borders cannot survive as a nation any more than a nation that fails to cherish its young!

In my home county of Kern in California, thirty per cent of the population speaks Spanish and twenty per cent live below the poverty level. Perhaps this makes me more sensitive to the problem than our legislators, none of which live in poverty but many of which like Gray Davis and Mayors Willie and

Jerry Brown depend on welfare, illegal aliens, and bad-mouthing conservatives like me for their political base.

With visions of the Nazi Gestapo dancing in their heads, university liberals and their allied politicians and attorneys, all good university graduates from the right schools, are horrified that our government might begin to pay serious attention to illegal aliens and those like the scum that were welcomed by these universities, these institutions being far above the laws governing us poor civilians, who drove those planes into the Towers and the Pentagon. But leave it to the universities to graduate the kinds of attorneys that had those who attacked America survived, would have their years of defenses and appeals in the courts no matter how many innocent lives they had taken. If only those poor, misguided Germans been tried in our courts rather than before that Nuremberg tribunal. If only Hitler had lived to face our court system and had a Johnny Cochran… but I digress.

I'm not sure why this makes me think of Gary Condit preparing to run for reelection. He is, you know. Given the reputation of Congress and politicians in general, why shouldn't an immoral, hypocritical scumbag like Condit go for it and find himself welcome? There are always more interns and ever-greater opportunities with so much going on since the Attack on America to get money the old fashioned way by stealing it. I never tire of quoting Sam Clemens who said: "Judas Iscariot was only a premature Congressman" and "An honest politician is one that hasn't had time to sell out."

Who doubts that the WTC and Pentagon was only the first blow and that more are to follow? I don't think Ali Salem, the well known and much respected Egyptian writer, would disagree since he has called attention to the fact (a fact that I have repeated many times) that with the Attack on America East and West are on a collision course in which I am of the opinion that America will eventually find itself primarily alone. Attack Iraq, Iran, Syria, Somalia, Lebanon, North Korea, and every other nation, an estimated nearly sixty of them, harboring and abetting terrorism, working on WMD (meaning Weapons of Mass Destruction, our latest addition to the NWV meaning "New World Vocabulary").

The International Red Cross says that killing Osama bin Laden is against humanitarian law. I am quite certain that I am not the only one who appreciates the philosophical difficulties encountered when struggling with the issues raised while trying to be civilized in the face of such a thing as the barbarism of terrorism. Does justice have anything to do with this? What does justice demand in the case of an Osama bin Laden? Was the issue settled in Nuremberg? I think not.

First Lady Laura Bush is certainly correct in pointing out that the issue of equal rights for women is crucial to any government in Afghanistan. What she neglected to point out was that this is an issue that needs to be addressed in all Moslem nations. It could take a few decades to happen, but it's a good thing the First Lady didn't say "equal value" for women since America and most of the world is still working on this problem with no end in sight.

Ok, so I'm a writer, an author, a philosopher, albeit not the most traditional kind. I enjoy the subtleties of complex questions and the many areas of inquiry such questions arouse. Like Clara Bow in respect to God and the "hereafter" I have the same question: Why can't we know?

But recalling WWII, I wrote President Bush and made the outrageous statement that if this is a real war our leadership had better make the case for it before making the demands that were made on us during those years of '41 through '45!

While I thoroughly enjoy the world of subtle ideas found in philosophical exploration, there are pragmatic questions requiring equally pragmatic answers facing us as a nation. I don't think Americans are ever going to be gulled by a lying scoundrel like Lyndon Johnson again; I don't think there will ever be room for any more Clintons (of either sex) in this crisis.

Americans, the whole civilized world, need leadership they can trust to fight this war to win. Now, it is up to the present leadership to make its case to us, a case that cannot look to the Ivory Tower or even Hollywood or Madison Avenue to make such a case. Like Phil Harris, I want to hear the leadership talking "American" without hiding behind the flag or either the University or God thing obfuscating the real issues at stake for my children and grandchildren.

***

NOVEMBER 30, 2001

SANTA

It seems the folk in a place called Kensington decided to eliminate Santa from its public Xmas display, their reason being that the emphasis was to be on American patriotism without any religious theme.

The mayor of this town, Lynn Raufaste, in commenting on the outcry and the thousands of responses across the country said "Somebody said they saw it on CNN, and I said 'Jeez, we've ousted the Taliban!'"

Even a spokesperson for the ACLU commented, "I doubt that a court would tell Kensington they could not have a Santa Claus."

At this point I decided to reprise a few remarks I made a few years ago about the jolly, old elf:

Two of the most endearing qualities of a child are trust and imagination. They will believe in magic, they thrill to stories of fairies and enchanted lands. Christmas, Santa Claus, the Easter Bunny, stories of birds and animals, enchanted islands and forests; these are the domain of childhood.

We don't forsake these things in adulthood. We continue to want our Merlins, Camelots, and enchanted glades. As parents, we enjoy making things like Santa and his elves and reindeer real to our children. All too quickly, we grow up and learn of the fantasies of childhood but the intent of parents in wanting their children exposed to the myths is the innocence of goodness.

Santa is the ultimate angel to a child. There isn't the slightest trace of evil connected to Santa; he could never do anything wrong or anything to hurt a child. Santa believes in children, in the innocence of childhood.

Our desire, as adults, to believe in angels follows the same pattern. We grow up and have to leave the myth of Santa, but we desperately want to continue to hold on to what he represents.

The emphasis of Santa relating to children is the basis of his enduring popularity. He personifies the love of children and the best of childhood as no other figure, historical or mythological.

Yes, Virginia, there is a Santa Claus. Who will forget these words to a little girl written by Francis Church for the New York Sun in 1897?

His concluding words to little Virginia:

Alas! How dreary would be the world if there were no Santa Claus. It would be as dreary as if there were no Virginias. There would be no childlike faith then, no poetry, no romance, to make tolerable this existence...the eternal light with which childhood fills the world would be extinguished...The most real things in the world are those that neither children or men can see.

Did you ever see fairies dancing on the lawn? Of course not, but that's no proof that they are not there. Nobody can conceive or imagine all the wonders there are unseen and unseeable in the world.

Thank God! He lives, and he lives forever. A thousand years from now, Virginia, nay, ten times ten thousand years from now, he will continue to make glad the heart of childhood.

The Christmas season with the distinctive music and decorations, the buying of gifts, the celebration of the hope of peace on earth, is something none of us would like to see disappear.

Singing Jingle Bells, Santa Claus is Coming to Town and reading 'TWas the Night Before Christmas celebrate the season. Children write letters to Santa and hang stockings with care and we watch A Christmas Carol, It's a Wonderful Life and Miracle on 34th Street. We have added The Grinch to the story of Scrooge, there is now a Charlie Brown Christmas, Frosty the

Snowman, The Little Drummer Boy, Rudolph and so many more with all the innocence, charm and fantasy of childhood.

The story of the North Pole, Santa's home and the workshop of elves, the magic of Santa's being able to visit every home with a child in a single night, going down chimneys, his Ho, Ho, Ho, children leaving cookies and milk for him and, very important, Santa knows if you have been bad or good, naughty or nice.

Believing in Santa is as natural to a child as faith and prayer.

Childhood is of so very short duration, such a short time in which to teach and encourage children in the things that will prepare them for adulthood. The whole concept of Santa is one of the things that will do this. We know that all too soon our children will face the realities of the denouement of Santa. But the lesson of goodness and the memory of the magic and innocence of childhood, like the healing power of a mother's kiss, should remain.

Of the greatest importance is the fact that Santa loves all children no matter the physical or mental differences, the race, religion or geography. This is what children learn from Santa.

The non-Christian world recognizes the jolly old elf, separating him from sectarian religious beliefs. He is welcome in Turkey, China, Cuba and even Iraq!

And unlike the cruel religious wars of Christianity, Judaism and Islam, none have ever been fought over Santa Claus.

December 1, 2001

War Is Fun!

(From The Weedpatch Cracker Barrel)

I was running low on cat food and the resident feline (otherwise affectionately known at times as "Damned Cat") must have known this as she realized she was getting short rations in her food dish. So, she left a very large, deceased gopher at my back door. Cats are great for their subtle behavior as any reader of Garfield can appreciate (But I do wonder who the fool was that told President Bush being seen with a dog on a leash made him appear "Presidential"?).

Of course, nature has always been "red in tooth and claw" but is humankind doing any better?

Because of the Attack on America, the world now realizes that Moslem nations are "family" as evidenced by the meeting and failure to get agreement in Germany. And even if some kind of coalition government is formed, check the odds in Vegas as to how long such a "government" will last? These families have been warring on each other for centuries, and largely because of ignorance and poverty it is a way of life for them and they enjoy it; to them (at least to the men) war is fun. The Christian Crusaders found this to be fun as well and, as usual throughout history, all in the name of God. This is always a nice touch to lend legitimacy to any war.

But we all know what can happen when any outsider steps into a family dispute. Is it any wonder that America is having some difficulty finding friendly faces in places like Saudi Arabia or Kuwait? And how long can Americans expect any other Moslem nation to remain "friendly" as the war continues, especially if we go after Iraq, Sudan, Somalia, etc.?

Ok, so we could care less about Islam and are not warring against the religion. But how do Moslem nations perceive this? To such nations it must sound like Hillary's reply (I believe) to her husband in retaliation for Monica: "But Bill, dearest, he was having sex, not me." At least I know ol' Bill would be able to appreciate, in his case even admire, his wife's parsing.

As to military tribunals vs. criminal courts I don't think any one wonders at salivating lawyers like Johnny Cochrane and others such as egotistical politicians not wishing to be cut out of the loop, a loop with lots of photo ops and full employment for those that make America the most litigious nation in history. Besides, if you ask these suckers at the public teat they will tell you that Americans really want to have the hundreds of millions of dollars it would cost to publicly try terrorists spent for such a purpose. But for those politicians, largely lawyers themselves, whose power base is welfare, illegal aliens, those here on fraudulent visas, etc., and giving away America for the dollars they pocket I have a bulletin: You didn't ask this American!

I know America has fallen on hard times when it comes to literacy and the reading of quality literature. Even so, you would think politicians are literate enough to know the classics having to do with "Justice Deferred." But, then, it seems most politicians would like to translate real justice as "Justice By Committee." I think Americans are getting more than a little weary of this, especially after things like the Simpson and Clinton debacles.

War has been "fun" since time immemorial and isn't likely to cease to be so for the foreseeable future. There has never been a lack of young cannon fodder to meet the call to the "high" of shooting at people and getting shot at in return, the "musket worshippers" as Emerson so well named them, and few young men want to trade their swords for a plow.

Since philosophers and psychologists have exhausted their repertoires in attempting to explain this phenomenon of human nature, it still remains that men make war, not women. By now you would think people worldwide would get the message. But not so because men lead the world, not women, and until women make their place in philosophy, denying men the sole purview of "explaining" and controlling the destiny of nations and by doing so become accepted as of equal value to men, this isn't likely to change.

What has changed due to September 11 is the fact that the world has become a much more dangerous place than civilized nations seem to have realized. Neither Americans nor Russians unleashed their atomic arsenals because the governments of both nations had systems that prevented religious mad men from controlling these arsenals.

But the whole picture has changed since the Attack on America and the civilized world now realizes that the fanaticism of religion, including the Nazi religion of Hitler, knows no bounds of civilized rules or behavior. You would have thought that the religious wars of the past, the fact that ignorance and poverty together with their concomitant denigration of women is the breeding ground of war being "fun" would have taught the more scientific, technological and civilized nations to beware and prepare.

It didn't happen, and now we have to face the ugly and brutal fact that prejudice, ignorance, and poverty do sow the seeds of destruction wherever they hold sway, whether in a home in America or in a nation.

Were it not so tragic in its consequences I could have laughed at the school district in Texas that is holding meetings on countering bullying in the schools and at the same time allows pupils to be struck with clubs, otherwise known as "paddles." You are going to try to teach non-violence to children and at the same time commit violence against children? Not an unusual position and paradox for those of the "Ivory Tower" or many politicians and parents that believe committing physical violence against children is a correct form of "discipline." So, speaking of ignorance...

While few would disagree that ignorance is a real killer, the enemies of the progress of civilization have remained a constant: prejudice, ignorance, and poverty. Crank in the factors of human nature such as envy, jealousy, greed and avarice, ego, regardless of the society or the position in society and you have the makings of continued warfare.

It is a truism that terrorism, being essentially mindless, can only be overcome by greater terror. Crude as it is, in the words of Hitler: You bash their heads in!

My, but don't we wish reason could prevail. But, terrorism being mindless is the expression of insanity and you cannot reason with insanity. And when God is used as the basis of the insanity, the situation is obviously hopeless.

We incarcerate people judged insane, but what to do about an insane nation or in the rapidly growing crisis of present events, the insanity of a number of nations? The present insanity is fomented by the factions considering Jerusalem a Holy City; and once you believe something holy, including the various books, Bibles, etc. you have removed yourself from any possibility of civilized, political "cures." Just let America declare that it does not go along with this "Holy" nonsense and we will quickly discover even Israel against us. Moslems and Jews will never acquiesce to any political or geographical plan that does not give Jerusalem to one or the other.

For that matter, Moslems know full well that America would come down on the side of Jews and Christians. The stupidity, to be charitable, of Clinton lighting a "National Menorah" last year spelled this out in unmistakable terms to all Moslems. Now I would be the first to vote for Santa since the jolly, old elf is welcome even in Iraq! And no religious war has ever been fought over Santa.

But as long as the drum is being beat for the myth of a "Judeo/Christian America" and Tom Paine is ignored, we can anticipate a "Post War World" that will include war continuing to be "fun" for untold millions for as long as religion is a basis for war.

Immediately following the Attack on America I voiced my wish that America's leadership had retaliated that same day with a nuclear cruise missile on Kabul. Like the two atomic bombs dropped on Japan, this would have made for a short war. Once America had proved by an immediate and appropriate response it would not tolerate attacks murdering our civilian population under any circumstances, the message to all other nations would have been unmistakable and what nation would have dared to oppose us?

But that opportunity was missed; a flash point of history was lost. Now? How many billions of dollars of American taxpayer's money will politicians give away to Moslem nations in order to appease them for the sake of their "friendship" and oil? And what fool believes that money will ever placate religious insanity?

There are an estimated one billion Muslims worldwide. Factor in the number of religious non-Moslem people that are equally committed to their superstitions not amenable to reason and like all strictly religious thinking not distinguishing between beliefs and facts, and you have a problem of unimaginable magnitude, you have the present problem of a "demon-haunted" world!

***

DECEMBER 3, 2001

THE WEEDPATCH CRACKER BARREL

I was reading the headlines of December 2 when something caught my attention. I thought it read: Daschle Fumigated. Knowing this was too good to be true, I looked at it again and realized it read: Daschle Suite Fumigated -

Funny how your eyes and mind work together to make sense of things. Now why, I wondered, couldn't the paper have made an error that worked in favor of the reader? Honestly now, how many people really believe politicians need fumigating? Silly me, if they didn't do it to Clinton and Condit… though a few carping critics might say politicians and their appointees have the potential of full time employment for several crews of pesticide companies.

It recently occurred to me for the umpteenth time that in all the years America's leaders have chased enemies of every description abroad, it never seems to have crossed the minds of any of these leaders to have Special Ops go after the domestic, home-grown terrorists in places like Watts or Southeast Bakersfield, areas where gangs terrorize entire neighborhoods at will and witnesses are murdered with impunity.

But given what some are already complaining about concerning the "Civil and Constitutional Rights" of terrorists and illegal aliens, I can certainly hear the howls rending the heavens should the police be given the tools necessary to bring law and order to places like Watts. Too many politicians depend on the universities and welfare populations for keeping them in office to even consider such a thing.

A California policy says sex offender status can be given to inmates who have been arrested, detained or charged with sex crimes. The Supreme Court recently upheld this policy in Garcia v Henry, 01-532. Having proposed a U. S. Constitutional amendment for the protection of children from molesters I would be the last person to fault this California policy. But it can readily be seen from this decision of the high court that there is little legal basis for "liberals" of any stripe to fault those actions necessary to protect our nation!

Hurrah! for the Santas of Kensington. They came and conquered! Santa is alive and well in the town that tried to ban him and make him a religious figure. And thanks to all of you folks that responded to my article on Santa, I never really held with the motto: Scrooge was right! I was particularly indebted to Sam Lerner who appeared in Kensington with a sign reading: Jews for Santa, Rockville Chapter. As I pointed out, religious wars have never been fought over Santa and he is even welcome in Iraq. Too bad he isn't the patron saint of politics in all nations. Children aren't the only ones that need Santa Claus.

December 7 is near at hand as I write and I always recall that date of 1941 vividly in spite of my being only six years old at the time. The memory of this date is indelible for many reasons, but largely because my stepfather was stationed in Pearl Harbor during the attack and my mother was with him. A shell landed in her kitchen and she still seemed to be in shock from the attack upon her return to the States a short time later.

I have a lot of pictures and keepsakes of the war years. When my mother died, I received two metal lamps fashioned like lighthouses that my stepfather, who was a navy machinist's mate, had made. Shortly before her death, my mother asked if there was anything special of hers that I wanted. The lamps and her scrapbook that she had started in 1939 and filled with pictures and mementos of the war years were the only items I requested.

Admiral Yamamoto upon learning that Japan's ultimatum was delivered fifty-five minutes after the attack on Pearl Harbor rather than the promised one-half hour before the attack: "I fear all we have done is to awaken a sleeping giant and fill him with a terrible resolve."

Those of us that Remember Pearl Harbor, that were growing up during the years of WWII know full well the truth of Yamamoto's dire prediction. The sneak attack on Pearl Harbor did indeed fill Americans with a terrible resolve, one that carried us through every demand our leaders made upon us for the war effort. No sacrifice was too great to destroy the vicious and cowardly enemy that had committed such a reprehensibly despicable atrocity! Americans did and gave all that was asked of them in order to win the war.

Of course, it would be many years later before we would learn of the mistakes our leaders had made, dreadful mistakes that had made the surprise attack so successful. Had we known of these at the time I am not so certain that some of our leaders would have received such whole-hearted cooperation; in fact, I'm not so certain but what some of them might have been shot or lynched by the homefolks! Some of these mistakes were the result of sheer ego, absolutely inexcusable! Had some of these military leaders been tried in open court I am certain they would have faced hanging or a firing squad! Some of the civilian leaders, politicians, would have needed "court tasters" for fear of being at the least poisoned!

I'm a good student of the history of events leading up to WWII and the things that took place during those years. For sheer stupidity, greed, and mistakes made through egos it is a matchless, at times shameful and disgraceful, piece of the history of America. Nothing can stain the history of those that fought and those that made the ultimate sacrifice for winning the war. Nothing can stain the history of those on the home front that did all they could sacrificially to provide what was needed by those that did the actual fighting. But among some of our leaders, civilian and military, there is enough stain to go around and then some.

Now, we Americans are being asked to support our civilian and military leaders once more following another "Pearl Harbor," a "Date that will live in Infamy" even more heinous than that of December 7, 1941 in that it was a purposeful and calculated attack on innocent civilians, not on our military. And that history of WWII with which I am so intimately familiar floods my mind with facts of both the heroism and sacrifices of Americans during that war together with the stupidity, greed, and egos on the part of so many of our leaders during that era.

Granted that we have made phenomenal advances in technology, I see no evidence that we have made any advances in changing human beings for the better, I see no evidence that humankind has overcome those factors of stupidity, greed, and egos so evident on the part of many of our leaders during WWII.

Example: The failure to take out Saddam Hussein by then President Bush, Sr., and the dismantling of our intelligence capability under the Clinton administration with the approval and cooperation of lapdog Reno and others. The ignoring of information, as with warnings about the attack on Pearl Harbor, by those under Clinton and Reno's control about al Qaeda and, as a result, becoming the Gang That Couldn't Shoot Straight was textbook egotistical stupidity! And who knows but what that early information that was spurned could have prevented September 11?

Now, with the Enron boondoggle and the principal being a FOG (Friend Of George) one Kenneth Lay, how will our President handle this one? Will he do the honorable thing and respond as Arianna Huffington and others have asked? Or will he evade and leave American taxpayers to foot this enormous bill spawned by the greed of industry and political leaders?

As a Californian, and with Enron having so much influence in my home state, I have a few reasonable questions of my governor Gray Davis: What did you know about Enron and Kenneth Lay and when did you know it? Did it have anything to do with the bankrupting utility bills and blackouts we faced? What part did you play in such an association that has left California in such deplorable financial condition?

You can see that the ego, greed, and stupidity factors concerning leadership have not changed since the time of WWII.

One thing is decidedly different from that era of WWII: The most fearful weapons of mass destruction, weapons of chemical and germ warfare now have to be considered in every decision made by our present leaders! And the seeming inexhaustible supply of stupidity, mistakes, and egos on the part of present leaders that marked some of those of the years of WWII hasn't lessened a whit by the passage of time. Not a fact from which any of us would derive any peace of mind or inspire Americans to make the sacrifices we made in the years '41 through '45 that this present war will, I firmly believe, eventually require.

Near the end of the war in the Pacific, a young Japanese pilot put my concern in words so eloquently poignant and precise that I can do no better than to quote his last thoughts:

Ensign Heiichi Okabe
22 February 1945

I am actually a member at last of the Kamikaze Special Attack Corps.

My life will be rounded out in the next thirty days. My chance will come! Death and I are waiting. The training and practice have been rigorous, but it is worthwhile if we can die beautifully and for a cause.

I shall die watching the pathetic struggle of our nation. My life will gallop in the next few weeks as my youth and life draw to a close...

...The sortie has been scheduled for the next ten days.

I am a human being and hope to be neither saint nor scoundrel, hero nor fool - just a human being. As one who has spent his life in wistful longing and searching, I die resignedly in the hope that my life will serve as a "human document."

The world in which I live was too full of discord. As a community of rational human beings it should be better composed. Lacking a single great conductor, everyone lets loose with his own sound, creating dissonance where there should be melody and harmony.

The knowledgeable reader will not confuse Ensign Okabe with the mad men that attacked America on September 11. Nor will such a reader confuse those that attacked innocent civilians with Ensign Okabe.

But this young pilot that gave his life for his nation did so on the basis of the stupidity, greed, and egos of some of his leaders, both civilian and military. And he did so with the same trust and confidence in these leaders that we had in our own during this time.

While giving himself freely to what we would consider an insane act, that rational part of his mind, with which I am certain we would all agree, was quite active in his parting remarks for posterity.

The last words of this brave, young man have haunted me for years. I can only wonder at what his thoughts would be considering the present world in which the discord has not only not lessened, but has increased to a most dangerous degree!

In the sixty years since Pearl Harbor I would like to believe our leaders are competent and trustworthy. But perhaps I've lived too long and know too much for me to be comfortable with such a belief. And the world lacking a "single great conductor" I suppose there are multitudes in America as well as other nations that share my concern.

I wonder about that young Russian Missileer that played a hunch and did not launch a nuclear attack on America some years ago. There are always those things that the film "Fail Safe" made so clear that haunt us. As technology and our reliance on technology increases, so does the potential for dreadful consequences in the event of failure increase; not everything falls into the category of Dean Kamen's "Ginger."

When you factor in the potential for such consequences based on the stupidity, mistakes, and egos that still plague humankind, it is indeed a very dangerous world, made even more so by the plagues of ignorance and poverty that holds sway in so much of the world!

With the most recent violence in Israel and that nation's retaliation the whole world is in an ever-increasing mode of worry and uncertainty. The stupidity of phrases like "cycle of violence" and "violence begets violence" makes it difficult for the voice of reason to be heard. Reason dictates that religious insanity will never be overcome by reason. Religious terror can only be met and overcome by a greater terror! Even the most pacifistic philosopher would have to agree with my dictum: The good will never overcome the evil until the good confronts the evil with equal determination to win!

Over the years since WWII, I have become increasingly aware of the remarkable "accident of birth" by which I am an American. I have become increasingly aware of the enormous responsibility this carries with it, a responsibility to be politically aware and active. After all, our leaders are a reflection of our nation and no one dares say we do not get the kind of leadership that is actively supported by the electorate.

But good leaders require good citizens. And there is no such thing as a good citizen that is not politically active and aware.

An "Enlightened Electorate." The need of this requirement for Democracy to work at its best hasn't changed since the time of our founding as a nation. Perhaps, after all is said and done, it is this that concerns me more than the potential for disasters based on the stupidity, mistakes, and egos on the part of some of our leaders.

***

December 5, 2001

The Weedpatch Cracker Barrel

Charlie Brown is absolutely correct: It's not wise to lie in bed at night asking yourself questions that you can't answer, Clara Bow's question concerning the hereafter: "Why can't we know?" for example.

But like most such good advice, we humans are not amenable to much of it; our minds seem wired to worry, and like Snoopy live lives of unsuffered consequences thereby lending this dimension of worry to lives of quiet desperation. Perhaps the world is only a stage and when not living in quiet desperation we human beings are determined to tread the boards committing ourselves to "sound and fury" whether it signifies anything or not. We want to believe our lives are meaningful, that there is a divine or at the very least intelligent plan to the universe as we search for answers to this thing called "life." Of such significance is the following:

Mike Devich, the editorial assistant of our local paper The Kern Valley Sun, just wrote an article that really warmed my heart. It concerned his struggle to determine whether the pumpkin was a fruit or a vegetable. Not being willing to go to the mundane and ordinary resources like a dictionary, Mike went to the web for an answer. Why get a relatively instant answer to weighty questions when you can go to the Internet and spend an hour with search engines and their suggested 50,000 plus possibilities?

Those of us who have become addicted to this miracle of electronic means and media via our online computers can certainly understand and appreciate the point of Mike's tongue-in-cheek parody. If you were a child who was fortunate enough to have adults that told you to "Look in the dictionary" you can readily appreciate the difference between the "that was then, this is now" approach of dictionaries and encyclopedias you could actually hold in your hands, turning the leaves of the pages and learning other things of consequence along the way in your book search for knowledge vs. computer searches.

The newspaper, like actual books you hold in your hands, will likely not be replaced by computers; that entire spectrum of tactile and visual sensations working in concert with the brain that print media affords will not likely give way to any electronic substitute. The local paper, like a good book, is a "friend" that you depend on to be there. Among those things that can hinder the intellectual development of a child is to be raised without books that become lifelong friends. And the child that is raised without resort to a local paper is certainly what I call a culturally deprived child. That paper, as with good books, should inspire questions as well as providing answers and current events.

Now I grant that as a child the first thing I learned to turn to in the newspaper was the "Funnies," especially on Sundays when those marvelous, color cartoons would open the world of adventure, laughter, excitement, and imagination to my brother and me. Next to those wonderful radio programs of yore and our comic books were the funny papers.

Of course, as I grew up and became a mature adult the comic books kind of faded away, the radio shows were supplanted by TV, and the first thing I would turn to in any newspaper was... the funny papers. Some things didn't change with age and maturity. And I will take this opportunity to thank The Washington Post, one of several papers I scan each day, for keeping the comics available online.

The right of American citizens to bear arms and the rights of free speech and a free press are the ultimate guarantees of freedom in this nation. America was enormously blessed by the Founding Fathers who in their wisdom recognized these as among the essentials upon which a free nation could be founded and kept free.

With that I want to congratulate and thank the Sacramento Bee for the excellent job it has done in recently validating the tremendous blessing of a free (and responsible) press by the following:

It seems I was too easy on California Governor Gray Davis when I only questioned him about the Enron dirt. The following day I read the article in the Sacramento Bee about the Governor being given some real help from U. S. District Judge Lawrence K. Karlton when he covered the backside of then Controller Gray Davis from damaging allegations more than five years ago.

Thanks to the efforts of the SacBee the 9th U. S. Circuit Court of Appeals finally decided that Judge Karlton should not have concealed the name of now Governor Davis and the part he may have played in the dirty politics and schemes that led to the indictment of then Costal Commissioner Mark L. Nathanson.

As part of a plea agreement of cooperation, Nathanson named Davis as seeking campaign contributions and favorable treatment for contributors at the commission. The Circuit Court found that protecting an official's name and reputation (Davis) "is an insufficient reason" to suppress free speech guarantees.

Once in a great while, I am forced to concede a modicum of common sense to judges. Of course, being human beings, I always have to reserve the logical attributes of egos, greed and avarice as well as the "sins of the flesh" to them as well. But in the case of Judge Karlton and our esteemed governor, perhaps I am just being a tad cynical. And maybe pigs will, after all, grow wings and feathers and be able to fly.

I'll take this opportunity to apologize for my earlier remarks about Clinton and Reno, calling them the Gang that couldn't shoot straight in respect to dealing with terrorists. Just the way they wiped out Randy Weaver's son and wife and those terrorists in Waco, men, women, and children…

I owe much to Walt Kelly (Pogo). In one strip he has Churchy comparing old-fashioned disasters like "The Dam has bust!" and "The Jute Mill has exploded!" to worries about those of a nuclear age. As Churchy had it, you just don't know how to prepare for nuclear disaster, whether to pack a light lunch or what to wear so 's to be found decent in case of such an event. Of course, the ancient admonition of being certain to have clean underwear kind of goes by the board if you are instantly converted to cosmic dust by a thermonuclear bomb.

But we are being told by the "experts" that a "dirty bomb" of simple TNT and nuclear waste is relatively innocuous and to take the attitude of Alfred E. Neuman of Mad Magazine: "What, me worry?" Being the curmudgeon that I am, I'm immediately reminded of Opus Penguin's writing of the "Elvis Diaries" and how readily accepted they were by the finest and most legitimate experts of Time Magazine and other noteworthy sources of factual information.

While I usually scan some twenty to thirty columnists each day, while I scan several papers each day and keep up my reading of good literature, I still find time to write books and articles, averaging some quarter-million words a year in print (of course I'm not married any longer and my children are grown). Which makes me find the claim of some pretenders that they are "writers" but have little to support such an accusation laughable, and I'm often surprised such a claim does not embarrass them. It's really very simple, a writer writes; that's what they do.

But speaking of columnists, I have never envied them their jobs though they provide an invaluable service to the American way of life. Nor have I ever envied those like Garry Trudeau that provide a like service through political cartooning, infuriating as he is at times, following the great tradition of Nast.

This forces me to admit that in spite of the occasional offer I've never felt comfortable accepting a deadline. And I have to admit that I probably would have great difficulty finding an editor or publisher whose ox I wouldn't find myself eventually goring. But I do admire those who have found a niche in publishing their views and are able to commit to those dreadful deadlines (and editors).

Which brings me to the subject (there really was one). Many years ago when I first began to write in earnest and become truly politically active, I quickly learned that the way to become privy to information from those in the limelight, regardless of position, was to never betray a confidence.

Now this would seem to be obvious, nevertheless it is something that many who should know better seem to not have learned or forget at some point. Like the fundamental lesson of primary sources as opposed to secondary, whether a history professor or a columnist, this thing of keeping a confidence too often goes astray if the price is right. So it is that larceny and plagiarism are as common to writers as they are to grad students and their professors.

As to politicians and columnists, I learned that they often want someone to talk with that they can trust. But some years ago while I was interviewing the CEO of a major concern, the most seemingly implausible thought came to my mind and I asked this man who controlled the lives of thousands: Don't you have anyone you can trust? His reply: No one!

You bet it's lonely at the top! It's lonely when you are a columnist or politician and find that anything you put in writing of a personal nature places you at risk. So, you keep your own counsel. And you remain lonely.

I have been able to obtain the cooperation of influential people at times because there is another fundamental lesson to be learned in working with such people: Never ask anything for yourself!

Politics is a dirty business, the rationale of Sam Clemens in his remarks opposing women being given the franchise. Sam had a view of women that many have faulted, accusing him of putting them on a pedestal.

I confess I have much the same view of women as that of Sam's. But this is too much like trying to save your cake and eat it too. I have to confess as well that if there is to be any peace in the world women must have a place of equal value to men and take an equal part on the basis of honoring the compatibility of differences in the decision-making processes of world governments.

Imagine, if you will, the present crises throughout the world and how women having an equal voice in the affairs of the various nations involved would impact them. Truly mind-boggling!

Yet who, of any civilized sensibility, can deny such a thing is needed?

Harking to my own counsel of respecting confidences, I will not divulge the names of prominent columnists, politicians, even world leaders who have responded to me about this issue. Like the personal replies of such people to my proposed U. S. Constitutional amendment for the protection of children from molesters, I would quickly find myself cut off from any responses on the part of these people if I were to ever betray their confidence; and understandably so.

Still, I can divulge the fact that for the greater part these prominent people admit the need of women on the basis of equal value to men in the decision-making processes of world governments, the need of women sitting in positions of authority at the United Nations.

Imagine, if you will, Bush, Hussein, Arafat, and Sharon consulting with women that held equal positions of authority in the respective governments. Imagine further that by denying an entire half of humankind, women, an equal position of authority in the decision making processes of governments that wisdom is absent, that knowledge plus wisdom equals peace...

If this should be the case, and logic and reason dictates that it is, why isn't it happening? I refer the reader to my opening comment, re: Charlie Brown.

***

DECEMBER 10, 2001

FROM THE WEEDPATCH CRACKER BARREL

Jon and Garfield are feeling "Christmasy" and it's a great way to feel. I'm grateful for our cartoonists that give us things like this along with Charlie

Brown, BC, Snuffy Smith, Hagar, Dilbert, The Wizard of Id, and others that bring a smile. God knows we need all the smiles we can get! I have made it a lifelong habit to read the "funnies" before reading the papers and columnists, kind 'a like the first cup of coffee to get me kick-started for the day.

I'm not surprised that those working at CERN did not find the "God Particle" (Higgs boson) that might have proved the missing link of matter. I'm sure that physicists will continue the search though they confess they aren't sure, without Higgs, where to look now. What would surprise me would be world leaders finding the missing "particle" (women) as of equal value to men in the decision making processes of governments.

But hey, that's ok. I still believe in Santa Claus and am filled with optimism for the future. One must believe in Santa to have such optimism.

While I smile and laugh at a lot of the same things the average person does, I'm aware that my sense of humor does take a different turn at times. I recall the literary award I received for a humor piece in which I play the role of a very self-righteous con man (some would say the "real" me) taking advantage of the greed and gullibility of teachers. A lot of people thought the piece was hilarious, but the educational hierarchy was, understandably, not amused.

But the real success of the story was based two facts: First, I had been a classroom teacher for so many years and really knew my subjects. Second, I was also acutely aware of the most fundamental characteristic of the successful con man; that is one who truly believes in his own virtue; which, understandably, brings me to the subject of politics.

In today's mail I received a very nice hand addressed card from The White House. With a first class stamp and beautiful gold-embossed White House seal, it's impressive and I feel suitably honored.

The President thanked me for writing about the acts of war committed against the United States on September 11. The note continued in very nice phraseology to proclaim the greatness of our nation and Americans.

Unlike some of the personal correspondence I had received from President Bush while he was governor of Texas, this was a "form" note rather than a personal response to the four-page letter I had written him right after the Attack on America.

I know the President is a busy man so I didn't take offense. But one item in his note did cause me some concern. To wit: "We must remember that our Arab and Muslim American citizens love our nation and must be treated with dignity and respect."

Ok, so it's the political thing to say. Perhaps. Then why do I find myself questioning this? Maybe it's because I don't see Arab and Muslim Americans "loving" our country? Admittedly it would be easier to believe if I heard such people and their leaders screaming with outrage at the Attack on America as though they really loved America.

This reminded me of the day not long ago that I was standing at my back door looking out at the trees, rocks, quail and squirrels that make for my small corner of the world and thinking to myself: This is not my America; this is not the America I knew as a child!

When Sir Walter Scott finally realized that the highland chiefs he had romanticized were no better than freebooters, his writing began to evidence a pronounced emphasis on the ordinary characters in his novels. It was these ordinary people he made the real heroes and heroines to whom he gave real life, that went about the ordinary tasks of living without claims of the past, rather than the mechanical and stilted characters of nobility to whom the past was all important.

It wasn't that Scott didn't understand and accept the importance of the history of his people and leaders, quite the contrary. But he came to realize, just as did Washington and Lincoln, that it was the ordinary people that make a nation and a culture. Scott, as with Emerson, knew the story of Jove and Minerva, how the goddess argued that human beings "...had a blur or indeterminate aspect, seen far or near; if you called them bad, they would appear so; if you called them good, they would appear so; and there was no person or action among them, which would not puzzle her owl, much more all Olympus, to know whether it was fundamentally bad or good."

As a child, I was taught a history of America that had heroes like Washington and Lincoln. We celebrated Thanksgiving with highly romanticized stories of the Pilgrims; we celebrated July 4th with romanticized stories of the Founding Fathers.

But among those things completely absent during such celebrations was any history that included Arabs and Muslims being involved with the founding of America, let alone romanticized.

William McGowan has an interesting book: Coloring the News. I do believe that by the media's bowing to the "god of diversity" there is too much emphasis on those people and agendas that separate, rather than bring together, the things that made America a great nation.

If President Bush means to make Arabs and Muslims among those citizens that "love America," he has a most difficult task making this believable to Americans like me. These latecomers to America don't equate for me as belonging to our history, any more than do those that cross our borders illegally, primarily from Mexico. These "foreigners" have no tradition steeped in the founding of our nation and can hardly be expected to "love" the America I was born into that included a history of the War for Independence, the Civil War, the First and Second World Wars, all that history and sacrifice that made the America I knew as a child.

Is the President's message to be understood as advocating "diversity" to the point that America has no identifiable character or image? A nation that cannot control its borders and without a national identity or national purpose has no future any more than does a nation that fails to cherish its young; surely the President knows this. Or does he?

If I'm ruthlessly honest with myself, I don't see foreigners coming to America interpreting our flag as anything but representing a dollar sign, all the spin of "fleeing oppression" aside. To make a better life? Why of course! And to the world that "better life" is a dollar sign having nothing to do with those things I learned as a child that made the America I knew as a child, the America that I understood our flag represented.

No, I'm sorry Mr. President; I'm not buying the line of these foreigners "loving" the America I knew as My America. Perhaps in my soul I know the consummate con man is one that believes his own con. But even at their best, no con man will ever make me believe that those who have a higher allegiance to their religion, whether that of Jews, Christians, or Muslims, and another nation or culture than they do to the America I knew as a child really "love" the America I knew as a child.

Nor do I believe there are any that love the America that I knew as a child who think perversion or the color of their skin is more important than that America I knew, the America I called My America. Is it the intention of all these "foreigners" and "hyphenated Americans" to "diversify" the America I used to know out of existence? I have to wonder? If so, just what kind of "America" do they want in its stead? I doubt any would call it "iconoclastic anarchy." But isn't that the direction of such "diversity?"

Just what is an "enlightened electorate?" Most would agree this would include people who can read and write at the very least a requirement of such. Does it include the babies of criminals being given instant citizenship based on their flaunting the laws of America? But what nation in history with a national identity has printed its ballots in foreign languages? Just what claim does such a nation have to an enlightened electorate?

Insane, to use a charitable term, as providing ballots in a foreign language is, perhaps you have seen the spot on TV: 25% of adults cannot read a story to their children!

Not everyone of even my advanced age was raised on Shakespeare, the King James Bible, Sir Walter Scott, and Emerson. But for the most part reading was encouraged both at home and in the schools. Popular magazines like Liberty, Colliers, and the Saturday Evening Post, film and music publications were very popular and encouraged reading, not to mention the newspapers.

The practice of reading stories to children made them want to learn to read as well. Just listening to my great-grandmother read marvelous stories to me made me want to learn to read them for myself.

"What I Did During My Summer Vacation" was a typical writing exercise when you returned to school. While many children didn't always appreciate this, it did place emphasis on writing skills, though I don't recall any of us as children jumping with joy at diagramming sentences at the blackboard.

Another discipline that was encouraged was memorization, not only of the multiplication tables, the essential foundation of arithmetic and learning mathematics but also of poetry and prose.

Well, we have a generation that cannot read, write, spell, punctuate, do arithmetic, and knows virtually nothing of the America I knew as a child, let alone great literature. What they have learned because of people like the Clintons, Reno, Condit, Andrea Yates, John Walker, et al. is that "no one is personally responsible for anything!" And, by extension, we have a generation that isn't even responsible for being illiterate.

Thoreau wrote that he had not learned anything of consequence or true wisdom from his elders. Taken in context, he was correct. Can our children, considering the context of continued warfare, say they have learned anything of consequence or true wisdom from their elders?

I recall attending a seminar for my doctorate sometime in 1972. Being a class in human behavior, one young woman was decrying the "old" emphasis on proper dress and grooming when applying for a job. This was an unfair and discriminatory practice and would have to be changed in her opinion.

There were twenty-two people in attendance at this seminar, but I was the only one that asked: What is wrong with proper dress and grooming? The class fell silent, unable or unwilling to counter my question. But I remind myself that this class represented those that believed it was no longer necessary that children should be taught to read, write, spell, punctuate properly, memorize times tables and do arithmetic, or, in short, be held personally responsible for their actions, let alone knowing anything about the real history of America except that approved of universities given to politically correct interpretations of America's history.

If the iconoclastic anarchy toward which America is heading is to be avoided, that "class" in Congress is going to have to answer the question of "What's wrong with proper dress and grooming?"

Politicians are notorious for ambiguity. But there is no avoiding this question. Some things are simply right no matter what the spinners of diversity howl to the contrary.

Should Clint Eastwood be condemned for not providing suitable accommodations for the handicapped? Is there anything in today's America from which even an ordinary citizen can escape litigation? Has government such control of our lives as Americans that personal responsibility is inescapably relegated to the America of the past, the America I knew as a child?

Alice had an easy time of it in Wonderland compared to the America in which we now live.

I grant you that since I have no job or empire to protect that I can say some of the hard things the average American wishes he or she could say, I can say some of the things that those in positions of power and influence wish they could say but cannot out of fear.

There is a lesson in this, one that our Founding Fathers had learned and put into practice, one that still allows of a private American citizen such as myself to put into practice. But it was their intention that such freedom of expression would be used responsibly and to better our nation, to advance civilization and not to promote perversion and anarchy. Now, how many children are required to even memorize the Preamble to our Constitution, and how many "foreigners" including those homegrown have done so, providing they can read, and read in English, and really know what the Founding Fathers intended it to mean? Just who, now, are We the People of the United States?

***

DECEMBER 13, 2001

FROM THE WEEDPATCH CRACKER BARREL

Who needs more than four dogs? Well, apart from those riding to the hounds, operating dog sled teams or a kennel, anyone on welfare, own very large junkyards, or deals drugs. My home county of Kern in California is planning to have residents apply for conditional permits if they are to have more than four dogs. If you have ever experienced the misfortune of irresponsible neighbors that care nothing about the barking of their dogs…

My daughter Karen, the most beautiful girl in the world (I use her picture on the covers of some of my books) owns *Black Ives Rottweilers*. She has earned an international reputation raising and training these animals for police agencies as well as home protection. There are few things that so brighten my day as to visit my daughter and grandkids and have a 165-pound Rottweiler crawl up on my lap like the little 5-pound Pomeranian Karen uses to teach the big dogs not to eat cats or little dogs.

So, while I am more of a cat than a dog person (plays hell with the *macho* image), I tolerate the beasts and if someone wants a dog, so be it. But the law long ago recognized the fact that a cat is not "owned." Dogs, however, are. As a consequence of this obvious discrimination against dogs, it isn't any wonder pooches develop an attitude toward felines who have their own *nayh, nayh, nayh* attitude toward dogs (not to mention people).

For some reason this reminds me of the attitude of little girls when I was growing up who always seemed to have given the impression they were somehow better than boys. These strange creatures had a "thing" about being clean, they never spit, shot marbles or told jokes, and would wear odd clothing that seemed to prevent their doing sensible things like playing in dirt. And there was this totally, sex-discriminating thing about not hitting girls. They had more delicate heinies than boys (Suzie to Calvin). I always wondered about this?

That little ditty about little girls being "sugar and spice and everything nice" whereas little boys were made of "sniffles and snails and puppy dog tails" didn't do much to dispel this "I'm better than you are" attitude of little girls. Just who, I've always wondered, was the nitwit that memorialized: "Words will never harm me"?

Oh, well, I've always been a critter person and my little girl is a chip off the old block, this aberration about cats vs. dogs notwithstanding. It's just that dogs are so, well, servile and compliant compared to cats. It's no fun trying to stare down a dog or play with their minds. And any aficionado of Garfield knows what Odie represents with the drool, etc. Besides, if I take off somewhere for a week, the resident cat, sometimes known as "damned cat," that was a "dumpee" at my back door will still be here when I return and won't have starved to death. It's the dependence vs. independence thing I like about cats; you know, that "go to hell, you only exist for my comfort" attitude. Now about cats and women; no, not going there.

I love to write about critters, far more than I like to write about people. But admittedly cats, especially those like lions and tigers, contribute so much to nature red in tooth and claw. This is one of my arguments against God(s) doing a good job in creation. To me there were either errors in creation or there was an attitude on the part of such beings like "Let's try this and see what happens?"

I had the good fortune to spend much of my boyhood living on a mining claim in the Sequoia National Forest with thousands of acres as my personal wilderness. My home was with the critters that inhabited the forest and I often felt theirs the better society to that of humans. Seeming to have been born to solitude rather than society, the forest was truly like home to me and I reveled in the stories of Leatherstocking and Kit Carson whom I envied. Much as I love Sam Clemens, I'll never excuse his disparaging remarks about James Fenimore Cooper.

While the years have passed, the memories of those years in the forest are as vibrant to me today as they were while living them. Would that all children could have been so blessed. But while I vividly recall the quail I provided for one Thanksgiving feast, the breasts baked on top of dressing in an iron pot in our wood stove, now I simply enjoy watching and listening to these beautiful and charming birds, my "wild, diminutive chickens."

So the reader will understand my difficulty in dealing with so many of the lessons learned about humankind vs. the critters. The birds and animals of the forest had clearly defined roles; their instincts were predictable and, many times, delightful, like the hoot of an owl, the barking antics of tree squirrels or the chittering of raccoons.

But for those of us that grew up during WWII there was no escaping the ugliness of the behavior of some humans. While nature was indeed red in tooth and claw, as I grew up I had cause to wonder if humankind was any better?

In my "golden years" I find it increasingly difficult to pry myself away from walkabouts and looking out at my miniature wilderness of the trees, rocks, and critters and pay attention to the news of the day. This morning I had to go out and break the ice so the birds and critters (including the resident cat) would have water. This was a good thing to do; I took pleasure in doing it. Unlike the problems Emerson so well enumerated when it comes to the giving of "gifts," the critters reward my efforts with their company; there is a true balance between them and me. I don't doubt that if they could speak, a simple "Thank you" without any thought of accruing debt of any kind would prove sufficient.

Then, I turn to the news of the day (after fortifying myself with BC, Peanuts, Garfield, Hagar, etc.). And unlike the beauty of the hills, trees, rocks, the company of my feathered and furred companions, much of the ugliness of the world confronts me.

I recalled a film in 1943: *Bataan* with Robert Taylor. I saw the film as a boy and recently it was on TCM. So, I watched it again, trying to recapture what it had meant to me way back then.

No good. Unlike my memories of life in the forest, I couldn't quite watch this film with the same eyes of the boy that had first seen it. Too much has happened through the intervening years, I have lived too long and I know too much.

We trusted our leaders, our government in WWII; as a boy I watched Bataan and the enemy was clear. *All Quiet On The Western Front*, 1930, many critics declared the greatest anti-war film ever made. But it didn't prevent WWII, Korea, or Vietnam. Neither that sniper's bullet and butterfly at the end of All Quiet nor the hammering machine gun at the end of Bataan had lessened humankind's determination to hate and kill; whether in the name of God or whatever.

There is the devastating Attack on America to deal with where, unlike Bataan, the enemy is not clear; at least he does not seem to be clear to our leaders. And unlike 1943 I don't have the same trust in our leaders, I don't think the majority of Americans do have the kind of trust we had back then. After the revelations about Kennedy, after Johnson and Nixon, after the Clintons and Reno, with Gary Condit still welcome in Congress and thinking he can win another election while telling the media and We the People to go to hell, how can I have such trust?

Come to think of it, people like the Clintons, Reno, and Condit have become too representative of government now for me to have the kind of confidence and trust I used to have, let alone anything approaching respect. I don't have that kind of confidence and trust in our present leadership to successfully prosecute this war, even granting them the same capability and capacity of stupidity, greed, and egos with which we contended in WWII, I don't feel they have earned the right to demand the sacrifices we made during that war; Enron, etc., only making my distrust and resentment all the deeper.

Part of this lack of trust and confidence in the present leadership is engendered by my belief that the enemy is just as clear as he was in 1943 but leaders are unwilling to acknowledge this. By trying to propagandize Americans to accept any religion as being harmless to democracy there is, to me, a clear and present danger. And a religion that is so well represented by Osama bin Laden particularly in regard to women (not that any religion makes women of equal value to men), to try to make that religion and its devotees favorable to democracy is nothing less than being lied to by the leadership. Or even far worse, is not recognized by the leadership as representing a threat to democracy!

Don Feder is absolutely correct: "People are discovering Islam the hard way!" This is something I mentioned right after the Attack on America, something I included in my four-page letter to President Bush, copies sent to Prime Minister Tony Blair among several others. But our leaders don't seem able to grasp or are unwilling to comprehend this enemy of democracy. Our leaders and citizenry during WWII wouldn't have had any problem dealing with a John Walker or an Osama bin Laden. Or any other enemies of America back then.

I do not admire Geraldo; he's an opportunist, a lackey and toady to any that will give him favorable TV time. In this, admittedly, he is no worse than many others. Kathleen Parker had a great column about the lengths some will go to in order to get "air time" and I loved her closing line: "By all means, Geraldo, do have your people get in touch with Sabiha's people. We'll be watching."

I cannot admire the Chairman of the JDL, Irv Rubin, when he wants to practice terrorism while hiding behind the guise of thwarting anti-Semitism. Despicable! His real motives? To make the world safer for theocratic Israel and further a theocratic America favorable to Jews rather than Muslims? Who knows? He can't be trusted any more than Geraldo…too much of the vices of human nature regardless of religion or ethnicity.

Wonderfully insightful piece by Phyllis Schlafly (The Visa Scandal) about the power of the universities, a power I have been warning of for years but no one listens. The universities remain the one real sacred cow of America that no one dares touch. I won't wonder at any attacks to come on Schlafly as a result of her comments. Who but those of the universities could get away with placing their welfare above that of the American people, even at the risk of encouraging further terrorism like the Towers and the Pentagon?

But I know the universities; I know the thinking of those in these institutions that has little to do with the welfare of America. The very insanity of those in these institutions making every attempt to make America an amoral and socialist nation while living on the largess of a capitalistic society should tell our leaders something. "A New McCarthyism" is the howl of these institutions as government leaders try to get a handle on the enemies of America.

But as I pointed out, our leaders are loath to make the enemies of America clear, largely through fear of the universities, or worse they do not really recognize the enemy.

As for calling on the help of Hollywood as per Bataan, forget it! Tom Hanks can't glorify perversion in one film and come off believable in "Bataan." And I like most of the characters Hanks has portrayed, I really like him paired with Meg Ryan (whom I really like, but then what man doesn't?). But a Clark Gable or a Robert Taylor he isn't… then, when it comes to Gable, who is?

Which brings another thought to mind, one that only contributes to the confusion that generates an Irv Rubin and others: *Exodus* and *Schindler's List* were marvelous propaganda pieces. But talk about shooting yourself in the foot, how is Hollywood with its too blatantly obvious Jewish dominance, even in TV films, sitcoms, and commercials where every niece, nephew, and grandmother wants to draw a check or have a crack at stardom, and with this kind of propaganda behind it, going to make believable propaganda for this present war? There is no Clark Gable left in Hollywood and a Jeff Goldblum could never make the cut no matter how much "Jewish influence." The American public knows what it likes and it liked Clark Gable. Given the present circumstances, Debbie Schlussel has it right: "Get Hollywood out of the 'War on Terrorism.'"

But even if a Gable were available, after so many years of making Arabs the enemy how could Hollywood ever be expected to pull off propaganda that successfully mimics Taylor's *Bataan* or Gable's *Command Decision*, let alone lay to rest Pat Buchanan's accusation of Congress being "Israeli occupied territory?" Bullies are never loved, but despised. And any one or group that uses their position of wealth or influence, whether in politics, religion, industry, the media, education, entertainment to exaggerate their power or silence dissent is recognized as a bully. And no amount of "labeling" like "anti-Semitic, racist" or "homophobic" will change the facts.

Arab leaders, including Hussein and Arafat, are not stupid, though their religion, like religion in general, makes them appear so. An obvious bias is an obvious bias, and the enemies of democracy remain the enemies of democracy regardless their "lifestyle" or religion whether Jewish, Christian, or Moslem. What could be more antithetical to reason and the progress of civilization than to believe the nonsense of "holy this" or "sacred that" whether of a person, a people, a city, or a book?

For people to use religious beliefs as the basis for murder in the name of God, what else to call this but the tyranny of religion leading to insanity and insane actions? For the sake of civilization the enemies of civilization must be identified and dealt with; and if democracy is to be the friend of civilization, the enemies of democracy must be identified and dealt with.

Even the most obtuse must recognize the conundrum facing us. We may kill bin Laden but the thousands of those that believe in his war are still out there, including those right here in America. Given the propaganda that has demonized Arab nations, given the Jewish influence in America far out of proportion to the actual numbers, as with homosexuals, and the bias toward Israel, given a leadership we cannot trust in too many instances for whatever reason, given that our "friendship" toward Arab nations is based on oil and they know this, given the Hollywood bias toward advocating perversion, given the cynicism of people in general due to these and many other factors like corrupt and immoral politicians, how can Hollywood make believable propaganda in this present war? Who envies the task?

For the sake of democracy and the progress of civilization a criteria of friendship to these is needed. And that friendship cannot be based on adherence and allegiance to Race, Torah, Bible, or Koran together with their imprecatory "prayers" and "scriptures" and barbarisms of religion like the mutilating of babies, male or female, through circumcision or teaching children to hate those that are "different" because of the color of their skin. Perhaps when these things cease to be the criteria by which people live, the "toys" of children will cease to be so-called "Action" figures, guns, and knives.

Fat is ugly. No amount of propaganda will make it otherwise. As we listen to the horror stories of fat children in America, their understandable lack of self-esteem and health problems, nothing will take the place of proper diet and exercise to reverse the trend. There simply is no magic bullet for obesity. The "Fat American" is not a poster child for America's concern for those who are starving in other nations, for those that hate Americans for whatever reason.

The very hypocrisy of attempting to appear concerned on the part of Americans for these others is not lost on them. "You're a beautiful person but you're fat!" No, I've never met the woman yet that could buy this line, and I've never met the woman yet in whom I could have a romantic interest that outweighed me.

Then how, I ask myself, can we expect those in other nations to buy the line that they should love a "Lardo?"

Obesity is often evidence of self-indulgence. I'm a good enough psychologist to recognize why people substitute food for any number of things wrong, real or perceived, in their lives. But if perception is everything, and in many cases this is true, try if you will to perceive America in this light as seen by other nations, particularly as they perceive us through Hollywood and our TV commercials! Then try to explain why Americans spend billions on both food and weight control, let alone the billions on cars, stock portfolios, cosmetics and pet food, categories of national self-destructive propaganda all to themselves. At that point the American flag representing a dollar sign and a selfishly indulgent lifestyle leading to obesity is unmistakable.

We Americans are not responsible for all the evils in the world. We are not responsible for the misery and suffering brought on others through the tyranny of religious beliefs leading to ignorance and poverty in so many other nations.

But we are the leaders of the world, and as such have the responsibility to avoid the appellation of "bullies" and lead in fairness and justice; we have the responsibility to keep ourselves both strong and educated in order to lead properly. We have the responsibility to avoid hypocrisy in all cases, whether political or religious.

If we do not exercise this responsibility to the world without hypocrisy, if we refuse to accept personal responsibility for our lives and actions from the level of the ordinary citizen to the President, we cannot lead others in fairness and justice, we cannot expect success in leading others out of their lives of ignorance and poverty.

America, the world, needs a criteria of democracy and the progress of civilization, one that clearly defines both the friends and the enemies of these and one that includes what is perhaps the most daunting item of all: That of women having a place of equal value to men in the establishing of such criteria.

Knowledge plus Wisdom equals Peace. Until the world knows peace, we must accept the fact that we lack wisdom. The world has become far too small and dangerous for any more allowing the hatreds and prejudices based on things like gender, race, and religion to hold sway any longer. Wisdom dictates that this historic condition of humankind must be abandoned, that new criteria of a global nature are established and a new path followed.

***

December 16, 2001

From The Weedpatch Cracker Barrel

Of course I'm not surprised that the universities would welcome a course about the *Simpsons*; anyone knowledgeable of life in the Ivory Tower knows there is nothing too hare-brained for inclusion in programs designed to prepare the ruling elite of America. And one only has to watch TV for a very short time to realize the ruling elite of today was raised on shows like the Simpsons. If you think this criticism too harsh, just read some of the interviews in foreign countries having to do with life in America.

In spite of my criticism of politicians I was gratified to receive the White House Xmas card. It was quite lovely and done in very good taste, the message not one that should offend anyone. Now I have been enjoying BC since its inception and will continue to do so, but how I wish Johnny Hart had taken a note from the White House and didn't abuse his position by such blatant Christian propaganda like this Sunday's strip. Blessed birth of Jesus? I don't think so. Nor do billions of other people that Hart offends by such propaganda. Make mine Santa Claus.

A very lengthy article by Abraham Cooper of the Wiesenthal Center in the Times caught my attention, and the Sunday BC strip was right in tune with it. Now why, I had to ask myself after reading the article, should Cooper exhibit any surprise at the offerings of Al Jazeera designed as anti-Semitic propaganda? Whether Hart, Cooper, or those in control of Al Jazeera, the purpose of propaganda is often to demonize your enemy and glorify your cause.

Taken all together, Christian, Jew, Moslem, and Hindu, it makes for a demon-haunted world as long as any propaganda exists that demonizes those with whom you disagree. Especially when such propaganda is intended to make people hate other people for whatever reason.

Chris Matthews calls bin Laden and Al Qaeda the Moslem version of Pat Robertson and his 700 Club. While I have no love for those like Robertson, Falwell, or any other "Gospel Peddlers," where is Matthews coming from by such a statement? Well, from the same position as Hart, Cooper, and Al Jazeera of course. Among the clueless are those that don't seem to know that neither Moslems nor Jews will ever agree on Jerusalem, which makes a farce of Israel's "terrific offer" to Arafat. Nor will Christians, Jews, or Moslems ever agree on the supremacy of their respective gods, their prophets, or their holy scriptures.

Among the clueless are those that don't seem to realize that these are religious issues leading to a religious war and Christians suffer the delusion that they are on the side of God in supporting Israel. Now that is successful propaganda, but propaganda that Moslems rightly hate and are attempting to counter by means such as those TV offerings Cooper writes about of Al Jazeera.

Hitler and Goebbels well recognized the power of the media in controlling propaganda. Wall Street and Madison Avenue take full advantage of such as well.

It is natural enough to hate Osama bin Laden and all those and all that he represents. There are not pejoratives enough in any language to describe a creature like bin Laden. It is a relatively simple task to demonize a demon. But if I point out the obvious in regard to those like Hart and Cooper, ah, that is different, the angels are obviously on their side and I should be demonized for pointing out such things that detract from their holiness and the righteousness of their cause.

Which calls to mind *To Kill A Mockingbird*. Please bear with me and I'll get to it.

Reading the LA Times this morning I was delighted to discover that I have been living a privileged life of meditation for years now, and at far less expense than the "Meditation Camp" people are paying big bucks to attend. I had long ago been turned on to vegetarianism as being preferable to the eating of animals, which had become "inconvenient to my imagination" long before I read *Walden* and diet for the sake of health wasn't a consideration. And my life in the Sequoia National Forest gave me a running start on meditation long before I knew anything about chic Zen.

Letters to my children; this was my explanation to my kids a few years ago when they asked about their dad's writing. Knowing that my generation was unique in many ways, that the era of WWII was unique in so many ways,

I felt a responsibility to bequeath a kind of history to my children that only people like me were qualified to leave behind.

But unlike *The Screwtape Letters*, it was my purpose to write letters from a very human perspective that would help to explain the human conditions and motives of a man that lived a very unique life in a very unique era of history.

I realized that my own life has been unique in many ways; very few even of my age were raised with coal oil lamps and outhouses. Not many my age had spent years of childhood on a mining claim in a forest then made the transition through experiences of early train travel cross country, road travel on old Route 66, living in early Las Vegas, then to the *Camelot* of California's South Bay of the early 50s.

The universities being what they are, media bias being what it is largely as a result of the universities, the actual truth of American society isn't told by the university-trained pundits or university historians. The real truth of my generation's America can only be told by people like myself, people that lived it through the magic of Hollywood's making film stars like Hedy Lamarr, Humphrey Bogart, and Clark Gable, and the magic of radio shows that required functioning imaginations, the early funny papers, and comic books with real heroes that my generation grew up with, all the things like rationing and constant war news and so much more that made the era of WWII so indelibly memorable.

People of my era know the power of propaganda in a way that this present generation, the generation of my children cannot possibly know. People my age may not remember James Fenimore Cooper winning libel suits against newspapers but we knew about that telephone survey that did in the *Literary Digest* and recall the headlines of Dewey *winning* over Truman and we have lived long enough to know that we cannot trust the media and we cannot trust politicians, to always tell the truth. Not that my children trust these, but their distrust isn't born of the transition through WWII that my generation lived through.

It took the experiences of the betrayal of so much that my generation had been taught was honorable and right, those things for which so many of the Great Generation gave their lives to protect, to reach the point of cynicism that my children have reached. It took the betrayal of what I had been taught as a child was the real America for my children to accept, as a matter of course, our Governor Gray Davis claiming he wouldn't endorse either Gary Condit or Dennis Cardoza because they were both "friends." In this context, my children will remember why some in Congress would not go along with ousting a scoundrel like Clinton.

When politicians like Davis have friends like Condit whom they cannot or will not disavow, I can easily understand the cynicism of my children. Those of my children's generation have come to accept as a matter of course the lack of any real integrity on the part of politicians.

From Weedpatch to Little Oklahoma, to the Polish Ghetto of Cleveland and St. Joseph's Military Academy in Florida, to Las Vegas, San Francisco and Oakland, to the Sequoia National Forest then to the magical South Bay of Sandra Dee my brother and I got to see a lot of America during the 30s, 40s, and 50s that most people only saw on the Silver Screen or read about in books and magazines.

I can't help wishing I could see *Snow White, The Wizard of Oz*, and *Bambi* again for the first time. I wish I could read *The Great Gatsby* and *The Last of the Mohicans* again for the first time. I wish I could be a child again, listening to the marvelous stories my great-grandmother and grandparents would tell my brother Ronnie and me. I wish I could recapture the romance and excitement of WWII that surrounded us as children; protected as we were from experiencing first-hand the actual horror of war.

I can tell my eldest son "You had to be there" but that won't make him understand what I'm talking about. He, like others his age, will argue as though he had been there, that he understands. But he doesn't and can't; and it would be foolish of me to expect him to. You really did have to be there.

The generation of my children probably won't learn any more of the truly essential lessons from history than my own did. But the lesson that each generation must learn the things of that one past seems lost to this generation that can't write, spell, or do arithmetic as mine could and this worries me.

But my generation wouldn't have countenanced even the most remote idea of bin Laden on the cover of *Time* as "Man of the Year." But the pundits of this generation, being trained by and reflecting the betrayal by the universities of the America I knew, made those like the Clintons and Condit possible, made possible the bin Ladens and those at Time that do countenance such a thing.

My generation wouldn't have countenanced perversion as an "alternative lifestyle." But those of my generation that betrayed my America and what those of the Great Generation died to protect in places like Okinawa and the beaches of Normandy are largely university graduates. Unlike *Willie and Joe*, the betrayers of the America I knew have no allegiance to that America. As a result, Tom Hanks couldn't represent me; he couldn't represent Willie and Joe, he couldn't represent those that paid the price for his being able to prostitute himself for fame and fortune; small wonder that those of Hollywood in general support politicians like the Clintons and Gray Davis.

Imagine, if you will, Steinbeck writing about "Okies" from a desk in an office in New York, having never even seen the Dust Bowl or California. Now you get a perspective of what I'm talking about when it comes to the pundits trying to escape the influence of the universities in their lives as they attempt to write about the America I'm talking about, the America I experienced as a child during the 30s and 40s.

This is the obligation I feel in my *Letters to my children*. They will not learn of the real America I knew from university texts or university-trained columnists and politicians, they will not understand the conundrum little Scout faced in To Kill A Mockingbird trying to make sense of the attitude of her Jewish teacher toward Negroes or why a jury would convict an obviously innocent man. You had to be there, you had to have lived this kind of history in the America I knew, the America that was betrayed by the universities and those trained by these institutions.

I don't envy the task of honest columnists, of honest people in politics, of honest people in Hollywood as they try to get a handle on the crises facing America and the world today. If they didn't live it as I did, there is no way they are going to understand any more than little Scout could, or my eldest son can. You had to be there.

If only there was a "royal path to knowledge." But there isn't, and as a result there is no escaping the judgmental, even condemnatory, attitude of those that don't like my telling of the America I knew as a child, the America so many of the Great Generation died to protect.

But Scout had the extreme good fortune to have a father like Atticus, a father that would stand for what was right and would try to explain things to her. As a result, Scout would be able, in spite of all the evil about her, even the evil of good people, to understand that the situation that presented itself in respect to Boo would be "sort of like shootin' a mockingbird."

I had the extreme good fortune of being surrounded by good people that would explain things to me as I was growing up. Like Scout, I would be able to see situations like that of Boo Radley and understand the frailties of good people, the frailties of the law that cannot at times escape being unjust. I would be able to understand that there are times when a strict adherence to the letter of the law would result in "shootin' a mockingbird."

So it is that there are good people today that are attempting to adhere to the letter of the law, good people that are going to wind up "shootin' mockingbirds" and convicting "Tom Robinsons" all done perfectly legal, and in far too many cases with an easy conscience, swearing their respective oaths with hands on Bible. There are going to be juries and those like Miss Gates that will never understand, let alone accept, their own hypocrisy.

But what good and civilized people like Atticus and Heck Tate could not do because of the constraints of law a mad man could do in order to balance the scales of justice. There is no way of escaping the lessons of Dostoevsky, Tolstoy, and Harper Lee. The very madness inherent to the letter of the law makes essential, at times, the madness of a Boo Radley the only source of justice.

The world too often represents the lynch mob that only a little girl like Scout could disperse. In the words of Atticus: "… maybe we need a police force of children…."

I have the extreme good fortune to be able to go back and look at the America I used to know with the eyes and memories of a child who understands what Atticus meant, who understands how Scout could understand what Sheriff Tate meant and put it in the perspective of "kind 'a like shootin' a mockingbird."

At the same time I can understand those who are "all grown up" that censure me as being naïve and altruistic, even anachronistic in my view of that America I knew as a child.

But those that really know anything about me would never accuse me of trying to simplify what are enormously complex issues. I'm too acutely aware of what the extremes of both poverty and wealth can do in warping attempts at objectivity; I'm too well schooled in the subject of human behavior to be guilty of attempts to simplify what are enormously complex issues of the human psyche, I'm too well schooled in the subject of human cultures and human nature to not understand the perspective of either a bin Laden, an Irv Rubin, or a Gary Condit; in short, I am not naïve to those factors that make for a devil or a saint, recognizing as I do the same struggles in myself that both Hawthorne and Melville attempted to deal with, those issues that Harper Lee dealt with so successfully in her masterful book.

As a result I'm not naïve to the ignorance and prejudices that held sway in the America of my childhood, the ugly things, many of which have been righted, that made that America unjust in many ways.

But as there remain good and faithful to the facts lessons of our Founding Fathers and the founding of this nation, so there remain the good things of that America of my childhood that should be taught and honored, many of which led to our stand for democracy and our victory over the Axis powers of WWII, the things inherent to our character as a nation that led us to helping those that were our enemies during that world war once they had been vanquished. Of such are the things that made me proud, and grateful, to be an American!

It takes the memories of such an America as that I knew as a child to make me, as an American, so angry with those that flaunt their perversion and those like the Clintons and Condit that have so dishonored that America. But how to distinguish that America I knew from the one my children know? Hence the letters to my children.

***

December 20, 2001

From The Weedpatch Cracker Barrel

I don't feel my manhood is threatened by telling folks that I tolerate cats but do not like dogs. Nor do I feel it threatened by telling folks that I like Longfellow, Wordsworth, films like *Steel Magnolias*, and occasionally watch PBS, though much of so-called "public broadcasting" has fallen to the level of Bowflex and SaladShooter commercials, or at its worst Winning Ben Stein's Money.

But last Tuesday night I caught the segment on "She Says, women in the news." I'm glad I did, and women like Judy Woodruff, for example, are easy to admire. Still, women are not immune from Bernard Goldberg's accusations in his book "Bias." Both men and women, largely due to the influence of the universities and Hollywood, are susceptible to this cancer in the media.

Without argument, there is no escaping the fact that the media needs the views of both men and women in order to provide balance. But being human, neither is exempt from certain other facts of history and human nature, and I do wish media owners would fire some of those that believe perversion is a proud monument to America and "diversity" rather than qualifications is good for education.

Walter Williams' excellent piece "Education Fraud in Philadelphia" points up one of the greatest flaws in education. Having experienced this fraud first hand as a teacher in Watts, having fought the battle for years, I can only say: Good luck Walter! No one really cares and certainly no one is going to be able to do anything about it until some sacred cows in the universities are slain! Just try that one on legislators.

But let's face it; until children become a national priority in fact rather than politics, nothing of substantive value can be accomplished to reverse the downward spiral of illiteracy. And as far as holding the schools accountable financially, you might as well try to audit the IRS. You remember how far the GAO got on that one. I sound like a broken record on this but you never solve problems by asking the people who created the problems for solutions.

If we want to analyze "authority-bound" in regard to keeping uppity women in their place we have only to look to Hitler's Germany for the *sine qua non* of the essentials. Not that other nations throughout history including

America haven't been successful in keeping women in their place, but Hitler deserves special recognition in this regard, not to mention those nations that continue to encourage the murder of girl babies.

If the "men know everything" syndrome permeates a culture and women are made to believe this from childhood, it is on the basis of the fact that men make war, not women, and historically war has been the ultimate authority. As I mentioned in a previous article, war is fun for men and they are war-lovers. As a consequence of its being a man's world, a large part of the authority of men has evolved from the fact that war has always been their approved method of relieving boredom and settling disputes. If women try to make their voices heard against war they are told, and made, to butt out through this authority of men (who know everything). As a result, a full half of humankind is excluded from any ultimately effective representation in world governments or the United Nations.

Religion, more than any other invention of men, has been enormously successful in keeping the poor from killing the rich; like war, religion (which has made its contribution to so many wars, including the one current) also has a terrific track record for keeping women in their place. The "Women are no damned good, unclean, and sin by definition" doctrines of all the major religions have done a real number on women in stifling their self esteem and keeping them subjugated to men. Spurgeon's comment about women preachers is still the dominant view: They remind me of a dog being trained to walk upright on its hind legs. I don't wonder that it does it poorly; I wonder that it does it at all?

Hitler's "natural order of things" included his beliefs in the inferiority of women. In this respect, his natural order is still reflected in world governments and the United Nations, and Hitler had only to point to the King of Disciplines, Philosophy, which excludes women to make his point since it is philosophy that guides the course of history and nations. The result, since philosophy is the "thinking discipline," being the "proof" that women are incapable of the kind of thinking worthy of guiding the course of history and nations.

To date, the "Fuhrer's" beliefs regarding women is still the norm by their lacking a place in philosophy and are still reflected throughout the world's governments, notwithstanding the occasional blips on the screen of history. And women like Senator Hillary Clinton who lacks not only any sense of shame but also the good sense to wipe the smirk from her face and Representative Nancy Pelosi of San Francisco, who is endorsing Gary Condit, go a long way toward enforcing Hitler's viewpoint (just today Pelosi shifted to "neutral" on Condit).

When I was a boy and trying to make sense of why some things were "girl things" and some were "boy things," my great-grandmother was of inestimable help. She pointed out that just as there was nothing wrong with my brother and I learning to sew and cook, so there was nothing wrong with a girl liking to hunt or fish (or even build a model airplane). But I still believe my great-grandmother was right about there being things appropriate for boys and girls. Grandma wouldn't have gone along with girls becoming soldiers or as police wearing guns and thumping heads right there with the "boys," or with boys putting on rouge, lipstick, and wearing dresses.

Grandma would have gotten a real kick out of Yale's Alison Hornstein's "revelation" that the Attack on America required a moral judgment that some things are actually wrong, in spite of the amoral stand by the universities that nothing is intrinsically wrong of itself. Leave it to the universities to blame America for the ills of the world, thus inviting the "Holy and Righteous Attack on America."

Toward year's end the WTC death toll has been reduced to 2,992. That's the good news. The bad news is that Stalin continues to be proven correct: *The murder of one* (or maybe a paltry few thousand) *is a crime, the murder of millions a statistic*. Therefore, it only remains for those that hate America, with the approval of the universities, to ratchet the numbers upward far enough. And thanks to number 92 of the Periodic Table, as Michio Kaku and others have warned, this is certainly possible, if not in fact probable.

There is something about the Enron debacle that reminds me of this historic keeping women in their place. The rich get richer and the poor get poorer. If you don't belong to that "circle" you are going to lose your shirt when you don't have the chips (the right pedigree and political clout) to buy into the game. Lacking a place in philosophy, women have never had the chips to buy into the game.

But nearly every attempt on my part to call the attention of women to this fact has been met with the kind of attitude that I was saying they are without influence or calling their value as human beings into question. Why is it, I have to ask myself, that women continue to confuse equal rights with equal value? For you ladies that like to believe in a "male conspiracy," try this one.

Granted women (in America at least) have come a long way since they got the vote and *Liberty Magazine* asked whether a *Flapper* would make a good wife. But until I see women making their place in philosophy and the decision making processes of world governments; which reminds me that neither Jews nor Moslems have any actual, legitimate facts of history on their sides to "prove" their claims of religious or ethnic superiority, let alone that of those of any religion making claims of speaking for God, which, you would think is too ludicrous for any civilized mind to entertain. And unlike Egypt and Greece, there are no proud monuments of such antiquity as claimed by either Jews or Arabs. If one discounts their "scriptures" there is little to substantiate any such claims of prominence and influence that begins to compare with either Egypt or Greece.

But this doesn't prevent Jews and Arabs, or Christians, from proclaiming Jerusalem a "holy city," thereby precluding any hope of a civilized political solution to their historic hating and killing in the name of God, which they apparently relish and cherish. Had Hitler won the war, God would have been on his side according to such thinking.

Such is the power of religion in the human attempts to give meaning to existence, even though it most often leads to forsaking reason and in many instances the culmination of such "meaning for existence" the hating, even killing, those that do not agree with the fanatical beliefs of Paine's "Black Coats" of whatever irrational persuasion.

Some have asked by what "miracle" I was delivered from my own Christian Fundamentalist beliefs, beliefs I used to teach and preach as the very word of God, including the plenary verbal inspiration of the Bible. To such I have never been able to give a satisfactory answer.

It does seem that the circumstances of my life, after many years, eventually led to my finally admitting of the legitimate questions for which no religion has ever been able to supply satisfactory answers. Gradually, these questions led to my disavowing religion as having any place in a legitimate and honest quest for legitimate answers to the How? and the Why? of the universe.

I never received an answer from then Colorado Governor Romer concerning the paternity of JonBenet. I still believe DNA would show either Mr. or Mrs. Ramsey (my guess, Mr. Ramsey) not the biological parent. Gary Condit still refuses to submit to a proper lie detector test and many questions concerning his bizarre behavior surrounding the disappearance of Chandra Levy remain unanswered.

It may be that my "deliverance" from the tyranny of religion is peculiar only to those that are compelled to seek answers to questions that don't seem to trouble others. But such is the way of philosophical thought and speculation.

I do believe we humans have an "instinct to believe." It seems natural to pray and call out to God *in extremis* especially. But in far too many cases religious systems, as Emerson so well pointed out, become mechanisms to escape both personal responsibility and responsibility for confronting and overcoming evil.

I once submitted a question to a physics symposium concerning the Big Bang theory. The question had to do with the formation of water, an absolute essential for life. I can imagine the universe beginning as a "seed." But a seed needs water to vitalize it. Since a liquid cannot be compressed, I wondered how water came about? I'm still waiting for an answer.

In *To Kill A Mockingbird*, little Scout makes the observation that she didn't believe the state of Alabama intended education to be twelve years of unrelieved boredom. That was in the 30s. There are many children now over sixty years later that would agree with Scout concerning the schools in general.

But Scout's complaint was based on school not being challenging enough, and through poor teacher preparation (that hasn't changed, only gotten far worse) made it boring to her. Imagine comparing the complaints of today's children if they were required to learn rather than be entertained!

Adding to the dilemma is TV. Since this has supplanted books and real learning, parents should not be unreasonable in expecting the schools, even if they had qualified personnel, to overcome the Sports is King and Entertainment is Queen mentality of an entire society. Like Hollywood and perversion, you can't have it both ways, and Americans are going to have to make the choice as to whether they want the schools to entertain and baby-sit children or educate them.

As it is, since fully one-third of teachers in America could not pass a qualifying test in reading, writing, spelling, punctuation, arithmetic, science, and history, the task of educating America's children is a truly daunting one, and one that has to start at the university level as well as educating parents and politicians to the real problems and holding them responsible for the part they must take in this.

And speaking of illiteracy, we in America may laugh at Arafat's claim that the attack on us was an Israeli plot. But if enough people in the world believed this, the myth becomes fact. Much of the religious history of both Jews and Arabs falls into this category. But the "winner" being Christianism so long ago, this system having its roots in the myths of Jewish history, it boggles the mind to imagine the fallout if the views of biblical "minimalists" should prove to be true! In fact there is no proof of Abraham or Moses ever existing; there is no proof of the Exodus. But there is very good reason to believe that "Hellenists" wrote very believable propaganda and historians are still prone to make their heroes larger than life.

For example, how much "history" is being learned from Hollywood? How many "facts" are being learned from Hollywood due to films like *The Ten Commandments*? Multiply such "facts" by some unnumbered thousands and you get the point.

About dissent- I'm glad Joel Mowbray spoke his piece cautioning John Ashcroft not to stifle dissent. But, of course, such caution from those in the media (the bias thing) usually excludes dissent against those things and people that make America look like it loves perversion and is at least as Jewish as it is Christian. Given so much Jewish representation in government, Hollywood, and those like Greenspan who hold so much power over America's economy and is ever before the world's cameras it isn't surprising that Arab nations in particular distrust America. The bias leading to stifling any dissent against perversion and coercive Jewish influence in America is strictly a taboo of Hollywood, the media, government, and the universities.

If Hollywood in particular wants to express "patriotism" it is going to have tough going with this American, as well as the rest of the world. Those in Hollywood can't save their cake and eat it too any more than those in government, the universities, or the media can.

So, rather than suffer trying to get something past the editors of Time or CNN and risk labels like *homophobic* and *anti-Semitic*, pundits take on the rest of the world and tell all other nations to go to hell! After all, if they don't agree they must be anti-American!

But I don't have to get past an editor and those that don't like what I say only have to hit the "delete" on their computers. Some might be tempted to send me a nasty message, but being a well-educated and "connected" man I'm not so easily dismissed for fear of admitting bias and there is a certain amount of caution on the part of those that would otherwise be calling me names and telling me to go to hell! Besides, I speak for many that fear such labeling as homophobic and anti-Semitic and can't get past their editors.

Robert Novak is right to question whether Congress is prepared for provoking that can of worms by opening an investigation into what went wrong in our Intelligence leading to the Attack on America. Questions remain unanswered from world wars one and two, the Kennedys, the Clintons, and so much more I for one have no confidence whatsoever in any committee to bring out the real truth to the public. As a citizen I have been lied to so much by those in government how can I have any confidence that the truth will out?

***

December 22, 2001

From The Weedpatch Cracker Barrel

I'm gratified of course that the column of December 20 caught the attention of so many. It certainly spawned several critical comments concerning my views of religion especially. According to several writers I succeeded in surpassing Scrooge and the Grinch.

Before getting to that, on the same date Representative Nancy Pelosi of San Francisco, taking a hint from Governor Gray Davis, decided to shift into "neutral" on Gary Condit. Politics as usual; if you won't do the right thing, be "neutral." Now why does this remind me of something to do with the phrase "The last resort of scoundrels?"

As I write, the number of WTC victims has fallen to 2,963. I hope the numbers continue to go down. Congratulations to Debbie Schlussel who, along with some others, helped bring down Professor Sami Al-Arian of the University of South Florida, who just happened to be Islamic Jihad's U.S. chief and encouraged and applauded the Attack on America.

When I hear "Only in America!" I often think of the universities. Only in America would such enemies of America and democracy be given such freedom to attack those that "feed" them. And not only feed them, but also give them tenure and positions of honor; but why not? Only America (actually America's politicians, following the lead of the universities) allows, even encourages, criminals to cross its borders by multiplied thousands and even gives the babies born to such criminals instant citizenship and continued welfare!

So why shouldn't other enemies of America like Al-Arian think they should be welcome by the "stupid Americans"? When you consider how John Walker is being debated instead of being treated as the traitor he is, I don't wonder that those of other nations think us stupid! After all, with the Clintons and mass murderers as examples, isn't it the American way to treat people as though there is no such thing as personal responsibility for anything in this country? Had the Nuremberg trials been held in America with Congressional Committees getting the "facts" and American attorneys like Johnnie Cochran... well, just the bad luck of those like Himmler, et al.

I read something this morning about "cut and paste" news. The writer apparently never worked for Child Protective Services where this has been the norm long before computers or before columnists and journalists discovered it. As a supervisor told me when I worked in the agency: We aren't here for creative thinking or writing. But, I've expounded on this at length in time past and won't belabor it here. Suffice it to say that CPS, like the schools, politics, the Clintons and John Walker exemplify the "Nobody is personally responsible for anything" rule in America. God forbid we ever have to contend with "I was just following orders!" of the magnitude of WWII.

Now to get to the topic of Scrooge and the Grinch; I never assume malice for what stupidity can explain; thank you Bill O'Reilly for sticking up for Santa Claus, the difference between genius and stupidity remains that genius has its limits and those that want to worship "diversity" and get rid of Santa could give lessons to stupid. And dumb as they appear compared to cats at times, unlike Foghorn Leghorn I never whistle at chained dogs just to watch them run and gag themselves on their collars. But if you think there is good in everybody, you haven't met everybody. As to happiness, I'm happy wrinkles don't hurt.

I admire Sinclair Lewis tremendously. But the flaw in *Elmer Gantry* was that Lewis had never been a true believer in Fundamentalist Christianism. I've pointed out the same flaw in Robert Duvall's *The Apostle.*

My college career really began at Biola College where it was my intention to study for the ministry. Having been born and raised into Fundamentalism, having been "saved" by making my "decision for Christ" and properly baptized into this religion, believing in the plenary verbal inspiration of the Bible, that is that every word of the Bible was "God-breathed" and totally without error, I have an understanding of the flaws in the works of Lewis and Duvall.

I was among those that "witnessed for Christ" and tried to win others to Christ. I was in the business of "saving" others, a "soul-winner."

During all those years as a fundamentalist I amassed a personal library of over 5,000 volumes of the very best of Biblical scholarship, some books being quite rare and my library rivaling that of the best seminary. I memorized well over 3,000 verses of "scripture" as well as some full chapters and studied Hebrew and Greek; I studied German so I could read Luther and German theologians in the original.

I studied the religions of the world; not for appreciation, but like the cults of Mormons and Jehovah's Witnesses so that I could refute these other religions quoting chapter and verse to prove them wrong according to the Bible.

In short, I truly understand those like Kennedy, Robertson, and Falwell. And I came to understand those like Schuller and Copeland, Swaggart and Baker as well. I could quote chapter and verse better than all these in justifying my point of view. A stint with Roman Catholicism as a child gave me further understanding of the religious mindset. For those that think themselves good Catholics, I can tell you from experience that until you have lived in the Polish Ghetto of Cleveland you don't know what a good Catholic is.

While at Biola I came to know Charles Lee Feinberg, Th. D., Ph. D., who was then the Dean of Talbot Seminary. Dr. Feinberg was to become my spiritual mentor and academic advisor. More than this he became a real friend.

"Uncle Charles," as he insisted I call him, was expert in Semitic languages. He became the head of the translating committee for The New American Standard Bible. One of my most precious possessions is the autographed copy of the pilot edition of this work that Dr. Feinberg gave to me. He was also the editor for the revision of the Scofield Reference Bible.

It was Dr. Feinberg who advised me to leave Biola and continue my education in secular universities. His reason being that by the time I had begun my college career I had more Bible knowledge than the professors at Biola. A further reason he gave was that I was too fundamental to be a liberal, and too liberal to be a fundamentalist. In Dr. Feinberg's opinion, I was right where he thought I should be.

Though I did go on to pastorates in fundamentalist (Bible-believing) churches, I never forgot Dr. Feinberg's assessment. In time, his evaluation of me came to pass in fact. I had become too fundamental to be a good liberal, and too liberal to be a good fundamentalist. Uncle Charles had been even wiser than I thought, and a better friend than I had believed. I love and miss him.

If our loved ones and friends now gone on before us can influence us, I believe Uncle Charles has been such an influence guiding me to the position I now hold as a Deist. Had his own prejudices and biases been overcome in his lifetime, I don't doubt he would have come to the same position.

This is in no way to detract from the integrity of such a great man and Bible scholar, a man that was not only a mentor, but also a good friend. I could say the same of another such good man, Dr. James Vernon MaGee. I have no doubt that Dwight L. Moody was such a man like Uncle Charles and MaGee.

Can good people, even among the most gifted, well intentioned and intelligent, be wrong? Yes, most sincerely wrong!

In making the transition between fundamentalism and deism, the biggest obstacle was the feeling that I was betraying those, including my grandparents, who had loved me and meant me no harm in teaching me the things they had concerning religion.

But they had been sincerely wrong. I know that; and I think they know that now as well, and I believe they have been influential in helping me to come to my present position as a deist. If those gone on before us can have any influence in our lives, it is these people that loved me that now continue to guide me as I struggle with so many questions and continue to seek answers to the How? and the Why? of the universe.

Perhaps Dr. Feinberg recognized this "seeking" characteristic in me long before I was aware of it? I don't know. But I do know he was the kind of man that could recognize such a thing. And perhaps he also knew that I would have to remove myself from the influence of a school like Biola, even that of the seminary, in order to do what he himself may have longed to do but because of the circumstances of his life was unable to do.

There is no doubt in my mind that good people can find themselves unable to extricate themselves from a system of belief. How do you find within yourself the means to renounce the beliefs of a lifetime? Still, it may have been this very thing that led Aquinas to come to the end of his life saying: All that I have done is nothing but straw!

Thoreau made the statement that it is never too late to give up one's prejudices. While true enough, it is a most difficult task in practice.

As a result of having never been true believers, neither Lewis nor Duvall could bring the dimension of a true believer to their respective works in spite of their gifts and talents. Lewis, for example, could have the wife of that pastor wondering to herself about the virgin birth. But he couldn't make it really "live." As expert as he was in understanding and portraying the hypocrisy of an Elmer Gantry, the overriding hypocrisy of the best of people, good people like those that would have lynched Tom Robinson and sat on the jury that convicted him in *To Kill A Mockingbird*, who are trapped in a system of real belief was beyond him, it is beyond anyone who has never been a true believer, one that has been born and raised to such a system of belief.

To my detractors I would say you cannot cast me in the mold of Scrooge or the Grinch. I take the position of Dickens who was roundly castigated for not making Jesus the center of *A Christmas Carol.*

I'm well qualified to point out that Christianism was the invention of the Apostle Paul. Without Paul as the "Goebbels" of Jesus, there would never have been a system of "Christianity." I'm well qualified to point out that the entire system that Paul formulated was based on the myths of Judaism, myths that lack any historical evidence in many instances, let alone any claims of "miracles."

If I'm to be made Scrooge or the Grinch, let me point out in my defense my support of the Christmas season. I'm all for the doctrine of the "brotherhood" of mankind (but quick to point out how such terms insult women, "generics" aside), I'm all for what Christians claim to be the message of the Gospel, though they deny such a claim in actual practice. The Pope, Billy Graham, and Jerry Falwell, for example, may preach "brotherhood" but they really mean a brotherhood of Christians.

But please allow me as well to point to the antiquity of the celebration of the winter solstice, the "Yule" season graced with logs, candles, and evergreens, allow me to point out the making of "Christmas" as we now celebrate it that includes the modern inventions of Scrooge, Santa (from Saint Nicholas) and his reindeer (*'T Was The Night Before Christmas*)," of the personification of Santa thanks to Nast, of the celebration of Santa from *It's A Wonderful Life* and *Miracle On 34th Street, Frosty, A Charlie Brown Christmas,* and songs like *Santa Claus Is Coming To Town* and *Rudolph The Red-nosed Reindeer.*

I certainly don't think it fair to vilify me for pointing out that Santa is far more suitable as a "saint," especially for children, than a Jesus, the belief in whom has led to so much suffering through wars and hypocrisy, just as that of other religions like Judaism and Islam.

There are some commentators and columnists that are taking advantage of the season to stick up for Baby Jesus. Not that many years ago I was in their camp. Not any longer.

Like Dickens, I would stick up for the spirit of the season, wishing that the whole world would come to an awakening to goodness such as Scrooge experienced, such as the story of Jesus is supposed, but fails, to exemplify.

But I'm tragically aware that as long as those of any religiously fanatical beliefs such as I once held, such as so many still hold, continue to encourage and make wars possible, so long will children suffer in spite of Baby Jesus and what so many call the "spirit of the season."

The real spirit of Christmas will never be a "Humbug" to me; but for those that believe religion of any kind means "peace on earth" and holds an answer to the threats of the bin Ladens of the world, my message remains: Not true! Unlike Sinclair Lewis and Robert Duvall, I understand the "bin Ladens" of religion regardless their propaganda of "peace and brotherhood" all too well.

I miss believing in the mythology of *Little Town Of Bethlehem* and *Silent Night*, the story of the birth of Jesus in Luke, and no one would like to believe in angels more than I. Belonging to a society such as that of a church is something else that I miss sorely.

But just as my friendship is not based on those agreeing with me, so I wish that others were of the same mind. This, more than any myths of religion, would exemplify what Dickens wrote about and what Santa and the spirit of the season represents.

I still want to believe in fairies and elves, the Merlins and enchanted glades and lands of childhood. I want the Easter Bunny and Tooth Fairy to still be real in my life. I want the "comfort zone" of a belief system that flies in the face of empirical evidence to the contrary. In these things I am no different than most folks, and since people choose to believe what they will, often despite facts to the contrary, I choose to believe that those loved ones and friends gone on before do guide and counsel me.

As I grew older and had to forsake the marvelous stories of things in fact, I never forsook them in spirit. So it is with Christmas, and while all the wishing in the world won't make wishes come true, I'll continue to wish just like you. And it is in that spirit I will wish all of you A Merry Christmas.

***

December 26, 2001

From The Weedpatch Cracker Barrel

I once asked my daughter Karen if she had any comment on my writing. She replied: "Just keep writing the way you are, dad."

That was praise and encouragement enough for me. And beyond any accolades of my writing over the past years, those words of my little girl (you know daughters never become all grown up to their dads) remain the most precious of all.

But I wouldn't want any reader to blame Karen for some of the things I put in print or to think she approves all such things. Being a person in her own right with her own opinions, there are times when I know she is too polite and caring of my feelings to voice disagreement. This is certainly not the case with some other readers, and I'm sure I will catch some flack from this issue of the WCB. What do you expect from someone whose birth certificate reads "Weedpatch?"

As long as the Post-Its don't begin to look like wallpaper and memory still serves me, I'll keep trying to say the things in print that colleagues in the writing game wish they could say but can't get past their editors. And following the wise advice of one of the greatest writers and natural born liars that ever blessed America, Sam Clemens, I'll keep writing without pay until someone offers pay.

Still, I'm ever mindful of the price to be paid when offending those that buy ink by the barrel. But my detractors say I seem more concerned at offending those that buy their wine by the gallon. A vile canard, of course, in view of my humble and self-effacing nature... In fact, in my defense a colleague once pointed out that in his opinion I had the greatest and deepest thoroughly untapped well of humility of any man he had ever known.

Time Magazine has validated my credentials as an irascible and crusty curmudgeon. I resented those at the magazine even considering Osama bin Laden for the cover. When they gave us the opportunity to vote, one of the selections offered was The American People. This must have been only a sop since it didn't seem to have a chance against Rudy Giuliani, a man proclaimed a "hero" which only proved how little that term means to the media, as we have seen too often since the WTC attack, and those at Time especially. Their "Person of the Year" only did what any politician would have done given the "opportunity" that fell in his lap as a result of the Attack on America.

Time chose a man that couldn't even be trusted to keep his marriage vows and he becomes their Person of the Year solely on the basis of serendipity, but of such a nature that made it a happy confluence of events only for the mayor and bin Laden. In true Clintonesque fashion, the mayor will make all the political hay he can out of Time's selection. In short order I expect him to betray his present "love" and start parsing "is." But I don't think his wife and children would have voted for him. I'm sure as hell one American that didn't!

Another aspect of my curmudgeonliness is my resentment of calling cops and firefighters "heroes" when they do exactly what they become cops and firefighters to do. But didn't Giuliani do what any mayor would be expected to do as well? Performing their duties, and performing them well which is what they sign up for and get paid or elected to do, does not make heroes of any of these people who purposely choose risk occupations. Those that fought the skyjackers and those that charged into machine gun fire on the beaches of Normandy, citizen soldiers; those were heroes in the American tradition, not "Giulianis." To call the mayor especially a "hero" is not only despicable, but a thoroughgoing cheapening of the term beyond description!

As for infidelity, the betrayal of marriage vows, this has become such a commonplace in America that it seems Time Magazine may have gotten it right in this regard. This seems to fit the thinking of those at the magazine. But damned if it fits mine!

There are three subjects you never bring up in a bar: Religion, Politics, and the Civil War. Infidelity is one of those things you never bring up in print.

Like most of you that write for publication, I like the occasional "attaboy." But those that have followed my writing for any length of time realize there are subjects I cover that alienate a broad spectrum of readers. This subject of marital infidelity is certainly a sore subject to many and some will take real exception to the value I place on the marriage vows.

But for those that object, I call your attention to the fact that those my age were raised with such values. In spite of a "Norman Rockwell America" having become a quaint anachronism when not being used as a downright pejorative phrase by the professional intellectual in many cases, without any intent to be condescending I still prefer that view of America.

Were it not so tragic in its consequences, I could laugh at so many "studies" that show children suffer from marital infidelity and divorce. Not to mention the fact that children are far more likely to suffer forms of abuse like molestation as a result of infidelity and divorce than in the normal, stable home with the natural father and mother. And before any object, yes I use the word "normal" without apology rather than the euphemism "traditional."

Admittedly I love the music of Stephen Foster, Irving Berlin, and Jerome Kern. I remember when I first heard Kate Smith sing *God Bless America* on the radio and it isn't likely that any song approaching our national anthem as representative of Norman Rockwell's America will ever supersede it. And just as I heartily resent any "stylizing" of our anthem, I equally resent any such emasculation of God Bless America.

Having gotten that off my chest, it seems fitting that I turn to prayer. Seems more and more "science" is finding prayer to be effectual for its healing power. Well, such stuff gets the attention of people but why should it come as a surprise to anyone that something that promotes peace and serenity of the mind should prove effective for its healing power? The psychology of this has been proven for many decades. What science could do to help is to make the connection between brain function and the mind's ability to promote physical well being and healing irrespective of any religious connotations.

But a physician's pat on the head and encouraging a belief in prayer and angels, together with keeping the bowels of the elderly regular, effectual as they may be begs the science of what is actually at work in the mind and body in concert through prayer, meditation, yoga, laughter, thinking lofty thoughts, etc.

Neither should it be surprising to any that a stable home, the extended family, close loved ones and friends contribute much to peace of mind and even to longevity in many cases.

My good friend and soul brother Henry Thoreau pointed out that a man is rich according to those things he can afford to live without. But there is one thing that lends a slightly hypocritical tinge to Henry's remark. Above earthly riches, Henry wanted recognition of his genius as a poet and writer.

While Emerson went out on a limb at times for his young friend and disciple, there was no way he could give Henry what he earnestly wanted most. In his eulogy of Thoreau, Emerson pointed out the weakness of his friend, that of not making the most of his gifts and talents, counting this as "almost a fault" in his friend. In this Emerson was alluding to Thoreau's not being willing to submit to the rigors of self discipline and perseverance required for the kind of success Henry wanted and, in Emerson's opinion, could have had if he had only applied himself. After all, Henry had showed himself more than capable of these in his education and mastery of languages.

There is far too much of Emerson in Thoreau's writings to discount this opinion, far too much to justify Lowell's harsh criticism that Henry spent his life picking up the windfalls in Emerson's orchard.

I continue a lifetime habit of reading my friends Emerson and Thoreau with great profit. The two, together, are my yin and yang of literature. The exquisite phrasing of Emerson, the deep thoughts of this intellectual giant are food and drink to my mind and soul, a continual challenge to my own thinking processes as well as language usage.

Henry, on the other hand, is the far more "readable." I find much of myself in Henry as the impractical free spirit, yet a man that could use his hands as well as his mind. I learned to build houses and overhaul engines, to run a lathe and mill as well as acquiring academic degrees and credentials. But like Henry, I would rather spend the six weeks getting my daily bread for the year and spending the rest of the time in nature and considering my thoughts of many things including thoughts about the How? and the Why? of the universe.

Like Henry, once it was possible for me to do so without harm to others, I chose a life of simplicity, being rich according to those things I could certainly live without.

But in a very real sense, I can't help believing that it takes the two, both Emerson and Thoreau, to make the complete man. The lack in the one seems to me fulfilled in the other.

If I'm honest with myself, I admit to thoughts like those of Thoreau's "Indian" who believed that once he had taken the trouble to make baskets, others were obligated to buy them: In Henry's mind, far better to remove oneself from the necessity of making baskets.

The problem, however, was that Henry didn't seem to realize that his wish to remove himself from any necessity of dependence on "market realities" left him dependent on those like Emerson to sustain him. I can't begin to imagine what might have become of Henry had he not been able to rely on Emerson. It isn't likely, for example, that without Emerson there would ever have been opportunity for Henry to produce a book like *Walden*. And had it not been for family that assured Henry's education, he could hardly have accomplished what he did.

But as Melville carped: The wolf remained at the door. So, he found himself constrained to write for pay because "The truth, it don't pay."

Henry, on the other hand, because of the good spirit and beneficence of his friend and mentor could take the time for "the truth" and his experiment in simplicity of living, an experiment that has done good for untold millions. Irrespective of the sheer impracticality of Henry's philosophy in many ways, how refreshingly timeless his thoughts are in the midst of so much complexity in our modern age.

The philosophical questions remain in spite of the complexity of our age. For example, this spirit of acquisition that imbues so many and leads to those chains that bound Scrooge's partner in *A Christmas Carol*. Thoreau would point out the enormous cost of life to obtain a dwelling on the part of the civilized man as opposed to that of the savage who obtained his from the bark of trees.

I recall writing a letter once to a friend, a California Senator, to whom I posed the question of whether it wouldn't be far more effectual to allow a person to buy a couple of acres and unhindered of restrictive building codes, to build what they could and own it outright rather than to be forever burdened by a mortgage?

The sense of the thing had to do with the personal responsibility of ownership and an incentive to build for ones heirs as opposed to rents of any kind. In spite of all the arguments to the contrary, I still believe in such a thing as being far better than "owing your soul to the company store."

While we haven't discussed it, I believe one of the things Karen likes about her dad's writing is our both being "critter oriented." We love birds and animals; we love nature with the trees, bunnies and butterflies. I certainly enjoy writing about such things.

I keep water outside my cottage just so I can enjoy watching my feathered and furred companions take advantage of this provision for their necessity. I have a family of redheaded woodpeckers that entertain me with their antics. The quail and doves, finches, and such a variety of other birds are a delight to watch.

It's a wonderful thing to be an "impractical" man in these surroundings I presently enjoy. I've always been the kind of person that too readily turns aside from practical things at the bark of a squirrel or the call of a quail. I resent the personal necessities of keeping house, such as it is, the things like preparing food and doing laundry (once a month, if that), and am prone to delaying all excursions that take me from the writing and observing nature; I resent whatever intrudes on my thoughts of things like human nature and the universe and a commitment a day or week ahead hangs over me like a dark cloud. I hate a knock at the door, the ring of the phone and vastly prefer the modern marvel of email.

I have no illusions about "wilderness living" having lived it, and prefer indoor plumbing to outdoor and I'm grateful for not having to rub dry sticks together for fire. So when I write about the things I have enjoyed from the past and the enjoyment of simplicity in living, it isn't that of "having to sit on a pumpkin which is only shiftlessness."

But I love to delve into works like Stephen Hawking's "The Universe In A Nutshell" and Martin Rees' "Our Cosmic Habitat." Letting my mind roam into the possibilities posed by multiple universes and time travel are challenging to my imagination. And being a compulsive writer, thoughts generated by such material find themselves expressed in much of my writing. Since a writer "lives in his/her head," it isn't surprising that once I have seized on some thought that commands my attention, I am loath to leave it for any reason. And a writer needs to see their thoughts on paper.

For example, knowing that our universe is of comparatively simple construction compared to the lowest life form of an insect conjures up all sorts of thoughts. We have yet to be able to explain what, exactly, life is? We are no further in being able to explain or understand what lies beyond the grave than any of our ancestors. In spite of all the artifacts and writings of ancients we don't know why we seem to have an instinct for prayer and to believe in a hereafter.

But lest you get the wrong impression, I have always loved Rex Stout's *Nero Wolfe*, and am really grateful for the series on TV.

Why don't we know the really important questions to ask when we are young? I suppose this is one of the reasons I write. My "letters to my children" are a way of telling them some things and answering some questions that I know won't be important to them until it's too late for them to realize how important some of these things are. Like, for instance, I wish I could quiz grandad about his stint with the circus as a "barker" and his role as a gambler in silent film. I would ask my mother about her aspirations for show business and her short-lived career as a chorus girl (all I was ever told was that she fell off a stage and broke her leg). This is really important stuff! And now it's too late to ask and I wish they had been writers. And this is a not too subtle hint for some of you.

I know it's important for my children to have the stories about my seeing that mountain lion in the forest and the time the skunk went off in the cabin on the mining claim. It's important for them to know about how I acquired some of the stories I picked up from people I met in bars and other places.

When all is said and done, the personal vignettes of our lives are the really important things that make for that unique and most important foundation of civilization, this thing we call "family." It is this dimension of the past, a history of my childhood, that led me to write my only novel: *Donnie and Jean, an angel's story.*

***

December 31, 2001

From The Weedpatch Cracker Barrel

Here it is folks, New Year's Eve as I begin this issue of the WCB. Not to trivialize the year but it has been one hell of! And it's been said over and over since 9-11: The world will never be the same! None capable of seeing the larger picture will disagree.

Doesn't seem that long since the doomsayers were predicting all hell breaking loose at the beginning of Y2K. They should have waited.

Once more I have forestalled any New Year's Resolutions. Somewhere along the line I surprised myself by living long enough to obey the Eleventh Commandment: Thou Shalt Not Sweat The Small Stuff! September 11 certainly proved the wisdom of this.

My gratitude to those that continued to express interest in my writing over the year, and I'm grateful for those conservative columnists that make up townhall.com. For some others I admire that don't swing to the right, I'm grateful for those that appear in the LA Times and Washington Post.

In spite of the extreme gravity of the issues facing us, in spite of the fact that those like Michio Kaku may prove correct about the threat of #92 of the Periodic Table causing some concern about our reaching Y2003, my feathered and furred companions still call my place "home."

If I have a "patron saint" of literature, he is Samuel Clemens and his alter ego Mark Twain. He said he would choose Shakespeare for the only work on a desert island. I would need both the Bard of Avon and the Bard of America. It may well be that Hemingway was correct, that distinctly American literature began with Sam Clemens' Huckleberry Finn. Whether or no, none would dispute the legacy of Clemens to literature in many ways, and none should fail to understand his claim based on his knowledge and experience of tragedy that the only pure and unalloyed gift of God was death.

There is a line in the classic film "Death Takes A Holiday" starring Frederic March that death may be kinder and far less complicated than life. It may have been this view that Clemens was referring to; at least I choose to believe this, knowing Sam as I do, and regardless all the philosophical speculation on the subject it does seem a comforting belief.

Sam could illustrate the corrosive hypocrisy of religion in the words: He was as happy as though he had just gotten out of church. Sam could spell out the corrosive role of money in politics as none other, calling Judas Iscariot a "premature congressman." And he could spell out in the most searing satire the kind of morality that distinguished Huck saying he guessed he couldn't obey the law and turn Jim in with the words: All right then, I'll go to hell.

I think most of us would agree that the "other place" Huck chose, the place with which his friend Tom was threatened, was vastly preferable to the kind of heaven the churches preached and, too often, made available only to those that could obey the kinds of laws which so disturbed Huck's conscience and Thoreau said shamed America. After all, what kind of government could make a legitimate claim of "democracy" and be both the government of the slave and that of the free man?

As to the "heaven" of the churches, if it were made to be half as friendly and exciting as hell the churches would be full! So it was that Justin Kaplan recently said he thought Satan was Twain's hero. While I take exception to Kaplan's remark, there is no denying that the hypocrisy of religion made it an attractive target of Sam's wit and had much to do with his sharing the observation of Ben Franklin that the human species might not be worthy or deserving of preservation.

Children are cheated, who have been denied Tom Sawyer and Huckleberry Finn. Though consistently among the books political correctness bans from libraries and classrooms, let alone being books recommended for children, they are books that children should read, not only for the sake of adventure and great literature, if for no other reason than to force adults to explain them to children.

While no knowledgeable person would ever consider disparaging or attempt to minimize the debt we have to English writers or to those American writers that followed in that tradition before Clemens' landmark book to which Hemingway referred, the voice which was distinctly Mark Twain was distinctly American. To deny that voice to children is to cheat and deprive them of an unsurpassed work of literature, one that will continue to stand the test of real art, the test of time.

I have to suppose that Sam would get a real kick out of those in some churches burning Harry Potter books. I suppose he would understand, though be appalled by, the surge in people buying Bibles due to 9-11.

Mona Charen and a few other women rightly share their gratitude in print for there still being real men around in spite of the attempts of the universities and political correctness to emasculate the species. But real men start from the boyhoods of those like Tom Sawyer and Huckleberry Finn, and later, the Jeremy Finches of To Kill A Mockingbird.

Sam Clemens didn't deal in statistics as important as these are; he dealt in stories that made statistics come alive. And being subject to common human weaknesses and failings, the very contradictions in himself throughout his life helped him to make his characters live and breathe on the printed pages of his works.

I've said many times that men and women are seldom as bad as their divorce papers indicate. So it is that neither Michael Jordan nor Michael Jackson is America and if I never hear of either of them again that will suit me right down to the ground; which brings me to Bill O'Reilly. He usually makes a lot of sense to me in spite of his religious views, the kind that taints other well-meaning guys like William Bennett and Pat Buchanan. I trust my readers of longstanding will forgive some repetition of past remarks in the following for the sake of those recently onboard.

The myth of God supposedly telling humankind to subdue the earth has real merit, but every Dominion Theology following, being religious, has never been able to overcome the fatal flaw of dualistic thinking that makes God responsible for both good and evil. Hawthorne and Melville, despite their genius, both made shipwreck on this paradoxical rock.

But the fable of the Garden included Adam and Eve being vegetarians and the shedding of the blood of animals being the result of disobedience to the will of God. Our teeth, for example, are far better designed for the masticating of cereals, fruits, and vegetables than that of predators for the tearing and rending of flesh. Still, both Judaism and Christianism continue as what are called "blood" religions demanding sacrifice whether of animals or Jesus.

Indeed we should subdue the earth and have dominion over it. We are capable of doing so, we are capable of eliminating the weeds and thistles, the beasts of prey, of an agriculture that would be more than sufficient for our needs once problems like birth control, both human and animal, are acknowledged, confronted and overcome.

And it isn't just the argument that it takes eight pounds of grain to produce one pound of meat that is at issue; particularly when you factor in the issue of unproductive mouths, an issue that does have to be considered necessitating birth control. What is needed is an entirely new way, a new philosophy if you will, of thinking about diet that incorporates all the logical factors impinging on health. Logically it makes no sense for any culture to encourage non-productive welfare births, for example, which have little chance at success, but on the contrary are more likely to sap the resources of a society and enlarge a criminal population, a distasteful fact, but still a fact.

An incontrovertible fact is that the better-educated and civilized populations do engage in birth control. What works against such efforts are the large populations of the poor, ignorant, and religiously superstitious that do not practice birth control. The host of abysmally ignorant and religiously superstitious illegal aliens crossing the borders of America has made California in particular a study in a failed "social experiment." But we have both a state and federal government that will not face this fact and, insanely, even encourages such a thing because so many politicians derive their power base from such obviously selfish insanity, much as the so-called "war on drugs" provides such a base in too many instances.

With the enormous financial demands made on the middle class in California by burgeoning social, medical, legal, criminal, police, and education bureaucracies through which political power is gained and maintained as a result of the hordes of criminal and welfare poor "vandals and barbarians" in the state, it isn't any wonder that a seeming Alice In Wonderland view of the situation seems endemic to the political structure.

Unwieldy political structures like those of California or the federal structure of America lend themselves to an implosion due to the kind of instability that lacks any true accountability. It may only be a matter of time when these enormous bureaucracies will collapse because they lack a foundation of accountability.

For example, the political rhetoric of jobs and education fails when jobs are scarce and education is not possible. This is the present situation in California where government at all levels is dependent on a fast-diminishing middle class to support it and an enormous growth in ignorant, religiously superstitious, unproductive mouths to feed and house.

I live in an area called "Welfare Valley." The reason being that the cost of housing is relatively affordable and Bakersfield sends their welfare people here; the area is largely recreational and supported by retired people for the most part. The quality of life is good only because there are no large minority populations fighting over drug turf. As a result we do not suffer the gang wars and drive-by shootings.

The "quality of poverty" is better here due to mild weather and affordable housing. But if I were to attempt to do a study of the quality of life and the low incidence of violent crime here on the basis of a lack of racial "diversity" and illegal aliens it would be impossible to find a publisher. But this wouldn't change the facts.

Nor does telling people to get jobs when there are no jobs to be had do any good. This is much like toughening high school graduation requirements while attempting to meet the demands of "diversity" and a failed system of education. This has led to my saying in regard to education: We couldn't have better designed a system for failure had we done so intentionally!

Knowing what I do of such matters, it isn't any wonder that Swift's "Modest Proposal" often comes to mind as well as the "Let Them Eat Cake" mentality of California's State Legislature together with that of Congress.

A recent article detailing Wisconsin's much heralded effort at welfare reform, for example, has little to do with what we in California face. Much of the failure of both welfare and education reform in California has to do with these hoards of ignorant and religiously superstitious people from a culture like that of Mexico where both personal and government corruption is a way of life. Factor in the generations of welfare-dependent communities like Watts and you get an idea of the magnitude of the problem.

To use the term "civilized" in America is to hearken to a uniquely European concept, not that of Africa, Mexico, South America, India, or China. Intelligent and educated people without bias will acknowledge this without resort to labels like "Anglophile" or "Xenophobic."

But rather than address such inflammatory facts, responsible people and the leadership lack the will to confront it, blaming instead institutions such as the schools and social services for not performing miracles. I am not a friend of the way our schools and social services do business. But in all fairness, they are asked to do the impossible under the circumstances.

Such a thing as the failure of responsible birth control measures is patently and inherently unhealthy for any culture or society. Any discussion of "human rights" must begin to take into account those that have no regard for personal responsibility for their actions or the rights and property of others. Here in America we are encouraging hoards of barbarians and vandals by insanely encouraging irresponsibility and a lack of accountability on the part of individuals, the media, and on the part of the leaders of our institutions and government for not controlling our borders or facing the question of forced birth control, the specter of Hitler's eugenics, like the race card, being the boogeyman of the universities and Hollywood.

It would be legitimate for those being forced to pay the bill for welfare to ask this question: Who made the decision that welfare as a way of life should include "reproductive rights" without hope of being able to support the resulting children and assure them a good education?

A vegetarian world of people and beasts… In all logic, what's wrong with the idea? I do believe a generation born and raised in such a manner would consider the previous generations of animal killers and eaters savage and barbaric! But, then, just looking at the violence now so graphically portrayed in films, "games," and TV would quickly convince them of that. Not to mention that people considering themselves "civilized" are still killing one another in the name of God because of their religious prejudices, and over something some call a "Holy Land."

August 26, 2001

Legalized Extortion!

In March of 1997 the Bakersfield Californian ran an article of mine in Community Voices concerning divorce. Since that time, more than a thousand studies and books have been published on the subject together with seemingly endless debates on talk shows and the consensus is that children do better in a two-parent home. Surprise!

Life is unfair. God (should He/She be there) made some really stupid mistakes in creating people the way they are. Ben Franklin and Sam Clemens would agree. In a perfect creation every woman would be attractive and every man handsome, none of us would grow old and wrinkled, there would be no genetic injustices. In a perfect creation the sex drive wouldn't come upon us before we were able to handle a job and a mortgage. And, of course, in a perfect world there would be no racial or religious hatreds and prejudices, and women would be of equal value to men.

But life is unfair; we are imperfect people living in a far from perfect world. God(s) really blew it and like earthly parents undoubtedly wishes He/She had done a better job.

No one ever asked me if I wanted to be held responsible for someone else's child, if I wanted to make child support payments for someone else's baby. But thanks to Big Brother Welfare, for many decades now I have had to support other people's children. Big Brother has made certain that I will be the one put in prison if I don't make these legalized blackmail payments through taxation, a tax where I was never given any choice as to how this extorted money was to be spent.

When I complained that the mothers and fathers of these other babies should be held accountable, not me, Big Brother either threatened or ignored me. When I suggested that contraception should be a condition of welfare, a judge said: Oh, we do not interfere with the "Reproductive Rights" of people in America!

Reproductive Rights? I wondered where that was guaranteed in the Constitution? Perhaps it is with the same section or article that says people can get divorced and if they have children, they become my responsibility to care for instead of the parents, it is my responsibility to provide child care for these other people's children, it is my responsibility to provide food and shelter for these other parents that decided they didn't want to be married any longer, or hadn't even been married to begin with?

To add insult to injury, there are some that preach I should be held accountable for slavery in this country, that further extortion by Big Brother, Caesar, should be legalized to make blackmail payments to those that want a free ride on my sweat! I would ask those that preach such a hellish doctrine to clean up their own mess of crime, drugs, and alcohol, molestation and rutting like barnyard animals with no thought for the future of the resulting children!

I don't think we are going to see Al Sharpton run for President on such a "reform" platform. But given the likes of "leaders" like the Clintons/Condits, why should he? And why play Lotto when Big Brother pays off with far better odds?

Life is unfair. Perhaps I should have been born in Mexico and have become an illegal alien. Big Brother would have given me "victim" status like those crying for reparations, like those that have babies and extort the money from me to support them.

But I find myself, inexplicably, in a different kind of victim status: that of a person that lived responsibly without Big Brother handouts, never "Caesar's dog" feeding at his table, that got an education at his own expense and supported a family and raised children with no thought that they should be someone else's responsibility. As a "victim" I thought this was what America was all about: Personal freedom with personal responsibility. But America's "leadership" has shown me the error of such thinking.

A little boy, Rodney McAllister of St. Louis, was torn apart by a pack of dogs. What to do? The child was the result of a welfare society and no one was responsible or to be held accountable for him. The dogs, no one was responsible or to be held accountable for them. Such things "happen." But in a responsible and accountable America such things would not "happen!"

The cry of "more money" is heard across the land to "fix" the problems, whether in education, welfare, housing the homeless, and the list goes on and on. What is not being heard are the voices raised on behalf of responsibility and accountability, either for individuals or bureaucracies… but a few voices, mine included, are warning that we are fast approaching that point where we will no longer be able to either endure the problems or their solutions and all the cries of "Hitlerian" will prove to have been empty ghosts.

In time past I have pointed out the fact that the Mother Teresas and Albert Schweitzers have not changed the world. Nor can they. Only when evil is met with equal determination by the good to prevail will the world be changed. While I sometimes cringe at the dogmatisms of some philosophers, even those like Emerson much as I respect him, this is one dogma that I cling to personally.

When I ran for California State Senate, I did so on a platform of education reform. But no one would support me on that basis; they kept telling me that it was the economy. People couldn't seem to understand that education was the economy; they didn't understand that accountability in education would have such a far-reaching impact on other aspects of society as a whole, including the economy.

But to really understand that would require an enlightened electorate, and America does not have that. To really understand that would require enlightened legislators, and America does not have those.

Tom Daschle is saying a high school diploma is of no consequence when hiring people to work in airport security. What is that message to those that even now are considering dropping out of school? The schools lie routinely about money and dropout rates, just as the large cities lie about their crime rates, and for far too long it has been recognized that a high school diploma is of little merit educationally. Even college degrees are viewed with such a suspicion now. But for Tom Daschle to even further minimize the value and need of education is deplorable and destructive!

Neither politicians nor those in the universities are capable of solving the dilemma of our failed system of education. Nor can we trust politicians with foreign aid any more than we can trust them to solve the problems of feeding and housing the countless unproductive mouths in our own country. "In God We Trust" makes a nice euphemism but there is nothing of a definitive nature in government to encourage such a belief.

The current battle in Kentucky over the Decalogue is founded in the sheer hypocrisy of attempts to force a Taliban-like interpretation of American history. God forbid, no pun intended, that any state or federal requirement to "worship" someone's religious superstition ever be law. But I am concerned about those in Congress that would make the word "desecrate" a part of law concerning our flag. I fervently wish such supporters in Congress would avail themselves of a dictionary.

I have an acquaintance that visits me regularly. He is a very religious man and the only reason I tolerate his visits is the fact that he lacks the power to enforce his religious beliefs on me. But if he had the power to do so, I have no doubt that he would, ever as much as some Nazi fanatic would have done in Hitler's Germany.

A fanatic is a fanatic. We have no lack of such fanatics in the universities, in government, in churches, synagogues, mosques, in Hollywood or the media. It seems a full time job to counter such fanaticism, but I live in hope that as long as a free press prevails in America there is always room for hope.

Of one thing we can all be certain, no amount of political rhetoric will avail until those things like meaningful control of our borders and enforced birth control measures tied to welfare are dealt with realistically. Until such a time little boys for whom no one is responsible will continue to be torn apart by dogs for which no one is responsible and both meaningful welfare and education reform will remain impossible of attainment.

***

So many have asked why I have not weighed in on the proposed fees for the use of campgrounds at Lake Isabella that I have decided in spite of the many articulate and well-reasoned articles already printed to offer my reasons for not having done so.

Some years ago as I was driving home to the Valley from Bakersfield, I saw gang graffiti spray-painted on a large limb of an old Cottonwood hanging out over the river. I was furious! So much so that when I got home I immediately wrote a letter to then Assemblyman Trice Harvey, whom I knew quite well. I even wrote then State Senator Don Rogers, whom I also knew well.

Since the late 30s and through the 40s on it wasn't that unusual for me to see "John loves Mary" occasionally painted on a rock along the canyon road and the river, but to deface a tree with gang graffiti, that was outright *sacrilege*! To me, this was an indication of where our beautiful canyon and Valley were headed; hence the political approach to the problem.

Alas, nothing could be done. The lesson learned was that nothing could be done when there is no reasonable threat of consequences for actions.

Now the Kern Valley Sun has always responded to my requests that its "Shopper" not be thrown on the road where I live since it becomes car and wind-blown trash unless I go out, pick it up and dispose of it properly. But the Sun cannot be expected to be responsible for the irresponsible riff raff that throw trash from their cars, or while they are walking, along the roadway.

So how do you make those behave responsibly that are irresponsibly to blame for trash and graffiti? Only by force of law, and at that, law that can be enforced. The bottom line: No enforceable penalty; no consequences for actions.

Were it not so tragic in its consequences I could laugh at the recent articles about so-called *Welfare Reform.* When I taught in Watts, it was obvious that such communities were being paid off by the political system to "keep those people in their place." And the system had been doing so for generations, thus making welfare a way of life.

But what were the options? These people were going to continue to live on the dole since education and job opportunities were virtually non-existent. Crime and welfare were a way of life that was not subject to change without education and jobs. The politicians may wring their hands over not being able to institute meaningful welfare reform, any more than they can education reform. But such reform is not possible where there is no accountability. And do not expect what never was and never will be: Accountability without penalty for the failure to be accountable.

The "welfare mentality" is an inherently irresponsible one; which brings me to the point about fees for camping. By charging such fees, regardless of the legitimate double and triple taxation apologetics, there will be less trash and graffiti. Further, a means may be provided to go after those that refuse to be personally responsible.

I'm sure some of you realize that the problem goes far beyond the charging of fees, it goes to the very core of a society that has for far too long rewarded indolence and irresponsibility. And given the Clintons, Condits, and locally the Wentlands of Belridge School District infamy, it isn't going to change by expecting those with a socialist welfare mentality to do right simply because it is the right thing to do.

Do you parents reward your children for picking up after themselves? Do you reward them for chores and cleaning up their rooms? Do you really expect people to do the right thing when they have nothing to gain by doing so? Not in today's America.

But then, since the beginning of recorded history there has never been a free lunch, and that which costs little is lightly esteemed. It has always been the case in a socialist/welfare society that when too many of those that cannot or will not provide for themselves are getting a free ride on the backs of workers, the bills (taxation) escalate. And as with true political, welfare, or education reform, there must be accountability or nothing will avail.

About the Author

Samuel D. G. Heath, Ph. D.

Other books in print by the author:

BIRDS WITH BROKEN WINGS
DONNIE AND JEAN, an angel's story
TO KILL A MOCKINGBIRD, a critique on behalf of children
THE AMERICAN POET WEEDPATCH GAZETTE for 2008
THE AMERICAN POET WEEDPATCH GAZETTE for 2007
THE AMERICAN POET WEEDPATCH GAZETTE for 2006
THE AMERICAN POET WEEDPATCH GAZETTE for 2005
THE AMERICAN POET WEEDPATCH GAZETTE for 2004
THE AMERICAN POET WEEDPATCH GAZETTE for 2003
THE AMERICAN POET WEEDPATCH GAZETTE for 2002

Presently out of print:
IT SHOULDN'T HURT TO BE A CHILD!
WOMEN, BACHELORS, IGUANA RANCHING, AND RELIGION
HEY, GOD! What went wrong and when are you going to fix it?
THE MISSING HALF OF HUMANKIND: WOMEN!
THE MISSING HALF OF PHILOSOPHY: WOMEN!
THE LORD AND THE WEEDPATCHER
CONFESSIONS AND REFLECTIONS OF AN OKIE INTELLECTUAL or Where the heck is Weedpatch?
MORE CONFESSIONS AND REFLECTIONS OF AN OKIE INTELLECTUAL

Dr. Heath was born in Weedpatch, California. He has worked as a manual laborer, mechanic, machinist, peace officer, engineer, pastor, builder and developer, educator, social services practitioner (CPS), professional musician and singer. He is also a private pilot and a columnist.
Awarded American Legion Scholarship and is an award winning author.
He has two surviving children: Daniel and Michael. His daughters Diana and Karen have passed away.

Academic Degrees:
Ph. D. – U.S.I.U., San Diego, CA.
M. A. – Chapman University, Orange, CA.
M. S. (Eqv.) — U.C. Extension at UCLA. Los Angeles, CA.
B. V. E. – C.S. University. Long Beach, CA.
A. A. – Cerritos College. Cerritos, CA.

Other Colleges and Universities attended:
Santa Monica Technical College, Biola University, and C.S. University, Northridge.

Dr. Heath holds life credentials in the following areas:
Psychology, Professional Education, Library Science, English, German, History, Administration (K-12), Administration and Supervision of Vocational Education and Vocational Education-Trade and Industry.

In addition to his work in public education, Dr. Heath started three private schools, K-12, two in California and one in Colorado. His teaching and administrative experience covers every grade level and graduate school.

Comments by some who have read the author's works

Your writing is very important. You are having an impact on lives! Never lose your precious gift of humor. V. T.

You raise a number of issues in your material ... The Church has languished at times under leaders whose theology was more historically systematic than Biblical ... (But) The questions you raise serve as very dangerous doctrines. John MacArthur, a contemporary of the author at Biola/Talbot and pastor of Grace Community Church in Sun Valley.

You have my eternal gratitude for relieving me from the tyranny of religion. D. R.

Before reading your wonderful writings, I had given up hope. Now I believe and anticipate that just maybe things can change for the better. J. D.

I started reading your book, The Lord and the Weedpatcher, and found I couldn't put it down. Uproariously funny, I laughed the whole way through. Thank you so much for lighting up my life! M.G.

Doctor Heath, every man with daughters owes you a debt of gratitude! I have had all three of my girls read your Birds With Broken Wings book. D. W.

I am truly moved by your art! While reading your writing I found a true treasure: Clarity! I felt as if I was truly on fire with the inspiration you invoked! L. B.

You really love women! Thank you for the most precious gift of all, the gift of love. Keep on being you! D. B.

Your writing complements coffee-cup-and-music. I've gotten a sense of your values, as well as a provocativeness that suggests a man both distinguished and truly sensual. Do keep up such vibrant work! E. R.

Some men are merely handsome. You are a beautiful man! One of these days some wise, discerning, smart woman is going to snag you. Make sure she is truly worthy of you. Desirable men like you (very rare indeed) who write so sensitively, compellingly and beautifully are sitting ducks for every designing woman! M. G.

Now, poet, musician, teacher, philosopher, friend, counselor and whatever else you have done in your life, I am finally realizing all the things you say people don't understand about a poet. They see, feel, write and talk differently than the rest of the world. Their glasses seem to be rose colored at times and other times they are blue. There seems to be no black or white in the things they see only soft pastel hues. Others see things as darker colors, but these are not the romantic poets you speak of. C. M.

You are the only man I have ever met who truly understands women! B. J.

Dr. Heath,
You are one of the best writers I've had the privilege to run across. You have been specially gifted for putting your thoughts, ideas, and inspirations to paper (or keyboard), no matter the topic.
Even when in dire straits, your words are strong and true. I look forward to reading many more of your unique writings. T. S.